D1241296

WOMAN, CHURCH AND STATE

UNABRIDGED EDITION

MATILDA JOSLYN GAGE

WITH AN INTRODUCTION BY
SALLY ROESCH WAGNER

CLASSICS IN WOMEN'S STUDIES

Humanity Books

an imprint of Prometheus Books
59 John Glenn Drive, Amherst, New York 14228-2197

Cover image: Courtesy Matilda Gage Foundation

Published 2002 by Humanity Books, an imprint of Prometheus Books

Introduction copyright © 2002 by Sally Roesch Wagner.

Inquiries should be addressed to
Humanity Books
59 John Glenn Drive
Amherst, New York 14228–2197
VOICE: 716–691–0133, ext. 207
FAX: 716–564–2711

06 05 04 03 02   5 4 3 2 1

Library of Congress Cataloging-in-Publication Data

Gage, Matilda Joslyn, 1826–1898.
    Woman, church, and state / Matilda Joslyn Gage ; with an
introduction by Sally Roesch Wagner.—Unabridged ed.
        p. cm.—(Classics in women's studies series)
    Originally published: Chicago : C.H. Kerr, 1893.
    Includes bibliographical references.
    ISBN 1–59102-007-7 (paper : alk. paper)
    1. Women's rights. 2. Women—Social conditions. I. Title.
II. Classics in women's studies.

HQ1236 .G34 2002
305.42—dc21   2002020756

Printed in the United States of America on acid-free paper

MATILDA JOSLYN GAGE was born on March 24, 1826, in Cicero, New York. An only child, she was raised in a household dedicated to antislavery. Her father, Dr. Hezekiah Joslyn, was a nationally known abolitionist, and the Joslyn home was a station on the Underground Railroad.

In 1845 she married merchant Henry Hill Gage, with whom she would have four children. They eventually settled in Fayetteville, New York, near Syracuse, and their home became a station on the Underground Railroad. Although occupied with both family and antislavery activities, Gage was drawn to a new cause: the woman's suffrage movement. Her life's work would become the struggle for the complete liberation of women.

Unable to attend the first Woman's Rights Convention held in Seneca Falls, New York, in 1848, Gage attended and addressed the third national convention in Syracuse, New York, in 1852. She became a noted speaker and writer on woman's suffrage.

During the Civil War, Gage was an enthusiastic organizer of hospital supplies for Union soldiers. In 1862 she predicted the failure of any course of defense and maintenance of the Union that did not emancipate the slaves.

Gage, along with Susan B. Anthony and Elizabeth Cady Stanton, was a founding member of the National Woman Suffrage Association and served in various offices of that organization (1869–1889). She helped organize the Virginia and New York state suffrage associations, and was an officer in the New York association for twenty years. From 1878 to 1881 she published the National Citizen and Ballot Box, the official newspaper of the NWSA.

In 1871 Gage was one of the many women nationwide who unsuccessfully tried to test the law by attempting to vote. When Susan B. Anthony successfully voted in the 1872 presidential election and was arrested, Gage came to her aid and supported her during her trial. In 1880 Gage led 102 Fayetteville women to the polls when New York State allowed women to vote in school districts where they paid their taxes.

During the 1870s Gage spoke out against the brutal and unfair treatment of Native Americans. She was adopted into the Wolf Clan of the Mohawk nation and given the name Ka-ron-ien-ha-wi (Sky Carrier). Inspired by the Six Nation Iroquois Confederacy's form of government, where "the power between the sexes was nearly equal," this indigenous practice of woman's rights became her vision.

Gage coedited with Stanton and Anthony the first three volumes of the six-volume *The History of Woman Suffrage* (1881–1887). She also authored the influential pamphlets *Woman as Inventor* (1870), *Woman's Rights Catechism* (1871), and *Who Planned the Tennessee Campaign of 1862?* (1880).

Discouraged with the slow pace of suffrage efforts in the 1880s, and alarmed by the conservative religious movement that had as its goal the establishment of a Christian state, Gage formed the Women's National Liberal Union in 1890, to fight moves to unite church and state. Her book *Woman, Church and State* (1893) articulates her views.

While Gage remained a supporter of woman's rights throughout her life, she spent her elder years concentrating on religious issues. A staunch supporter of the separation of church and state, she opposed the religious right's attempt to turn the United States into a Christian nation. She also concentrated on the church's role in creating and maintaining the oppression of women.

Gage died in Chicago, Illinois, on March 18, 1898, five days after suffering a stroke. Her lifelong motto appears on her gravestone in Fayetteville: "There is a word sweeter than Mother, Home or Heaven; that word is Liberty."

INTRODUCTION

We have seen our country gradually advancing in recognition
of broader freedom, fewer restrictions upon personal liberty,
and the peoples of all nations looking towards us as the great
exemplar of political and religious freedom. But of late a
rapidly increasing tendency has been shown towards the
destruction of our civil liberties . . . we are confronted by the
fact that our form of government is undergoing a radical
change, with a well organized body greedy for power. . . . This
. . . is a vast help to those persons who wish to incorporate certain religious dogmas in the Federal constitution.[1]

I t is 1890 and the speaker is Matilda Joslyn Gage, longtime
woman's rights advocate who has left the increasingly conservative suffrage ranks in order to focus her attention on what she
identifies as the true enemy of freedom: the church. Addressing
the founding convention of her new organization, the Woman's
National Liberal Union, Gage warns that this growing presence
of the Religious Right is the great "danger of the hour."

With only four months' planning, Gage has brought together representatives from thirty-three states calling for an absolute separation of church and state, and no prayer or religious instruction in the public schools. "That every Church is the enemy of liberty and progress," the convention resolves, "and the chief means of enslaving woman's conscience and reason, and, therefore, as the first and most necessary step toward her emancipation, we should free her from the bondage of the Church."[2]

Who was Matilda Joslyn Gage and why has history lost her name? "Mrs. Gage has been conspicuous, and united with Mrs. Stanton since the early days; and the three names, Stanton, Anthony and Gage, linked together in the authorship of 'The History of Woman Suffrage,' will ever hold a grateful place in the hearts of posterity," predicted the *Woman's Journal* in 1888. Considered part of the "triumvirate" of the nineteenth-century U.S. woman's movement with Elizabeth Cady Stanton and Susan B. Anthony, Gage in many ways combined the qualities of her two coworkers. Stanton was essentially a theoretician; Anthony an activist. Gage was both. When the National Woman Suffrage Association (NWSA) impeached the government for its treatment of women on July 4, 1876, for example, Gage and Stanton penned "The Declaration of Rights of Women," while Gage and Anthony made the illegal presentation of the document at the Centennial celebration in Philadelphia. Gage wrote the story of the incident. The three women held comparable positions of responsibility in the NWSA from its founding in 1869 until it merged with the American Woman Suffrage Association in 1890. Stanton typically was president and Anthony, first vice president, while Gage was chair of the Executive Committee.[3]

Editor of a suffrage paper for four years and correspondent for newspapers around the country, Gage documented the activities of the woman's rights movement. She failed, however, to credit her own work. "Mrs. Gage as journalist and historian of the movement in which she has been a prominent actor, has omitted or crowded out the record of her own services which we hope some other chronicler will surely supply," a suffrage paper, the *New Era*, worried.[4]

Gage did, however, celebrate the triumphs of other women. "She always had a knack of rummaging through old libraries, bringing more startling facts to light than any woman I ever knew," Stanton once said of Gage. In writing *Woman as Inventor*, Gage maintained that the cotton gin owed its origin to a woman, Catherine Littlefield Greene, and not to Eli Whitney, as was generally believed. Greene didn't patent the machine, Gage explained, because "to have done so would have exposed her to the ridicule and contumely of her friends and a loss of position in society, which frowned upon any attempt at outside industry for women." In "Who Planned the Tennessee Campaign of 1862?" Gage revealed strong evidence that this brilliant military strategy, which changed the course of the Civil War, was planned in detail by a woman, Anna Ella Carroll.[5]

Gage charted new territory in her analysis. In a resolution she introduced at the 1878 NWSA convention, Gage drew an economic analogy for the position of women:

> RESOLVED: that the question of capital and labor is one of special interest to us. Man standing to woman in the position of capitalist has robbed her through the ages of the results of her toil. No just settlement of this question can be attained until the right of woman to the proceeds of her labor in the family and elsewhere be recognized, and until she is welcomed into every industry on the basis of equal pay for equal work.[6]

While president of the NWSA in 1875, she penned a series of articles for the New York papers applauding the superior form of government practiced by the Six Nations of the Iroquois Confederacy, in which "the power between the sexes was nearly equal."[7] "The common interest of the confederacy were arranged in councils," she explained, "each sex holding one of its own, although the women took the initiative in suggestion, orators of their own sex presenting their views to the council of men."[8]

When the Grand Council of the Confederacy opposed an attempt by New York to force citizenship upon Native American men, Gage supported the council's position, pointing out the government's hypocrisy in an editorial in her newspaper.

> Over one hundred chiefs and warriors of the different nations took part in this discussion. This council of Indians at Onondaga Castle, in the center of the great Empire State, and the convention of the women of the country at Washington in January, the one protesting against citizenship about to be forced upon them, because with it would come further deprivation of their rights,— the other demanding citizenship denied them, in order to protect their rights, are two forcible commentaries upon our so-called republican form of government.[9]

Gage expressed her support of treaty rights:

> That the Indians have been oppressed,—are now, is true, but the United States has treaties with them, recognizing them as distinct political communities, and duty towards them demands *not an enforced citizenship* but a faithful living up to its obligations on the part of the Government.[10]

Suffragists, she suggested, should take a lesson in tactics from Native American men:

> A delegation of Indians called at the White House on New Year's day. As a sarcasm of justice, on their "Happy New Year" cards were inscribed extracts from various treaties made with them, and disregarded rights guaranteed them in treaty by the Government.
>
> The women of the nation might take hint from the Indians and on July 4th, send to the legislative, judicial and executive bodies, cards inscribed with such sentiments as "Governments derive their *just* powers from the *consent* of the governed." "Taxation without representation is tyranny," and others of like character.[11]

She ended her editorial with a look at the juncture of race and gender, where injustice met.

The black man had the right of suffrage conferred upon him without his asking for it, and now an attempt is made to force it upon the red man in direct opposition to his wishes, while women citizens, already members of the nation, to whom it rightfully belongs, are denied its exercise. Truly, consistency is a jewel so rare its only abode is the toad's head.[12]

Gage's interest in the Haudenosaunee (Iroquois) dovetailed with her examination of indigenous societies. In an 1890 *Twentieth Century* article, she reported that the position of women had not always been the inferior one found in Christian nations.

Persons unacquainted with the present phase of historical knowledge assume that woman's place in the family has always been that of an inferior and dependent; man's that of a superior and ruler. But this is not true either of the family, of the State, or in religion. The earliest phase of family life was entirely dependent upon woman; she was the principal factor in it, man having no place whatsoever except as son or dependent. The mother was one through whom blood relationship ran, not alone in the family, but the tribe was united through her. Social, political, and religious life were all in harmony with the idea of woman as the primal power. The matriarchate existed long before the patriarchate. . . . Mother and children constituted the family, woman gave laws to the State, and in all early religions when a goddess and god are mentioned it was mother and son, the mother ever holding superior position.[13]

The subordinate position of Christian women was not biological, inherent, or universal, she reasoned. Neither was morality.

Aside from general historical facts we are thus learning the evolution of morality, finding to our amazement that no absolute standard exists, but morality is relative, depending upon the general condition of society, and what is looked upon as right in one age of the world is regarded as wrong in a preceding or succeeding one.[14]

"Never was justice more perfect, never civilization higher than under the Matriarchate," Gage contended three years later in *Woman, Church and State*. Anticipating the current scholarship on the Iroquois influence on democracy, she noted,

> the most notable fact connected with woman's participation in governmental affairs among the Iroquois is the statement of Hon. George Bancroft that the form of government of the United States was borrowed from that of the Six Nations. Thus to the Matriarchate or Mother-rule is the modern world indebted for its first conception of inherent rights, natural equality of condition, and the establishment of a civilized government upon this basis.[15]

Trained early to think for herself in her parents' abolitionist household, Gage entered the freethought movement in the 1870s, joined the American Theosophical Society the following decade, and became a student of the occult in the 1890s.

Gage spoke at her first freethought convention in 1878. It was that "political religion," Christianity, that Gage had come to see as the chief enemy of woman's rights. The subordination of women was not peripheral to Christianity; it was its centerpiece, Gage asserted:

> You have heard spoken here the wrongs men have felt by the trenching of the Church on their rights. Can one of you tell me what is the foundation doctrine of the Christian church to-day? Does one of you know what is the foundation principle of the three great divisions of the Christian Church—Catholic, Protestant, and Greek? The foundation is not upon Christ; not upon Paul; not upon the doctrine of immersion; it is not upon any of these, but the Christian Church is based upon the fact of woman servitude; upon the theory that woman brought sin and death into the world, and that therefore she was punished by being placed in a condition of inferiority to man—a condition of subjection, of subordination. This is the foundation to-day of the Christian Church.[16]

Gage joined theory and practice when she introduced a series of resolutions at the 1878 NWSA convention holding the church responsible for woman's lack of rights:

RESOLVED: That as the duty of every individual is self-development, the lessons of self-sacrifice and obedience taught women by the Christian church have been fatal not only to her own highest interests, but through her have also dwarfed and degraded the race.

RESOLVED: That the fundamental principle of the Protestant reformation, the right of individual conscience and judgment in the interpretation of Scripture, heretofore conceded to and exercised by men alone, should now be claimed by woman and that in her most vital interests she should no longer trust authority, but be guided by her own reason.

RESOLVED: That it is through the perversion of the religious element in woman, cultivating the emotions at the expense of her reason, playing upon her hopes and fears of the future, holding this life with all its high duties forever in abeyance to that which is to come, that she and the children she has trained, have been so completely subjugated by priest-craft and superstition.[17]

The resolutions passed, much to the dismay of clergy, who denounced them from their pulpits. The press followed suit, the *New York World* declaring: "Never was there a clearer illustration of the evil tendencies of the Woman's Rights movement than in the resolutions adopted at the Rochester convention."[18]

Ten years later, at the 1888 International Council of Women, Gage was still challenging Christianity from the woman's rights platform. "In view of all the past and present continuous revisions of the Bible and its many thousand acknowledged mistakes and interpolations . . . it is folly to expect from women an undoubted belief in man's theological statements and biblical interpretations," she admonished.[19]

Like many in her day, she was thinking through theology for

herself. Gage began her speech on *Women in the Early Church* by remarking, "One of the most notable things connected with this Council has been the almost universal unanimity with which the delegates, both ministerial and lay, in invocation and speech, have ignored the feminine in the Divinity. The morning when I presided over its proceedings I was in some little trouble to find the woman far enough advanced in theology to recognize the divine mother-hood," she continued, "but eventually, in Isabella Beecher Hooker, I secured such person for the invocation with which the programme of the Council demands all proceedings should be opened." Hooker was the half-sister of Henry Ward Beecher, the best-known minister in America. He did not preach to a female God.[20]

Spirituality needed no external authority, Gage suggested. "By no external miracle is the world to be taught truth. The kingdom of heaven lies within; each person can hasten its advent for himself, herself." Gage went on to cast the creation story in gender-inclusive language:

> God, that is Father-Mother, said: "Let us make man in Our image, after Our likeness." So God, Father-Mother, created man, male and female created He-She, them, and called their name Adam, a generic term signifying "red"; or, as has been interpreted, "the one who blushes." In addition, the woman, possessing the feminine attributes of the Divinity, received a specific name, signification of spirit, of life: Eve in our transla-tion, Zoe in the Greek, both signifying life, the one who holds or gives life, the life-giver, the creative principle, in which respect the woman possesses superiority over the man.[21]

Gage had been studying the challenge to religion that science was making in the area of biology.

> While the Church has opposed every demand of woman for higher opportunities, on the ground of feminine inferiority and secondary creation, the more recent biological discoveries, prove exactly the contrary. . . . Not only are the primal forms of life feminine, but as far as has been discovered, the great under-lying creative principle is solely and distinctively feminine.[22]

As a Theosophist, Gage believed that events relegated to the "occult" followed a natural law, which could be studied and scientifically proven, like any other natural event. A student of the supernatural, she kept careful records of the predictions of astrologers, mediums, and psychics she had consulted, in order to determine their accuracy. Gage saw the occult not as a new religious superstition which would further enslave people's minds, but as a rediscovered science through which events could be predicted, allowing people to take greater control of their lives.

Gage shared her process of study, along with the depth of her personal spirituality, in a letter to her son, Thomas Clarkson—who, incidentally, was named after a famous English abolitionist.

> I am much interested in microscopy. . . . You know Theosophy says—I think Esoteric Buddhism—that *matter, space, motion and duration* constitute one and the same eternal substance of the Universe. There is nothing else eternal absolutely. . . . In these observations of science I find many things confirmatory of Theosophy. . . . *I* "get satisfaction" in seeing the wonderful progress and advance of the world in all occult, hidden and spiritual things. *The church* has darkened man's understandings by prohibiting free thought, and by asserting as true things of which it knew nothing.
>
> I think. I judge for myself, and I as fully believe that all of me that is of value is *spiritual* as I do that this world and its existences are full of limitations and yet a place for study & growth. . . . I think after a few more years of investigation the world will be spiritually wiser than now.[23]

While her intellectual investigation revealed to Gage a female creative principle, moral relativity, and spirituality residing not in external authority but in personal integrity, a religious backlash was rising up in the country that challenged this emerging theology.

The country moved toward the Right in the late 1880s, carried along by a conservative religious movement that had as its goal the creation of a Christian state. Rather than fall into discouraged silence, Gage decided it was time to launch a full-scale attack on the church. Stanton agreed. Believing that the danger to religious liberty and a secular state was immediate, Gage and Stanton began talking of the need for a feminist antichurch organization. At the same time Anthony was moving toward a single-minded focus on obtaining the vote.

Although much of their energy went into working for the vote, Gage and Stanton never saw suffrage as an end in itself. Never for a minute did they believe that gaining the vote would, in and of itself, change women's lives for the better. Gage and Stanton agreed that the ballot was "the lever with which to lift one-half of humanity from the depths of degradation" caused by "the four-fold bondage of women" at the hands of the state, the church, the capitalist, and the home. Increasingly they were "sick of the song of suffrage."[24]

As the two major theoreticians grew more restive over a focus limited to the vote, a new army of suffrage recruits entered the movement. The Women's Christian Temperance Union (WCTU), under the banner "For God and Home and Native Land," represented a conservative army of "organized mother-love" devoted to cleaning up the country's impurities, especially the liquor traffic. When praying and singing failed to accomplish their goals, Frances Willard received divine inspiration (she said) to work for woman suffrage. With the ballot in their hands, the mothers of America could then legislate morality. Willard joined the American Woman Suffrage Association, as did many WCTU members.[25]

Beyond temperance, however, the WCTU plan embraced the agenda of the religious right: mandatory prayers in the public schools, mandatory Sunday rest, and, most chilling, the Constitution amended to recognize Christ as "the author and head of government."

Religious conservatives had a well-orchestrated program. Bills were introduced in Congress requiring school prayers and a closure of all public facilities on Sunday. Supported by the WCTU, a Prohibition Party sprang up with a preamble calling on "Almighty God as the source of all power in government." One of their platforms called for the establishment of uniform national laws governing marriage and divorce based on the conservative

Christian notion that marriage was a divine union which could not be broken, even if a woman's life was in danger from her husband. Gage warned, "This looks like a return to the Middle Ages and proscription for religious opinions, and is the great danger of the hour." Stanton believed that the conservative Christian women failed to see that their plan could produce a police state of enforcement, writing:

> These women do not seem to see that all this special legislation about faith, Sabbaths, drinking, etc., etc., is the entering wedge to general governmental interference which would eventually subject us to an espionage that would soon become tyrannical in the extreme.[26]

The Prohibition Party also included a suffrage plank, calling for the states (not the federal government) to restore the right of suffrage to all who would meet "moral and educational qualifications." The "moral evidently to be twisted church-wise," Gage worried. The WCTU wanted women to get the vote for reasons diametrically opposed to the plans of the NWSA, as an old-time reformer explained:

> I am a woman suffragist through and through, because I believe in human rights, in human liberty. The orthodox party are woman suffragists, because they want to get the power to suppress both.[27]

In the meantime, Anthony was following a path destined to bring her into conflict with the other two suffrage leaders. With her eye on creating a united front of all suffrage advocates, Anthony led her followers in merging the two existing suffrage groups, the AWSA and NWSA, thereby bringing in the conservative WCTU forces. Anthony justified her action to Olympia Brown:

> I suppose your feeling of my change is the same as that of Mrs. Gage and Mrs. Stanton—that is because I am not as intolerant of the so-called Christian women as they are—that therefore I

have gone, or am about to go over to the popular church. I do not approve of their system of fighting the religious dogmas of the people I am trying to convert to my doctrine of equal rights to women. But if they can afford to distrust my religious integrity, I can afford to let them.[28]

Becoming less active in the day-to-day work of the organization, Stanton stayed on the sidelines while Gage organized opposition to the merger. As chair of the NWSA Executive Committee, "I need money," she wrote her son. The association "has been steered into an orthodox pit-hole by Miss Anthony & her aids—and it needs not only a strong will, but money to put us back. . . . The opposition has money and spends it freely. I have brains, will & the sustaining hand of many."[29]

Gage's assets weren't enough, however, to challenge Anthony successfully. In Gage's absence (Anthony didn't send her enough money to travel to the convention), the NWSA Executive Committee voted to merge with the AWSA by a vote of 30 to 11.[30]

Unable to stop the merger, Gage dropped out of the suffrage ranks and focused her energy on forming the National Woman's Liberal Union, an organization to challenge the religious right. Stanton chose not to join Gage in this work, accepting instead the presidency of the merged suffrage organization, the National American Woman Suffrage Association.

Made up of anarchists, prison reformers, labor leaders, and feminists, the Woman's National Liberal Union was viewed as one of the most radical organizations in the country, certainly by the government, which intercepted Gage's mail. Anthony denounced Gage's "secession" (as she called it) from the suffrage ranks, and Gage spent the final eight years of her life estranged from most of her movement allies and friends of the previous forty years.[31]

Gage did work again with Stanton, however, as a member of the revising committee for Stanton's *Woman's Bible*, which analyzed the Bible from a feminist perspective. In her interpretations of Kings and Revelations, Gage speculates that the Bible is a "record of ancient mysteries hidden to all but initiates," and she interprets the occult meaning of names, numbers, and symbols used in the Bible. Revelations, she posits, is "a purely esoteric work, largely referring to woman, her intuition, her spiritual powers, and all she represents," which can only be explained through a knowledge of astrology.[32]

Gage was not antireligion per se. She was, in fact, deeply religious, believing that "to undo the heavy burdens and let the oppressed go free, is the truest religion." Christianity could become a force for liberation if it was stripped of its triple doctrine of obedience to authority, woman's subordination to man, and original sin, and was based instead on equality, individual responsibility, and freedom. That was not the way it had developed, however, Gage contended:

> The doctrine of woman's secondary creation and subordination was a part of Judaism engrafted upon Christianity, soon becoming a component part of the new religion, in fact its corner-stone; for, without the doctrine of the fall, and the consequent need of a Savior, the whole Christian super-structure drops into nothingness.[33]

Gage's analysis held first that the foundation of woman's oppression was the church and second (and most startling) that the foundation of the church was the oppression of women. Common law was based on canon law, firmly setting women legally, politically, socially, and economically in the subordinate position in which Christianity had placed them religiously. It would take a revolution beyond any seen yet in the world, Gage maintained, to free women:

> During the ages, no rebellion has been of like importance with that of Woman against the tyranny of Church and State; none has had its far-reaching effects. We note its beginning; its progress will overthrow every existing form of these institutions; its end will be a regenerated world.[34]

"Even if I should slip out, my chief life work, my *Woman, Church and State* is done, ready for the printer," Gage wrote her son in February 1893. The book was on the market by July, published by the socialist firm of Charles Kerr in Chicago. The cloth edition sold for $2.00 and a half-leather cover edition cost $3.00.[35] When asked by a reporter why she wrote the book, Gage answered:

> My long work of over forty years in the Woman Suffrage reform, holding there the most important offices, both in the state and national societies, [and] having appeared before many congressional and legislative committees, taught me that the great obstacle to woman's enfranchisement lay in the teachings of the church, both Catholic and Protestant, that woman was created inferior to man, brought sin into the world and was therefore under an especial "curse." Knowing these teachings to be false I deemed it my duty to break the bonds which hold both men and women captive.[36]

Gage then went on to share the most important lesson of her life, which ultimately led her to write the book:

> People are trained to believe what the church teaches, without examining for themselves. . . . If there has been one education of more value to me than all others, it was the training I received from my father to think for myself.[37]

Gage presented a copy of *Woman, Church and State* to the school library in her hometown of Fayetteville, New York. A school-board member prominent in the local Roman Catholic church sent the book to Anthony Comstock (chief enforcer of the obscenity laws bearing his name) asking him to render an opinion on the book. Comstock threatened to arrest the school-board members if they placed the book in the school library.[38]

"The Book Has Bitter Enemies and Warm Friends," a headline read, and those who loved the book (most of whom were women) had as much good to say about it as those who hated it had bad things to say. Victoria Woodhull Martin's English magazine, the *Humanitarian,* applauded the vigor and directness with which Gage "swept away the theological cobwebs which for ages have obscured the light."[39]

The ideas in her book, Gage contended, should be studied and contemplated, not accepted or rejected on anyone's say: "I do not ask anyone to accept my work alone. I have given abundant proof of my assertions in the very copious notes with which the book abounds."[40]

Ten years after its publication, in 1913 (Gage died in 1898), the book was still in print and a bibliography of the National American Woman Suffrage Association denounced *Woman, Church and State* as: "Fanatical and solemn without impressiveness; an uncompromising and unpersuasive attack on church and state—especially church—for their attitude towards woman." The woman's movement had become religiously respectable (Stanton's *Woman's Bible*, from which the organization had earlier disassociated itself, is not even mentioned on the list) and the process of eliminating the far more radical suffragist Matilda Joslyn Gage from history was nearly complete.[41]

Woman, Church and State stayed in print until 1917 and then was lost to history, as was its author. When the book was reissued in 1980 by a feminist publishing house (Persephone Press), the second wave of the woman's movement, hungry for the ideas, greeted it with open arms. It quickly gained a reputation as a feminist classic, "indispensable" according to Mary Daly in her foreword, "for an understanding of the women's movement today."[42]

Reviews exclaimed: "A visionary work that belongs in every woman's library and in every women's studies program"; ". . . anticipates many of the themes of recent feminist scholarship"; ". . . indispensable for scholars of nineteenth-century feminism and religion"; "Why was this book allowed to go out of print? Why has this woman's work been lost to us?" The author was lauded as "one of the most witty and brilliant social theorists that America has yet produced."[43]

Now, a new audience has discovered Gage. A century after her death, her views create a cultural bridge, and Native Americans are "discovering" Matilda Joslyn Gage as they confront, and heal from, the damage Christianity has done to them.

"I received the name of Ka-ron-ien-ha-wi, or 'Sky Carrier,'" Gage described her adoption into the wolf clan of the Mohawk nation in 1893, the year *Woman, Church and State* was published. Her Mohawk sister said "this name would admit me to the Council of Matrons, where a vote would be taken, as to my having a voice in the Chieftainship," Gage wrote. How amazing this must have been to a woman who went to trial the same year for registering to vote in a public school board election. Considered for full voting rights in her adopted nation, she was arrested in her own nation for preparing to exercise that right.[44]

Tehanetorens (Ray Fadden), founder of the Akwesasne Mohawk Counselor Organization and the Six Nations Museum in Onchiota, New York, wrote in 1988 when he first read *Woman, Church and State*, "I wish that every person in the country would read that book, it is great, believe me."[45]

Today the Matilda Joslyn Gage Foundation, headquartered in her Fayetteville, New York, home, carries on the mission of restoring this remarkable woman to her rightful place in history.

Gage remained hopeful to the end of her life, judging that the fundamentalist backlash against a religion of freedom was simply a last-gasp effort by religious conservatives. The world was changing and women would one day be free, she believed.

> The night of ignorance, credulity, and despair is nearly at an end; the dawn is at hand; the feminine will soon be fully restored to this rightful place in creation and in religion as well as in law, in the divinity as well as in humanity, we shall find recognition of the sexual duality of all life, of the motherhood as well as the fatherhood of God.[46]

Sally Roesch Wagner
Matilda Joslyn Gage Foundation
Fayetteville, New York

Notes

1. Speech of Matilda Joslyn Gage at the Woman's National Liberal Convention, "Dangers of the Hour," February 24, 1890, Matilda Joslyn Gage Papers, Schlesinger Library, Radcliffe College (hereafter cited as Gage Papers).

2. *Woman's National Liberal Union Convention for Organization Resolutions*, Gage Papers.

3. *The Woman's Journal*, 28 March 1888. Wendy Martin, ed., *The American Sisterhood* (New York: Harper and Row, 1972), p. 83. Martin, one of the few contemporary suffrage historians to recognize the importance of Gage, uses this term.

4. *New Era*, December 1885.

5. Matilda Joslyn Gage, *Woman as Inventor*, Woman Suffrage Tracts, no. 1 (Fayetteville, N.Y.: F. A. Darling, Printer, 1870).

6. *National Citizen and Ballot Box*, August 1878.

7. Matilda Joslyn Gage: "The Onondaga Indians," *New York Evening Post*, 3 November 1875; "The Remnant of the Five Nations," *Evening Post*, 24 September, 1875; "Msickquatash," *Appleton's Journal* (1875); "The Burning of the White Dog, *Appleton's Journal* 15, no. 373 (1876): 628–29. Scrapbook of Gage's published writings, Gage Papers.

8. "The Remnant of the Five Nations."

9. Matilda Joslyn Gage, "Indian Citizenship," *Syracuse (N.Y.) National Citizen and Ballot Box*, May 1878, p. 2.

10. Ibid.

11. Ibid.

12. Ibid.

13. Matilda Joslyn Gage, "The Matriarchate," *Twentieth Century*, 25 December 1890.

14. Ibid.

15. Matilda Joslyn Gage, *Woman, Church and State* (1893; reprint, South Dakota: Sky Carrier Press, 1998), p. 6.

16. Address of Mrs. Gage, the Watkins Convention (1878), Free Thought Collection, New York Public Library.

17. NWSA Convention July 19, 1878 held in Rochester, New York, on the thirtieth anniversary of the first woman's rights convention. Resolutions in Elizabeth Cady Stanton, Susan B. Anthony, and Matilda Joslyn Gage, *History of Woman Suffrage* (1886; reprint, Salem, N. H.: Ayer Company, 1985), 3:124.

18. *National Citizen and Ballot Box*, August/September 1878.

19. Matilda Joslyn Gage, "Woman in the Early Christian Church," International Council of Women; Religious Symposium, April 1, 1888. Report of the International Council of Women, assembled by the National Woman Suffrage Association, Washington, D.C., March 25 to April 1, 1888 (Washington, D.C.: National Woman Suffrage Association, 1888), pp. 400–407.

20. Ibid.

21. Ibid.

22. Gage, Matilda Joslyn, "The Church, Science, and Woman," *Index*, 29 April 1886.

23. Matilda Joslyn Gage to Thomas Clarkson Gage, 3 February 1888, Gage Papers.

24. Stanton, Anthony, and Gage, preface to *History of Woman Suffrage*, 3: vi.

25. Frances E. Willard, *Glimpses of Fifty Years* (Chicago: Woman's Temperance Publication Association, 1889), pp. 442–45.

26. Anna Gordon, *The Beautiful Life of Frances Willard* (Chicago: Woman's Temperance Publishing Association, 1898), pp. 114–15; Gage to Stanton, 13 July 1888, Gage Papers; Alma Lutz, *Created Equal* (New York: John Day Company, 1940), p. 276.

27. WCTU and Prohibition Party information in *Woman's Tribune* throughout the fall, 1888.

28. Susan B. Anthony to Olympia Brown, 11 March 1889, Brown Papers, Schlesinger Library, Radcliffe College.

29. Matilda Joslyn Gage to Thomas Clarkson Gage, 26 May 1888, Gage Papers.

30. Matilda Joslyn Gage, "A Statement of Facts, Private. To Members of the NWSA Only," Gage Papers.

31. Susan B. Anthony to Eliza Wright Osbourne, 5 February and 5 March 1890, Garrison Papers, Sophia Smith Library, Smith College.

32. Matilda Joslyn Gage, Comments on Revelations in Elizabeth Cady Stanton and the Revising Committee, *The Woman's Bible* (New York: European Publishing Company, 1898), p. 176.

33. Gage, "The Church, Science, and Woman."

34. Gage, *Woman, Church and State*, p. 324.

35. Promotional material inserted in first edition of *Woman, Church and State* (Chicago: Charles Kerr, 1893), author's collection.

36. "Mrs. Gage's Book, *Woman, Church and State*," *Fayetteville Weekly Recorder*, 1893, Gage Papers.

37. Ibid.

38. Ibid.

39. Ibid.

40. Ibid.

41. Margaret Ladd Franklin, *The Case for Woman Suffrage: A Bibliography* (New York City: National College Equal Suffrage League, 1913), p. 67.

42. Mary Daly, Foreword to *Woman, Church & State: The Original Expose of Male Collaboration Against the Female Sex* (Watertown, Mass.: Persephone Press, 1980), p. vii.

43. Carol P. Christ, "Book Review," *Religious Studies Review* 8, no. 1 (January 1982); Mary Casey, "Tough, Creative Vision," *Plexus* (October 1981); Marcia Womangold, "Review," *Equal Times* (23 November 1980).

44. Matilda Joslyn Gage to "My dear Helen," 11 December 1893, Gage Papers; "They Want to Vote," *Syracuse Sunday Herald*, 29 October 1893.

45. Tehanetorens (Ray Fadden) to the author, 23 November 1988, cited by permission.

46. Gage, "Woman in the Early Christian Church," p. 407.

WOMAN,
CHURCH AND
STATE

This Book is Inscribed to the Memory of my Mother, who was at once mother, sister, friend:

Dedicated to all Christian women and men, of whatever creed or name who, bound by Church or State, have not dared to Think for Themselves:

Addressed to all Persons, who, breaking away from custom and the usage of ages, dare seek Truth for the sake of Truth. To all such it will be welcome; to all others, aggressive and educational.

This work explains itself and is given to the world because it is needed. Tired of the obtuseness of Church and State; indignant at the injustice of both towards woman; at the wrongs inflicted upon one-half of humanity by the other half in the name of religion; finding appeal and argument alike met by the assertion that God designed the subjection of woman, and yet that her position had been higher under Christianity than ever before: Continually hearing these statements, and knowing them to be false, I refuted them in a slight *résumé* of the subject at the annual conventIon of the National Woman Suffrage Association, Washington, D.C., 1878.

A wish to see that speech in print, having been expressed, it was allowed to appear in *The National Citizen*, a woman suffrage paper I then edited, and shortly afterwards in "The History of Woman Suffrage," of which I was also an editor. The kindly reception given both in the United States and Europe, to that meager chapter of forty pages confirmed my purpose of a fuller presentation of the subject in book form, and it now appears, the result of twenty years investigation, in a volume of over five hundred and fifty pages.

Read it; examine for yourselves; accept or reject from the proof offered, but do not allow the Church or the State, to govern your thought or dictate your judgment.

CONTENTS

Chapter I—The Matriarchate

Tendency of Christianity from the first to restrict woman's liberty. Woman had great freedom under the old civilizations. The Matriarchate; its traces among many nations; it preceded the Patriarchate. The Iroquois or Six Nations under reminiscences of the Matriarchate. Government of the United States borrowed from the Six Nations. To the Matriarchate, or Mother-rule, is the world indebted for its first conception of "inherent rights," and a government established on this basis. Malabar under the Matriarchate when discovered by the Portuguese. The most ancient Aryans under the Matriarchate. Ancient Egypt a reminiscence of the Matriarchal period. Authority of the wife among the most polished nations of antiquity. As Vestal Virgin in Rome, woman's authority great both in civil and religious affairs. Monogamy the rule of the Matriarchate. Polygamy, infanticide and prostitution the rule of the Patriarchate 39

Chapter II—Celibacy

Chapter III—Canon Law

Chapter IV—Marquette

Chapter V—Witchcraft

Chapter VI—Wives

Chapter VII—Polygamy

Chapter VIII—Woman and Work

Chapter IX—The Church of Today

Chapter X—Past, Present, Future

Chapter I

The
Matriarchate

W oman is told that her present position in society is
entirely due to Christianity; that it is superior to that
of her sex at any prior age of the world, Church and State both
maintaining that she has ever been inferior and dependent, man
superior and ruler. These assertions are made the basis of opposition to her demands for exact equality with man in all the relations
of life, although they are not true either of the family, the church,
or the state. Such assertions are due to nonacquaintance with the
existing phase of historical knowledge, whose records the majority
of mankind have neither time nor opportunity of investigating.

Christianity tended somewhat from its foundation to restrict
the liberty woman enjoyed under the old civilizations. Knowing
that the position of every human being keeps pace with the religion and civilization of his country, and that in many ancient
nations woman possessed a much greater degree of respect and
power than she has at the present age, this subject will be presented

from a historical standpoint. If in so doing it helps to show man's unwarranted usurpation over woman's religious and civil rights, and the very great difference between true religion and theology, this book will not have been written in vain, as it will prove that the most grievous wrong ever inflicted upon woman has been in the Christian teaching that she was not created equal with man, and the consequent denial of her rightful place in Church and State.

The last half century has shown great advance in historical knowledge; libraries and manuscripts long inaccessible have been opened to scholars, and the spirit of investigation has made known many secrets of the past, brought many hidden things to light. Buried cities have been explored and forced to reveal their secrets; lost modes of writing have been deciphered, and olden myths placed upon historic foundations. India is opening her stores of ancient literature; Egypt, so wise and so famous, of which it was anciently said: "If it does not find a man mad it leaves him mad," has revealed her secrets; hieroglyph inscribed temples, obelisks and tombs have been interpreted; papyri buried 4,000 and more years in the folds of bandage-enveloped mummies have given their secrets to the world. The brick libraries of Assyria have been unearthed, and the lost civilization of Babylonia and Chaldea imparted to mankind. The strange Zuni's have found an interpreter; the ancient Astec language its Champollion, and the mysteries of even our western continent are becoming unveiled. Darkest Africa has opened to the light; the colossal images of Easter Island hint at their origin; while the new science of philology unfolds to us the history of peoples so completely lost that no other monument of their past remains. We are now informed as to the condition of early peoples, their laws, customs, habits, religion, comprising order and rank in the state, the rules of descent, name, property, the circumstances of family life, the position of mother, father, children, their temples and priestly orders; all these have been investigated and a new historic basis has been discovered. Never has research been so thorough or long-lost knowledge so fully given to the world.

These records prove that woman had acquired great liberty

under the old civilizations. A form of society existed at an early age known as the Matriarchate or Mother-rule. Under the Matriarchate, except as son and inferior, man was not recognized in either of these great institutions, family, state or church. A father and husband as such, had no place either in the social, political or religious scheme; woman was ruler in each. The primal priest on earth, she was also supreme as goddess in heaven. The earliest semblance of the family is traceable to the relationship of mother and child alone. Here the primal idea of the family had birth.[1] The child bore its mother's name, tracing its descent from her; her authority over it was regarded as in accord with nature; the father having no part in the family remained a wanderer. Long years elapsed before man, as husband and father, was held in esteem. The son, as child of his mother, ranked the father, the mother taking precedence over both the father and the son.[2] Blood relationship through a common mother preceded that of descent through the father in the development of society.[3] This priority of the mother touched not alone the family, but controlled the state and indicated the form of religion. Thus we see that during the Matriarchate, woman ruled; she was first in the family, the state, religion, the most ancient records showing that man's subjection to woman preceded by long ages that of woman to man. The tribe was united through the mother; social, political and religious life were all in harmony with the idea of woman as the first and highest power. The earliest phase of life being dependent upon her, she was recognized as the primal factor in every relation,[4] man holding no place but that of dependant.

Every part of the world today gives evidence of the system; reminiscences of the Matriarchate everywhere abound. Livingstone found African tribes swearing by the mother and tracing descent through her. Marco Polo discovered similar customs in his Asiatic voyages, and the same customs are extant among the Indians of our own continent. Backofen[5] and numerous investigators[6] agree in the statement that in the earliest forms of society; the family, government, and religion, were all under woman's control; that in fact society started under woman's absolute authority and power.

The second step in family life took place when the father, dropping his own name, took that of his child. This old and wide-spread custom is still extant in many portions of the globe; the primitive peoples of Java, Australia and Madagascar are among those still continuing its practice.[7] By this step the father allied himself to both mother and child, although still holding an inferior position to both. The Matriarchal family was now fully established, descent still running in the female line. Thus, as has been expressed, we find that woman's liberty did not begin today nor under modern religions or forms or government, but that she was in reality the founder of civilization, and that in the most remote times woman enjoyed superiority of rights in all the institutions of life.[8] And yet so difficult is it to break away from educated thought, so slight a hold have historical facts upon the mind when contrary to preconceived ideas, that we find people still expressing the opinion that man's place has always been first in government. Even under those forms of society where woman was undisputed head of the family, its very existence due to her, descent entirely in the female line, we still hear assertion that his must have been the controlling political power. But at that early period to which we trace the formation of the family, it was also the political unit. And when peoples became aggregated into communities, when tribal relations were ultimately recognized, woman still held superior position, and was the controlling power in government, and never was justice more perfect, never civilization higher than under the Matriarchate. Historians agree as to the high civilization even today of those nations or tribes still preserving traces of Matriarchal customs. Even under its most degenerate form, the family, governmental and religious rights of women are more fully recognized than under any phase of Christian civilization. In all the oldest religions, equally with the Semetic cults, the feminine was recognized as a component and superior part of divinity, goddesses holding the supreme place. Even at much later periods woman shared equally with man in the highest priestly offices, and was deified after death. In Egypt, Neith the Victorious, was worshiped as mother of the gods, and in the yearly festival held in her honor, every family took part for the time holding a priestly office. To neglect this duty was deemed an omission of great irreverence.[9] The most ancient occultism recognized the creative power as feminine and preceding both gods and men.

Under the Matriarchate, monogamy was the rule; neither polyandry or promiscuity existed.[10]

For long years after the decline of the Matriarchate we still discover that among many of the most refined nations, woman still possessed much of the power that belonged exclusively to her during that early period. Ancient Egypt, recognized as the wisest nation since the direct historic period, traced descent even to the throne in the female line. To this reminiscence of the Matriarchate are we indebted for the story of Moses and his preservation by an Egyptian princess in direct contravention of the Pharaoh's orders, as told by the Bible and Josephus. She not alone preserved the child's life but carried him to the king as her son given to her by the bounty of the river and heir to his throne. As showing woman's power in that kingdom, the story is worthy of being farther traced. Josephus says that to please his daughter, the king took the child in his arms, placing his crown on the baby head, but the chief priest at that moment entering the room, in a spirit of prophecy cried aloud, "Oh King; this is the child of whom I foretold danger; kill him and save the nation," at the same time striving to take the babe from the king. But the princess caught him away thus setting both kingly and priestly power at defiance, taking this step by virtue of her greater authority, protecting him until he reached manhood and causing him to be educated in all the wisdom of the Egyptians, in a college under her own control. Nor in the supreme hour of the nation's peril, when the king, too old to lead his armies to battle, demanded Moses as heir to the throne in his place, would she give him up until she had exacted an oath from her father, the potent Pharaoh, that he meant the youth no harm.

The famous Iroquois Indians, or Six Nations, which at the discovery of America held sway from the great lakes to the Tombigbee river, from the Hudson to the Ohio, and of whom it has been said that another century would have found them master of all tribes to the Gulf of Mexico on the south, and the Mississippi on the west, showed alike in form of government, and in social life, reminiscences of the Matriarchate. The line of descent, feminine, was especially notable in all tribal relations such as the election of Chiefs, and the Council of Matrons, to which all disputed questions were referred for final adjudication. No sale of lands was valid without consent of the squaws and among the State Archives at Albany, New York, treaties are preserved signed by the "Sachems and Principal Women of the Six Nations."[11] The women also possessed the veto power on questions of war. Sir William Johnston mentions an instance of Mohawk squaws forbidding the warpath to young braves. The family relation among the Iroquois demonstrated woman's superiority in power. When an Indian husband brought the products of the chase to the wigwam, his control over it ceased. In the home, the wife was absolute; the sale of the skins was regulated by her, the price was paid to her. If for any cause the Iroquois husband and wife separated, the wife took with her all the property she had brought into the wigwam; the children also accompanied the mother, whose right to them was recognized as supreme. So fully to this day is descent reckoned through the mother, that blue-eyed, fair-haired children of white fathers are numbered in the tribe and receive both from state and nation their portion of the yearly dole paid to Indian tribes. The veriest pagan among the Iroquois, the renowned and important Keeper of the Wampum, and present sole interpreter of the Belts which give the most ancient and secret history of this confederation, is Ephraim Webster, descended from a white man, who, a hundred or more years since, became affiliated through marriage with an Indian woman, as a member of the principal nation of the Iroquois, the Onondagas. As of yore, so now, the greater and lesser Council Houses of the Iroquois are upon the "mountain" of the Onondaga reservation a few miles from the city of Syracuse, New York. Not alone the Iroquois but most Indians of North America trace descent in the female line; among some tribes woman enjoys almost the whole legislative authority and in others a prominent share.[12] Lafitte and

other Jesuit missionary writers are corroborated in this statement
by Schoolcraft, Catlin, Clark, Hubert Bancroft of the Pacific coast,
and many students of Indian life and customs. But the most
notable fact connected with woman's participation in governmental affairs among the Iroquois is the statement of Hon.
George Bancroft that the form of government of the United
States, was borrowed from that of the Six Nations.[13] Thus to the
Matriarchate or Mother-rule is the modern world indebted for its
first conception of inherent rights, natural equality of condition,
and the establishment of a civilized government upon this basis.
Although the reputation of the Iroquois as warriors appears most
prominent in history, we nevertheless find their real principles to
have been the true Matriarchal one of peace and industry. Driven
from the northern portion of America by vindictive foes, compelled to take up arms in self-protection, yet the more peaceful
occupations of hunting and agriculture were continually followed. Their history was preserved by means of wampum, while
under their women the science of government reached the
highest form known to the world. Among the Zunis of Mexico,
woman still preserves supreme religious and political authority;
the Paramount Council consisting of six priests under control of
a supreme priestess who is the most important functionary of the
tribe.[14] This form of government is traceable to their earliest civilization at which period their cities were grouped in sevens, six
of them constructed upon a uniform plan; the supreme seventh
containing six temples clustered about a supreme central seventh
temple. While male priests ruled over the six primal cities the central and superior seventh was presided over by a priestess who not
alone officiated at the central temple, but to whom the male
priests of the six cities and six inferior temples were subservient.
The ancient Lycians, the Sclavs, the Basques of Spain,[15] the Veddas
of Ceylon,[16] the inhabitants of Malabar, the aborigines of widely
separated lands, all show convincing proof of woman's early superiority in religion, in the state, and in the family. Monogamy was
a marked feature of the Matriarchate; Backofen, who has written
voluminously upon the Matriarchate, recognizes it as peculiarly

characteristic of woman's government. He also says the people who possessed the Mother-rule together with Gynaikokraty (girls' rule) excelled in their love of peace and justice. Under the Matriarchal family and tribal system even long after its partial supercedence by the incoming Patriarachate, the marriage relation was less oppressive to woman than it has been under most centuries of christian civilization. Daughters were free in their choice of husbands, no form of a force or sale existing.[17]

One of the most brilliant modern examples of the Matriarchate was found in Malabar at the time of its discovery by the Portuguese in the XV century. The Nairs were found to possess a fine civilization, entirely under the control of women, at a period when woman's position in England and on the Continent of Europe, was that of a household and political slave. Of Malabar it has been said, that when the Portuguese became acquainted with the country and the people, they were not so much surprised by the opulence of their cities, the splendor of all their habits of living, the great perfection of their navy, the high state of the arts, as they were to find all this under the entire control and government of women. The difference in civilization between christian Europe and pagan Malabar at the time of its discovery was indeed great. While Europe with its new art of printing, was struggling against the church for permission to use type, its institutions of learning few, its opportunities for education meagre; its terrible inquisition crushing free thought and sending thousands each year to a most painful death, the uncleanliness of its cities and the country such as to bring frequent visits of the plague; its armies and its navies with but one exception, imperfect; its women forbidden the right of inheritance, religious, political, or household authority;—the feminine principle entirely eliminated from the divinity—a purely masculine God the universal object of worship, all was directly the opposite in Malabar. Cleanliness, peace, the arts, a just form of government, the recognition of the feminine both in humanity and in the divinity were found in Malabar. To the question of a Danish missionary concerning their opinion of a Supreme Being, this beautiful answer was given.

The Supreme Being has a Form and yet has no Form; he can
be likened to nothing; we cannot define him and say that he is
this or that; he is neither Man or Woman; neither Heaven or
Earth, and yet he is all; subject to no corruption, no mortality
and with neither sleep nor rest, he is Almighty and Omnipo-
tent without Beginning and without End.[18]

Under the Missionaries sent by England to introduce her
own barbaric ideas of God and man, this beautiful Matriarchal
civilization of Malabar soon retrograded and was lost.

The ancient Mound Builders of America, of whom history
is silent and science profoundly ignorant, are proven by means of
symbolism to have been under Matriarchal rule, and Motherhood
religion. Anciently motherhood was represented by a sphere or
circle. The circle like the mundane egg which is but an elongated
circle, contains everything in itself and is the true microcosm. It
is eternity, it is feminine, the creative force, representing spirit.
Through its union with matter in the form of the nine digits it is
likewise capable of representing all natural things.[19] The perfect
circle of Giotto was an emblem of divine motherhood in its
completeness. It is a remarkable fact—its significance not recognized,—that the roughly sketched diameter within the circle,
found wherever boys congregate, is an ancient mystic sign[20] signifying the male and female, or the double-sexed deity. It is the
union of all numbers, the one within the zero mark comprising
ten, and as part of the ancient mysteries signifying God, the creative power, and eternal life; it was an emblem of The All.

In many old religions, the generative principle was regarded as
the mother of both gods and men. In the Christian religion we
find tendency to a similar recognition in Catholic worship of the
Virgin Mary. The most ancient Aryans were under the Matriarchate, the feminine recognized as the creative power. The word
"ma" from which all descendants of those peoples derive their
names for mother, was synonomous with "Creator." Renouf, the
great antiquarian authority upon the Aryan's,[21] gives the songs and
ceremonies of the wedding. In these, the woman is represented as

having descended to man from association with divine beings in whose custody and care she has been, and who give her up with reluctance. In Sanscrit mythology,[22] the feminine is represented by Swrya, the Sun, the source of life, while the masculine is described as Soma, a body. Soma, a beverage of the gods especially sacred to Indra was the price paid by him for the assistance of Vâyu, the swiftest of the gods, in his battle against the demon Vritra. A curious line of thought is suggested. The marriage of the man to the woman was symbolized as his union with the gods. Soma, a drink devoted to Indra, the highest god, signified his use of a body, or the union of spirit and body. In the same manner, woman representing spirit, by her marriage to man became united with a body. As during the present dark age, the body has been regarded more highly than the spirit, we find a nonrecognition of the woman, although the union of spirit and body is symbolized in the Christian church by the sacrament of bread and wine. During the purest period of Aryan history marriage was entirely optional with woman and when entered into, frequently meant no more than spiritual companionship. Woman equally with man was entitled to the Brahminical thread; she also possessed the right to study and preach the Vedas, which was in itself a proof of her high position in this race. The Vedas, believed to be the oldest literature extant, were for many ages taught orally requiring years of close application upon part of both teacher and student.

The word "Veda" signifies *to know*; the latter from "Vidya" meaning *wise*. The English term widow is traceable to both forms of the word, meaning a wise woman—one who knows man. Many ages passed before the Vedas were committed to writing.[23] At that early day the ancestral worship of women—departed mothers—was as frequent as that of departed fathers, women conducting such services which took place three times a day. In the old Aryan Scriptures the right of woman to hold property, and to her children, was much more fully recognized, than under the Christian codes of today. Many of the olden rights of women are still extant in India. The learned Keshub Chunder Sen vigorously protested against the introduction of English law into India, upon the ground that it would destroy the ancient rights of the women of that country. It was primal Indian law that upon the death of the husband the wife should heir all his property. Marriage was regarded as an eternal union, the two, by this act, having so fully become one, that upon the husband's death, one half of his body was still living. The property and the children were held as equally belonging to the husband or the wife.

Colebrook's *Digest of Hindoo Law*, compiled from the writings of the Bengal Pundit Jergunnat, 'Na Tercapancháma, from those of Vasist ha, Cátayana, and other Indian authorities says:

> In the Veda, in Codes of Law, in sacred ordinances, the wife is held as one person with the husband; both are considered one. When the wife is not dead, half the body remains; how shall another take the property when half the body of the owner lives? After the death of the husband the widow shall take his wealth; this is primeval law.
>
> Though a woman be dependent, the alienation of female property, or of the mother's right over her son by the gift of a husband alone[24] is not valid in law or reason;
>
> The female property of wives like the property of a stranger, may not be given, for there is want of ownership.
>
> Neither the husband, nor the son, nor the father nor the brother, have power to use or alien the legal property of a woman.
>
> We hold it proper that the wife's co-operation shall be required in civil contracts and in religious acts under the text.
>
> A gift to a wife is irrevocable.

The collection of East Indian laws made under authority of the celebrated Warren Hastings, 1776, is of similar character. The kinds of property a wife can hold separate from her husband at her own disposal by will, are specified.

During long centuries while under Christian law the Christian wife was not allowed even the control of property her own at the time of marriage, or of that which might afterwards be given her, and her right of the disposition of property at the time of her death was not recognized in Christian lands, the Hindoo wife, under immemorial custom could receive property by gift alike from her parents, or from strangers, or acquire it by her own industry, and property thus gained was at her own disposal in case of her death. Another remarkable feature of Indian law contrasting with that of Christian lands was preference of woman over man in heirship. In case of a daughter's death, the mother heired in preference to father, son, or even husband.

> That is called a woman's property; First. Whatever she owns during the Agàmini Shàdee, i.e. Days of Marriage; . . .
>
> Whatever she may receive from any person as she is going to her husband's home or coming from thence.
>
> Whatever her husband may at any time have given her; whatever she has received at any time from a brother; and whatever her father and mother may have given her.
>
> Whatever her husband on contracting a second marriage may give her to pacify her.
>
> Whatever a person may have given a woman for food or clothing.
>
> Whatever jewelry or wearing apparel she may have received from any person; also whatever a woman may receive from any person as an acknowledgment of payment for any work performed by her. Whatever she may by accident have found anywhere.
>
> Whatever she may gain by painting, spinning, needlework or any employment of this kind.
>
> Except from one of the family of her father, one of the family of her mother, or one of the family of her husband, whatever she may receive from any other person. Also if the father or mother of a girl give anything to their son-in-law, saying at the same time: "This shall go to our daughter," and even without any words to this purpose at the time of making the gift, if they merely have it in their intention that the thing thus given should revert to their daughter, all and every one of these articles are called a woman's property.

Her right of final disposal by will is also specified. Her effects acquired during marriage go to her daughters, in preference to her sons, and possessing no daughters, to her mother.

When a woman dies, then whatever effects she acquired during the Agàmini Shàdee, even though she hath a son living, shall go first to her unmarried daughter; if there is but one unmarried daughter she shall obtain the whole; if there are several unmarried daughters, they all shall have equal share.

Property under the three forms of marriage, if no unmarried daughters and others mentioned here, goes to her mother before to her father; and if neither, to her husband, and if no husband to husband's younger brother, or several younger brothers, (if several).

The specification of gifts of intention is remarkable in securing property to the wife that was seemingly given by the parents to the husband alone. An equally remarkable fact is the father's heirship in preference to the husband's, and the heirship of the daughters and mother in preference to any male relative however near, and is in striking contrast to Christian law in reference to woman's property. If a husband neglect to provide his wife necessary food and clothing, the East Indian wife is allowed to procure them by any means in her power. Maine has not failed to recognize the superior authority of the eastern wife in relation to property over that of the Christian wife. He says:

"The settled property of a married woman incapable of alienation by her husband, is well known to the Hindoos under the name of Stridham."

It is certainly a remarkable fact that the institution seems to have developed among the Hindoos at a period relatively much earlier than among the Romans. The *Mitakshara*, one of the oldest and most revered authorities of the Hindoo judicial treatises, defines Stridham, or woman's property, as that which is given to the wife by the father, the mother, or a brother at the time of the wedding, before the nuptial fire.

But adds Maine:

"The compiler of Mitakshara adds a proportion not found elsewhere; also property which she may have acquired by inheritance, purchase, partition, seizure, or finding, is denominated woman's property. . . . If all this be Stridham, it follows that the ancient Hindoo law secured to married women an even greater degree of proprietary independence than that given to them by the modern English Married Woman's Property Act.

Property is common to the husband and the wife. The ample support of those who are entitled to maintainance, is rewarded with bliss in heaven; but hell is the portion of that man whose family is afflicted with pain by his neglect. Therefore the Hindoo husband is taught to maintain his family with the utmost care. Maxims from the sacred books show the regard in which the Hindoo woman is held:

> He who despises woman despises his mother.
> Who is cursed by woman is cursed by God.
> The tears of a woman call down the fire of heaven on those who make them flow.
> Evil to him who laughs at woman's sufferings; God shall laugh at his prayers.
> It was at the prayer of a woman that the Creator pardoned man; cursed be he who forgets it.
> Who shall forget the sufferings of his mother at his birth shall be reborn in the body of an owl during three successive transmigrations.
> There is no crime more odious than to persecute woman.
> When women are honored the divinities are content; but when they are not honored all undertakings fail.
> The households cursed by women to whom they have not rendered the homage due them, find themselves weighed down with ruin and destroyed as if they had been struck by some secret power.
> We will not admit the people of today are incapable of comprehending woman, who alone can regenerate them.

The marriage ceremony is of the slightest kind and under three forms:

1. Of mutual consent by the interchange of necklaces or strings of flowers in some secret place.

2. A woman says, "I am become your wife," and the man says, "I acknowledge it."

3. When the parents of a girl on her marriage day say to the bridegroom: "Whatever act of religion you perform, perform it with our daughter," and the bridegroom assents to this speech.

The comparatively modern custom of suttee originated with the priests, whose avaricious desires created this system in order thereby to secure the property of the widow. The Vedas do not countenance either suttee or the widow's relinquishment of her property, the law specifically declaring "If a widow should give all her property and estate to the Brahmins for religions purposes, the gift indeed is valid, but the act is improper and the woman blamable." An ancient scripture declares that "All the wisdom of the Vedas, and all that has been written in books, is to be found concealed in the heart of a woman." It is a Hindoo maxim that one mother is worth a thousand fathers, because the mother carries and nourishes the infant from her own body, therefore the mother is most reverenced. A Hindoo proverb declares that "Who leaves his family naked and unfed may taste honey at first, but shall afterwards find it poison." Another says, "A wife is a friend in the house of the good."

Ancient Egypt worshiped two classes of gods; one purely spiritual and eternal, the other secondary but best beloved, were believed to have been human beings who from the services they had rendered to humanity were upon death admitted to the assembly of the gods. Such deification common in ancient times, is still customary in some parts of the earth. Within the past few years a countryman of our own was thus apotheosized by the Chinese to whom he had rendered valuable service at the time of the Tae-ping rebellion.[25] Ancient Egyptians recognized a masculine and feminine principle entering in all things both material and spiritual. Isis, the best beloved and most worshiped of the secondary gods, was believed by them to have been a woman who at an early period of Egyptian history had rendered that people invaluable service. She was acknowledged as their earliest law-maker, through whose teaching the people had risen from barbarism to civilization. She taught them the art of making bread[26] from the cereals theretofore growing wild and unused, the inhabitants at an early day living upon roots and herbs. Egypt soon became the grain growing portion of the globe, her enormous crops of wheat not alone aiding herself, but rendering the long stability of the Roman Empire possible. The science of medicine was believed to have originated with Isis; she was also said to have invented the art of embalming, established their literature, founded their religion. The whole Egyptian civilization was ascribed to the woman-goddess, Isis, whose name primarily Ish-Ish, signified Light, Life.[27] Isis, and Nepthys—the Lady of the House—were worshiped as the Beginning and the End. They were the Alpha and Omega of the most ancient Egyptian religion. The statues of Isis bore this inscription:

> I am all that has been, all that shall be, and none among mortals has hitherto taken off my veil.

Isis was believed to contain germs within herself for the reproduction of all living things. The most universal of her 10,000 names was, "Potent Mother Goddess."[28] This Egyptian regard for Isis is an extremely curious and interesting reminiscence of the Matriarchal period. Her worship was universal throughout Egypt. Her temples were magnificent. Her priests, consecrated to purity, were required to bathe daily, to wear linen garments unmixed with animal fibre, to abstain from animal food, and also from those vegetables regarded as impure.[29] Two magnificent festivals were yearly celebrated in her honor, the whole people taking part. During one of these festivals her priests bore a golden ship in the procession. The ship, or ark,[30] is peculiarly significative of the feminine principle, and wherever found is a reminiscence of the Matriarchate. The most sacred mysteries of the Egyptian religion, whose secrets even Pythagorus could not penetrate, to which Herodotus alluded with awe, and that were unknown to any person except the highest order of priests, owed their institution to Isis, and were based upon moral responsibility and a belief in a future life. The immortality of the soul was the underlying principle of the Egyptian religion.

Isis seems to have been one of those extraordinary individuals, such as occasionally in the history of the world, have created a literature, founded a religion, established a nationality. She was a person of superior mentality, with power to diffuse intelligence.

Moses, "learned in all the wisdom of the Egyptians," borrowed much from Isis. The forms and ceremonies used in her worship were largely copied by him, yet lacked the great moral element—immortal life—so conspicuously taught as a part of Egyptian religion. The Sacred Songs of Isis were an important part of the literature of Egypt. Plato, who burned his own poems after reading Homer, declared them worthy of the divinity, believing them to be literally 10,000 years old.[31] All orders of the priesthood were open to women in Egypt; sacred colleges existed for them, within whose walls dwelt an order of priestesses known as "God's Hand," "God's Star." Its ranks were recruited from women of the principal families, whose only employment was the service of the gods. "Daughter of the Deity," signified a priestess.

Women performed the most holy offices of religion, carrying the Sacred Sistrum and offering sacrifices of milk, both ceremonies of great dignity and importance being regarded as the most sacred service of the divinity. Such sacrificial rites were confined to queens and princesses of the royal household. Amés-Nofri-Ari, a queen who received great honor from Egyptians, spoken of as the "goddess-wife of Amun," the supreme god of Thebes, for whose worship the wonderful temple of Karnak was founded by a Pharaoh of the XII dynasty, is depicted on the monuments as the Chief High Priest—the Sem, whose specific duty was offering sacrifices and pouring out libations in that temple. By virtue of her high office she preceded her husband, the powerful and renowned Rameses II. The high offices of the church were as habitually held by women as by men; Princess Neferhotep, of the

fifth dynasty, was both a priestess and a prophetess of the goddesses
Hathor and Neith, the representatives of celestial space, in which
things were both created and preserved.

A priestess and priest in time of the XIII Pharaoh represented
on a slab of limestone, in possession of the Ashmolean Library of
Oxford, England, is believed to be the oldest monument of its
kind in the world, dating to 3500 B.C.

Queen Hatasu, the light of the brilliant XVIII dynasty, is
depicted upon the monuments as preceding in acts of worship,
the great Thotmes III, her brother, whom she had associated with
herself upon the throne, but who did not acquire supreme power
until after her death.[32] The reign of Hatasu was preeminent as the
great architectural period of Egypt, the engraving upon monuments during her reign, closely resembling the finest Greek
intaglio. Egypt so famous for her gardens and her art of forcing
blossoms out of season, was indebted to this great queen for the
first acclimatizing of plants. Upon one of her voyages she brought
with her in baskets filled with earth several of those Balsam trees
from Arabia, which were numbered among the precious gifts of
the Queen of Sheba to King Solomon. The red granite obelisks
erected by Hatasu before the gates of Karnak, the most magnificent and loftiest ever erected in Egypt, were ninety-seven feet in
height and surmounted by a pyramid of gold.

As early as the XI Pharaoh, II dynasty, the royal succession
became fixed in the female line. A princess was endowed with
privileges superior to a prince, her brother, her children reigning
by royal prerogative even when her husband was a commoner; the
children of a prince of the Pharaonic house making such marriage were declared illegitimate.

From the highest to the most humble priestly office, women
officiated in Egypt. A class of sacred women were doorkeepers of
temples, another order known as "Sacred Scribes" were paid great
deference. The Pellices or Pellucidæ of Amun were a remarkable
body of priestesses whose burial place has but recently been discovered. They were especially devoted to the service of Amun-
Ra, the Theban Jove. Egypt was indebted to priestesses for some

of its most important literature. To Penthelia, a priestess of Phtha[33] the God of Fire, in Memphis, Bryant ascribes the authorship of the Illiad and the Odyssey, Homer[34] in his travels through that country by aid of a suborned priest, having stolen these poems from the archives of the temples of Phtha where they had been deposited for safe keeping.

The priestly class of prophetesses was large in Egypt, their predictions not infrequently changing the course of that country's history. To his daughter, the prophet-priestess Athryte, was the great Rameses II indebted for the prophesy which led him into his conquering and victorious career. Known as one of the four great conquerors of antiquity,[35] reigning sixty years, he greatly added to the wealth and renown of Egypt.

The class of priestesses called Sibyls, were early known in Egypt, India, and other portions of the ancient world. They were regarded as the most holy order of the priesthood and held to be in indirect communion with the gods, who through them revealed secrets to the lower order of priests; the word Sibyl originating from Syros, i.e. God. The learned Beale defines Sibyl as thought, therefore a woman in possession of God's thought. The names of ten renowned Sibyls have come down to our day. The Sibyline Books for many years governed the destinies of Rome. Oracles were rendered from the lips of a priestess known as the Pythia; the famous Delphian Shrine for ages ruling the course of kings and nations.

Upon the monuments of Egypt, those indisputable historic records, queens alone are found wearing the triple crown, significant of ecclesiastical, judicial and civil power, thus confirming the statement of Diodorus that queens were shown greater respect and possessed more power than kings: the pope alone in modern times claiming the emblematic triple crown. A comparison between the men and women of the common people of this country shows no less favorably for the latter. Women were traders, buying and selling in the markets while the men engaged in the more laborious work of weaving at home. Woman's medical and hygienic knowledge is proven by the small number of

infantile deaths.[36] At the marriage ceremony the husband
promised obedience to the wife in all things, took her name, and
his property passed into her control; according to Wilkinson great
harmony existed in the marriage relation, the husband and wife
sitting upon the same double chair in life and resting at death in
the same tomb.

Montesquieu says:

> It must be admitted although it shocks our present customs,
> that among the most polished peoples, wives have always had
> authority over their husbands. The Egyptians established it by
> law in honor of Isis, and the Babylonians did the same in time
> of Semiramis. It has been said of the Romans that they ruled
> all nations but obeyed their wives.

Crimes against women were rare in Egypt and when
occuring were most severely punished.[37] Rameses III caused this
inscription to be engraved upon his monuments:

> To unprotected woman there is freedom to wander through
> the whole country wheresoever she list without apprehending
> danger.

A woman was one of the founders of the ancient Parsee religion, which taught the existence of but a single god, thus intro-
ducing monotheism into that rare old kingdom. Until the introduction of Christianity woman largely preserved the liberty
belonging to her in the old civilizations. Of her position under
Roman law before this period Maine, (Gaius), says:

> The juriconsulists had evidently at this time assumed the
> equality of the sexes as a principle of the law of equity. The
> situation of the Roman woman whether married or single
> became one of great personal and proprietary independence;
> but Christianity tended somewhat from the commencement to
> narrow this remarkable liberty. The prevailing state of religious
> sentiment may explain why modern jurisprudence adopted

these rules concerning the position of men which belong to an imperfect civilization. No society which preserves any tincture of Christian institutions is likely to restore to married women the personal liberty conferred on them by middle Roman law. Canon law has deeply injured civilization.

Rome not only secured remarkable personal and proprietary rights to woman, but as Vestal Virgin she held the highest priestly office. No shrine equalled that of the Vestals in sanctity; none was so honored by the state. To their care the sacred Fire was entrusted, and also the Palladium; those unknown articles upon whose preservation not alone the welfare but the very existence of Rome was held to depend. The most important secrets of state were entrusted to them and their influence in civil affairs was scarcely secondary to their religious authority. In troubled times, in civil wars, in extreme emergencies of the commonwealth they acted as ambassdors, or were chosen umpires to restore peace between the parties. In state ceremonies, in the most solemn, civil or religious meetings they performed important duties. They were superior to the common law or the authority of the consul. The most important secrets were entrusted to them, wills of the emperors and documents of state confided to their care; offenses against them were punished with death. If meeting a criminal on his way to execution, he was pardoned as a direct intervention of heaven in his behalf. Among their important privileges was exemption from public taxes, the right to make a will, interment within the city walls, the right to drive in the city where no other carriage was allowed; even the consuls were obliged to make room for them to pass. Chosen from noble families when between the ages of six and ten, their terms of service was thirty years.

The order of Vestal Virgins flourished eleven hundred years having been founded seven hundred years before the Christian era and continuing four hundred years afterwards. But those women all young, all between the ages of six years and forty, so closely guarded the secrets of the Penetralia that to this day they still remain as unknown as when in their charge. The order was destroyed in the fourth century, but the ruins of their temple recently discovered, prove that when obliged to flee from the sacred enclosure they first demolished the most holy portion where the secrets of Rome were hidden.[38] Recent important archæological discoveries at the Atrium Vertæ in the Forum, corroborate history in regard to the high position and extraordinary privileges of the Vestals. Several statues have been found representing the sacred maiden with the historic fillet about her head and the cord beneath her breast. Medallions worn upon the breast of their horses have also been unearthed. The wealth of the order was extremely great, both its public and private property being exempt from that conscription which in times of war reached all but a few favored individuals.

The names by which Imperial Rome was known were all feminine; Roma, Flora, Valentia; nearly its first and greatest goddess was Vesta.[39]

Sacred and secret were originally synonymous terms. All learning was sacred, consequently secret, and as only those possessed of learning were eligible to the priestly office it is readily seen that knowledge was a common heritage of primitive women. Letters, numbers, astrology, geography and all branches of science were secrets known only to initiates. The origin of the most celebrated mysteries, the Eleusinian, and those of Isis, were attributed to woman, the most perfect temple of ancient or modern times, the Parthenon, or Temple of the Virgins, was dedicated to the goddess Minerva.

Chryseis was priestess of Juno in Argo. This office was of great civil as well as religious importance regulating their dates and chronology. To the present day in China, woman assists at the altar in ancestral worship, the prevailing form of religious adoration. The mother of a family is treated with the greatest respect[40] and the combined male and female principle is represented in god under the name Fou-Fou, that is, Father-Mother.[41] When the Emperor acting as high priest performs certain rites he is called Father-Mother of the people. Woman is endowed with the same political powers as man.[42] The wife presides like her husband at family councils, trials, etc. As Regent, she governs the Empire with wisdom, dignity, power, as was shown during the coregency of the Empresses of the East and of the West, their power continuing even after the promotion of a boy-heir to the throne.

A Thibetan woman empire extant between the VI and VII centuries A.D. is spoken of by Chinese writers. An English author, Cooper, seems to have visited this region, meeting with an amusing venture while there.[43]

Under the law of the Twelve Tables, founded A.U.C. 300, woman possessed the right of repudiation in marriage. The code itself was ascribed to a woman of that primitive Athens founded and governed by women long years previous to the date of modern Athens. The change in woman's condition for the worse under Christianity is very remarkable and everywhere it is noticed. Among the Finns, before their conversion, the mother of a family took precedence of the father in the rites of domestic worship. Under the Angles, a wound inflicted upon a virgin was punished with double the penalty of the same injury inflicted upon a man, remarkable as showing the high esteem and reverence in which women were held. Before the introduction of Christianity, the Germans bound themselves to chastity in the marriage relation; under Catholocism the wife is required to promise the devotion of her body to the marital rite. German women served as priestesses of Hertha, and during the time of Rome's greatest power, Wala or Valleda,—this title being significative of a supremely wise woman, a prophetess,—was virtual ruler of the Germanic forces; Druses when about invading Germany was repelled by her simple command to "Go Back." But under Christianity the German woman no longer takes part in public affairs, education is denied, the most severe and degrading labor of field, streets and mine falls upon her, while in the family she is serf to father, brother, husband.

The women of ancient Scandinavia were treated with infinite respect; breach of marriage promise was classed with perjury; its penalty was outlawry. Marriage was regarded as sacred and in many instances the husband was obliged to submit to the wife.[44]

Those old Berserkers reverenced their Alruna, or Holy Women, on earth and worshiped goddesses in heaven, where, according to Scandinavian belief, gods and goddesses sat together in a hall without distinction of sex.

The whole ancient world recognized a female priesthood, some peoples, like the Roman, making national safety dependent upon their ministration; others as in Egypt, according them pre-eminence in the priestly office, reverencing goddesses as superior to gods; still other as the Scandinavians, making no distinction in equality between gods and goddesses; others governing the nation's course through oracles which fell from feminine lips; still others looking to the Sibylline Books for like decision.[45] Those historians anxious to give most credit to the humanizing effect of Christianity upon woman are compelled to admit her superiority among pagan nations before the advent of this religion.[46]

The Patriarchate under which biblical history and Judaism commenced, was a rule of men whose lives and religion were based upon passions of the grossest kind, showing but few indications of softness or refinement. Monogamous family life did not exist, but a polygamy whose primal object was the formation of a clan possessing hereditary chiefs ruling aristocratically. To this end the dominion of man over woman and the birth of many children was requisite. To this end polygamy was instituted, becoming as marked a feature of the Patriarchate as monogamy was of the Matriarchate. Not until the Patriarchate were wives regarded as property, the sale of daughters as a legitimate means of family income, or their destruction at birth looked upon as a justifiable act. Under the Patriarchate, society became morally revolutionized, the family, the state, the form of religion entirely changed. The theory of a male supreme God in the interests of force and authority, wars, family discord, the sacrifice of children to appease the wrath of an offended (male) deity are all due to the Patriarchate. These were practices entirely out of consonance with woman's thought and life. Biblical Abraham binding Isaac for sacrifice to Jehovah, carefully kept his intentions from the mother Sarah. Jeptha offering up his daughter in accordance with his vow, allowing her a month's life for the bewailment of her virginity, are but typical of the low regard of woman under the Patriarchate. During this period the destruction of girl children became a widely extended practice, and infantile girl murder the custom of many nations. During the Matriarchate all life was regarded as holy; even the sacrifice of animals was unknown.[47] The most ancient and purest religions taught sacrifice of the animal passions as the great necessity in self-purification. But the Patriarchate subverted this sublime teaching, materializing spiritual truths, and substituting the sacrifice of animals, whose blood was declared a sweet smelling savor to the Lord of Hosts.

Both infanticide and prostitution with all their attendant horrors are traceable with polygamy—their origin—to the Patriarchate or Father-rule, under which Judaism and Christianity rose as forms of religious belief. Under the Patriarchate woman has ever been regarded as a slave to be disposed of as father, husband or brother chose. Even in the most Christian lands, daughters have been esteemed valuable only in proportion to the political or pecuniary advantage they brought to the father, in the legal prostitution of an enforced marriage. The sacrifice of woman to man's baser passions has ever been the distinguishing characteristic of the Patriarchate. But woman's degredation is not the normal condition of humanity, neither did it arise from a settled principle of evolution, but is a retrogression, due to the grossly material state of the world for centuries past, in which it has lost the interior meaning, or spiritual significance of its own most holy words.

Jehovah signifies not alone the masculine and the feminine principles but also the spirit or vivifying intelligence. It is a compound word indicative of the three divine principles.[48] Holy Ghost although in Hebrew, a noun of either genders, masculine, feminine, neuter, is invariably rendered masculine by Christian translators of the Bible.[49] In the Greek, from whence we obtain the New Testament, spirit is of the feminine gender, although invariably translated masculine. The double-sexed word, Jehovah, too sacred to be spoken by the Jews, signified the masculine-feminine God.[50] The proof of the double meaning of Jehovah, the masculine and feminine signification, Father-Mother, is undeniable. Lanci, one of the great orientalists, says:

> Jehovah should be read from left to right, and pronounced Ho-Hi; that is to say He-She (Hi pronounced He,) Ho in Hebrew being the masculine pronoun and Hi the feminine. Ho-Hi therefore denotes the male and female principles, the *vis genatrix*.[51]

Kingsford says:

> The arbitrary and harsh aspect under which Johovah is chiefly presented in the Hebrew Scriptures is due not to any lack of the feminine element either in His name or in His nature, or to any failure on the part of the inspired leaders of Israel to recognize their equality but to the rudimentary condition of the people at large, and their consequent amenability to the delineation of the stern side only of the Divine Character.[52]

The Hebrew word "El Shaddai," translated, "The Almighty" is still more distinctively feminine than Iah, as it means "The Breasted God," and is made use of in the Old Testament whenever the especially feminine characteristics of God are meant to be indicated.[53]

The story of the building of the tower of Babel and and the subsequent confusion of language possesses deep interior significance. The word (Babel) meaning "God the Father" as distinct and separate from the feminine principle. The confusion which has come upon humanity because of this separation has been far more lamentable in its results than a mere confounding of tongues.[54] In the earliest religions the recognition of the feminine principle in the divinity is everywhere found. "I am the Father and Mother of the Universe" said Krishna in the Bhagavad Gita.

An Orphic hymn says: "Zeus is the first and the last, the bead and the extremities; from him have proceeded all things." He is a man and an immortal nymph, i.e. the male and female element.

The Sobar declares "the ancient of the ancient has a form and has no form."

The Holy Spirit, symbolized by a dove, is a distinctively feminine principle—the Comforter—and yet has ever been treated by the Christian Church as masculine, alike in dogmas propounded from the pulpit, and in translations of the Scriptures. A few notable exceptions however appear at an early date. Origen expressly referred to the Holy Ghost as feminine, saying: "The soul is maiden to her mistress the Holy Ghost." An article upon the "Esoteric character of the Gospels" in Madam Blavatsky's "Lucifer" (November 1887) says:

> Spirit or the Holy Ghost was feminine with the Jews as most ancient peoples and it was so with the early Christians; Sophia of the Gnostics and the third Sephiroth, Binah (the female Jehovah of the Cabalists) are feminine principles "Divine Spirit" or *Ruach*, "One is She the spirit of the Elohim of Life," is said in Sepher Yetzirah.[55]

An early canonical book of the New Testament known as "The Everlasting Gospel" also as "The Gospel of the Holy Ghost" represents Jesus as saying, "My mother the Holy Ghost, took me by the hair of my head up into a mountain."

The word "sacred" simply meaning secret, having its origin as shown at the time when knowledge was kept hidden from the bulk of mankind, only to be acquired by initiation in the mysteries, so also the word "holy" simply means whole, that is, undivided. In its ignorance, unwisdom, and fear of investigation, mankind has allowed a division of the two divine principles, male and female, to obtain firm hold in their minds. Prejudice, which simply means prejudgment, a judgment without proof, has long ruled mankind, owing chiefly to that bondage of the will inflicted by a tyrannous self-seeking priesthood. But we have now reached a period in history when investigation is again taking the place of blind belief and the truth, capable of making man free, is once more offered. It is through a recognition of the divine element of motherhood as not alone inhering in the great primal source of life but as extending throughout all creation, that it will become possible for the world, so buried in darkness, folly and superstition, to practice justice toward woman. Not legislation but education will bring about the change; not external acts but internal thought. It is but a few years since the acknowledgment of a feminine element even in plants was regarded by the church as heretical. Yet though still perceiving but partial truth, science now declares the feminine principle to inhere in plants, rocks, gems, and even in the minutest atoms; thus in some degree recognizing the occult axiom, "As it is above, so it is below."

Notes

1. The first state of primitive man must have been the mere aggregation. The right of the mother was therefore most natural; upon the relationship of mother and child the remotest conception of the family was based.—*Wilkin*, p. 869.

2. Where a god and goddess are worshiped together they are not husband and wife, but mother and son. Neither does the god take pre-eminence, but the mother or goddess. This condition dates from the earliest days of society, when marriage in our sense of the word was unknown, and when kinship and inheritance were in the female line. The Babylonian Ishtur of the Izdobar legend is a deity of this type.—*W. Robertson Smith: Kinshiship in Ancient Arabia.*

3. Dr. Th. Achelis.—Article on Ethnology: (*The Open Court*).

4. In a country where she is the head of the family, where she decides the descent and inheritance of her children, both in regard to property and place in society in such a community, she certainly cannot be the servant of her husband, but at least must be his equal if not in many respects his superior.—*Wilkin.*

5. *Motherright.*

6. Lubbuck.—*Pre-Historic Times and Origin of Civilization. Wilkin.*

7. Among many people the father at birth of a child, especially a son, loses his name and takes the one his child gets. Tylor—*Primitive Culture.* Also see *Wilkin.*

8. "Thus we see that woman's liberty did not begin at the upper,

but at the lower end of civilization. Woman in those remote times were endowed with and enjoyed rights that are denied to her but too completely in the higher phase of civilization. This subject has a very important aspect, i.e. the position of woman to man, the place she holds in society, her condition in regard to her private and public (political) rights."

9. "Among the monogamous classic nations of antiquity, the maternal deity was worshiped with religious ceremonies."

10. We find the mother's right exclusively together with a well-established monogamy.—*Bachofen.*

11. *Documentary History of New York.*

12. Alexander: *History of Women.*

13. *History of the United States,* Vol. I.

14. *Cushing.*

15. "What is most to be considered in this respect are the political rights which women in time of the Matriarchate shared with the men. They had indeed the right to vote in public assemblies still exercised not very long ago among the Basques in the Spanish provinces."

16. That the Veddas are the aborigines of Ceylon may be assumed from the fact that the highly civilized Singalese admit them to be of noble rank. *Pre-Historic Times.*—Lubbuck.

17. "We find in some instances this independence of the maiden in regard to disposing of her hand, or selecting a husband as a memento of the time of the Matriarchate. . . . The most remarkable instance of the self-disposition of woman we find among the ancient Arabs and the Hindoos; among the latter the virgin was permitted to select her own husband if her father did not give her in marriage within three years after her maturity."

18. *Account of the religion, Manners, etc., of the People of Malabar, etc.,* translated by Mr. Phillips, 1718.

19. Among the illustrative types of interior realities and the elementary geometric forms, point, direct line and deflected line, the last of which is a true arc produces the circle when carried to its ultimate, this circle representing the triune order of movement; the point in the line, the line in the curve, and the curve in the circle.—*The Path.*

20. The phallus and lingum (or lingum and yoni), the point within the circle or diameter within the circle.—*Volney's Ruins.*

21. *Chips from a German Work-Shop.*—Max Muller.

22. All mythology has pertinently been characterized as ill-remembered history.

23. In the Rig-Veda, a work not committed to writing until after that movement of the Aryans, which resulted in the establishment of Persia and India. . . . There is nothing more striking than the status of woman at that early age. Then the departed mothers were served as faithfully by the younger members of the family as departed fathers. The mother quite as often, if not more frequently than the father, conducted the services of the dead ancestry, which took place three times a day, often consisting of improvised poetry.—*Elizabeth Peabody on the Aryans.*

24. There are but few of the United States in which the authority of the father to bind out a living child or to will away an unborn one, is not recognized as valid without the mother's consent.

25. Ward, the American who rendered such service to the Chinese Emperor, has been deified. The Emperor, in a recent edict, has placed him among the major gods of China, commanding shrines to be built and worship to be paid to the memory of this American. The people are worshiping him along with the most ancient and powerful deities of their religion as a great deliverer from war and famine—as a powerful god in the form of man. In every household, school and temple, his name will be thus commemorated.—*Newspaper Report.*

26. *Diodorus Siculus.*

27. "I am nature, the parent of all things, the sovereign of the elements, the primary progeny of time, the most exalted of the deities, the first of the heavenly gods and goddesses, the queen of the shades, the uniform countenance who dispose with my rod the innumerable lights of heaven."

28. The salubrious breezes of the sea, and the mournful silence of the dead, whose single deity the whole world venerates in many forms with various rites and many names. The Egyptians, skilled in ancient lore, worship me with proper ceremonies and call me by my true name—Queen Isis.

29. Leeks, garlic, onions and beans.

30. All the ancient nations appear to have had an ark or archa, in which to conceal something sacred.—Godfrey Higgins, *Anacalypsis* I, 347.

31. The Sacred Song of Moses and Miriam was an early part of Jewish literature; the idea was borrowed, like the ark from the religion of Isis.

32. The throne of this brilliant queen who reigned 1600 years B.C. has recently been deposited in the British Museum. Her portrait, also brought to light, shows Caucasian features with a dimpled chin.

33. Bryant was an English writer of the last century, a graduate of Cambridge who looked into many abstruse questions relating to ancient history. In 1796, eight years before his death, he published *A Dissertation Concerning the War of Troy*.

34. That Homer came into Egypt, amongst other arguments they endeavor to prove it especially by the potion Helen gave Telemachus—in the story of Menalaus—to cause him to forget all his sorrows past, for the poet seems to have made an exact experiment of the potion Nepenthes, which he says Helen received from Polymnestes, the wife of Thonus, and brought it from Thebes in Egypt; and indeed in that city, even at this day, the women use this medicine with good success, and they say that in ancient times the medicine for the cure for anger and sorrow was only to be found among the Diospolitans, Thebes and Diospolis being affirmed by them to the and the same city.—*Diodorus Siculus*, Vol. I, Chap. VII.

35. The remaining three were Cyrus, Nebuchadnezzar and Alexander. Cyrus met defeat and death at the hands of Tomyris, queen of the Scythians, who caused him to be crucified, a punishment deemed so ignominious by the Romans that it was not inflicted upon the most criminal of their citizens. Because of his barbarity, Tomyris caused the head of Cyrus to be plunged into a sack of blood "that he might drink his fill."

36. Very few mummies of children have been found.—Wilkinson, *Ancient Egyptians*.

37. In relation to women the laws were very severe; for one that committed a rape upon a free woman was condemned to have his privy member cut off; for they judged that the three most heinous offenses were included in that one vile act, that is wrong, defilement and bastardy.—*Diodorus*, Vol. I, Chap. VII.

38. *Ancient Rome in the Light of Recent Discoveries*. Chapter on the Vestals.—Lanciani.

39. *The Anacalypsis* II, 241.

40. According to Commissioner of Education, Chang Lai Sin, Chinese women can read and write, and when a husband wishes to do anything he consults with his wife, and when the son comes home, although he may be prime minister, he shows his respect to his mother by bending his knee. "I claim that the Chinese institutions and system of education, both with regard to men and women, are far superior to those of any of the neighboring nations for a great many centuries, and that

it is only within this century that China, after having been defeated by so many reverses in her arms, has turned to a foreign country—to the United States—for example and instruction."

41. The Shakers hold that the revelation of God is progressive. That in the first or antediluvian period of human nature God was known only as a Great Spirit; that in the second or Jewish period he was revealed as the Jehovah. He, she or a dual being, male or female, the "I am that I am"; that Jesus in the third cycle made God known as a father; and that in the last cycle commencing with 1770, A.D., "God is revealed in the character of Mother, an eternal Mother, the bearing spirit of all the creation of God."—*W. A. Parcelle.*

42. In China the family acting through its natural representative is the political unit. This representative may be a woman. The only body in China that may be said to correspond with our law-making assemblies is the Academy of Science and Letters of Pekin, and women are not excluded from that learned conclave. *La Cité Chinoise.*—G. Eugene Simon.

43. *Art Letters*, p. 322.—Bachofen.

44. *Journal of Jurisprudence*, Vol. XVI, Edinburg, 1872.

45. The divine element, according to the idea of the ancient world, was composed of two sexes. There were *dei femma*, and hence temples sacred to goddesses; holy sanctuaries where was celebrated mysteries in which men could not be permitted to participate. The worship of goddesses necessitated priestesses, so that women exercised the sacerdotal office in the ancient world. The wives of the Roman Consuls even offered public sacrifices at certain festivals. The more property the wife had, the more rights she had.—*M. Derraimes.*

46. The superiority of woman's condition in Europe and America is generally attributed to Christianity. We are anxious to give some credit to that influence, but it must not be forgotten that the nations of Northern Europe treated women with delicacy and devotion long before they were converted to the Christian faith. Long before the Christian era women were held in high estimation, and enjoyed as many privileges as they generally have since the spread of Christianity. Nichols.—*Women of All Nations.*

47. When I go back to the most remote periods of antiquity into which it is possible to penetrate, I find clear and positive evidence of several important facts: First, no animal food was eaten; no animals were sacrificed. *Higgins.*—*Anacalypsis* II, p. 147.

48. Observe that I. H. U. is Jod, male, father; "He" is female, Binah, and U is male, Vau, Son.—*Sepher Yetzirah*.

49. *The Perfect Way*.—Kingsford.

50. I. A. H. according to the Nabbalists, is I. (Father) and A. H. (Mother); composed of I. the male, and H. the mother. Nork.—*Bibl. Mythol. I*, 164–65 (note to *Sod* 166, 2, 354.)

51. Nork says the "Women clothed with the sign of the Sun and the Moon is the bi-sexed or male-female deity; hence her name is Iah, composed of the masculine I and the feminine *Ah. Sod*.—Appendix 123.

52. *The Perfect Way*, p. 78.

53. That name of Deity, which occurring in the Old Testament is translated the Almighty, namely El Shaddai, signified the Breasted God, and is used when the mode of the divine nature implied is of a feminine character. Kingsford.—*The Perfect Way*, p. 68.

54. A chief signification of the word Babel among Orientals was "God the Father." The Tower of Babel therefore signifies the Tower of God the Father—a remarkable indication of the confusion, not alone of tongues, but of religious ideas arising from man's attempt to worship the father alone.—*E. L. Mason*.

Injustice to the sex reached its culmination in the enthronement of a personal God with a Son to share his glory, but wifeless, motherless, daughterless.—*Dr. William Henry Channing*.

55. Those who have studied the ancient lore of Cabalistic books, know that in the ineffable name Yod-he-vau (or Jehovah), the first letter *yod* signifies the masculine, the second letter *hu* or *ha* the feminine, while the last letter *vau* or *vaud* is said by Cabalists to indicate the vital life which fills all the throbbing universe from the union of eternal love with eternal wisdom. It is this ineffable holy (or whole) Mother and Father, which must be exalted and imaged forth in family and government with the woman-force more strongly emphasized, before even human society can be filled with that new creation with which the iridescent subtle mother-essence infuses and enwreathes all other realms of the pulsing universe.

No man seems shaken at hearing of the fatherhood of Jehovah. Is motherhood less divine? Nothing but a male-born theology evolved from the overheated fires of feeling would have burned away all recognition of the fact that the presence of the "Eternal Womanly" in yod-he-vau being is necessary to full-sphered perfection; none but those whose degraded estimate of woman has caused them to desecrate her holy office of high priestess of life will see anything more sacrilegious in a recognition of "Our Mother in Heaven," and in offering her the prayer "hallowed be thy name, thy will be done on earth as it is in heaven," than in saying the same things to the Father there.

Those who choose to search will discover that the "Eternal Fatherhood of God," in regard to which Protestant theologians talk so much, has been balanced in all ancient religions as well as in the nature of things by the eternal Motherhood in Jehovah's being, without which Fatherhood would be impossible. This Motherhood has always and everywhere been the preserver and creator of the omnipresent life of all kinds which fills the throbbing universe. Yod-he-vau's *Lost Name* can never be hallowed (made whole) without the Mother is there. E. L. Mason.—*The Lost Name.*

CHAPTER II

CELIBACY

W hile the inferior and secondary position of woman early became an integral portion of Christianity, its fullest efforts are seen in Church teachings regarding marriage. Inasmuch as it was a cardinal doctrine that the fall of Adam took place through his temptation into marriage by Eve, this relation was regarded with holy horror as a continuance of the evil which first brought sin into the world, depriving man of his immortality.[1] It is a notable fact that the expected millennium of a thousand years upon earth with its material joys has ever had more attraction for Christians than the eternal spiritual rapture of heaven. Many of the old Fathers taught that "the world is a state of matrimony, but paradise of virginity."[2] To such extent was this doctrine carried it was declared that had it not have been for the fall, God would have found some way outside of this relation for populating the world, consequently marriage was regarded as a condition of peculiar temptation and trial; celibacy as one of especial holiness.

The androgynous theory of primal man found many supporters, the separation into two beings having been brought about by sensual desire. Jacob Bœhme and earlier mystics of that class recognized the double sexuality of God in whose image man was made. One of the most revered ancient Scriptures, "The Gospel according to the Hebrews," which was in use as late as the second century of the Christian era, taught the equality of the feminine in the Godhead; also that daughters should inherit with sons. Thirty three fragments of this Gospel have recently been discovered. The fact remains undeniable that at the advent of Christ, a recognition of the the feminine element in the divinity had not entirely died out from general belief, the earliest and lost books of the New Testament teaching this doctrine, the whole confirmed by the account of the birth and baptism of Jesus, the Holy Spirit.[3] The feminine creative force, playing most important part. It was however but a short period before the church through Canons and Decrees, as well as apostolic and private teaching, denied the femininity of the Divine equally with the divinity of the feminine. There is however abundant proof that even under but partial recognition of the feminine principle as entering in the divinity, woman was officially recognized in the early services of the church, being ordained to the ministry officiating as deacons, administering the act of baptism dispensing the sacrament, interpreting doctrines and founding sects which received their names.[4]

The more mystical among priests taught that before woman was separated from man, the Elementals[5] were accepted by man as his children and endowed by him with immortality, but at the separation of the androgynous body into the two beings Adam and Eve, the woman through accident was also endowed with immortality which theretofore had solely inhered in the masculine portion of the double-sexed being. These mystics also taught that this endowment of woman with immortality together with her capability of bringing new beings into existence also endowed with immortal life, was the cause of intense enmity toward her on the part of the Elementals, especially shown by their bringing suffering and danger upon her at this period.

Still another class recognizing marriage as a necessity for the continuance of the species, looked upon it with more favor attributing the fall to another cause, yet throwing odium upon the relation by maintaining that the marriage of Adam and Eve did not take place until after they had been driven from Paradise. This doctrine was taught by the Father Hieronymus.[6] Thus with strange inconsistancy the church supported two entirely opposing views of marriage. Yet even those who upheld its necessity still taught woman's complete subordination to man in that relation; also that this condition was one of great tribulation to man, it was even declared that God caused sleep to fall upon Adam at the creation of Eve in order to prevent his opposition.[7] Lecky speaking of the noxious influences of ascetics upon marriage, says it would be difficult to conceive anything more coarse and repulsive than the manner in which the church regarded it; it was invariably treated as a consequence of the fall of Adam and regarded from its lowest aspect.[8] But having determined that evil was necessary in order to future good, the church decided to compel a belief that its control of this contract lessened the evil, to this end declaring marriage illegal without priestly sanction; thus creating a conviction of and belief in its sacramental nature in the minds of the people. Despite the favoring views of a class regarding marriage, celibacy was taught as the highest condition for both man and woman, and as early as the third century many of the latter entered upon a celibate life, Jerome using his influence in its favor. Augustine, while admitting the possibility of salvation to the married, yet speaking of a mother and daughter in heaven, compared the former to a star of the second magnitude, but the latter as shining with great brilliancy. The superior respect paid to the celibates even among women is attributed to direct instruction of the apostles. The "Apostolic Constitutions" held even by the Episcopal church as regulations established by the apostles themselves, and believed to be among the earliest christian records, give elaborate directions for the places of all who attend church, the unmarried being the most honored. The virgins and widows and elder women stood or sat first of all.

The chief respect shown by the early fathers towards marriage was that it gave virgins to the church, while the possibility of salvation to the married was at first recognized, was denied at later date even to persons otherwise living holy lives. The Emperor Jovinian banished a man who asserted the possibility of salvation to married persons provided they obeyed all the ordinances of the church and lived good lives.[9] As part of this doctrine, the church taught that woman was under an especial curse and man a divinely appointed agent for the enforcement of that curse. It inculcated the belief that all restrictions placed upon her were but parts of her just punishment for having caused the fall of man. Under such teaching a belief in the supreme virtue of celibacy—first declared by the apostle Paul—was firmly established. To Augustine is the world indebted for full development of the theory of original sin, promulgated by Paul as a doctrine of the Christian Church in the declaration that "Adam first created was not first in sin." Paul brought up in the strictest external principles of Judaism did not lose his educational bias or primal belief when changing from Judaism to Christianity.[10] Neither was his character as persecuter changed when he united his fortunes with the new religion. He gave to the Christian world a lever long enough to reach down through eighteen centuries, all that time moving it in opposition to a belief in woman's created and religious equality with man, to her right of private judgment and to her personal freedom. His teaching that Adam, first created was not first in sin, divided the unity of the human race in the assumption that woman was not part of the original creative idea but a secondary thought, an inferior being brought into existence as an appendage to man.

Although based upon a false conception of the creative power, this theory found ready acceptance in the minds of the men of the new church. Not illiterate, having received instruction at the feet of Gamaliel Paul was yet intolerant and credulous, nay more, unscrupulous. He was the first Jesuit in the Christian church, "Becoming all things to all men." The Reformed church with strange unanimity has chosen Paul as its leader and the accepted exponent of its views. He may justly be termed the Prostestant Pope, and although even among Catholics rivalling Peter in possession of the heavenly keys, yet the Church of Rome has accepted his authority as in many respects to be more fully obeyed than even the teachings of St. Peter.[11] Having been accepted by the Church as the apostolic exponent of its views upon marriage, it was but to be expected that his teachings should be received as divine. That Paul was unmarried has been assumed because of his bitterness against this relation, yet abundant proof of his having a wife exists. For the membership of the Great Sanhedrim, marriage was a requisite. St. Clement of Alexandria positively declared that St. Paul had a wife. Until the time of Cromwell, when it was burned, a MS. letter of St. Ignatius in Greek, was preserved in the old Oxford Library; this letter spoke of "St. Peter and Paul and the apostles who were married." Another letter of St. Ignatius is still extant in the Vatican Library. Tussian and others who have seen it declare that it also speaks of St. Paul as a married man.[12] But tenderness toward woman does not appear in his teachings; man is represented as the master, "the head" of woman. In consonance with his teaching, responsibility has been denied her through the ages; although the Church has practically held her amenable for the ruin of the world, prescribing penance and hurling anathemas against her whom it has characterized as the "door of hell."

At a synod in Winchester in the eighth century, St. Dunstan, famed for his hatred of women, made strenuous efforts to enforce celibate life. It was asserted to be so highly immoral for a priest to marry, that even a wooden cross had audibly declared against the horrid practice.[13] Although in the third century marriage was permitted to all orders of the clergy,[14] yet the very ancient "Gospel of the Egyptians," endorsed as canonical by Clement of Alexandria, taught celibacy. These old christian theologians found the nature of woman a prolific subject of discussion, a large party classing her among brutes without soul or reason. As early as the sixth century a council at Macon (585), fifty-nine bishops taking part, devoted its time to a discussion of this question, "Does woman possess a soul?" Upon one side it was argued that woman should not be called "homo"; upon the opposite side that she should, because, *first*, the Scriptures declared that God created man, male and female; *second*, that Jesus Christ, son of a woman, is called the son of man. Christian women were therefore allowed to remain human beings in the eyes of the clergy, even though considered very weak and bad ones. But nearly a thousand years after this decision in favor of the humanity of the women of Christian Europe, it was still contended that the women of newly discovered America belonged to the brute creation, possessing neither souls nor reason.[15] As late as the end of the sixteenth century an anonymous work appeared, arguing that women were no part of mankind, but a species of intermediate animal between the human and the brute creation. (*Mulieres non est homines, etc.*) Mediæval Christian writings show many discussions upon this point, the influence of these old assertions still manifesting themselves.

Until time of Peter the Great, women were not recognized as human beings in that great division of Christendom known as the Greek church, the census of that empire counting only males, or so many "souls"—no woman named. Traces of this old belief have not been found wanting in our own country within the century. As late as the Woman's Rights Convention in Philadelphia, 1854, an objector in the audience cried out: "Let women first prove they have souls; both the Church and the State deny it."

Everything connected with woman was held to be unclean. It is stated that Agathro desired the Sophist Herodes to get ready for him the next morning a vessel full of pure milk, that is to say which had not been milked by the hand of a woman. But he perceived as soon as it was offered to him that it was not such as he desired, protesting that the scent of her hands who had milked it offended his nostrils. In the oldest European churches great distinction was made between the purity of man and woman. At an early date woman was forbidden to receive the Eucharist into her naked hand on account of her impurity,[16] or to sing in church on account of her inherent wickedness. To such an extent was this opposition carried, that the church of the middle ages did not hesitate to provide itself with eunuchs in order to supply cathedral choirs with the soprano tones inhering by nature in woman alone. One of the principal charges against the Huguenots, was that they permitted women to sing in church, using their voices in praise of God contrary to the express command of St. Paul, Catherine de Medicis reproaching them for this great sin.[17] The massacre at St. Bartholomew, when 30,000 men, women and children lost their lives, and the entire destruction of many families of purest character took place, with an additional great loss to France from the self-imposed banishment of hundreds more, may be traced to the teaching of St. Paul that woman should keep silence in the church. This doctrine also crossed the ocean with the Puritan Fathers, and has appeared in America under many forms.[18]

The Christianity of the ages teaching the existence of a superior and inferior sex, possessing different rights under the law and in the church, it has been easy to bring man and woman under accountability to a different code of morals. For this double code the church is largely indebted to the subtle and acute Paul, who saw in the new religion but an enlarged Judaism that should give prominence to Abraham and his seed from whom Christ claimed descent. His conversion did not remove his old Jewish contempt for woman, as shown in his temple service, the law forbidding her entrance beyond the outer court. Nor could he divest himself of the spirit of the old morning prayer which duly led each Jew to thank God that he was not born a heathen, a slave or a woman.

He brought into the new dispensation the influence of the old ceremonial law, which regarded woman as unclean. The Jewish exclusion of forty days from even the outer court of the sanctuary to the woman who had given birth to a son, and of twice that period, or eighty days, if a daughter had been born, was terminated in both religions by a sin-offering in expiation of the mother's crime for having, at the peril of her own, brought another human being into life.[19] This Old Testament teaching degraded the life-giving principle exemplified in motherhood, and in a twofold way lessened the nation's regard for womanhood. *First*, through the sin-offering and purification demanded of the mother; *second*, by its doubling the period of exclusion from the temple in case a girl was given to the world.[20] The birth of girls even under Christianity has everywhere been looked upon as an infliction, and thousands have been immured in convents, there to die of despair or to linger through years,[21] the victim alike of father and of priest.

The influence of Judaism extended through Christendom. The custom of purification after maternity inherited by the church from Judaism brought with it into Christianity the same double restriction and chastening of the mother in case her infant proved a girl, a gift as propitiation or expiation being required. Uncleanliness was attributed to woman in every function of her being; the purification of the Virgin Mary, who was not exempt, when after the birth of a God, being used as an incontrovertible argument in proof. A festival of the purification of the Virgin Mary, adopted from paganism, was introduced into Rome at an early date, thus perpetuating a belief in the uncleanliness of motherhood. The Church in the Roman Empire soon united with the State[22] in imposing new restrictions upon women. Since the Reformation the mother's duty of expiation has been confirmed by the Anglican Church and is known in England as "churching. " Directions as to the woman's dress at this time was early made the subject of a canon.[23] She was to be decently appareled. This term "decently," variously interpreted, was at times the occasion of serious trouble. In 1661, during the reign of James I, the Chancellor of Norwich ordered that every woman who came to be churched, should be covered with a white veil. A woman who refused to conform to this order was excommunicated for contempt. She prayed a prohibition, alleging that such order was not warranted by any custom or Canon of the Church of England. The judges of the civil court, finding themselves incompetent to decide upon such a momentous question, requested the opinion of the archbishop of Canterbury. Not willing to trust his own judgment, that dignitary convened several bishops for consultation. Their decision was against the woman, this Protestant Council upon woman's dress, declaring that it was the ancient usage of the Church of England for women who were to be churched to come veiled, and a prohibition was denied.

The doctrine that woman must remain covered when in the sacred church building shows itself in the United States.[24] In many instances under Christianity, woman has been entirely excluded from religious houses and church buildings. When Pope Boniface[25] founded the abbey of Fulda he prohibited the entrance of women into any of the buildings, even including the church. This rule remained unbroken during the tenth and eleventh centuries, and even when in 1131 the Emperor Lothair went to Fulda to celebrate Pentecost, his empress was not permitted to witness the ceremonies. When Frederick Barbarossa, 1135, proposed to spend his Easter there, he was not even allowed to enter the house because of having his wife with him. In 1138 Boniface IX, at the request of the abbot, John Merlow, relaxed the rule and permitted women to attend the services of the church. Shortly afterwards the building was destroyed by lightning, which was looked upon as evidence of the divine displeasure at the desecration. The monastery of Athos under the Greek church, situated upon an island, does not permit the entrance of a female animal upon its confines. Even in America woman has met similar experience.[26]

At certain periods during the middle ages, conversation with women was forbidden. During the Black Death, the Flaggellants, or Brotherhood of the Cross, were under such interdict.[27] In this last decade of the nineteenth century, the Catholic church still imposes similar restrictions upon certain religious houses. Early in 1892 the queen-regent of Spain visited the monastery of Mirzaflores; its rules not allowing a monk to speak to a woman, the queen was received in silence. Her majesty immediately telegraphed to the pope asking indulgence, which was granted, and during four hours the monks were permitted the sin of speaking to a woman. It is curious to note that the first sentence uttered by one of the monks was a compliment upon the simplicity of her majesty's attire. But the most impressive evidence of the contempt of the church towards all things feminine was shown in a remark by Tetzel the great middle-age dealer in indulgences. Offering one for sale he declared it would insure eternal salvation even if the purchaser had committed rape upon the mother of God.[28]

A knowledge of facts like these is necessary in order to a just understanding of our present civilization, especially as to the origin of restrictive legislation concerning woman. The civilization of today is built upon the religious theories of the middle ages supplemented by advancing freedom of thought. Lea, declares thus,

> The Latin church is the great fact which dominates the history of modern civilization. All other agencies which molded the destinies of Europe were comparatively isolated or sparodic in their manifestations.

The influence of church teaching is most strikingly manifested in the thought of today. Without predetermined intention of wrongdoing, man has been so molded by the Church doctrine of ages and the coordinate laws of State as to have become blind to the justice of woman's demand for freedom such as he possesses. Nor is woman herself scarcely less bound, although now torn by the spirit of rebellion which burned in the hearts, of her fore-mothers, so cruelly persecuted, so falsely judged, during past ages, when the most devout Christian woman possessed no rights in the church, the government or the family. The learning which had been hers in former periods, was then interdicted as an especial element of evil. Her property rights recognized in former periods then denied; as a being subordinate to man she was not allowed a separate estate or control over the earnings of her own hands. Her children were not her own but those of a master for whose interest or pleasure she had given them birth. Without freedom of thought or action, trained to consider herself secondary to a man, a being who came into the world not as part of the great original plan of creation but as an afterthought of her Creator, and this doctrine taught as one of the most sacred mysteries of religion which to doubt was to insure her eternal damnation, it is not strange that the great body of women are not

now more outspoken in demanding equal religious and governmental rights with man. But another phase of heredity shows
itself in the eagerness with which woman enter all phases of
public life which does not place them in open antagonism with
Church or State. Education, industries, club life and even those
great modern and religious organizations which bring them
before the public, throwing active work and responsibility upon
them, would be entirely unexplainable were it not for the tendency of inherited thought to ultimately manifest itself.

The long continued and powerfully repressing influence of
church teaching in regard to the created inferiority of women,
imposed upon millions of men and women a bondage of thought
and action which even the growing civilization of the nineteenth
century has not yet been able to cast off. To this doctrine we can
trace all the irregularities which for many centuries filled the
church with shame; practices more obscene than those of
Babylon or Corinth, dragged Christendom to a darkness blacker
than the night of heathendom in the most pagan countries—a
darkness so intense that the most searching efforts of the historian
but now and then cast a ray of light upon it;—a darkness so profound that in Europe from the seventh to the eleventh centuries
no individual thought can be traced, no opinion was formed, no
heresy arose. All Christendom was sunk in superstition. Lange[29]
says "The disappearance of ancient civilization in the early centuries of the Christian era is an event the serious problems of
which are in great part still unexplained." Had Lange not been
influenced by the subtle current of heredity which unwittingly
influenced nations and systems equally with individuals, he could
easily have discovered the cause of this disappearance of olden
civilization, to be in the degradation of the feminine element
under Christianity. While this darkness of Christian Europe was
so great that history knows less of it a thousand years since than
it does of Egypt 5,000 years ago, one corner of that continent was
kept luminous by the brilliance of Mahommedan learning. The
Arabs alone had books from the eighth to the thirteenth centuries
of the Christian era. The Moors of Spain kept that portion of

Europe bright, while all else was sunk in darkness. Universities existed, learning was fostered and women authors were numerous. For many hundred years Rome possessed no books but missals and a few Bibles in the hands of priests. Men were bound by church dogmas looking only for aggrandisement through her. The arts ceased to flourish, science decayed, learning was looked upon as a disgrace to a warrior,[30] the only occupation deemed worthy of the noble.

The priesthood who alone possessed a knowledge of letters, prostituted their learning to the basest uses; the nobility when not engaged against a common foe, spent their time battling against each other; the peasantry were by turns the sport and victim of priest and noble, while woman was the prey of all. Her person and her rights possessed no consideration except as she could be made to advance the interest or serve the pleasure of priest, noble, father, husband; some man-god to whose lightest desire all her wishes were made to bend. The most pronounced doctrine of the church at this period was, that through woman sin had entered the world; that woman's whole tendency was towards evil, and had it not been for the unfortunate oversight of her creation, man would then be dwelling in the paradisal innocence and happiness of Eden, with death entirely unknown. When the feminine was thus wholly proscribed, the night of moral and spiritual degradation reached its greatest depth, and that condition ensued which has alike been the wonder and the despair of the modern historians, whose greatest fault, as Buckle shows, has been the reading of history from a few isolated facts rather than building up its philosophy from an aggregation of events upon many different planes.

Under all restrictions woman did not fail to show her innate power even within the fold of the church. She founded devout orders,[31] established and endowed religious institutions, and issued her commands to the pope himself, in more than one instance seating that holy personage in the papal chair.[32] From St. Paulina, whose life was written by St. Jerome, to the promulgation of the dogma of the Immaculate Conception of the Virgin Mary by the Ecumenical Council under Pius IX, and the later canonization of Joan of Arc, woman has not failed to impress even the Christian world with a sense of her intellectual and spiritual power. Yet despite the very great influence exerted by so many women in the affairs of the church—notwithstanding the canonization of so many women, she has only been able to show her capacity at an immense expenditure of vital force against constant priestly opposition and the powerful decrees of councils. Subtle and complex as are the influences that mould thought and character, we cannot comprehend the great injustice of the church towards woman in its teaching of her mental and spiritual inferiority without a slight examination of the great religious institutions that have been under her charge. Of these none possess more remarkable history than the Abbey of Fontervault,[33] founded in 1099, for both monks and nuns. It belonged in the general rank of Benedictines, and was known as the Order of Fontervault. It was ruled by an abbess under title of General of the Order, who was responsible to no authority but that of the pope himself. Forming a long succession of able women in thirty-two abbesses from the most eminent families of France, woman's capacity for the management of both ecclesiastical and civil affairs was there shown for six hundred years. It was the abbess who alone decided the religious fitness of either monk or nun seeking admission to the order. It was the abbess who decreed all ecclesiastical and civil penalties; who selected the confessors for the different houses of the order throughout France and Spain; who managed and controlled the vast wealth belonging to this institution; it was the abbess who drew up the rules for the government of the order, and who also successfully defended these privileges when attacked. For neither the protection of the pope, the wealth of the order, or the family influence connected with it, prevented priestly attack,[34] and no argument in favor of woman's governing ability is stronger than the fact that its abbesses ever successfully resisted these priestly assaults upon the privileges of their order. The abbey of Fontervault, with its grounds of forty or fifty acres, was surrounded by high walls; its soil was tilled by the monks of the abbey, who received even their food as alms from the nuns, returning all fragments for distribution to the poor.[35] The authority of women was supreme in all monasteries of the order. The ecclesiastical power maintained by these abbesses is the more remarkable, as it was in direct contravention of the dictates of the early councils, that of Aix-la-Chapelle, 816, forbidding abbesses to give the veil or take upon themselves any priestly function; the later council of Paris, A.D. 824, bitterly complained that women served at the altar and even gave to people the body and blood of Jesus Christ.

Among the convents controlled by women, which have largely influenced religious thought, was that of the Paraclete in the twelfth century under Heloise. Its teachings that belief was dependent upon knowledge, attacked the primal church tenet that belief depends upon faith alone. The convent of Port Royal des Champs during the seventeenth century exerted much influence. Its abbess, the celebrated Mother Angélique Arnault, was inducted into this office in her eleventh year upon death of her abbess-aunt, whose co-adjutrix she had been. This convent, both in person of the nuns as well as the monks connected with it, became a protest against the jesuitical doctrine of the seventeenth century and, like the Paraclete, is intimately connected with reform questions in the Catholic Church. Notwithstanding such evidences of woman's organizing mind and governing qualities under the most favorable conditions, as well as of piety so unquestioned as to have produced a long calendar of female saints, the real policy of the church remained unchanged; nor could it be otherwise from its basis of woman's created inferiority and original sin. The denial to women of the right of private judgment and the control of her own actions, the constant teaching of her greater sinfulness and natural impurity, had a very depressing effect upon the majority of women whose lowly station in life was such as to deprive them of that independence of thought and action possible to women of rank and wealth. Then, as now, the church catered to the possessors of money and power; then, as now, seeking to unite their great forces with its own purpose of aggrandizement, and thus the church has ever obstructed the progress of humanity, delaying civilization and condemning the world to a moral barbarism from which there is no escape except through repudiation of its teachings. To the theory of "God the Father," shorn of the divine attribute of motherhood, is the world beholden for its most degrading beliefs, its most infamous practices. Dependent upon and identified with lost motherhood is the "Lost Name" of ancient writers and occultists. When the feminity of the divine is once again acknowledged, the "Lost Name" will be discovered and the holiness (wholeness) of divinity be manifested.[36]

As the theory of woman's wickedness gathered force, her representative place in the church lessened. From century to century restrictive canons multiplied, and the clergy constantly grew more corrupt, although bearing bad reputation at an early date.[37] Tertullian, whose heavy diatribes are to be found in large libraries, was bitter in his opposition to marriage.[38] While it took many hundreds of years for the total exclusion of woman from the christian priesthood, the celibacy of the clergy during this period was the constant effort of the Church. Even during the ages that priestly marriage was permitted, celibates obtained a higher reputation for sanctity and virtue than married priests, who infinitely more than celibates were believed subject to infestation by demons.[39]

The restriction upon clerical marriages proceeded gradually. First the superior holiness of the unmarried was taught together with their greater freedom from infestation by demons. A single marriage only was next allowed, and that with a woman who had never before entered the relation.[40] The Council of A.D. 347, consisting of twenty-one bishops, forbade the ordination of these priests who had been twice married or whose wife had been a widow.[41] A council of A.D. 395, ruled that a bishop who had children after ordination should be excluded from the major orders. The Council of A.D. 444, deposed Chelidonius, bishop of Besancon, for having married a widow. The Council of Orleans, A.D. 511, consisting of thirty-two bishops, decided that monks who married should be expelled from the ecclesiastical order. The Church was termed the spouse of the priest. It was declared that

Peter possessed a wife before his conversion, but that he forsook her and all worldly things after he became Christ's, who established chastity; priests were termed holy in proportion as they opposed marriage.[42] The unmarried among the laity who had never entered that relation, and the married who forsook it, were regarded as saintly. So great was the opposition to marriage that a layman who married a second time was refused benediction and penance imposed.[43] A wife was termed "An Unallowed Thing."

So far from celibacy producing chastity or purity of life, church restrictions upon marriage led to the most debasing crimes, the most revolting vices, the grossest immorality. As early as the fourth century (370) the state attempted purification through a statute enacted by the emperors Valentinian, Valerius and Gratian, prohibiting ecclesiastics and monks from entering the houses of widows, single women living alone, or girls who had lost their parents.[44] The nearest ties of relationship proved ineffectual in protecting woman from priestly assault, and incest became so common it was found necessary to prohibit the residence of a priest's mother or sister in his house.[45] This restriction was renewed at various times through the ages. The condemnation of the Council of Rome, Easter, 1051, under the pontificate of Pope Leo IX, was not directed against married priests, but against those who held incestuous relations. Yet although the Church thus externally set her seal of disapprobation upon this vice, her general teaching sustained it. Gregory, bishop of Venelli, convicted of this crime by the Council of Rome, was punished by excommunication, but in a short time was restored to his former important position. The highest legates were equally guilty with the inferior priests. Cardinal John of Cremona, the pope's legate to the Council of Westminster 1125, sent by Pope Honorius for the express purpose of enforcing celibacy, became publicly notorious and disgraced, and was obliged to hastily leave England in consequence of his teaching and his practice being diametrically opposed.[46]

Through this clerical contempt of marriage, the conditions of celibacy and virginity were regarded as of the highest virtue. Jerome respected marriage as chiefly valuable in that it gave virgins to the church, while Augustus in acknowledging that marriage perpetuated the species, also contended that it also perpetuated original sin.

These diverse views in regard to marriage created the most opposite teaching from the church. By one class the demand to increase and multiply was constantly brought up, and women were taught that the rearing of children was their highest duty. The strangest sermons were sometimes preached toward the enforcement of this command. Others taught an entirely different duty for both men and women, and a large celibate class was created under especial authority of the church. Women, especially those of wealth, were constantly urged to take upon themselves the vow of virginity, their property passing into possession of the church this helping to build up priestly power. Another class held the touch of a woman to be a contamination, and to avoid it holy men secluded themselves in caves and forests.[47] Through numerous decretals confirmation was given to the theory that woman was defiled through the physical peculiarities of her being. Even her beauty was counted as an especial snare and temptation of the devil for which in shame she ought to do continual penance.[48] St. Chrysostom, whose prayer is repeated at every Sunday morning service of the Episcopal church, described woman as a "necessary evil, a natural temptation, a desirable calamity, a domestic peril, a deadly fascination, and a painted ill." But to escape her influence was impossible and celibacy led to the most direful results. Monks and hermits acknowledged themselves tormented in their solitary lives by visions of beautiful women. Monasteries were visited by an illness to which celibacy imparted a name,[49] and impurity of body and soul spread throughout Christendom. The general tone of the church in regard to marriage; its creation of a double code of morality; its teaching of woman's greater sinfulness, together with that of her absolute subordination to man, subverted the moral character of the Christian world within whose borders the vilest systems of immorality arose which the world has ever known; its extent being a subject of historical record.[50]

According to the teaching of men who for many hundreds of years were molders of human thought, priests, philosophers and physicians alike, nature never designed to procreate woman, her intention being always to produce men. These authorities asserted that nature never formed the feminine except when she lost her true function and so produced the female sex by chance or accident. Aristotle[51] whose philosophy was accepted by the church and all teaching of a contrary character declared heretical, maintained that nature did not form woman except when by reason of imperfection of matter she could not obtain the sex which is perfect.[52] Cajetan enunciated the same doctrine many hundred years later.[53] Aristotle also denied creative power to the mother.[54] While throughout its history the course of the Christian Church against marriage is constantly seen, no less noticeable are the grossly immoral practices resulting from celibacy. Scarcely a crime or a vice to which it did not give birth. Celibacy was fostered in the interests of power, and in order to its more strict enforcement barons were permitted to enslave the wives and children of married priests.[55] Those of Rome were bestowed upon the Cathedral church of the Lateran, and bishops throughout Christendom were ordered to enforce this law in their own dioceses and to seize the wives of priests for the benefit of their churches. At no point of history do we more clearly note the influence of the Church upon the State than in the union of the temporal power with the ecclesiastical for purposes of constraining priestly celibacy.

Under reign of Philip I of France, a council was held at Troyes which condemned the marriage of priests.[56] In 1108, the following year, King Henry I of England[57] summoned a council to assemble in London for purpose of upholding priestly celibacy, urging its enforcement upon the bishops, and pledging his kingly honor in aid. A new series of canons was promulgated, strengthened by severe penalties and the cooperation of the king. Finding it impossible either through spiritual or temporal power to compel absolute celibacy[58] the king for the benefit of his exchequer established a license for concubinage upon the payment of a tax known as cullagium.[59]

Notwithstanding all the powerful enginery of the church, priestly celibacy, so contrary to nature, was not rendered absolutely imperative until the thirteenth century. The Fourth Lateran Council, (Twelfth Ecumenical), 1215, under pope Innocent III, is especially famous because of its final settlement of the policy of the church in regard to priestly marriage. This was a large council, 1300 prelates taking part in the adjudication of this question. While with St. Augustine acknowledging that marriage was requisite for the preservation of the race, it strictly confined this relation to the laity.

The subject of celibacy as we see had agitated the church from its foundation. A more renowned council even than the Twelfth Ecumenical, namely, the First Nicene or Second Ecumenical, having seriously discussed it, although after prolonged debate pronouncing against celibacy and in favor of priestly marriage. St. Paphinutius, the martyr bishop of Thebes, although himself a celibate advocated marriage which he declared to be true chastity, the council adopting his opinion. Although the tendency of the church for so many hundred years had been towards celibacy yet when adopted as a dogma, a belief in its propriety or its scriptural authority was by no means universal even among the most eminent members, but in no instance has the control of the church over the consciences and will of its adherents been more forcibly illustrated. Many illustrious and learned theologians as Gratian the Canonist, St. Thomas Aquinas and Giraldus Cambrensis, Arch-Deacon of St. Davids, while thereafter sustaining celibacy *as a law of the church* declared it had neither scriptural nor apostolic warrant; St. Thomas affirming it to be merely a law of human ecclesiastical origin.[60]

Absolute celibacy of the priesthood proved very difficult of enforcement. At the great council of London, 1237, twenty-three years afterwards, Cardinal Otto deplored the fact that married men still received holy orders and held office in the church, and in 1268 only fifty-three years after the great council confirming celibacy as a doctrine of the church, another great council was convened in London, when Cardinal Legate Ottoborn, the direct representative of the Pope, demanded the establishment of concubinage for priests. The institutions of Otto and Ottoborn long remained the law of the English church. Yet to their honor be it remembered that despite council and cardinal, pope and church, there were priests who still persistently refused either to part from their wives or to relinquish their priestly functions, and who when excommunicated for contumacy, laughed at the sentence and continued their priestly offices.[61] Others sufficiently conformed to the edicts to lock up their churches and suspend their priestly administrations, yet refusing to part with their wives. The relatives of wives also exerted their influence against the action of the church.

The struggle was bitter and long. New canons were promulgated and celibacy enforced under severe penalties, or rather marriage was prohibited under severe penalties. The holy robbery which made slaves of the wives and children of priests confiscating their property to the church, had more effect in compelling celibacy than all anathemas upon the iniquity of marriage. Priests who retained their wives preferring the chastity of this relation to the license allowed celibates, were prohibited from their offices and their wives denounced as harlots. If this did not suffice, such priests were finally excommunicated. But a way of return was left open. In case this measure coerced them into abandoning wives and children, a short penance soon restored the priestly rank with all its attendant dignities. Nor was the reinstated priest compelled to live purely. So little was it expected that the tax upon concubinage soon became a component part of the celibate system. So gross and broadspread became the immorality of all classes that even the Head of the Church pandered to it in the erection by Pope Sixtus V of a magnificent building devoted to illicit pleasure.[62]

The example of Christ himself was pointed to in favor of celibacy, even upon the cross saying to his mother, "Woman, what have I to do with thee?" The saints of the Old Testament as well as the New, were quoted as having opposed marriage. Abel, Melchisedeck, Joshua, Elias, Jonah, Daniel, St. John the Baptist, St. John the Evangelist, St. Paul with his disciples, and all saintly personages were declared to have been celibates.

A concubinage tax was exacted from all the clergy without exception, and rendered compulsory even upon those priests who still kept their wives, or who lived chastely outside of the marital relation. Protests were of no avail. Those whom disinclination, age or ill health kept chaste, were told the privilege of unchastity was open to them; the bishop must have the money and after payment they were at liberty to keep concubines or not.[63] Under concubinage the priest was free from all family responsibility; his mistress possessed neither present nor future claim upon him; children, who according to church teaching followed the condition of the mother, were born to him, but for their education and maintenance neither ecclesistical nor civil law compelled him to provide.[64]

For many centuries this immoral tax brought enormous sums into the treasuries of both Church and State. Although the laws against the marriage of priests were enacted on pretense of the greater inherent wickedness of woman, history proves their chief object to have been the keeping of all priestly possessions under church control. It was openly asserted that the temporal possessions of the church were imperilled by sacerdotal marriage, and it has been declared with every proof of truthfulness that edicts against the marriage of priests were promulgated to prevent the alienation of property from the church.[65] The saying of Paul was quoted: "He that is married careth for his wife, but he that is unmarried for the Lord." Married bishops were occasionally confirmed in their sees upon condition that their wives and children should not inherit their property, which upon their death should fall to the church.[66]

The struggle against the absolute celibacy of the priesthood was bitter. A few priests still kept their benefices while retaining their wives and acknowledging their children as legitimate. The sons of such contumacious priests were declared forever incapable of taking holy orders, unless by a special dispensation. The church showed almost equal determination in the establishment of concubinage as in the enforcement of priestly celibacy, each of these systems tending to its enrichment.

Opposition proved of no permanent avail. Holding control

over the conscience of men, asserting the power to unlock the doors of heaven and hell, a strongly organized body working to one end, it is not a subject of astonishment that the church, its chief object the crushing of body and soul, should in the end prove conqueror, and the foulest crimes against woman receive approval of the entire christian world. Many notable consequences followed the final establishment of celibacy as a dogma of the church.

First. The doctrine of woman's inherent wickedness and close fellowship with Satan took on new strength.

Second. Canon Law gained full control of civil law.

Third. An organized system of debauchery arose under mask of priestly infallibility.

Fourth. Auricular confession was confirmed as a dogma of the church.

Fifth. Prohibition of the Scriptures to the laity was enforced.

Sixth. Crime was more openly protected, the system of indulgences gained new strength becoming the means of great revenue to the church.

Seventh. Heresy was more broadly defined and more severely punished.

Eight. The Inquisition was established.

When Innocent III completed the final destruction of sacerdotal marriage, it was not upon disobedient priests the most severe punishment fell, but upon innocent women and children.[67] Effort was made to force wives to desert their husbands. Those who proved contumacious were denied christian burial in an age when such denial was looked upon as equivalent to eternal damnation; property left such wives was confiscated to the church; they were forbidden the eucharist; churching after childbirth was denied them; they were termed harlots and their children bastards, while to their sons all office in the church was forbidden. If still contumacious they were handed over to the secular power for condign punishment, or sold as slaves for the benefit of the church. They were regarded as under the direct control of Satan himself, as beings who iniquitously stood between their husbands and heaven.

At numerous times in the history of the church women have been brought to despair by its teachings, and large numbers driven to suicide. A similar period was inaugurated by the confirmation of priestly celibacy. The wives of such men, suddenly rendered homeless and with their children classed among the vilest of earth, powerless and despairing, hundreds shortened their agonies by death at their own hands. For all these crimes the church alone is responsible.

Under celibacy, auricular confession, and extended belief in witchcraft, a new era of wrong toward woman was inaugurated. From thenceforth her condition was more degraded than even during the early centuries of christianity. Accusations of heresy, which included witchcraft as well as other sins against the church were constantly made against that being who was believed to have brought sin into the world. Whosoever dared question the infallibility of the church by use of their own judgment, even upon the most trivial subjects, immediately fell into condemnation.

Canon Law gaining full control over civil law, the absolute sinfulness of divorce, which maintained by the church has yet been allowed by civil law, was fully established. Woman was entirely at the mercy of man, the Canon Law maintaining that the confession of a guilty woman could not be received in evidence against her accomplice, although it held good against herself[68] and the punishment due to both was made to fall on the woman alone.[69] The best authorities prove that while the clergy were acquainted with the civil codes that had governed the Roman Empire, they made but little use of them.[70] Upon coming to the throne, Justinian[71] had repealed the law of the Patriarchate which gave the father sole right and title to, and interest in the children of legal marriage, but this was soon again subverted by ecclesiasticism and under Canon Law a mother was prohibited all authority over her child, its relationship to her even being denied. While under Common Law children followed the condition of their fathers, who if free transmitted freedom to their children, yet in the interests of priestly celibacy, under church legislation, an entire reversal took place and children were held to follow the condition of their mothers. Thus serf-mothers bore serf-children to free-born fathers; slave mothers bore slave children to their masters; while unmarried mothers bore bastard children to both priestly and lay fathers, thus throwing the taint of illegitimacy upon the innocent child, and the sole burden of its maintenance upon the mother. This portion of Canon Law also became the law of the State in all Christian countries[72] and is in existence at the present time, both civil codes and statue laws enforcing this great wrong of the Church.[73] The relations of men and women to each other, the sinfulness of marriage, and the license of illicit relations for the priesthood, employed the thought of the church. The duty of woman to obey, not alone her male relatives, but all men by virtue of their sex, was sedulously inculcated. She was trained to hold her own desires and even thoughts in abeyance to those of man, as to one who was rightfully her master. Every holy principle of her nature was subverted by this degrading assumption.

When auricular confession became confirmed as a dogma of the church, it threw immense power over the family into the hands of the priesthood, a power capable of being converted to many ends, but was specially notable in its influence upon morals.[74] Although auricular confession was not established as a dogma until the Council of 1215, it had been occasionally practiced at early date, carrying with it the same immorality in lesser form as that which afterwards became so great a reproach to the church.[75] Through its means the priesthood gained possession of all family, social and political secrets, thus acquiring information whose power for evil was unlimited. The spirit of evil never found a more subtle method of undermining and destroying human will, its most debasing influences falling upon woman, who through fear of eternal damnation made known her most secret thoughts to the confessor, an unmarried and frequently a youthful man. It soon became a source of very great corruption to both priest and woman.

Another effect of this council was the formal prohibition of the scriptures to the laity, and thenceforth the Bible was confined to the priest who explained its teachings in the interests of his own order, adding to, or taking from, to suit his own interests; the recent new version showing many such interpolations.[76] Nothing was held sacred by these men, who sacrificed everything to their own advancement and that of their order.

The insolence of the priesthood was that of all periods; claiming direct inspiration from God, they taught their own infallibility and in name of Him, whom they professed to serve, the grossest crimes were perpetrated, and this profession became a protecting sanctuary to men whose villainous lives would otherwise have brought them to the gallows.[77]

With conviction of woman's supreme wickedness, increased through the formal recognition of celibacy as a dogma of the church, with the establishment of auricular confession, and the denial of the Bible to the laity, the persecution of woman for witchcraft took on new phase. The belief that it was the ordinary method through which the devil won souls, together with the persuasion that woman through her greater wickedness fell more readily than men into such practices, acquired a firmer seat in theology. Heresy, of which witchcraft was one phase, became a greater sin; the inquisition arose, and the general characteristics of the christian world rapidly grew more inimical to humanity, and especially to woman's freedom, happiness and security.

The influence of the church daily grew more unfavorable to all virtue; vice was sustained, immorality dignified. The concubines of priests called "wives," in bitter mockery of that relation in which the legal wife was termed concubine, were known as "The Hallowed Ones," "The Honored Ones." No stigma attached to such a life; these women formed quite a class in mediæval society, themselves and their children ranking the wives of ordinary laymen;[78] the touch of a priest had sanctified them. In the estimation of the church an immoral life led with a priest was more honorable than marriage with a layman, and all the obligations such a relation implied. Priests assumed immunity from wrongdoing. So far from celibacy causing purity of life, through it the priesthood grew to look upon themselves as especially set apart for indulgence in vice. Did not history so faithfully portray this condition, it would seem impossible that it had existed among people asserting the highest morality, and is proof of the danger of irresponsible power to possessor and victim alike, and the ease with which the true meaning of right and wrong is lost under such circumstances.

The theory of the church that as the fall and sin really existed, priestly immorality became a necessity in order to perpetuate the world even through a continuance of the original sin, was a species of fine casuistry for which the church in all ages has been remarkable. The general tenor of the church against marriage, together with its teaching of woman's greater sinfulness, were the chief causes which undermined the morality of the christian world for fifteen hundred years. With these doctrines were also taught the duty of woman to sacrifice herself in every way for man, a theory of which the present century is not unfamiliar. The loss of chastity in woman was held as light sin in comparison to the degradation that marriage would bring to a priest, and young girls ruined by some candidate or priest, considered themselves doing God service in refusing a marriage that would cause the expulsion of the priestly lover from the ecclesiastical order. With woman's so-called "divine," but rather demoniac self-sacrifice, Heloise chose to be deemed the mistress of Abelard rather than by acknowledging their marriage destroy his prospects of advancement in the church.[79]

The State sustained the Church in its opposition to marriage, and we find the anomaly of marriage for political reasons where the parties forever separated at the altar. St. Jerome, and at a later date St. Dunstan, sustained the policy of such marriages. The history of Britain gives instances of early queens thus separating from their newly made husbands at the close of the ceremony, dedicating their lives to celibacy and their fortunes to the church.

Nor did this institution neglect that large class of women to whom marriage was made impossible because of the numbers of men to whom it was forbidden. After the Lateran Council had permanently settled the action of the church in favor of priestly celibacy, great effort was made to draw women of wealth into a monastic life. Religion was the chief method of acquiring power, and as an abbess of a religious institution it opened opportunity for power to women scarcely possible outside the church. The two highest womanly virtues inculcated by the church were a celibate life and liberality to religious houses. It was taught if anything could possibly mitigate woman's sin through Eve's transgression, it was the observance of these two conditions.

To the student this is the most remarkable period in the history of the church, not merely as a culmination of the effort of centuries in finally deciding the questions of celibacy, so long agitated with such varying results, but in the immediate change and permanent settlement it brought about in regard to other church dogmas, as well as its pronounced influence in causing the Lutheran Reformation.

It was asserted that the spiritual office of the priest sanctified sin; it became a maxim that whatever a priest might do was holy; by their taking part in lasciviousness it became consecration. To disobey a priest was to endanger salvation; it was libellous and treasonable to question the purity of a priest's motives, hence religion became a screen for all vice and a source of moral degradation to all women. To such extent was belief carried in the superior purity of a celibate life that but little more than 300 years since a man was burned at the stake in England for asserting the lawfulness of priestly marriage.[80] The action of the council of 1215, so powerfully sustaining the olden claims of the superior holiness of celibacy soon created a belief in the inability of a priest to commit sin. During the middle ages his infallibility was constantly maintained, his superior sanctity in consequence of his celibacy universally asserted. It was impossible not to connect the idea of great wickedness with those incapable of entering this holy office, and as woman by virtue of sex was prohibited priestly functions, and as her marriage had been declared a necessity for the world, these conditions were used as arguments against her. The conscience and morality of tens of thousands were destroyed by these teachings, enforced as they were by all the dread authority of the church. The christian world was under entire control of a class whose aim was chiefly that of personal aggrandizement, and that hesitated at no means for securing wealth and power.

The Inquisition was firmly established; under its reign six hundred methods of torture were known, and it was conducted with such secrecy that not until dragged before it were many of its victims aware they were under suspicion. Even when imprisoned in its torture chambers, the charges against them were kept secret in hopes thereby to compel self-accusation upon other points. The inferiority of woman, her proneness to evil and readiness to listen to all suggestions of Satan, was taught with renewed vigor and power for evil.

The priest regarded himself as the direct representative of divinity; the theory of infallibility was not confined to the pope, but all dignitaries of the church made the same claim, asserting themselves incapable of wrongdoing, maintaining an especial sanctification by reason of their celibacy, priests nevertheless made their holy office a cover for the most degrading sensuality. Methods were taken to debauch the souls as well as the bodies of women. Having first taught their special impurity, it was now maintained that immorality with a priest was not sin, but on the contrary hallowed the woman, giving her particular claim upon heaven. It was taught that sin could only be killed through sin.[81] The very incarnation was used as a means of weakening woman's virtue. That Christ did not enter the world through the marriage relation, stamped with christian honor a system of concubinage in the church, for whose warrant woman was pointed to the Virgin Mary. As an enforcement of her duty of absolute surrender of soul and body to the will of the priest the course of the Virgin was adduced, "who obeyed the angel Gabriel and conceived without fear of evil, for impurity could not come of a spirit."[82] The chastity of concubinage and the unchasteness of marriage was constantly asserted by the church, and thus the mysteries upon which its foundations were laid were used by it for the degradation of woman who was at all times depicted as a being of no self-individuality, but one who had been created solely for man's pleasure. As late as the seventeenth century, it was taught that a priest could commit no sin. This old doctrine took new strength from the Illumes, who claimed an inner divine light.[83]

We find reference to priestly immorality and claim of infallibility among old writers, Boccacio in many of his stories, putting arguments of this kind in the mouth of his priestly characters.[84]

It was asserted too, that sin was of the body alone, the soul knowing nothing, partaking nothing of it. As an argument in favor of woman's throwing herself entirely in the hands of priests for immoral purposes, it was declared that: "The devout having offered up and annihiliated their own selves exist no longer but in God; thenceforth they can do no wrong. The better part of them is so divine that it no longer knows what the other is doing."

In confirmation of this doctrine it was said that Jesus threw off his clothing and was scourged naked before the people. The result of this teaching was the almost universal immorality of christendom. Under such religious doctrine it could but be expected that the laity would closely imitate the priesthood. Europe became a continent of moral corruption, of which proof is overwhelming. Could we but relegate christian immorality to the dark ages we might somewhat palliate it under plea of ignorance. But unfortunately for such claim ample proof is found to show that the enlightenment of modern civilization has not yet been able to overthrow the basic idea upon which this immorality rests. Amid the material and intellectual advancement of the last hundred years we find spiritual darkness still profound in the church and the true foundation of immorality almost unrecognized.

As long as the church maintains the doctrine that woman was created inferior to man, and brought sin into the world, rendering the sacrifice of the Son of a God a necessity, just so long will the foundation of vice and crime of every character remain. Not until the exact and permanent equality of woman with man is recognized by the church, aye, even more, the greater power and capacity of woman in the creative function, together with the accountability of man to woman in everything relating to the birth of a new being, is fully accepted as a law of nature, will vice and crime disappear from the world. Until that time has fully come, prostitution in its varied forms will continue to exist, together with almshouses, reformatories, jails, prisons, hospitals and asylums for the punishment, reformation or care of the wretched beings who have come into existence with an inheritance of disease and crime because of church theory and church teaching.

The system of celibacy produced its same effects wherever preached. So constant was the system of debauchery practiced in England during the reign of Henry VII that the gentlemen and farmers of Carnarvonshire laid complaint against the clergy of systematically seducing their wives and daughters.[85] Women were everywhere looked upon as slaves and toys, to obey, to furnish pleasure and amusement, and to be cast aside at will. Under the religious teaching of christendom it could not but be expected that the laity would closely imitate the priesthood and to victimize women became the custom of all men.[86] When a priest failed to take a concubine his parishoners compelled him to do so in order to preserve the chastity of their own wives and daughters. Draper[87] tells us that in England alone 100,000 women became victims of the priests. Houses of vile character were maintained for especial use of the priesthood. The marriage of a priest was called a deception of the devil who thus led him into an adulterous relation[88] for sake of alienating property from the church.

This mediæval doctrine that sin can only be killed through sin, finds expression today not alone in religion[89] but in society novels.[90] Its origin like many other religious wrongs, being directly traceable to the teaching of St. Paul.[91]

The incontinence of these celibate priests ultimately became so great a source of scandal to the church that it was obliged to take action. Edicts and bulls were fulminated from the papal chair, although the facts of history prove that Rome itself, its popes, and its cardinals, to have been sunk in the grossest immorality. Spain the seat of the Inquisition, and at that period the very heart of Christendom, was the first country toward which investigation was turned, Pope Paul IV issuing a bull against those confessors who solicited women, provoking them to dissolute action. When this bull of investigation first appeared in Spain, it was accompanied by an edict commanding all those who knew of monks or priests that had thus abused the confessional to make it known within thirty days under grievous penalty. The terrible power of the church intimidated those who otherwise for very shame would surely have buried the guilt of their priests in oblivion, and so great was the number of women who thronged the palace of the Inquisition in the city of Saville alone, that twenty secretaries with as many Inquisitors were not sufficient to take the deposition of the witnesses. A second, a third and a fourth thirty days were appointed for investigation, so great were the number of women making complaint.[92] So large a number of priests were implicated, that after a four months' examination, the Holy Tribunal of the Inquisition put a stop to the proceedings, commanding that all those immoralities and crimes against womanhood only rendered possible in the name of religion, and which has been proven by legal evidence, should be buried in eternal oblivion. The deposition of thousands of women seduced by their confessors, was not deemed sufficient evidence for removal of the guilty priests from their holy offices. Occasionally a single priest was suspended for a short time but in a few months restored again to his priestly position.[93]

It was not uncommon for women to be openly carried off by priests, their husbands and fathers threatened with vengeance in cases of their attempted recovery.[94] During the height of the Inquisitorial power it was not rare for a family to be aroused in the night by an ominous knock and the cry "The Holy Fathers, open the door!"

To this dread mandate there could be but one reply, as both temporal and spiritual power lay in their hands. A husband, father or son might thus be seized by veiled figures; or as frequently a loved wife or young daughter was dragged from her bed, her fate ever to remain a mystery. When young and beautiful these women were taken to replenish the Inquisitional harem the "dry pan," "boiling in oil," and similar methods of torture, threatened, in order to produce compliance upon part of wretched victims. No Turkish seraglio with bow-string and sack ever exhibited as great an amount of diabolical wickedness as the prison-harems of the Inquisition. As late as the seventeenth century Pope Gregory

XV commanded strict enforcement of the bull against priestly lechery not alone in Spain, but in all other parts of the Christian world. In England after the reformation, the same condition was found to exist.[95] But edicts against lasciviousness were vainly issued by a church whose foundation is a belief in the supremacy of one sex over the other, and that woman brought sin into the world through having seduced man into the marriage relation. Despite the advance of knowledge and civilization the effect of such teachings are the same now as during the middle ages, as fully proven at time of separation between the temporal and spiritual power in Italy;[96] and these proofs are taken from Catholic sources. In 1849 when the Roman people opened the palace of the Inquisition there was found in the library a department entitled "Summary of Solicitations," being a record of cases in which women had been solicited to acts of criminality by their confessors in the pontifical state.[97] The testimony of Luther as to the moral degradation of the church at time of the Reformation has never been invalidated,[98] and is entirely in accord with its character throughout history.

That the same iniquities are connected with the confessional today, we learn from the testimony of those priests who have withdrawn from the communion of the Catholic Church. Father Hyacinthe publicly declaring that ninety-nine out of one hundred priests live in sin with the women they have destroyed. Another priest following the example of Father Hyacinthe in marrying, asserted that he took this step in order to get out of the ultramontane slough and remain an honest man.[99] That the Catholic Church of the present day bears the same general character it did during the middle ages is proven from much testimony. Among the latest and most important witnesses, for minuteness and fullness of detail, is Rev. Charles Chiniquy in his works *The Priest, The Woman and the Confessional; Fifty years of Rome*, etc. Now over eighty years of age Rev. Mr. Chiniquy was for more than fifty years a catholic priest of influence and high reputation, known in Canada, where thousands of drunkards reformed under his teaching, as the "Apostle of Temperance."

Becoming convinced of the immorality of the Romish Church, he left it in 1856 taking with him five thousand French Canadians with whom be settled at St. Anne, Kankakee County, Illinois. Having united with a branch of the Protestant church he was invited to Scotland to take part in the Tercentary of the Reformation, and later to England where he lectured on invitation of ministers of every evangelical denomination.[100] His "Fifty Years of Rome," indissolubly links his name with that of Abraham Lincoln, through the information there made known regarding the Catholic plot for President Lincoln's assassination.

It is as fully a law of moral as of material nature that from the same causes the same effects follow. In his work upon the confessional[101] Rev. Mr. Chiniquy relates incidents coming under his own personal knowledge while he was still a catholic priest regarding its present abuses. The character of the questions made a duty of the priest to ask during confession, are debasing in the extreme, their whole tendency towards the undermining of morality. Too broadly indelicate for translation these priestly instructions are hidden in Latin, but are no less made the duty of a priest to understand and use. In 1877, a number of prominent women of Montreal, Canada, addressed a declaration and protest to the bishop of that diocese against the abuses of the confessional of which their own experience had made them cognizant.

DECLARATION
To His Lordship Bourget, Bishop of Montreal

Sir:—Since God in his infinite mercy has been pleased to show us the errors of Rome, and has given us strength to abandon them to follow Christ, we deem it our duty to say a word on the abominations of the confessional. You well know that these abominations are of such a nature that it is impossible for a woman to speak of them without a blush. How is it that among civilized christian men one has so far forgotten the rule of common decency as to force women to reveal to unmarried men, under the pains of eternal damnation, their most secret thoughts, their most sinful desires and their most private actions?

How unless there be a brazen mask on your priest's face dare they go out into the world having heard the tales of misery which cannot but defile the hearing, and which the women cannot relate without having laid aside modesty and all sense of shame. The harm would not be so great should the Church allow no one but the woman to accuse herself. But what shall we say of the abominable questions that are put to them and which they must answer?

Here, the laws of common decency strictly forbid us to enter into details. Suffice it to say, were husbands cognizant of one-tenth of what is going on between the confessor and their wives, they would rather see them dead than degraded to such a degree.

As for us, daughters and wives from Montreal who have known by experience the filth of the confessional, we cannot sufficiently bless God for having shown us the error of our ways in teaching us that it was not at the feet of a man as weak and as sinful as ourselves, but at the feet of Christ alone that we must seek salvation. Julia Herbert, Marie Rogers, J. Rocham, Louise Picard, Francoise Dirringer, Eugenie Martin, and forty-three others.[102]

In reply to a letter of inquiry addressed by myself to Rev. Mr. Chiniquy, the following answer was received.

St. Anne, Kankakee County, Illinois
January 4, 1887
"MRS. MATILDA JOSLYN GAGE,
Madam;

In answer to your honored letter of the 29th Dec. I hasten to say: *First*. The women of Montreal signed the declaration you see in *The Priest, the Woman and the Confessional*, in the fall of 1877. I do not remember the day. *Second*. As it is ten years since I left Montreal to come to my Missionary field of Illinois, I could not say if these women are still in Montreal or not. Great, supreme efforts were secretly made by the Bishop of Montreal to show that these names were forged in order to answer and confound me, but the poor Bishop found that the document was too correct, authentic and public to be answered and attacked, and he remained mute and confounded, for many of these woman were well known in the city.

Third. You will find the answer to your other questions, in the volume *Fifty Years in the Church of Rome*, which I addressed you by today's mail.

Respectfully yours in Christ,
C. Chiniquy

The same assertion of priestly infallibility is made today as it was centuries ago, the same declaration of change of nature through priestly celibacy. Upon this question Mr. Chiniquy says:

> If any one wants to hear an eloquent oration let him go where the Roman Catholic priest is preaching on the divine of auricular confession. They make the people believe that the vow of perpetual chastity changes their nature, turns them into angels and puts them above the common faults of the fallen children of Adam. With a brazen face when they are interrogated on that subject, they say that they have special graces to remain pure and undefiled in the midst of the greatest dangers; that the Virgin Mary to whom they are consecrated is their powerful advocate to obtain from her son that superhuman virtue of Chastity; that what would be a cause of sin and perdition to common men is without peril and danger for a true son of Mary.[103]

A work entitled *Mysteries of the Neapolitan Convents*, its author Henrietta Carracciola, a woman of the purest blood of the princes of Italy, daughter of the Marshal Carracciola, Governor of the Province of Pasi in Italy, is quoted from, by Rev. Mr. Chiniquy, in confirmation of his statements as to the continued impurity of the confessional.

> Finally another priest, the most annoying of all for his obstinate assiduity, sought to secure my affections at all cost. There was not an image profane poetry could afford him, nor a sophism he could borrow from rhetoric, no wily interpretation he could give to the word of God, which he did not employ to convert me to his wishes. Here is an example of his logic:

"Dear daughter," said he to me one day, "knowest thou who thy God truly is?"

"He is the Creator of the Universe," I answered dryly.

"No-no-no-no! that is not enough" he replied laughing at my ignorance; "God is Love, but love in the abstract which receives its incarnation in the mutual affection of two hearts which idolize each other. You must then not only love God in the abstract existence, but must also love him in his incarnation, that is, in the exclusive love of a man who adores you. *Quod Deus est amor nec colitus nisi amando.*"

"Then," I replied, "a woman who adores her own lover would adore Divinity itself?" "Assuredly," reiterated the priest over and over again, taking courage from my remark and chuckling with what seemed to him the effect of his catechism.

"In that case," said I hastily, "I should select for my lover rather a man of the world than a priest."

"God preserve you, my daughter! God preserve you from that sin. To love a man of the world, a sinner, a wretch, an unbeliever, an infidel! Why, you would go immediately to hell. The love of a priest is a sacred love, while that of a profane man is infamy. The priest purifies his affections daily in communion with the Holy Spirit . . . If you cannot love me because I am your confessor, I will find means to assist you to get rid of your scruples. We will place the name of Jesus Christ before all our affectionate demonstrations and thus our love will be a grateful offering to the Lord and will ascend fragrant with perfume to Heaven like the smoke of the incense of the Sanctuary. Say to me for example 'I love you in Jesus Christ, last night I dreamed of you in Jesus Christ, and you will have tranquil conscience, because in doing this God will sanctify every transport of your love.'"

Rev. Mr. Chiniquy who in his fifty years of Romish priesthood possessed every opportunity for knowing the truth, does not hesitate to affirm that the popes are today of the same general immoral character they were in the earlier centuries of the Church. He says:

Let not my readers be deceived by the idea that the popes of Rome in our days are much better than those of the ninth, tenth, eleventh and twelfth centuries. They are absolutely the same—the only difference is that today they take a little more care to conceal their secret orgies. Go to Italy and there the Roman Catholics themselves will show you the two beautiful daughters whom the late Pope, Pius IX had from two of his mistresses. Inquire from those who have personally known Pope Gregory XVI the predecessor of Pius IX; after they will have given you the history of his mistresses, one of whom was the wife of his barber, they will tell you that he was one of the greatest drunkards in Italy.[104]

The views of the Catholic Church in regard to marriage of the priesthood was recently demonstrated in the United States, 1885, by the persecution of a priest of the Uniate Greek Church sent as a missionary from Austria to Pennsylvania. The Greek Church, it must be remembered, permits a single marriage to a priest. The Uniate while in this respect following the discipline of the Greek Church, yet admits the supremacy of the Pope which the regular Greek Church does not. The Uniate Greek Church accepts, as binding, all the decisions of Rome subsequent to the division between the eastern and the western parts of christendom. Endowed with authority from both branches, Father Wolonski came to this country accompanied by his wife, in full expectation of fellowship with his catholic brethren. His first contrary experience occurred in Philadelphia when Archbishop Ryan of the Cathedral, refused all intercourse with him because of his marriage. Reaching Shenandoah where commissioned by his own Austrian Bishop, he discovered himself still under ban; the resident priest of the catholic church having warned his congregation under pain of excommunication to shun both himself and his church, upon the ground that the Roman Church under no circumstances tolerated a married priest. Eventually the subject grew to such proportions that Father Wolonski was recalled, and an unmarried priest sent in his stead.[105]

From the experience of Father Wolonski less than a decade

since, with the bitter hostility shown by the church towards Father Hyacinthe we find that a belief in the special holiness of celibacy is as dominant in the Catholic church today, as at any period of its history; concurrent testimony teaching us that its greatest evils remain the same as of old. It is less than twenty years since the whole christian world was interested in a suit brought against the heirs of the deceased Cardinal Antonelli in order to secure recognition of his daughter's claim to inheritance. This girl was everywhere spoken of by the Catholic Church as "a sacrilegious child," that is, a being who had violated sacred things by coming into existence. The destruction of her mother's life, her own illegitimacy, the wrong done to her mother's family and to society were held as of no moment beside the fact that her claims, if allowed, would take property from the church. The love of the Great Cardinal for this girl's mother was fully proven, but the church having established celibacy in order that it might control the property of its priests, was not inclined to permit any portion to be diverted from that source. Honesty, justice, and the ties of natural affection, now as of yore are not part of the Church system. In consequence, this suit of the illegitimate child of the Great Cardinal Secretary, filled not alone Italy, but the whole Catholic world with disgrace.

Among the countries now striving to free themselves from Church dominion is Mexico. A letter to the *New York Herald*, winter of 1892, regarding the revolution there in progress, said of Diaz:

> Instead of his being assisted by the Church it has been his bitterest and most relentless enemy and opponent. The Church in Mexico is opposed to all enlightenment of the people. The clergy, if they can be honored with that name, fight all improvements. They want no railways or telegraphs and when he adopted a system of compulsory education the war began in earnest. Diaz was determined, however, and he retaliated by closing up the convents and prohibiting the establishment of monasteries. Being further opposed in his efforts at reform and defied by the priests he put hundreds of them in Pueblo in jail

and prohibited the ringing of Church bells in certain localities. He forcibly impressed on them the fact that he was running Mexico, not they. He gave them to understand that his ideas of Christianity was, that priests should preach Christ crucified and not revolution and infraction of the laws.

In Mexico, priests can keep mistresses with impunity. From a church to a gambling-table is but a step, and the priests gamble with the rest. The rentals of houses of ill-fame, of gambling-houses, of bull-pens all go to a church which is supposed to teach religion. Because Diaz, a catholic himself, will not tolerate such crimes under the guise of religion he is fought by the church and is the recipient of their anathemas.

Take the leading church in Monterey outside of the cathedral. You step from the church-door to a plaza owned by the church and in which stands fifty tents in which are conducted monte, roulette and other games of chance. Behind this stands the bull-pen, and the profits and rentals go to the Church.

With all these lights the most plausible inference or theory is that the clerical party, as they see all these privileges being swept away, will cheerfully contribute the sinews of war with which to carry on a revolution against Diaz. They have agents in Europe and the money can come through that source without detection.

The agents of the Clerical Party in Europe is the Church itself. As a body, it has ever opposed advancement and reform. It anathematized the printing press as an invention of the devil and has steadily opposed education of the people. Its work is best done in the darkness of ignorance and superstition. For this cause it has opposed all new discoveries in science, all reforms of whatever character.[106] Not by the Catholic Church alone, but under the "Reformation," as we have seen, the same prohibition of the Bible to common people, has existed the same resistance to education of the masses, the same opposition to antislavery, to temperance, to woman's demand for equality of opportunity with man. The general nature of the church does not change with change of name. Looking backward through history we even find the same characteristics under the patriarchate; love of power, greed for money, and intense selfishness combined in a general disregard for the rights of others.

M. Renan's novel of *L'Abbesse de Jouarre* was written because he wished to prove the worthlessness of those vows imposed on catholic priests and nuns, as well as show the bondage under which they held the feminine conscience, while the masculine conscience throws them aside. It is not alone the nuns whose conscience is bound, but all feminine members of the catholic church are more closely held in a spiritual bondage, than the male members of that church. In 1885, a letter from Chili to the *New York Sun*, graphically pictured certain Chilian women penitents who are known by a peculiar dress they are required to wear.[107] Others whose sins are so great that they cannot be purged by a penitential dress, retire for a season to the "Convent of Penitents," where by mortification of the body they hope to gain absolution for the soul. Still more severe than this retreat are other convents known as "Houses of Detention," where wayward daughters are sent, and young mothers without husbands are cared for. But the whole country of Chili fails to show a similar dress, or house of penitence, or correction for men. Shame and penance, equally with sin, have been relegated by the church to women alone.

The confessional is not frequented by men, and mass is but seldom attended by them. For this laxity a double reason exists: *First*, immorality in men is not looked upon as contrary to its discipline. *Second*, through woman having been trained to a more sensitive conscience than man, the confessional wrests secrets from her lips, which gives the church knowledge of all it wishes to learn in regard to the family. No more certain system could have been devised for the destruction of woman's self-respect than the one requiring penance from her for sins the church passes lightly over in man. Nor would penance of this character be demanded from women were the offices of the church open to her the same as to man. No greater crime against humanity has ever been known than the division of morality into two codes, the strict for woman, the lax for man. Nor has woman been the sole sufferer from this creation of Two Moral Codes within the

Christian Church. Through it man has lost fine discrimination between good and evil, and the Church itself as the originator of this distinction in sin upon the trend of sex, has become the creator and sustainer of injustice, falsehood and the crimes into which its priests have most deeply sunken. Nor is this condition of the past. As late as the fall of 1892 a number of articles appeared in Canadian papers openly accusing the catholic priesthood of that province of the grossest immorality.[108] That priestly celibacy yet continues in the Romish Church is not a subject of surprise, when we realize the immense power and wealth it has been enabled to secure through its means; but it is one of astonishment, carrying with it a premonition of danger, that we now see a similar tendency in the ritualistic portion of the Episcopal Church, both in England and the United States. The evils of monasticism, although less potent than during the middle ages, are still great, and in finding entrance into Protestant denominations are a fresh warning of their dangerous tendency. The experience of the past should not appeal to us in vain. We have noticed the perils to society arising from those classes of persons who, under plea of religion, evade the duties of family and social life. No crime against the world can be greater than the deliberate divestment of responsibility by one's self, because tired of the warfare of life, that struggle which comes to every human being; the becoming "fascinated with the conceptions of an existence" outside of ordinary cares; and the entrance into an order in which one's own personal responsibility is largely surrendered to others is not alone a crime against the state, but a sin against one's own self and against humanity. An order which thereafter assumes the task of directing the thoughts and lives of its members into a channel of "repose and contentment" as certain protestant orders do, is one of the dangerous religious elements of the present day. No crime against one's self or against society can be greater than this. In the Ritualistic Episcopal Church are to be found monks and sisterhoods upon the celibate plan, confessors and penance, all of them primal elements in moral and spiritual degradation. If religion has a lesson to teach mankind, it is that of personal responsibility; it is that of the worth and duty of the individual; it is that each human being is alone accountable for his or her course in life; it is the lesson of the absolute equality of each human being with every other human being in relation to these cardinal points. The lesson should have been learned ere this, that ecclesiastical pretense of divinely appointed power has ever made the priesthood arrogant, coarse and tyrannical; the male laity dependent and dissimulating; woman, self-distrustful and timorous, believing in the duty of humiliation and self-sacrifice; that her life is not to be lived primarily for herself alone, but that her very right to existence is dependent upon the benefit thereby to accrue to some other person. Today, as of old, the underlying idea of monasticism, of "brotherhoods," "sisterhoods," and their ilk even in Protestant denominations, is the divine authority of some priestly superior, and that the power of remitting sins inheres in some system under control of some priest. The Ritualistic party of the Episcopal Church, equally with the Roman Catholic Church, makes frequent reference to these words of Christ—St. John XX, XXIII—"Whatever sins You remit they are remitted unto them, and whatsoever sins you retain are retained," thus premising the divine power of the priesthood.

Notes

1. It was a favorite doctrine of the Christian fathers that concupiscence or the sensual passion was the original sin of human nature. Lecky.—*Hist. European Morals.*

The tendency of the church towards the enforcement of celibacy was early seen. At the four Synods which assembled to establish the true faith in respect to the Holy nature of Christ's Humanity, the first one at Nice, 318, the second at Constantinople with forty bishops present; the third at Ephesus with two hundred bishops present; the fourth at Chaledonia with many bishops together, they forever forbade all marriage to the minister at the altar. *Monumenta Ecclesiastica.*

"To no minister at the altar is it allowed to marry, but it is forbidden to every one." *Ibid.*, p. 347.

2. According to Christianity woman is the unclean one, the seducer who brought sin into the world and caused the fall of man. Consequently all apostles and fathers of the church have regarded marriage as an inevitable evil just as prostitution is regarded today. August Babel.—*Woman in the Past, Present and Future.*

3. Spirit in the Hebrew, as shown in the first chapter, answers to all genders; in the Greek to the feminine alone. With Kabbalists the "Divine Spirit" was conceded to be the feminine Jehovah, that is, the feminine principle of the Godhead.

4. From Marcellina, in the second century, a body of the church took its name. Her life was pure, and her memory has descended to us free from calumny and reproach.

5. Lowest in the scale of being are those invisible creatures called by Kabbalists the "elementary." . . . The second class is composed of the invisible antitypes of the men *to be* born. *Isis Unveiled*, I, 310.

6. Who maintained that Adam did not think of celebrating his nuptials till he went out of Paradise.

7. It was the effect of God's goodness to man that suffered him to sleep when Eve was formed, as Adam being endowed with a spirit of prophecy might foresee the evils which the production of Eve would cause to all mankind, so that God perhaps cast him into that sleep lest he should oppose the creation of his wife. *Life of Adam by Loredano.* Pub. at Amsterdam, 1696. See Bayle.

8. Lecky.—*Hist. European Morals.*

9. That marriage was evil was taught by Jerome.

10. So fully retaining it as to require the circumcision of Timothy, the Gentile, before sending him as a missionary to the Jews.

11. The Council of Tours (813) recommended bishops to read, and if possible retain by heart, the epistles of St. Paul.

12. Although Paul "led about" other "women" saluting "some with a holy kiss."

13. 964. Notion of uncleanliness attaching to sexual relations fostered by the church. Herbert Spencer.—*Descriptive Sociology, England.*

14. In the third century marriage was permitted to all orders and ranks of the clergy. Those, however, who continued in a state of celibacy, obtained by this abstinence a higher reputation of sanctity and virtue than others. This was owing to an almost general persuasion that they who took wives were of all others the most subject to the influence of malignant demons.—*Mosheim.*

15. Old (Christian) theologians for a long time disputed upon the nature of females; a numerous party classed them among the brutes having neither soul nor reason. They called a council to arrest the progress of this heresy. It was contended that the women of Peru and other countries of America were without soul and reason. The first Christians made a distinction between men and women. Catholics would not permit them to sing in Church. *Dictionaire Féodal,* Paris, 1819.

16. By a decree of the Council of Auxerre (A.D. 578), women on account of their impurity were forbidden to receive the sacrament into their naked hands.

17. Catherine reproached the Protestants with this impious license as with a great crime. "Les femmes chantant aux *orgies* des huguenots, dit Georges l'apotre; apprenez donc, prédicans, que saint Paul a dit; *Mulieres in* ecclesiaétaccant; et que daus le chapitre de l'apocolypse l'evoque de Thyathire est menacé de la damnation pour avoir permis á une femme de parles a l'église. See *Redavances Seigneur.*

18. When part singing was first introduced into the United States, great objection was made to women taking the soprano or leading part, which by virtue of his superiority it was declared belonged to man. Therefore woman was relegated to the bass or tenor but nature proved too powerful, and man was eventually compelled to take bass or tenor as his part, while woman carried the soprano, says the *History of Music.*

19. *Leviticus 12:15.*

Dr. Smith characterizes a sin-offering as a sacrifice made with the idea of propitiation and atonement; its central idea, that of expiation, representing a broken covenant between God and the offender; that while death was deserved, the substitute was accepted in lieu of the criminal.—*Dictionary of the Bible.*

20. *The Talmud* (Mishna) declared three cleansings were necessary for leprosy and three for children, thus placing the bringing of an immortal being into life upon the same plane of defilement with the most hideous plague of antiquity.

21. The mean term of life for these wretched girls under religious confinement in a nunnery was about ten years. From the fifteenth century a sickness was common, known as Disease of the Cloisters. It was described by Carmen.

Jewish contempt of the feminine was not alone exhibited in prohibiting her entrance into the holy places of the temple, and in the ceremonies of her purification, but also in the especial holiness of male animals which alone were used for sacrifice. Under Jewish law the sons alone inherited, the elder receiving a double portion as the beginning of his father's strength. See Deut. 21:15. If perchance the mother also possessed an inheritance that was also divided among the sons to the exclusion of daughters. The modern English law of primogeniture is traceable to Judaism.

Even the commandments were made subservient to masculine ideas, the tenth classing a man's wife with his cattle and slaves, while the penalties of the seventh were usually visited upon her alone.

22. The reign of Constantine marks the epoch of the transformation of Christianity from a religious into a political system. Draper.— *Conflict of Religion and Science.*

23. "The woman that cometh to give thanks must offer accustomed offering in this kingdom; it is the law of the kingdom in such cases."

24. In the year 1867 the Right Rev. Bishop Coxe, of the Western Diocese of New York, refused the sacrament to those women patients of Dr. Foster's Sanitarium at Clifton Springs, N.Y., whose heads were uncovered, although the rite was performed in the domestic chapel of that institution and under the same roof as the patient's own rooms.

During the famous See trial at Newark, N.J., 1876, the prosecutor, Rev. Dr. Craven, declared that every woman before him wore her head covered in token of her subordination.

25. The Catholic Congress of July, 1892, telegraphing the pope it would strive to obtain for the Holy See the recovery of its inalienable prerogative and territorial independence, was convened at Fulda.

26. "In the old days, no woman was allowed to put her foot within the walls of the monastery at San Augustin, Mexico. A noble lady of Spain, wife of the reigning Viceroy, was bent on visiting it. Nothing could stop her, and in she came. But she found only empty cloisters, for each virtuous monk locked himself securely in his cell, and afterward every stone in the floor which her sacrilegious feet had touched was carefully replaced by a new one fresh from the mountain top. Times are sadly changed. The house has now been turned into a hotel."

27. *Sacerdotal Celibacy.*—Lea.

28. *Studies in Church History.*—Lea.

29. *History of Materialism.*

30. Seals upon legal papers owe their origin to the custom of the uneducated noble warrior stamping the imprint of his clenched or mailed hand upon wax as his signature.

31. *St. Theresa* founded the Barefoot Carmelites, and it is but a few years since thousands of its members assembled to do honor to her name.

32. The annals of the Church of Rome give us the history of that celebrated prostitute Marozia of the tenth century, who lived in public concubinage with Pope Sergius III, whom she had raised to the papal throne. Afterwards she and her sister Theodosia placed another of their lovers, under name of Anastatius III, and after him John X, in the same position. Still later this same powerful Marozia placed the tiara upon the head of her son by Pope Sergius under name of John XI, and this before he was sixteen years of age. The celebrated Countess Matilda exerted no less power over popedom, while within this century the maid of Kent has issued orders to the pope himself.

33. The first abbess, Petrouville, becoming involved in a dispute with the powerful bishop of Angers, summoned him before the council of Chateraroux and Poicters, where she pleaded the cause of her order and won her case. In 1349 the abbess Théophegénie denied the right of the senaschel of Poiton to judge the monks of Fontervault, and gained it for herself. In 1500, Mary of Brittany, in concert with the pope's deputies, drew up with an unfaltering hand the new statutes of the order. Legouvè.—*Moral History of Women.*

34. No community was richer or more influential, yet during six hundred years and under thirty-two abbesses, every one of its privileges were attacked by masculine pride or violence, and every one maintained by the vigor of the women.—*Sketches of Fontervault.*

35. What is more remarkable the monks of this convent were under control of the abbess and nuns, receiving their food as alms.—*Ibid.*

36. "The Lord's Prayer," taught his disciples by Jesus, recognizes the loss, and demands restoration of the feminine in "Hallowed (whole) be Thy Name."

37. Woman should always be clothed in mourning and rags; that the eye may perceive in her only a penitent, drowned in tears, and so doing for the sin of having ruined the whole human race. Woman is the gateway of Satan, who broke the seal of the forbidden tree and who first violated the divine law.

38. Gildas, in the first half of the sixth century, declared the clergy were utterly corrupt. Lea.—*Studies in Church History.*

39. In the third century marriage was permitted to all ranks and orders of the clergy. Those, however, who continued in a state of celibacy, obtained by this abstinence a higher reputation of sanctity and

virtue than others. This was owing to the almost general persuasion that they who took wives were of all others the most subject to the influence of malignant demons.—*Mosheim*.

As early as the third century, says *Bayle*, were several maidens who resolved never to marry.

40. The priests of the Greek Church are still forbidden a second marriage.

In the beginning of the reign of Edward I, when men in orders were prohibited from marriage in England, a statute was framed under which lay felons were deprived of the clergy in case they had committed bigamy in addition to their other offenses; bigamy in the clerical sense meaning marriage with a widow or with two maidens in succession.

41. Pelagius II, sixty-fifth pope in censuring those priests, who after the death of their wives have become fathers by their servants, recommended that the culpable females should be immured in convents to perform perpetual penance for the fault of the priest. Cormenin.—*History of the Popes*, p. 84.

42. A priest's wife is nothing but a snare of the devil, and he who is ensnared thereby on to his end will be seized fast by the devil, and he must afterwards pass into the hands of fiends and totally perish.—*Institutes of Polity, Civil and Ecclesiastical*, pp. 438–42. *Canons of Ælfric and Ælfric's Pastoral Epistles*, p. 458.

43. *Monumenta Ecclesiastica. Institutes of Polity, Civil and Ecclesiastical.*

44. In order to understand the morals of the clergy of this period, it is important that we should make mention of a law which was passed by the emperors Valentinian, Valerius and Gratian toward the end of the year 370. It prohibited ecclesiastics and monks from entering the houses of widows and single women living alone or who had lost their parents. Dr. Cormenin.—*History of the Popes*, p. 62.

45. *Lecky* finds evidence of the most hideous immorality in these restrictions, which forbade the presence even of a mother or sister in a priest's house.

Lea says it is somewhat significant that when in France the rule of celibacy was completely enforced that churchmen should find it necessary to revive this hideously suggestive restriction which denied the priest the society of his mother and sister.—*Sacerdotal Celibacy*, p. 344.

46. He declared it to be the highest degree of wickedness to rise from a woman's side to make the body of Christ. He was discovered the

same night with a woman to the great indignation of the people and obliged to flee the country to escape condign punishment.

47. It is not difficult to conceive the order of ideas that produced that passionate horror of the fair sex which is such a striking characteristic of old Catholic theology. Celibacy was universally conceded as the highest form of virtue, and in order to make it acceptable theologians exhausted all the recourses of their eloquence in describing the iniquity of those whose charms had rendered it so rare. Hence the long and fiery disquisitions on the unparalleled malignity, the unconceivable subtlety, the frivolity, the unfaithfulness, the unconquerable evil propensities of woman. Lecky.—*Hist. European Morals.*

48. The Fathers of the Church for the most part, vie with each other in their depreciation of woman and denouncing her with every vile epithet, held it a degradation for a saint to touch even his aged mother with his hand in order to sustain her feeble steps. . . . For it declared woman unworthy through inherent impurity even to set foot within the sanctuaries of its temples: suffered her to exercise the function of wife and mother only under the spell of a triple exorcism, and denied her when dead burial within its more sacred precincts even though she was an abbess of undoubted sanctity. Anna Kingsford.—*The Perfect Way*, p. 286.

49. *Disease of the Cloisters.*

50. When the sailors of Columbus returned from the new world they brought with them a disease of an unknown character, which speedily found its way into every part of Europe. None were exempt; the king on his throne, the beggar in his hovel, noble and peasant, priest and layman alike succumbed to the dire influence which made Christendom one vast charnel house.

Of it, *Montesquieu* said: "It is now two centuries since a disease unknown to our ancestors was first transplanted from the new world to ours, and came to attack human nature in the very source of life and pleasure. Most of the powerful families of the South of Europe were seen to perish by a distemper that was grown too common to be ignominious, and was considered in no other light than that of being fatal. *Works*, I, 265.

51. St. Ambrose and others believed not that they (women) were human creatures like other people. Luther.—*Familiar Discourses*, p. 383.

52. When a woman is born it is a deficit of nature and contrary to her intentions, as is the case when a person is born blind or lame or with

any natural defect, and as we frequently see happens in fruit trees which never ripen. In like manner a woman may be called a fortuitous animal and produced by accident.

53. Cagetan, living from 1496 to 1534, became General of the Dominican Order and afterwards Cardinal.

54. "The Father alone is creator."

55. By decree of the Council of Lyons, 1042, barons were allowed to enslave the children of married clergy.—*Younge*.

56. In 1108 priests were again ordered to put away their wives. Such as kept them and presumptuously celebrated mass were to be excommunicated. Even the company of their wives was to be avoided. Monks and priests who for love of their wives left their orders suffering excommunication, were again admitted after forty days penance if afterwards forsaking them.

57. Dulaure.—*Histoire de Paris*, I, 387, note.

58. The abbot elect of St. Augustine, at Canterbury, in 1171, was found on investigation to have seventeen illegitimate children in a single village. An abbot of St. Pelayo, in Spain, in 1130, was proved to have kept no less than seventy mistresses.—*Hist. European Morals*, p. 350.

59. A tax called "cullagium," which was a license to clergymen to keep concubines, was during several years systematically levied by princes.—*Ibid*. 2, p. 349.

60. *Supplement to Lumires, 50th question, Art. III.*

61. St. Anselm, although very strict in the enforcement of the canons favoring celibacy, found recalcitrant priests in his own diocese whose course he characterized as "bestial insanity."

62. So says *Bayle*, author of the *Historical and Critical Dictionary*, a magnificent work in many volumes. Bayle was a man of whom it has justly been said his "profound and varied knowledge not only did much to enlighten the age in which he lived by pointing out the errors and supplying the deficiencies of contemporaneous writers of the seventeenth century, but down to the present time his work has preserved a repository of facts from which scholars continually draw."

63. Those who support celibacy would perhaps choose rather to allow crimes than marriage, because they derive considerable revenue by giving license to keep concubines. A certain prelate boasted openly at his table that he had in his diocese 1,000 priests who kept concubines, and who paid him, each of them, a crown a year for their license.—*Cornelius Aggrippa*.

64. For years in Germany the word Pufferkind signified "priest's bastard." *Montesquieu* declared celibacy to be libertinism.

65. *Amelot* (Abraham Nicholas), born in Orleans 1134, declared the celibacy of the clergy to have been established a law in order to prevent the alienation of the church estate.

66. Pope Pelaogius was unwilling to establish the Bishop of Sagola in his see because he had a wife and family, and only upon condition that wife and children should inherit nothing at his death except what he then possessed, was he finally confirmed. All else was to go into the coffers of the church.

67. Cardinal Otto decreed that wives and children of priests should have no benefit from the estate of the husband and father; such estates should be vested in the church.

68. In 1396 Charles VI forbade that the testimony of women should be received in any of the courts of his kingdom.

69. The council of Tivoli, in the Soisonnais, 909, in which twelve bishops took part, promulgated a Canon requiring the oath of seven witnesses to convict a priest with having lived with a woman; if these failed of clearing him he could do so by his own oath.

70. Though the clergy now and then made use both of the Justinian and Theodosian Codes, the former body of law, as such, was notwithstanding from the reign of the Emperor Justinian, or about the year of our Lord 560, till the beginning of the twelfth century, or the year of Christ, 1230 or thereabouts, of no force in the west in matter of government. Seldon.—*Dissertation on Fleta*, p. 112.

71. The codification of the laws under Justinian were largely due to his wife, the Empress Theodosia, who having risen from the lowest condition in the empire, that of a circus performer, to the throne of the East, proved herself capable in every way of adorning that high position.

72. By the Code Napoleon, all research into paternity is forbidden. The Christian Church was swamped by hysteria from the third to the sixteenth century. Canon Charles Kingsley.—*Life and Letters*.

73. Although under law the entire property of the wife became that of the husband upon marriage.

74. A treatise on Chastity, attributed to Pope Sixtus III, barely admits that married people can secure eternal life, though stating that the glory of heaven is not for them.

75. The Romish religion teaches that if you omit to name anything in confession, however repugnant or revolting to purity which you

even doubt having committed, your subsequent confessions are thus rendered null and sacrilegious. Chiniquy.— *The Priest, the Woman and the Confessional*, p. 202. Study the pages of the past history of England, France, Italy, Spain, etc., and you will see that the gravest and most reliable historians have everywhere found instances of iniquity in the confessional box which their order refused to trace. *Ibid.*, p. 175.

It is a public fact which no learned Roman Catholic has ever denied that auricular confession became a dogma and obligatory practice of the church only at the Lateran Council, in the year 1215, under Pope Innocent III. Not a single trace of auricular confession as a dogma can be found before that year. *Ibid.*, p. 239.

Auricular confession originated with the early heretics, especially with Marcius. Bellarmin speaks of it as something to be practiced. But let us hear what the contemporary writers have to say on this question: "Certain women were in the habit of going to the heretic Marcius to confess their sins to him. But as he was smitten with their beauty, and they loved him also, they abandoned themselves to sin with him."—*Ibid.*, p. 234.

76. *Disraeli*, who is most excellent authority, declared the early English edition of the Bible contained 6,000 errors, which were constantly introduced and passages interpolated for sectarian purposes or to sustain new creeds; sometimes, indeed, they were added for the purpose of destroying all scriptural authority by the use of texts.

The revisers of the New Testament found 150,000 errors, interpolations, additions and false translations in the King James or common verse.

77. Cardinal Wolsey complained to the Pope that both the secular and regular priests were in the habit of committing actions for which if not in orders, they would have been promptly executed.

The claim of direct inspiration from God exists equally among Protestants as among Catholics, and even among the Unitarians, who deny Christ's divinity. A notable instance of this kind, both because of the high scientific and moral character of the clergyman, took place in the pulpit of the May Memorial Church, Syracuse, N. Y., December 4th, 1887, as reported in the *Morning Standard* of the 5th.

Luther declared that priests believed themselves to be a superior to the laity in general, as males were held superior to females.

78. The legal wife of a priest was termed "An Unhallowed Thing," while mistresses and concubines were known as "The Hallowed Ones," "The Honored Ones." In parts of France, especially in Paris, the latter epithet was common as applied to a priest's mistress.—*Michelet*.

79. Heloise sacrificed herself on account of the impediments the church threw in the way of the married clergy's career of advancement. As his wife he would lose the ascending ladder of ecclesiastical honors, priory, abbacy, bishopric, metropolitane, cardinalade, and even that which was above and beyond all. Milman.—*Latin Christianity*.

80. In 1558 one Walter Mill was indicted, one article of his accusation being his assertion of the lawfulness of sacerdotal marriage. He was condemned to the stake and burned. Taine.—*English Literature*.

81. An old doctrine which often turns up again in the middle ages. In the seventeenth century it prevailed among the convents of France and Spain. Michelet.—*La Sercerle*, p. 258.

82. They made the vilest use of the doctrine that Christ was born of a Virgin, using this as an example for woman to be followed.—*Ibid.*, p. 259.

83. They must kill sin by being more humble and lost to all sense of pride through sin. This was the quietest doctrine introduced by a Spanish priest, Molines, who claimed it as the result of an inner light or illumination. He declared that "Only by dint of sinning can sin be quelled."

84. "Let not this surprise you," replied the abbot. "My sanctity is not the less on this account because that abides in the soul, and what I now ask of you is only a sin of the body. Do not refuse the grace that heaven sends you." Boccacio.—*Decameron*.

85. Taine.—*Eng. Lit.* I, 363.

86. The unmarried state of the clergy was in itself one of the chief causes of sexual excess. The enormously numerous clergy became a perilous plague for female morality in town and village. The peasants endeavored to preserve their wives and daughters from clerical seduction by accepting no pastor who did not bind himself to take a concubine. In all towns there were brothels belonging to the municipality, to the sovereign, to the church, the proceeds of which flowed into the treasury of proprietors.

87. Draper.—*Intellectual Development of Europe*, p. 498.

88. Men in orders are sometimes deceived by the devil that they marry unrighteously and foredo themselves by the adulteries in which they continue.—*Institutes of Polity, Civil and Ecclesiastical*, p. 437.

There is ground for the assumption that the Canon which bound all the active members of the church to perpetual celibacy, and thus created an impenetrable barrier between them and the outer world, was one of the efficient methods in creating and sustaining both the temporal and spiritual power on the Romish Church. Taine.—*English Literature*.

89. All steps are necessary to make up the ladder. The vices of men become steps in the ladder one by one as they are remounted. The virtues of man are steps indeed, necessary not by any means to be dispensed with, yet though they create a fair atmosphere and a happy future, they are useless if they stand alone. The whole nature of man must be used wisely by the one who desires to enter the way. Seek it by plunging into the mysterious and glorious depth of your inmost being. Seek it by testing all experience, by utilizing the senses in order to understand the growth of meaning of individuality and the beauty and obscurity of those other divine fragments which are struggling side by side with you and from the race to which you belong.—*Light on the Path*, Rule XX.

90. "What in the world makes you look so sullen?" asked the young man as he took his arm and they walked towards the palace. "I am tormented with wicked thoughts," answered Eugene gloomily. "What kind? They can easily be cured." "How?" "By yielding to them." *Dialogue in Balsac's Père Goriot*.

91. *1st Corinthians* VII, 36.

92. Limbrock.—*History of the Inquisition*.

93. Carema reported that the parish priest of Naples was not convicted though several women deposed that he had seduced them. He was, however, tortured and suspended for a year when he again entered his duties.

94. Lea.—*Sacerdotal Celibacy*, p. 422.

The secrecy with which the Inquisition worked may be conjectured from the fact that during the whole time its officers were busy gathering evidence upon which to condemn Galileo, his friends in Rome, none of whom occupied high position in the church, not only did not suspect his danger, but constantly wrote him in the most encouraging terms.

95. The acts of the Metropolital Visitation of the Archbishops of Wareham states that in the Diocese of Bangor and St. Davids, in time of Henry VIII, more than eighty priests were actually presented for incontinence.

96. Against this separation the bitter animosity of Pope Leo XIII was seen in his refusal of the gifts tendered him by the royal family of Italy at the time of his jubilee.

97. And the summary was not brief. Dwight.—*Roman Republic in 1849,* p. 115. Pope John XIII, having appeared before the council to give an account of his conduct, he was proved by thirty-seven witnesses, the greater part of whom were bishops and priests, of having been guilty of fornication, adultery, incest, sodomy, theft and murder. It was also proved by a legion of witnesses that he had seduced and violated 300 nuns.—*The Priest, Woman and Confessional,* p. 268.

Henry III, bishop of Liege, was deposed in 1274 for having sixty-five illegitimate children. Lecky.—*Hist. European Morals,* p. 350. This same bishop boasted at a public banquet that in twenty-two months fourteen children had been born to him. *Ibid.,* Vol. 2, p. 349. It was openly asserted that 100,000 women in England were made dissolute by the clergy. Draper.—*Intellectual Development of Europe,* p. 498.

98. *Familiar Discourses* and other works. In Rome are born such a multitude of bastards that they are constrained to build particular monasteries where they are brought up and the pope is named their father. When any great processions are held in Rome, then the said bastards go all before the pope.—*Familiar Discourses,* p. 383.

After Pope Gregory confirmed celibacy he found 6,000 heads of infants in a fish pond, which caused him to again favor the marriage of priests.—*Ibid.* Bishop Metz, to my knowledge, hath lost the annual revenue of 500 crowns, which he was wont to receive from the county for pardoning of whoring and adultery.—*Ibid.,* p. 260.

99. In 1874 an old Catholic priest of Switzerland, about to follow Père Hyacinthe's example in abandoning celibacy, announced his betrothal in the following manner: "I marry because I wish to remain an honorable man. In the seventeenth century it was a proverbial expression, 'As corrupt as a priest,' and this might be said today. I marry, therefore, because I wish to get out of the Ultramontane slough."—*Galignani's Messenger,* September 19, 1874.

100. See *Biographical Sketch.*

101. Pp. 86 to 140.

102. To be found in *The Priest, the Woman and the Confessional.*

103. *Ibid.,* pp. 77–78.

104. *Ibid.,* p. 287

105. A Shenandoah correspondent of the *Pittsburgh Commercial Advertiser,* June 5, 1885, wrote:

Shenandoah, Pa., June 5.—Father Wolonski, of this place, the only priest of the Uniate Greek Church in this country, has been recalled to Europe.

The Uniate Greek Church, it will be remembered, comprehends those Christians who, while they follow the Greek rite, observe the general discipline of the Greek Church and make use of the Greek liturgy, are yet united with the Church of Rome, admitting the double procession of the Spirit and the supremacy of the Roman Pontiff, and accepting all the doctrinal decisions subsequent to the Greek schism which have force as articles of faith in the Roman Church. The usage of the Church as to the law of celibacy is, with the consent of the Roman Pontiff, the same as among the other Greeks, and Father Wolonski brought a wife with him to Shenandoah when he came here last December. This fact has made both the priest and his religion, subjects of great importance here, and the attention they have received has resulted in his recall to Limberg, Austria, the see of the diocese from which he was transferred here.

FATHER WOLONSKI AND THE ARCHBISHOP

When Father Wolonski arrived in Philadelphia he visited the Cathedral and sought an interview with Archbishop Ryan, but when that gentleman discovered that he was married he refused to treat with him. The priest then came to Shenandoah, as directed by Bishop Sembratowicz, of Limberg, who sent him on his mission. Father O'Reilly, of the Irish Catholic Church, warned his congregation under pain of excommunication, to shun the church and priest, at the same time tacitly denying that the Roman Church recognized the right of any priest to marry. The matter led to great controversy, during which Father Wolonski established his congregation, and arrangements have been made for the erection of a church. To avoid further trouble, however, the Bishop of Limberg has selected and sent an unmarried priest to succeed him, and Father Wolonski will return to Austria. Father Wolonski is an intelligent and highly educated gentleman, and has made a large number of friends during the few months he has been here. He speaks several languages, and during his stay here acquired a remarkable knowledge of English. He has worked incessantly since his arrival here for the temporal as well as the spiritual comfort of his people, and has made a large circle of acquaintants, who will regret his departure from the town.

106. And yet the world "does move," and the experience of the church is much that of the big elephant Jumbo, who in opposing his vast form to a train of cars met his death at the engine.

107. The Chili mantas and skirts of white flannel are worn by penitentes, or women who have committed some heinous sin and thus advertise their penitence; or those who have taken some holy vow to get a measure nearer heaven, and go about the street with downcast eyes, looking at nothing and recognizing no one. They hover about the churches, and sit for hours crouched before some saint or crucifix, saying prayers and atoning for their sin. In the great Cathedral at Santiago, and in the smaller churches everywhere, these penitentes, in their snow-white garments, are always to be seen, on their knees, or posing in other uncomfortable postures, and looking for all the world like statues carved in marble. In the Santiago Cathedral they cluster in large groups around the confessionals, waiting to receive absolution from some fat and burly father, that they may rid their bodies of the mark of penitence they carry and their souls of sin. Some of them make vows, or are sentenced by their confessors to wear their white shrouds for a certain time, while others assume them voluntarily until they have assurance from their priest that their sin is atoned for. Ladies of the highest social position and great wealth are commonly found among the penitentes, as well as young girls of beauty and winning grace. Even the wives of merchants and bankers wander about the streets with all but their eyes covered with this white mantle, which gives notice to the world that they have sinned. The women of Chili are as pious as the men are proud, and this method of securing absolution is quite fashionable.

Those souls that cannot be purged by this penitential dress retire to a convent in the outskirts of the city called the Convent of the Penitents, where they scourge themselves with whips, mortify the flesh with sackcloth, sleep in ashes and upon stone floors, and feed themselves on mouldy crusts. Some stay longer and some a less time in these houses of correction, until the priests by whose advice they go there, give them absolution; but it is seldom that the inmates are men. They are usually women who have been unfaithful to their marriage vows, or girls who have yielded to temptation. After the society season, after the carnival, at the end of the summer when people return from the fashionable resorts, and at the beginning of lent these places are full, and throngs of carriages surround them, waiting to bear back to their homes the belles who are sent here and can find no room to remain.

For those whose sins have been too great to be washed out by this process, for those whose shame has been published to the world and are unfitted under social laws to associate with the pure, other convents are open, established purposely as a refuge or House of Detention. Young mothers without husbands are here cared for, and their babes are taken to an orphan asylum in the neighborhood to be reared by the nuns for the priesthood and other religious orders. It is the practice for parents to send wayward daughters to these homes, while society is given to understand that they are elsewhere visiting friends or finishing their education. After a time they return to their families and no questions are asked.

108. Too long have the people out of respect for the church, maintained silence in the presence of gross abuses, while their families have been ruined. I am a husband and a father, and I do not wish that the honor of my name and my family to be at the mercy of a wolf who may introduce himself with the viaticum in his hands. I am a father, and I do not wish that the sacred candor of my child should be exposed to the lecherous attempts of a wretch in a soutane. The religious authorities are on the eve of witnessing honest men follow their wives, their daughters, and even their little boys to the confessional, to assure themselves if the hand that holds there the balance of divine justice is the hand of a respectable man or the hand of a blackguard who should receive the lash in public with his neck in the pillory.—*Letter from a gentleman.*

A recent article in the Canada "Review" asks if after giving to the clergy riches, respect and the highest positions, it is too much to ask that they should leave to the people their wives? Our wives and daughters whom they steal from us by the aid of religion, and more especially of the confessional. An immediate, firm and vigorous reform is needed. Our wives and daughters must be left alone. Let the clergy keep away from the women, and religion and the Catholics will be better off. This must be done and at once.—*Montreal Correspondence of the Toronto Mail,* September 15, 1892.

CHAPTER III

CANON
LAW

T
he earliest Saxon laws were almost entirely ecclesiastical,[1]
their basis seeming to have been payment of titles to the
Church and support of the pope through what was known as the
"hearth penny" to St. Peter. Marriage was by no means allowed to
escape general ecclesiastical control, its legitimacy being made to
depend upon the sanction and services of a priest.[2] This we learn
from Reeves, whose authority is indisputable,[3] therefore we discover that even long before marriage was constituted one of the
sacraments, celibacy, or the confessional established, the Church
had perceived the great increase in its authority to be brought
about by gaining control of the marriage ceremony and making
its legitimacy depend upon the services of a priest. This was a
material step towards the subjugation of mankind; one whose dire
consequences has not yet received due consideration. When
Rome became a Christian State, and the phallic cross triumphed
over the gods and goddesses of old, the conditions of woman

under the civil law became more degraded. The change from ancient civilization to that renewed barbarism at an early age of the Christian era, which so many writers note without perceiving its cause, is to be found in the low conception of womanhood inculcated by the Church. Ignorance, superstition, falsehood and forgery united in creating new codes of law, new customs of society, new habits of thought, which, having for centuries been imposed upon mankind by the united force of the Church and the State, still continue their impress upon modern life and law.

Among general canons we find that "No woman may approach the altar." "A woman may not baptize without extreme necessity." "Woman may not receive the Eucharist under a black veil." "Woman may not receive the Eucharist in *morbo suo menstrule.*"

At the Synod or Council of Elvira,[4] 305 or 306, several restrictive canons were formulated against woman. Under Canon 81, she was forbidden to write in her own name to lay Christians, but only in the name of her husband. Women were not to receive letters of friendship from any one addressed only to themselves.

From the commencement of the fifth century, the Christian clergy acquired a powerful influence in Rome. Bishops and priests were the municipal magistrates of the Roman Empire, of which little now remained except its municipal government; thus the Church in reality became Rome, and Rome the Church. It has been declared difficult to fix with precision the period at which ecclesiastics first began to claim exemption from civil jurisdiction. The Synod of Paris, 615, seems to have secured to the clergy the privilege of being brought before mixed tribunals in all cases which had theretofore belonged to the civil judge alone. Bishops acquired greater power from having an oversight over the whole administration of justice committed to them, while their spiritual judgments were rendered more effective by the addition of excommunication to civil punishments. The State, at first holding repression over the Church, added to its powers by relieving the clergy from all civil duties,[5] thus tending to make of them a body exterior to the civil government. This division was further increased through the emperors giving confirmation to the decisions pronounced by bishops in ecclesiastical affairs, and also when they were chosen umpires in civil suits; the tendency of this action was towards the creation of an ecclesiastical law with separate powers from the civil law. Another step towards the separation of civil from ecclesiastical law and the supremacy of the latter, was made when in cases of discipline the clergy were allowed to come under the authority and supervision of the Spiritual Courts.[6]

As soon as Christianity became the religion of the State, this power was still further increased by the permission accorded ecclesiastics to accept gifts, inherit and hold property; the purity of clerical motives being thereby greatly lessened, as covetous and unscrupulous persons were forthwith attracted to this profession. The law of tithes was introduced by Charlemagne, and his edicts largely increased clerical power. The compilation of a Code of Canon Law was begun as early as the ninth century,[7] by which period the olden acknowledged rights of the clergy, those of superintending morals and interference on behalf of the unfortunate, had largely been lost sight of, or diverted from their proper course by a system of ecclesiastical tyranny which created an order of morals, whose sole design was that of building up priestly power.

The complete inferiority and subordination of the female sex was maintained both by civil and common law. It was a principle of common law that sons should be admitted to an inheritance before daughters.[8] This distinction created by the Church in the interests of the class which was alone admitted to the priesthood, thus placing the possession of wealth in the hands of man, did much towards keeping woman in a subordinate condition. In accordance with natural law, the person not owning property is less interested in the welfare of the State than the one possessing it, a denial of the rights of ownership acting prejudicially upon the individual.

Ecclesiastical or Canon Law[9] made its greatest encroachments at the period when Chivalry[10] was at its height; the outward show of respect and honor to woman under chivalry keeping pace in its false pretence with the destruction of her legal rights. The general conception in regard to woman was so degraded at this period, that a "Community of Women" was proposed, to whom all men should act in the relation of husbands.[11] This plan was advocated by Jean de Meung, the "Poet of Chivalry" in his famous *Roman de la Rose*. Christine of Pisa, a woman of learning and remarkable force of character, the first strictly literary woman of western Europe, wrote a work in defense of her sex against the general libidinous character of the age.[12] Her opposition to the debasing theories of the "Romance" marks the later period of woman's entrance into literature and is an era from which dates the modern intellectual development of Europe.[13] Efforts to utterly crush the moral rectitude of women through the adoption of those base ideas of phallic origin, having been the systematic course of the Church, the State and society through many hundred years, it is a most notable proof of her innate disbelief in this teaching that woman's first literary work of modern times was written in opposition to such a powerfully sustained theory as to her innate depravity. Christine asserted the common humanity of woman, entirely repudiating the sensual ideas of the times.

To the credit of mankind it must be recorded that the laity did not unresistingly yield to priestly power but made many attempts to take their temporal concerns from under priestly control. But under the general paucity of education, and the abnegation of the will so sedulously inculcated by the Church as the supreme duty of the laity, its dread power brought to bear in the enforcement of its teaching by terrifying threats of excommunication and future eternal torment, the rights of even the male portion of the people were gradually lost. The control of the priesthood over all things of a temporal as well as of a spiritual nature, tended to make them a distinct body from the laity. In pursuance of its aims for universal dominion, the Church saw the necessity of assuming control of temporal affairs. Rights were divided into those pertaining to persons and things; the rights of persons belonged to the priesthood alone, but inasmuch as every man, whatever his condition, could become a priest, and no woman however learned or pious or high in station could be admitted to its ranks, the whole tendency of ecclesiastical law was to divide mankind into a holy or divine sex, and an unholy or impious one.[14] Thus Canon Law still further separated those whose interests were the same, creating an antagonism in the minds of all men against all women, which bearing upon all business of ordinary life between men and women, fell with its greatest weight upon women. It corrupted the Common Law of England, and perverted the civil codes of other nations. Under Canon Law wives were deprived of the control of both person and property, while sisters were not allowed to inherit with brothers; property, according to old ecclesiastical language, going "to the worthiest of blood." Blackstone acknowledged that this distinction between brothers and sisters reflects shame upon England, and was no part of the old Roman law, under which the children of a family inherited equally without distinction of sex.[15] It was as late as 1879 before the Canon Law in regard to the sole inheritance of sons was repealed in one of the Swiss Cantons. The influence of this law in creating selfishness was manifested by the opposition it met, brothers piteously asserting ruin to themselves by this act of justice to their sisters. Whenever the Canon Law is analyzed it is found destructive to the higher moral sentiments of humanity. A woman was prohibited the priesthood, and as the property of men entering orders became forfeited to the Church, the real intent of this law—that of obtaining control of property—which otherwise might have escaped the grasping hand of the church, is easily discernible. From its first theory of woman's inferiority to its last struggle for power at the present day, the influence and action of the Patriarchate is clearly seen. The touch of the church upon family life, inheritance and education, increased the power of the Patriarchate.

As celibacy proved a lucrative method of bringing wealth into its coffers, so marriage was early made a source of revenue to the Church, Conon Law creating it a sacrament to be performed at the church door. Owing, however, to the innate sinfulness of marriage, this sacrament was not for many years allowed to take place within the sacred building dedicated to God and deemed too holy to permit the entrance of a woman within its sacred walls at certain periods of her life. In order to secure full control of this relation, marriage unblessed by a priest was declared to be concubinage, and carried with it deprivation of church privileges, which the ignorance of the people held to be of vital importance. In entering this relation the wife was compelled to relinquish her name, her property, the control of her person, her own sacred individuality, and to promise obedience to her husband in all things. Certain hours of the day to suit the convenience of priests were set aside as canonical, after which time no marriage could be celebrated.

Nor has this priestly control of marriage been confined to the Catholics alone. Similar laws were extant after the Reformation. In England 1603, Canon 62 instituted, that under penalty of suspension, people could not marry except between the hours of eight and twelve in the forenoon, nor was marriage then allowed in any private place but must be performed at the church door.[16] The rapid growth of the Canon Law in England must be ascribed to avarice; the denial to wives of any right of property in the marital union being an example. At this period Canon Law began to take cognizance of crimes, establishing an equivalent in money for every species of wrong doing. The Church not only remitted penalty for crimes already committed, but sold indulgences for the commission of new ones. Its touch soon extended to all relations of life. Marriages within the seventh degree were forbidden by the Church as incestuous,[17] but to those able to pay for such indulgences a dispensation for such "incestuous" marriage was readily granted. No crime was so great it could not be condoned for money. Thus through Canon Law was seen the anomaly of legal marriage between the laity pronounced concubinage, while the concubines of priests were termed "wives." As soon as the legality of marriage was made dependent upon priestly sanction the door of gross immorality was widely opened.[18] All restrictions connected with this relation were made to fall with heaviest weight upon woman. Husbands were secured the right of separation for causes not freeing wives; even the adultery of the husband was not deemed sufficient cause unless he brought his mistress into the same house with his wife.[19] Church and State sustained each other. Conviction of the husband for a capital crime gave the wife no release from the marriage bond, yet in case of the husband's treason, his innocent wife and children were robbed of all share in the estate of the criminal husband and father and were reduced to beggary, his estate escheating to the State. As under civil law so under ecclesiastical, the Church recognized but slight difference in the guilt of a contumacious husband and that of his pious wife and children.[20] It was a principle of the Church that the innocent must suffer for the guilty, especially when the innocent were women and children powerless to aid themselves. At its every step Canon Law injured woman. The clergy assuming to be an order of spiritual beings, claimed immunity from civil law and allowed for themselves an "arrest of judgment" ultimately enlarged so as to include all male persons who could read and write. This arrest known as "benefit of clergy" was denied to all women, who were liable to sentence of death for the first crime of simple larceny, bigamy, etc.[21] Men who by virtue of sex could become priests if able to read, were for the same crimes punished by simple branding in the hand, or a few months imprisonment, while a woman was drawn and burned alive. Did not history furnish much proof of this character it would be impossible to believe that such barbaric injustice was part of English law down to the end of the eighteenth century. Woman first rendered ineligible to the priesthood, was then punished for this ineligibility.

Blackstone recognizes as among the remarkable legal events of the kingdom, the great alteration in the laws through the separation of ecclesiastical courts from the civil. Matrimonial causes, or injuries respecting the rights of marriage are recognized by him as quite an undisturbed branch of ecclesiastical jurisdiction, from the Church having so early converted this contract into a sacramental ordinance.[22] During many centuries education was denied to woman in Christian countries for reasons connected with her ineligibility to the priesthood. The art of reading is by scholars believed to have been one of the ancient mysteries taught at Eleusis and other olden temples; learning, then, as at later periods, was in the hands of priests; therefore the fact of being able to read was synonymous with the right of entering the priesthood. This right appertained to women in many ancient nations even under the Patriarchate. Higgins shows that the word *Liber*, from which our words liberty, freedom, are derived, is one and the same as *liber*, a book, and had close connection with the intellectual, literary, and priestly class. As under Christian doctrine the priesthood was denied to woman, so under the same rule learning was prohibited to her.[23] To permit woman's education under Christianity would have been a virtual concession of her right to the priesthood. In not allowing her "benefit of clergy" the priests were but consistent with themselves and their pretensions as to the superior holiness of the male sex. That a woman should be burned alive for a crime whose only punishment for a man was a few months imprisonment, was in unison with the whole teaching of the Christian Church regarding woman. Under Canon Law many of the shields theretofore thrown about women were removed. Punishment for crimes against them lessened, while crimes committed by them were more severely punished. Rape, which in early English history was termed felony, its penalty, death, was regarded in a less heinous light under clerical rule.

Under the political constitutions of the Saxons, bishops had seats in the national council and all laws were prefaced by a formal declaration of their consent. By their influence it became a general law that a woman could never take of an inheritance with a man, unless perhaps by the particular and ancient customs of some cities or towns; while daughters at a father's death could be left totally unprovided for. A law was enacted in the reign of Edward VI that no son should be passed over in his father's will unless disinherited in plain terms and a just cause given. In case of daughters, sex was deemed "a just cause" for leaving them in poverty. The earlier laws of the Danish Knut, or Canute, show that the estate was then divided among all the children. Under Canon Law, the testimony of a woman was not received in a court of justice. She was depicted by the Church as the source of all evil, the mother of every ill.[24] Legislation had the apparent aim of freeing the clergy from all responsibility to the civil or moral law, and placing the weight of every sin or crime upon woman.

A council at Tivoli in the Soissainanes, A.D. 909, presided over
by twelve bishops, promulgated a Canon requiring the oath of
seven persons to convict a priest with having lived with a woman;
if their oath failed of clearing him he was allowed to justify himself upon his sole oath. Under Canon Law a woman could not
bring an accusation unless prosecuted for an injury done to herself. It is less than thirty years since this law was extant in Scotland; and as late as 1878, that through the influence of Signor
Morelli, the Italian Parliament repealed the old restriction existant
in that country regarding woman's testimony. Under Canon Law
a woman could not be witness in ecclesiastical or criminal suits,
nor attest a will.[25] To cast doubts upon a person's word is indicative of the most supreme contempt, importing discredit to the
whole character. That a woman was not allowed to attest a will,
nor become a witness in ecclesiastical suits, implied great degradation and is a very strong proof of the low esteem in which
woman was held both by State and Church. That a priest could
clear himself upon his own unsubstantiated oath, is equally significative of the respect in which this office was held, as well as
showing the degree in which all law was made to shield man and
degrade woman. When we find the oath of seven women
required to nullify that of one layman, we need no stronger testimony as to woman's inequality before the law. Canonists laid
down the law for all matters of a temporal nature whether civil
or criminal. The buying and selling of lands; leasing; mortgaging;
contracts; the descent of inheritance; the prosecution and punishment of murder; theft; detection of thieves; frauds; those, and
many other objects of temporal jurisdiction were provided for by
Canon Law. It was intended that the clergy should come entirely
under its action, governed as a distinct people from the laity. The
principal efforts of the Canon Law towards which all its enactments tended, was the subordination of woman[26] and the elevation of the hierarchy. To secure these two ends the church did not
hesitate at forgery. For many hundred years a collection of Decretals, or what were claimed as decrees of the early popes, carried
great authority, although later investigation has proven them forg-

eries.[27] Civil as well as ecclesiastical laws were forged in the interest of the priesthood; a noted instance, was the once famous law of Constantine which endowed bishops with unlimited power, giving them jurisdiction in all kinds of causes. This law declared that whatever is determined by the judgment of bishops shall always be held as sacred and venerable, and that in all kinds of causes whether they are tried according to the pastoral or civil law that it is law to be forever observed by all.

The famous Seldon known as the "Light of England," declares it to have been "a prodigious and monstrous jurisdiction" assumed by the priestly order, by means of falsehood and forgery.[28] The two classes of temporal affairs that Spiritual Courts especially endeavored to appropriate, were marriages, and wills, with everything bearing upon them. In these the greatest oppression fell upon women.[29] Canon Law gradually acquired enormous power through the control it gained over wills, the guardianship of orphans, marriage, and divorce.[30] As soon as ecclesiastical courts were divided from the temporal in England,[31] a new set of principles and maxims began to prevail. This was one of the first effects of the Conquest, but in 1272, Robert Kilmandy, Dean of Canterbury, gave directions for the restoration and observation of the ancient and neglected laws of Ecclesiastical Courts; of these the Court of Arches was one of the most ancient. It is almost impossible to fix the date of ecclesiastical rule, unless indeed we go back to the very foundation of the church. As noted, the early Saxons were largely governed by their priests. In 615, at the Paris synod, the clergy were given authority in matters theretofore under civil power, while in England we find priestly power to have been great during the fourth and fifth centuries. Bracton sets the one hundred and fifty years between the middle of the twelfth and end of the thirteenth centuries as the period when this power took its greatest strides. At this time it touched upon wills, inheritance, bequests, the legitimacy of children, the marriage relation, and all family concerns, having broken over many securities of the common law. This period covers the establishment of celibacy with the trains of evils noted in the preceding chapter, when the marriage of priests was declared invalid, their wives branded as immoral persons, and stain of illegitimacy thrown upon their children. Despite the guarantees of the Runnymede Charter, and the religious rebellion of the Eighth Henry, despite the vigor of Elizabeth who "bent both priest and prelate to her fiery will," the influence of this period moved down in line with the Reformation, and to the injury of woman, successfully incorporated its worst features into the common law; the new church, social and family life all partaking of this injustice. A great number of canons were enacted after the reformation. These, together with the foreign canons which had been adopted, were held as part of the law of England.[32] The Episcopal church appropriated numerous canons extant at the time of the Reformation, several of these having been created for purpose of sustaining the church at a period when the temporal power threatened encroachment.

The archdeacon of Surrey prepared a voluminous work upon this subject known as the Jurus,[33] proving that these canons, decrees, etc., when falling into disuse had been established by act of Parliament, as part of the law of England. The preface of his work declared that it had been prepared purely for the service of the clergy, and in support of the rights and privileges of the Church. Thus we have direct proof of the adoption of papal decrees as part of the government of the Protestant Episcopal church—the Anglican—and also as part of English law.

An act of Parliament at this age was regarded as synonymous with a law of God. The Bible and the English government were upon the same plane, each to be implicitly obeyed.[34] Canon Law thus firmly established by act of Parliament, the union of Church and State complete, England lost much of that civil freedom whose origin can be traced to the wise legislation and love of freedom inhering in two British queens, Martia and Boadicea. Suffering from cruel wrong, the latter rose in revolt against the Romans. Riding among the squadrons of her army she thus addressed them:

It will not be the first time, Britons, that you have been victorious under the conduct of your queen. I come not here as one of royal blood, to fight for empire or riches, but as one of the common people to avenge the loss of their liberty, the wrongs of myself and my children. If you Britons, will but consider the motives of our war, you will resolve to conquer or die. Is it not much better to fall in the defense of liberty, than to be exposed to the outrages of the Romans? Such at least is my resolution, you may if you please live and be slaves.

But many historians date the entire subordination of the common law to ecclesiasticism, to the reign of Stephen, who ascended to the throne 1135, the fourth of the Anglo-Norman kings. In order to keep the ranks of the church full, the bearing of children was enforced upon women as a religious duty. No condition of health or distaste for motherhood was admitted as exemption. Alike from the altar, the confessional, and at the marital ceremony,[35] was this duty taught, nor has such instruction even under the light of physiology and new regard for personal rights, yet ceased.[36] No less is the unresisting subjection of women in this relation indirectly or directly enforced by the Protestant and the Greek churches as the law of the Bible and God. "Increase and multiply"[37] has been the first commandment for woman, held as far more binding upon her than the "Ten Words" of Mount Sinai. Proof exists in abundance of a character impossible to present in this work.

Under the general absence of learning and the equally general reverence for whatever emanated from the church, minor ecclesiastics found it in their power to promulgate doctrines to suit every new set of circumstances; thus many laws aside from regularly promulgated canons, came from time to time into force. When once applied they assumed all the power of custom and soon bore all the force of common law. The evils of ecclesiastical law were soon increased through the unsparing use of forgery and falsehood. Lea says:

In the remodeling of, European Institutions, so necessary to the interests of Christianity and civilization, one of the most efficient agencies was the collection of Canons known as the False Decretals. Forgery was by no means a novel expedient to the church. From the earliest times orthodox and heretics had rivalled each other in the manufacture of whatever documents were necessary to substantiate their respective positions whether in faith or discipline. An examination of these Decretals tends to the conclusion that they were not the result of one effort or the work of one man. Their constant repetitions and their frequent contradiction would seem to prove this, and to show that they were manufactured from to time to time to meet the exigencies of the moment or to gratify the feelings of the writers. Interpolated into codes of law, adopted and amplified in the canons of councils and the decretals of popes, they speedily become part of the civil and ecclesiastical policy of Europe, leaving traces on the constitutions which they afflicted for centuries. . . . The pretenses and privileges which they conferred on the hierarchy became the most dearly prized and frequently quoted portions of the Canon Law. In each struggle with the temporal authority, it was the arsenal from which were drawn the most effective weapons, and after each struggle the sacerdotal combatants had higher vantage ground for the ensuing conflict. . . . theories of ecclesiastical superiority which left so profound an impress on the middle ages and which have in no slight degree molded our modern civilization.

Even Magna Charta, strengthened Canon Law, confirming many liberties of the Church, and injuring women by prohibiting appeal to them unless for the death of their husbands. While the general tenor of the church was against marriage, an unmarried woman unless dedicating her life to the church was regarded with more contempt than the married. To be under control of a husband was looked upon as the normal condition of women not living celibate lives. Consequently women were driven into marriage or monastic houses,[38] and no reproach so great as the term "old maid." The influence of custom is nowhere more discernable than in Blackstone himself. The great commentator while fully admitting the blending of Canon with Common law, also acknowledging its most prejudicial effects to have fallen upon woman, yet attempts to prove that the liberties of the English people were not infringed through ecclesiasticism. He is so entirely permeated with the church doctrine of woman's created inferiority as not to be willing to acknowledge the infringement of her natural liberty through it, although at the same time he declares that "whosoever would fully understand the Canon Law must study Common Law in respect to woman." Such benumbing of the moral faculties through her doctrines is among the greatest wrongs perpetrated by the church upon mankind. Nor is it alone in regard to woman. During the Franco-Prussian war a writer declared the great and absolute need of the French people to be education; that of moral character there was absolutely none, either in the higher or lower classes. Even the sons of aristocratic families educated in Jesuit schools, being at most taught that wrong can only be measured by a formal religious standard, and that every wrong can be wiped out by confession to the priest. French education, this writer declared to be that of two centuries ago, when might was looked upon as identical with justice. Nor can morality be taught while its basis in the church remains the same.

The priestly profession held the most brilliant promises of gratified ambition to every man that entered it. Not alone did he possess the keys of heaven and hell, but also those of temporal power. The laity were his obedient servants upon which he could impose penance and from whose coffers wealth could be made to flow into his own. Through long continued false teaching the people believed their fate in both worlds more fully depended upon the priesthood than upon their own course in life, God having deputed a share of his power to every priest and monk, no matter how debased; and that when he spoke it was not himself, but God, through his lips, as asserted by the priesthood themselves. This impious assertion so capable as shown, of being used for the most tyrannous purposes, came also into the Reformation, and is even heard from the lips of Protestant clergymen today.[39] Denied recognition of a right to decide for themselves whether the priest spoke from God, or from his own ambitious and iniquitous purposes, deprived of education as well as of free thought,—the latter a crime to be punished with death after the most diabolical torture—it is not a subject of surprise that the majority of the christian world was a prey to the vilest superstition. The claim of infallibility, which may be unsuccessfully combatted when urged by a single individual, became all-potent when advanced by a large powerfully organized and widely distributed class under guise of religion, into which the element of fear largely entered. No salvation outside of the church was a fundamental doctrine of that body. Hell was declared not to be peopled alone by the heathen, but by christian heretics, and the excommunicated who had died without obtaining forgiveness from the Church. These were depicted as in eternal torments of a more terrible character than even those whom birth had left ignorant of the plan of salvation. The strength of the church lay in its control of the conscience and the will. Upon the State it fastened double bonds; *first*, by its control of each individual member; *second*, in its capacity of secular ruler. Long before the days of Torquemada and Ximenes, the Inquisition had practically been brought to every man's door. The imagination, that faculty that in its perfection constitutes the happiness of mankind, was made the implement of excessive mental torture. Common Law as it exists today is the outgrowth of Ecclesiastical or Canon Law touching upon all the relations of life but falling with heaviest weight upon woman, as Blackstone so frankly admits.[40] From the tenth to the sixteenth centuries is the period when the features of the Canon Law most derogatory to woman, became thoroughly incorporated into English common law, since which period the complete inferiority and subordination of woman has been as fully maintained by the State as by the Church.

Common Law is not alone English law, it is the basic law of the United States. Chancellor Kent said of it, "Common Law is part of the fundamental law of the United States." It has been recognized and adopted as one entire system by the constitutions of Massachusetts, New York, New Jersey and Maryland. It has been assumed by courts of justice, or declared by statute, as the law of the land in every State, although its influence upon the criminal codes of England and the United States has but recently attracted the attention of legal minds. Wharton whose *Criminal Law* has been for years a standard work, did not examine this relation until its seventh edition. In the preface to this edition he gave a copious array of authors in English, German, Latin, in proof that the criminal codes of those two countries are permanently based upon Ecclesiastical Law.

An early council of Carthage thus ordained: "Let not a woman however learned or holy presume to teach a man in a public assembly." To this Canon may be ascribed the obstacles thrown in the way of women even during the present century, who have come before the world as public teachers in the pulpit, at the bar, in medicine, or the more customary branches of instruction. Advancing civilization of the present century is still hampered by the laws of an imperfect church, enacted many hundred years since. The trial of Mistress Anne Hutchinson in New England, during the seventeenth century, was chiefly for the sin of having taught men.

All modern legislation can be referred to the church for its origin although most especially noticable in reference to women legislated for as a class, distinct and separate from men. Under Church laws, the humble, the ignorant, the helpless have been the most oppressed, because of their powerlessness, but upon no part of humanity has this oppression so heavily fallen as upon her whom the church has declared to be the author of all the misery of human life.[41] The laws of bastardy and illegitimacy still extant in Christian countries which decree that a child born outside of marriage shall be known by its mother's name and she alone responsible for its support, and which do not allow it to inherit its putative father's property even when he acknowledges the child as his own, are of ecclesiastical origin. Enacted by the Church in its most powerful days, as protection to a celibate priesthood against all claim by mother or child, they are still a reminder of the Matriarchate when the sole right of the mother to the child was unquestioned. But under Church ruling this law that the child should follow the condition of the mother, herself but a slave, was the source of great injustice both to women and to thousands of innocent children. Under feudalism and during slavery the child of the feudal lord or powerful master by a serf woman, became at birth subject to all the restrictions of the mother while the father was freed from accountability of any nature. The Antonelli case referred to in the second chapter, in which the Countess Lambertini claimed heirship of Cardinal Antonelli's property as his daughter, was decided against her not upon denial of her paternity which was most fully proven, but because under church law this daughter had no claim upon her priestly father. Under Canon Law she was no more to be regarded as his child than as the child of any other man. She was "fatherless." She was "A sacrilegious child" having violated sacred things by coming into existence. Her "holy" father under Canon Law being entirely irresponsible for her birth.[42]

The reformation proved itself in many ways as restrictive towards woman as catholicism. The commencement of modern law dates to the reign of Elizabeth, who established the reformation upon a firm basis. The oppression of her reign exceed all that had been experienced under Catholicism. No cottager in England, was permitted to shelter his homeless mother or sister under penalty[43] because she was "masterless." The greatest amount of legislation both religious and secular under the Patriatchate, has had woman for its object, and this is especially noticeable in all countries where Christianity has been the dominant power, because she has not been regarded by the church as a component part of humanity, but as an offshoot whose rights and responsibilities were entirely different from those of man. Although among the Anglo-Saxons the priesthood possessed great influence yet after the Norman Conquest, ecclesiasticism gained much greater control in England, and Canon Law began to influence legislation, as has been shown, exercising its chief restrictive force upon woman. While under old Common Law,[44] a husband was compelled to leave his wife one-third of his property and could leave her as much more as he pleased, by Canon Law he was prohibited from leaving her more than one-third and could leave her as much less as he pleased. Thus ecclesiasticism presumed to control a husband's affections and placing its slimy fingers upon common law, allowed the husband to leave his wife in absolute poverty, notwithstanding that her property upon marriage, and her services under marriage, belonged exclusively to him. As early as the twelfth century, Glanville laid it down as a law of the British Kingdom that no one was compelled to leave another person any portion of his property, and that the part usually devised to wives, was left them at the dictate of affection and not of law. Thus early did the Church in England override Common Law to the detriment of woman. While thus legislating in opposition to family rights, the church continually favored its own increase of its own property.[45] The world has produced no system so thoroughly calculated to extend its own power and wealth, as this vast celibate organization which, under the guise of religion, appealed to man's superstition, and ruled his will under the assumption of divine authority, the family being its chief objective point of attack.

While under feudalism, his lord was to receive the best gift at the villein's death, the church the second best, in time the demands of the church overpowered those of the lord, as well as those of the family. So rapacious did the church at last become in its demand for valuable gifts and its claim of one third of a man's property upon his decease, that the civil law ultimately interfered, not however in the interests of wives, but of creditors. Canon Law nearly everywhere prevailed, having its largest growth through the pious fiction of woman's created inferiority. Wherever it became the basis of legislation, the laws of succession and inheritance, and those in regard to children, constantly sacrificed the interests of wives and daughters to those of husbands and sons. Church legislation created numerous and stringent enactments which rendered it impossible for woman to succeed to any considerable amount of property, forcing her to entire dependence upon man, either as a wife, or as a resident of a religious house; thus she entirely lost the freedom possessed by her in pagan Rome.[46]

While under Canon Law the dower of the wife was forfeited by attainder of the husband, yet the husband did not lose his right to the wife's property in case she was attainted of treason. Under Canon Law if for recognized just cause of the husband's cruelty the wife separated from him, she was returned upon his demand provided he gave security for treating her well.

Canon Law gave to the husband the power of compelling the wife's return if, for any cause, she left him. She was then at once in the position of an outlaw, branded as a runaway who had left her master's service, a wife who had left "bed and board" without consent, and whom all persons were forbidden "to harbor" or shelter "under penalty of the law." The absconding wife was in the position of an excommunicate from the Catholic Church, or of a woman condemned as a witch. Any person befriending her was held accessory to the wife's theft of herself from her husband, and rendered liable to fine and other punishment for having helped to rob the husband (master) of his wife (slave). The present formula of advertising a wife, which so frequently disgraces the press, is due to this belief in wife-ownership.

> Whereas my wife . . . has left my bed and board without just cause or provocation, I hereby forbid all persons from harboring or trusting her on my account.

By old English law, in case the wife was in danger of perishing in a storm, it was allowable "to harbor" and shelter her. It is less than fifty years since the dockets of a court in New York City, the great metropolis of the United States, were sullied by the suit of a husband against parties who had received, "harbored" and sheltered his wife after she left him, the husband recovering $10,000 damages.

In losing control, upon marriage, of her person and her property, woman's condition became that of an infant. No act of hers was of legal value. If she made a bargain her husband could repudiate it and the person with whom she had contracted was held to have taken part in a fraud. The denial under Common Law of her right to make a contract grew out of the denial of her right of ownership. Not possessing control of her inheritance or of her future actions, she was consequently held unable to make a binding contract.[47] Forbidden the right of acting for herself; deprived of the ownership and control of her own property or earnings, woman had little opportunity to prove her business capacity. Since the time of Aristotle the control of property has been recognized as the basis of social and responsible conditions. The great school of German jurists[48] teach that ownership increases both physical and moral capacity, and that as owner, actual, or possible, man is a more capable and worthy being than he would otherwise be.

Inasmuch as through both the ecclesiastical and civil laws of Christendom, woman was debarred from giving testimony in courts of law; sisters prohibited from sharing a patrimony with brothers; wives deprived of property rights both of inheritance and earnings, it is entirely justifiable to say that even the boasted Common Law, that pride of English-speaking peoples, has greatly injured civilization through its destruction of woman's property rights. Canon or Church laws were enacted upon the principle of protection for men alone and upon these civil laws gradually became wholly based. Herbert Spencer[49] has not failed to recognize this fact in England. No less in law than in religion is woman dealt with as a secondary being, for whom equal religious rights or equal civil rights are not designed. While under the Matriarchate justice and purity prevailed, and the inherent rights of man were preserved, we find an entirely contrary condition under the Patriarchate, that system enacting laws solely with intent to man's interest regardless alike of mother, sister, wife or daughter. The entire destruction under Canon and civil law, of woman's property rights, has not alone lessened her responsibility, but has also diminished her self-respect. As in common with a child, or a slave, her business agreements were held as of no binding force, she ultimately came to regard herself as incapable of business transactions. In England until a very recent date, and in the United States until when in 1839, Mississippi first placed the control of her own property in a married woman's hands (to be followed in 1848, by Pennsylvania, New York, and about the same period by Rhode Island), it was in the husband's power in every part of christian Europe and America, to repudiate any bargain, sale or gift made by the wife as of no binding legal force, and this, even though she had brought the entire property into the marital firm.[50] Therefore under christian laws the person with whom the wife made a contract, or to whom she made a gift was held as a criminal, or participant in a fraud. The wife under Canon Law belonged to the husband, and as a sequence to not owning herself she could not own property, and in her condition of servitude could possess no control over either her present or her future actions. Such is Common Law warped and changed by Canon Law.[51]

Property is a delicate test of the condition of a nation. It is a remarkable fact in history that the rights of property have everywhere been recognized before the rights of person. The American Revolution arose from an attack upon property rights and although the Declaration of Independence assumed the rights of person to be primal, this unique foundation for a system of government has not yet fully been admitted in practice, and woman is still denied its advantages and responsibilities. While the property owner unwittingly becomes a hostage for the security of the state itself, it needs governmental recognition of the rights of person, in order to create firm self-reliance and a feeling of strength and freedom. A proper self-respect cannot inhere in any person under governmental control of others. Unless the person so governed constantly maintains a system of rebellion in thought or deed, the soul gradually becomes debased, and the finest principles of human nature suffer a rapid process of disintegration. The integrity of elementary principles disappears, bad citizenship results, the general rights of humanity are ignored, selfish, personal, or family interests taking their place. Good citizenship requires individual personal responsibility in affairs of the state.

That property rather than person still receives recognition in governmental matters, owes its origin to the period when the rights of the common people in both property and person were ignored. The effort of the peasant was chiefly directed to securing property. To his clouded vision, the wealth of the lord created his power, and to a great extent such was the fact. Intuitively he felt that property rights were the basis of the rights of persons. The Church possessed enormous wealth, as did all his oppressors, and the peasant could but see that control of rights of property was a dangerous assault upon their rights of person. The foremost element of all slavery is the denial to the slave of right to the proceeds of his own labor. As soon as a colored slave in the United States, was permitted to hire his time, the door of freedom began to open for him. Thus when Canon Law so influenced Civil and Common Law that it forbade woman's inheritance and ownership of property, it placed its final touch upon her degradation; she virtually became a slave to her husband. Sir Henry Maine is outspoken in declaring that Christianity has thus deeply injured civilization, an injury from which he asserts there can be no recovery as long as society remains Christian. As a man of profound thought he does not fail to see that the prevailing religious sentiment created by the teachings of the church as to woman's created inferiority and subjection to man was the cause of that destruction of her property rights. The priests of pagan Rome held juster view regarding woman than did the Christian Church. Before the establishment of Christianity they had conferred the rights of woman to property; daughters inherited equally with sons. To such extent was woman's rights of property carried that at one period, as has been heretofore stated, the greater part of the real estate of the empire was in woman's possession.[52] The slavish condition of woman greatly increased through denial of her rights of inheritance, was more fully established through denial to her of the fruits of her own labor in the marriage relation. Under church law the wife was the husband's personal slave, all her time was absolutely his. Civil and ecclesiastical law held her as completely under his authority. Her property, her person, her time and services were all at the husband's disposal. Nor did the Reformation effect a change in this respect. Luther's ninety Theses nailed against the church door in Wurtzberg, did not assert woman's natural or religious equality with man. It was a maxim of his that "no gown or garment worse became a woman than that she will be wise." The home under the reformation was governed by the laws in force before that period.

First. She was to be under obedience to the masculine head of the household.

Second. She was to be constantly employed for his benefit.

Third. Her society was strictly chosen for her by her master and responsible head.

Fourth. This masculine family head was regarded as a general father-confessor to whom she was held as responsible in word and deed.

Fifth. Neither genius nor talent could free women from such control without his consent.

The Cromwellian period while exhibiting an increase of piety brought no amelioration to woman. The old Church doctrine of her having caused the expulsion of men from Paradise was still proclaimed from the pulpit, and warnings against her extreme sinfulness lost none of their invective strength from the lips of the new gospel. All kinds of learning and accomplishments for her fell under new reprobation and the old teaching as to her iniquities and the necessity for her to feel shame from the fact of her existence took new force after the rise of Melancthon, Huss, and Luther.[53] About this period it was said "she that knoweth how to compound a pudding is more desirable than she who skilfully compoundeth a poem."[54] Men thought it no shame to devote themselves to the pleasure of the table. Epicures and gluttons abounded, but to women was forbidden a seat at the world's intellectual board; she who secured learning did so at the peril of her social and religious position. Under no other system of religion has there been such absolute denial of woman's right to directly approach the divinity; under no other religious system has her debasement been greater.[55]

It cannot be asserted that the religious system teaching restrictive moral and civil laws regarding woman, is of the past. Its still great living influence is shown by the thousands of pilgrims who visited Italy during the Pope's jubilee and the presents of incalculable value that by tens of thousands poured into the papal treasury in commemoration of the fiftieth anniversary of the entrance of Pope Leo XIII into the priesthood. These were received from almost every civilized nation, Christian, Mohammedan, Catholic, Protestant. Even the President of the United States, head of a form of government which recognizes religion as entirely disconnected with the State, so far catered to superstition, so far conceded the assumptions of this system, as to send an elegant copy of the Federal Constitution to the Pope, through Cardinal Gibbons.[56] No stronger proof is required of the still powerful influence of that system based upon the degradation of woman, than the fact that the President of the United States, temporary head of a nation professedly based upon a recognition of equal civil, political and religious rights; the Queen of England head of the Anglican Church; the Sultan of Turkey representative of Mohammedanism; Sadogara, the celebrated Rabbi of Vienna, known as the "Pope of the Hebrews," were all found among the the number of persons outside of Catholicism who by gifts recognized this occasion. It was but ten years previously that Pope Plus IX celebrated his jubilee entrance into the Episcopal office with great pomp and ceremony, but the jubilee of Leo XIII exceeded in splendor and popular interest anything of the kind ever before known as the history of the church. With a religious clientelle of 200,000,000 behind him, and the ten thousand magnificent testimonials as to the justice of his claim as vicar of Jesus Christ, the world cannot fail to be impressed by the danger to human liberty still connected with this powerful organization; an organization that in its control of human thought and human will has ever been of incalculable injury to mankind. Portions of the daily press saw the continuing danger, declaring that:

> These facts are truly impressive indicating as they do the
> tremendous hold which the Roman ecclesiastical system has
> gained over the hearts and minds of men. Very striking, too, is
> the contrast between all this magnificence and pomp and man-

ifest aspiration for temporal power on the part of one who claims to be the representative on earth of the "meek and lowly Jesus," and the poverty, unostentation and self-denial of the "Son of Man," who had not where to lay his head.

This jubilee is an event of great moment to the nineteenth century, at once a warning and a proof of the life and strength of that scheme which has for its real end, not alone the spiritual but also the temporal subjugation of the entire human race. Since Italy under King Humbert secured its release from the temporal power, thus severing the last authoritative grasp of the pope upon temporal kingdoms, the attempt has been sedulously made to create a fictitious sympathy for the pope under claim of his imprisonment in the Vatican. Nor at the least supreme moment of his pride and glorification did the pope forget to call attention of the world to his temporal claims, by a refusal to receive the offered gifts of the king and queen who occupy the worldly throne he maintains to be especially his own.[57]

The doctrine of original sin and woman as the original sinner, transplanted from Judaism into Christianity by Paul in the statement that "Adam, first created, was not first in sin," was developed to its present evil proportions by the early Christian Fathers. To St. Augustine, whose youth was spent in company with the most degraded of womankind, is the world indebted for the full development of the doctrine of original sin. Taught as one of the most sacred mysteries of religion, which to doubt or to question was to hazard eternal damnation, it at once exerted a most powerful and repressing influence upon woman, fastening upon her a bondage which the civilization of the nineteenth century has not been able to cast off.

Reverence for the ancient in customs, habits of life, law, religion, is the strongest and most pernicious obstacle to advancing civilization. To this doctrine of woman's created inferiority[58] and original sin we can trace those irregularities which for many centuries filled the Church with shame, for practices more obscene than the orgies of Babylon or Corinth, and which dragged Christendom to a darkness blacker than the night of heathendom in pagan countries—a darkness upon which the most searching efforts of historians cast scarcely one ray of light—a darkness so profound that from the seventh to the eleventh century no individual thought can be traced.

Rev. Charles Kingsley, a canon of the English Church declared that from the third to the fifteenth centuries, Christianity had been swamped by hysteria in the practice of all those nameless orgies which made a by-word of Corinth during the first century. Every evil was traced to woman. A curious old black letter volume published in London, 1632, declares that "the reason why women have no control in Parliament, why they make no laws, consent to none, abrogate none, is their original sin."

Notes

1. Maine says the bodies of customary law which were built up over Europe were in all matters of first principles under ecclesiastical influence, but the particular application of a principle once accepted were extremely various.

2. The Council held at Winchester in time of Archbishop Le Franc contained a constitution that a marriage without the benediction of a priest should not be deemed a legitimate marriage. Ecclesiastical law as allowed in this country (Great Britain), from earliest times the presence of a priest was required to constitute a legal marriage. Reeves.—*History of English Law.*

3. Reeves *History of English Law* is a full and comprehensive history of the English law. Accurate and judicious as well as full. Lord Mansfield is said to have advised its author. In this work the student is presented with all that is necessary that he should know of the earliest law books. Bracton, Glanville and Fleta carefully collected and presented. Reeves *History of English Law*, says Chancellor Kent, contains the best account that we have of the progress of the law from the time of the Saxons to the reign of Elizabeth. Sherwood.—*Professional Ethics.*

4. Hefele's, *Acts of Councils.*

5. Church and priestly property is still untaxed in the United States. At an early day the clergy were not required to sit on juries nor permitted to cast a vote.

6. Giessler, *Ecclesiastical History.*

7. Doctrines in the Canon Law most favorable to the power of the clergy are founded in ignorance, or supported by fraud and forgery, of which a full account is found in Gerard. See *Mem. de l'Acad. des Inscript.*, Tom 18, p. 46. Also Voltaire's essay upon general history.

8. "Whenever Canon Law has been the basis of legislation, we find the laws of succession sacrificing the interests of daughters and wives." "Du Cange, in his Glossary, *voc Casia Christianitatis*, has collected most of the causes with respect to which the clergy arrogated an exclusive jurisdiction, and Giannone, in the *Civil History of Naples*, lib. 19, sec. 3, has arranged these under proper heads scrutinizing the pretentions of the church."

9. "Canons were made from time to time to supply the defects of the common law of the church; so were statutes added to enforce both Common and Canon Law. The greater part of the statutes made before the Reformation, which concerns the church and clergy, are directly leveled against violence committed against the possession or persons by the minister of the king, and against the encroachments of the Temporal Courts upon the spiritual jurisdiction."

10. "Phantastic romanticists and calculating persons have endeavored to represent this period as the age of morality and sincere reverence for woman. . . . The 'Service of Love' preached by French, German, and Italian knights, was supposed to prove the high respect paid to the women of that day. On the contrary, this period succeeded in destroying the little respect for the female sex which existed at its commencement. The knights both in town and country were mostly coarse, licentious men. . . . The chronicles of the times swarm with tales of rape and violence on the part of nobles in the country, and still more in the towns where they were exclusive rulers up to the thirteenth and fourteenth centuries, while those subjected to this degraded treatment were powerless to obtain redress. In the towns the nobles sat on the magistrates bench, and in the country criminal jurisdiction was in the hands of the lord of the manor, squire or bishop."

11. The first article of the famous Code of Love was "Marriage is not a legitimate excuse against love."

12. This was Christine's first work. Her success was so great that she supported a family of six persons by her pen.

13. Wright.—*Womankind in Europe*.

14. "The Fathers seem to have thought dissolution of marriage was not lawful on account of the adultery of the husband, but that it was not absolutely unlawful for a husband whose wife had committed adultery to remarry."

15. The preference of males over females in succession was totally unknown to the laws of Rome. Brothers and sisters were entitled to equal parts of the inheritance. Blackstone.—*Commentaries.*

16. No marriage could take place after twelve noon, which is even now the rule of the English Established Church. The decrees of the Plenary Council, Baltimore 1884, tend to the establishment of similar regulations in our own country.

17. The New Testaments of sixty years since, contained a list of relatives commencing with grandfather and grandmother, whom a man and woman might not marry.

18. The policy of the church was to persuade mankind that the cohabitation of a man and woman was in itself unholy, and that nothing but a religious bond or sacrament could render it inoffensive in the eyes of God. Pike.—*History of Crime in England,* I, 90.

19. This law held good in Protestant England until within the last decade.

20. The church visited its penalties upon the innocent as well as guilty; when any man remained under excommunication two months, his wife and children were interdicted and deprived of all doctrines of the church but baptism and repentance. Lea.—*Studies in Church History.*

21. In England, until the reign of William and Mary, women were refused the benefit of clergy.

22. In the hands of such able politicians it (marriage), soon became an engine of great importance to the papal scheme of an universal monarchy over Christendom. The innumerable canonical impediments that were invented and occasionally dispensed with by the Holy See, not only enriched the coffers of the church, but gave it a vast ascendant over persons of all denominations, whose marriages were sanctioned or repudiated, their issue legitimated or bastardized . . . according to the humor or interest of the reigning pontiff.—*Commentaries,* 3, p. 92.

23. The word *Liber,* free, the solar *Phre* of Egypt, and *Liber,* a book, being as has been shown, closely connected, the bookish men of Bac, Boc, Bacchus, were comparatively free from the rule of the warrior class, both in civil and military point of view, and thence arises our benefit of clergy. If the *benefit of clergy* depends upon a statute, it had probably been obtained by the priests to put their privilege out of doubt. It has been a declaratory statute, although, perhaps, every man who was initiated could not read and write, yet I believe every man who could read and write was initiated, these arts being taught to the initiated only in very early times. It has been

said that the privilege of clergy was granted to encourage learning. I believe it was used as a test, as a proof that a man was of, or immediately belonging to, the sacred tribe, and therefore exempt from the jurisdiction of the court in which he had been tried. If he were accused he said nothing; if found guilty he pleaded his orders and his reading. I have little doubt that the knowledge of reading and letters were a masonic secret for many generations, and that it formed part of the mysterious knowledge of Eleusis and other temples.—*Anacalypsis*, 2, pp. 271–72.

24. Woman was represented as the door of hell, as the mother of all human ills. She should be ashamed of the very thought that she is a woman. She should live in continual penance on account of the curses she had brought upon the world. She should be ashamed of her dress, for it is the memorial of her fall. She should especially be ashamed of her beauty, for it is the most potent instrument of the demon. . . . Women were even forbidden by a provincial council, in the sixth century, on account of their impurity, to receive the eucharist in their naked hands. Their essentially subordinate position was continually maintained. Lecky.—*Hist. European Morals*.

25. No woman can witness a will in the State of Louisiana today.

26. Blackstone says whosoever wishes to form a correct idea of Canon Law can do so by examining it in regard to married women.— *Commentaries*.

27. Blondell, a learned Protestant who died in 1659, fully proved Isidore's collection of the Decretal Epistles of the popes of the first three centuries, to be all forged and a shameless imposture, *says Collier*.

28. The famous law of Constantine, attached to the Theodosian Code, by virtue of which a prodigious and monstrous jurisdiction was formerly attributed to bishops, or to the hieratic order, though in reality that law was never a part of the aforesaid code, at the end of which it is found. Seldon.—*Dissertation on Fleta*, p. 101.

At time of Valentinian neither bishops nor the Consistories could, without the consent of the contracting lay parties, take cognizance of their causes. . . . Because, says that emperor, it is evident that bishops and priests have no court to determine the laws in, neither can they according to the imperial constitutions of Arcadius and Honorius, as is manifest from the Theodosian body, judge of any other matters than those relating to religion. Thus the aforesaid Emperor Valentinian. Neither do I think that the above sanction as extravagant, obtained a place at the end of the Theodosian Code, or was under the title of Episcopis, by any other manner posted into my manuscript, than by the frauds and deceits, constantly, under various pretenses, made use of by the hieratical orders, who endeavored to shape right or wrong, according to the custom of those ages, not to mention others, sovereign princes and republics of their authority and legal power, by this means under the cloak of religion, its constant pretext, most strenuously serving their own ends and ambition.—*Ibid.*, p. 107.

29. See Reeves.—*History of English Law.*

30. Draper.—*Conflict of Science and Religion.*

31. Reeves.

32. Declaration of judges in the famous case of Evans and Ascuith. Vaughn said in a later case of the same kind, "If Canon Law be made part of the law of this land, then it is as much a law of the land and as well, and by the same authority as any other part of the law of the land."

33. Gibson was archdeacon of Surrey, Rector of Lambeth, and Chaplain of his Grace the Lord Archbishop of Canterbury (Primate of all England and Metropolitan) to whom the Jurus was dedicated. The work said: "The foreign is what we commonly call the body of Canon Law, consisting of the Canons of Councils, Decrees of Popes and the like, which obtained in England by virtue of their own authority (in like manner as they did in other parts of the Western Church), till the time of the Reformation, and from that time have continued upon the foot of consent, usage and custom. For which distinction we have no less warrant than an act of Parliament, made at the very time when those foreign laws were declared to be no longer binding by their own authority. . . . We have a plain declaration that foreign laws became part of the law of England by long use and consent." Gibson.—*Codex Jurus Ecclesiasticum Anglican.*

34. English *Common Law Reports*, Hill vs. Gould, *Vaughn*, p. 327, says: "Whatever is declared by an Act of Parliament to be against God's law must be so admitted by us, because it is so declared by an Act of Parliament."

35. Under Catholic form the bride promises to consecrate her body to the marital rite.

36. Chiniquy.—*The Priest, the Woman and the Confessional.*

37. "The clergy formerly, and to this very day, declare those women evil who desire to limit self-indulgence and procreation."

38. See Lecky.—*Hist. of European Morals.*

39. In a sermon laudatory of the preachers office, delivered in the May Memorial, Unitarian Church, in Syracuse, N.Y., Sunday, Nov. 27,

1887, Rev. Mr. Calthrop, the pastor, said: "Noble words are your chief weapons of offense and defense. But remember it is not you that speak when you utter them, but the Holy Ghost." From "Report of Sermon," published in the *Daily Standard*, November 28th.

40. Whoever wishes to gain insight into that great institution, Common Law, can do so most efficiently by studying Canon Law in regard to married women.—*Commentaries*.

41. Distinction of class appears most prominently in all the criminal laws for which the clergy are responsible. It was for the man of low estate, the slave, and for women, that the greatest atrocities were reserved. If the thief was a free woman she was to be thrown down a precipice or drowned (a precedent without doubt for dragging a witch through a pond). If the thief was a female slave and had stolen from any but her own lord, eighty female slaves were to attend, each bearing a log of wood to pile the fire and burn the offender to death. Pike.—*Hist. of Crime in England*, pp. 49–51.

42. A correspondent of the *London Times* writes from Rome that he has not heard a single doubt expressed as to the paternity of the Countess Lambertini, and the line adopted by the Antonelli heirs tacitly confirms it. They strenuously oppose the production of any of the evidence the plaintiff has offered. They object to the depositions of the witnesses being heard and tested, and they have declared their intention of impugning as forgeries the documentary proofs tendered. These documents consist of some letters written by Antonietta Marconi to the Archpriest Vendetta, and particularly one dated April 1, 1857, wherein, asking him to prepare a draught of a letter to the Cardinal, she says that "Giacomo" does not send her money, although he knows that he has a daughter to support, and that Loretina is a cause of great expense. "Write to him forcibly," she says, "or I shall do something disagreeable." The extent of the scandal in Rome does not consist so much in the fact of a Cardinal in Antonelli's position having had one or more children, as in the lawsuit which has brought all the intimate details connected with the affair before the public. Antonelli was to all intents and purposes a layman, filling one of those civil departments of an ecclesiastical temporal Government to qualify for which it was indispensably requisite to assume the ecclesiastical habit. He accepted early in life those obligations without which no career would have been open to him, and, like many others, he regarded them as mere matters of form, for under the imperturbable mask of the ecclesiastical diplomat beat a heart filled with

the warmest domestic affections and instincts; and how strong those feelings were in him was fully demonstrated in his will, and is clearly shown in every incident of the story now revealed.

Dame Gervasi has been subjected to a rigid cross-examination by the counsel of the brothers Antonelli. The proceedings were conducted with closed doors, but a Roman correspondent of the *Daily News* seems in some manner to have wormed out the essential facts. When the mysterious "foreign young lady" went to lodge at Dame Gervasi's, Cardinal Antonelli—so the gossip runs—paid several visits to his protégé. "I remember," says the Dame, "that when I went to open the door to them I held in my hand a bowl of beef tea, which I was taking to the patient. Dr. Lucchini was the first to enter, and I soon recognized the second visitor to be Cardinal Antonelli, who wore a long redingote and a tall hat. He took the bowl, which I held in my hand. 'This is for the patient,' he said inquiringly, but before I had time to reply he had swallowed part of its contents." Dame Gervasi then proceeded to relate how Dr. Lucchini left the Cardinal alone with the foreign young lady. The witness put her ear to the keyhole, and heard distinctly the sound of kisses alternating, with sobs between the two. His Eminence, to console the patient, told her he had taken every precaution against the matter becoming known. "Don't be afraid," he said, "nobody will be a bit the wiser. You will be able to marry. As for the baby, that's my affair. I will take care of her, and I swear to you that she will never know the name of her mother." Dame Gervasi gave the names of the persons who had come to her on behalf of the brothers Antonelli, and these emissaries, she said, tried to make her disclose all she knew, and promised her large sums of money to bind her to silence as to the clandestine part played by Signora Marconi, and as to the Cardinal's relations with the "foreign young lady."—*N. Y. Tribune*, July 5, 1878.

43. See Reeves.—*Early English Law*.

44. *Hollingshed's Chronicles*.

The foundation of old common law seems traceable to Martia, the widow of Guilliame, left regent of her husband's kingdom, comprising a part of Britain, two hundred years prior to the christian era. This queen directed her attention to framing a system of laws, which acquired for her the surname of "Proba," or "The just." They were evidently one of the three parts under which the common law is divided, although under canon law the entire property of the wife became that of the husband upon marriage.

45. In England, in 1538, or even earlier, it was calculated that besides the tithes, one-third of the kingdom was ecclesiastical property, and that these vast possessions were devoted to the support of a body of men who found their whole serious occupation in destroying the virtue of women. Lea.—*Sacerdotal Celibacy*.

46. The pagan laws during the Empire had been continually repealing the old disabilities of women; and the legislative movement in their favor continued with unabated force from Constantine to Justinian and appeared also in some of the early laws of the barbarians. But, in the whole feudal legislation, women were placed in a much lower legal position than in the pagan Empire. In addition to the personal restrictions which grew necessarily out of the Catholic Christian doctrines concerning divorce, and the subordination of the weaker sex, we find numerous and stringent enactments, which rendered it impossible for women to succeed to any considerable amount of property, and which almost reduced them to the alternative of marriage or a nunnery. The complete inferiority of the sex was continually maintained by law; and that generous public opinion which in Rome had frequently revolted against the injustice done to girls, in depriving them of the greater part of the inheritance of their fathers, totally disappeared. Wherever the canon law has been the basis of legislation, we find laws of succession sacrificing the interests of daughters and of wives, and a state of public opinion which has been formed and regulated by these laws; nor was any serious attempt made to abolish them till the close of the last century. The French Revolutionists, though rejecting the proposal of Sieyès and Condorcet to accord political emancipation to women, established at least an equal succession of sons and daughters, and thus initiated a great reformation of both law and opinion, which sooner or later must traverse the world. Lecky.—*Hist. Morals*, Vol. II, pp. 357–59.

47. Sheldon Amos.—*Science of Law*.

48. *Ibid*.

49. Our laws are based on the all-sufficiency of man's rights. Society exists for man only; for women merely as they are represented by some man; are in the *mundt* or keeping of some man.—*Descriptive Sociology of England*.

50. This slavish condition of the wife yet prevails in over one-half the states of the union.

51. The relations in respect to property which exist between husband and wife in England, is solely grounded on her not being assumed

at common law to have sufficient command of her purse or of her future actions wherewith to procure the materials for making a contract. The legal presumption then is that she did not intend to make one, and therefore the allegation that she did make a contract would simply on the face of it be a fraud. Amos.—*Science of Law.*

52. The jurisconsults had evidently at this time assumed the equality of the sexes as a principle to the code of equity. The situation of the Roman woman, whether married or single, became one of great personal and proprietary independence; but Christianity tended somewhat from the very first to narrow this remarkable liberty. The prevailing state of religious sentiment may explain why modern jurisprudence has adopted those rules concerning the position of woman, which belong peculiarly to an imperfect civilization. No society which preserves any tincture of Christian institutions is likely to restore to married women the personal liberty conferred on them by middle Roman law. Canon law has deeply injured civilization.—Sir Henry Maine.

53. Under the Commonwealth, society assumed a new and stern aspect. Women were in disgrace; it was everywhere declared from the pulpit that woman caused man's expulsion from Paradise, and ought to be shunned by Christians as one of the greatest temptations of Satan. "Man," said they, "is conceived in sin and brought forth in iniquity; it was his complacency to woman that caused his first debasement; let man not therefore glory in his shame; let him not worship the fountain of his corruption." Learning and accomplishments were alike discouraged, and women confined to a knowledge of cooking, family medicines and the unintelligible theological discussions of the day. Lydia Maria Child.—*History of Woman.*

54. Many women made their entrance into literature through the medium of a cookbook, thus virtually apologizing for the use of a pen.

55. The slavish superstition under which church teaching still keeps the minds of men was no less shown by the thousands who visited the St. Anne relic in the United States. Nor are Protestants but little less under the same superstition, accepting the teaching of the church without investigation. An educated Protestant girl, upon her return from Europe, recently, gravely declared that during her absence she had seen the spear which pierced the Saviour's side.

56. The most interesting of all to Americans is the copy of the American Constitution that President Cleveland sent to the Vatican by Cardinal Gibbons. It is printed on vellum in richly illuminated English characters,

and bound in white and red. It is enclosed in a case of purple plush with gold hinges, and bears this autographic inscription by President Cleveland:

"Presented to his Holiness Pope Leo XIII, as an expression of congratulation on the occasion of his sacerdotal jubilee, with the profound regard of Grover Cleveland, President of the United States, through the courtesy of his Eminence Cardinal Gibbons, Archbishop of Baltimore.

Washington, D. C."

Upon the next page, beneath an American eagle printed in gold, is this inscription:

"The Constitution of the United States. Adopted Sept. 17, 1787."

The page bearing this inscription and all the fly leaves were of exquisite watered silk.

57. "Owing to the pope's refusal to accept the gifts of the king and queen of Italy on the occasion of his jubilee, all the members of the House of Savoy, including the Duke d'Aosta and the Princess Clotilde, have omitted to send offerings. This is the fly in the jubilee ointment of Pope Leo XIII, and settles the question of concessions of temporal power. Nevertheless, the day is passed when the claim of 'imprisonment in the Vatican' will further avail the pope."

58. When Linneaus published his sexual system of plants, in the eighteenth century, he was ridiculed and shunned as one who had degraded nature.

Chapter IV

Marquette

The minds of people having been corrupted through centuries by the doctrines of the Church in regard to woman, it became an easy step for the State to aid in her degradation. The system of feudalism arising from the theory that warfare was the normal condition of man, still oppressed woman by bringing into power a class of men accustomed to deeds of violence, who found their chief pleasure in the sufferings of others. To be a woman, appealed to no instinct of tenderness in this class. To be a woman was not to be protected unless such woman held power in her own right, or acted in place of some feudal lord. The whole body of villeins and serfs were under absolute dominion of the feudal lords. They were regarded as possessing no rights of their own; the priests had control of their souls, the lord, of their bodies. But it was not upon the male serfs that the greatest oppression fell. Although the tillage of the soil, the care of swine and cattle was theirs, the masters claiming half or more of everything, even to one-half of the wool shorn from the flock,[1] and all exactions upon them were great while their sense of security was slight, it was upon their wives and daughters that the greatest outrages were inflicted. It was a pastime of the castle retainers to fall upon peaceful villages, to the consternation of the women, who were struck, tortured, and made the sport of ribald soldiers.[2] "Serfs of the body," they had no protection. The vilest outrages were prepetrated by the feudal lords under the name of "rights." Women were taught by church and state alike that the feudal lord or seigneur had a right to them not only as against themselves, but as against any claim of husband or father. The custom known by a variety of names, but more modernly as "marchetta," or "marquette," compelled newly married women to a most dishonorable servitude. They were regarded as the rightful prey of the feudal lord for from one to three days after their marriage,[3] and from this custom, the oldest son of the serf was held as the son of the lord, "as perchance it was he who begot him."

From this nefarious degradation of woman the custom of Borough-English arose, the youngest son becoming the heir.[4] The original signification of the word *borough*, being *to make secure*, the peasant through Borough-English made secure the right of his own son to what inheritance he might leave, thus cutting off his property from the possible son of his hated lord. France, Germany, Prussia, England, Scotland, and all christian countries in which feudalism existed, held to the enforcement of marquette. The lord deemed this right his, as fully as he did his claim to half the crops of the land, or half the wool shorn from the sheep. More than one reign of terror arose in France from the enforcement of this law, and the uprisings of the peasants over Europe during the twelfth century and the fierce Jacquerie, or Peasants War, of the fourteenth century in France, owed their origin among other causes, to the enforcement of these claims by the lords upon the newly married wife. The Edicts of Marley securing the seigneural tenure in Lower Canada transplanted that claim to America when Canada was under the control of France.[5]

During the feudal period when chivalry held highest rank in the duties of the knight, women of the lower classes were absolutely unprotected. Both Church and State were their most bitter enemies; the lords even if in holy orders did not lessen their claims upon the bride. Most of the bishops and *chanonies* were also temporal lords. The Bishop of Amiens possessed this right against the women of his vassals and the peasants of his fiefs, of which he was dispossessed at the commencement of the fifteenth century, by an *arreet*, rendered at the solicitation of husbands.[6] Although the clergy, largely drawn from the nobility, whose portionless younger sons were thus easily provided for, sustained the corruptions of the lords temporal yet having connected themselves with the church, they did not fail to preserve their own power even over the nobility.

The canons of the Cathedral of Lyons, bore title of Counts of Lyons; sixteen quarters of nobility, eight on side of the father; eight on side of the mother. The marchetta or cuissage was still practiced by them in the fourteenth century at the time Lyons was reunited to the crown of France. It was but slowly, after a great number of complaints and arrests of judgment that the canons of Lyons consented to forego this custom. In several cantons of Piccardy, the curés imitated the bishops and anciently took the right of cuissage, but ultimately the peasants of this region refused to marry, and the priests gave up this practice which they had usurped when the bishop had become too old to take his right.[7] The resolution not to marry, surprised and confounded the lord "suzerains," who perceived it would cause the depopulation of their feifs. During the feudal period, bearing children was the duty preeminently taught women. Serf children increased the power and possessions of the lord, they also added to the power of the church, and the strangest sermons in regard to woman's duty in this respect fell from the lips of celibate monks and priests. She was taught that sensual submission to man, and the bearing of children, were the two reasons for her having been created, and that the woman who failed in either had no excuse for longer encumbering the earth. The language used from the pulpit for the enforcement of these duties, will not bear reproduction.[8] The villeins were not entirely submissive under such great wrongs, frequently protesting against this right of their suzerains. At one time a number of Piedmont villages rose in united revolt, compelling the lords to relinquish some of their powers. Although[9] the concessions gained were but small, not putting an end to the lord's claim to the bride but merely lessening the time of his spoliation, the results were great in establishing the principle of serf rights.

Marquette began to be abolished in France towards the end of the sixteenth century.[10] But an authority upon this question says that without doubt the usage still continued in certain countries, further asserting that even in this century it existed in the county of Auvergene, and several vassals plead to their lords against the continuance of this custom because of the great unhappiness it caused them. The lower orders of the clergy were very unwilling to relinquish this usage, vigorously protesting to their archbishops against the deprivation of the right, declaring they could not be dispossessed.[11] Bœms states that he was present at a spiritual council of the metropolitane of Bourges, and heard a priest claim the right upon ground of immemorial usage.[12]

Although feudalism is generally considered the parent of this most infamous custom, some writers attribute its origin to an evangelical council, or to precepts directly inculcated by the church,[13] whose very highest dignitaries did not hesitate to avail themselves of the usage. In 1471, quite the latter part of the fifteenth century, Pope Sixtus IV,[14] sought admission to the very illustrious Piedmont family, Della Rovere, which possessed the right of cuissage, allowing the lord absolute control of his vassals newly wedded bride for three days and nights; a cardinal of the family having secured the patent by which this outrageous and abominable right was granted them. The rights of the Lords spiritual in the *jus primæ noctis*, at first, perchance, confined to those temporal lords who holding this right entered the church, at last extended to the common priesthood, and the confessional became the great fount of debauchery. Woman herself was powerless; the church, the state, the family, all possessed authority over her as against herself. Although eventually redemption through the payment of money, or property, was possible, yet a husband too poor or penurious to save her, aided in this debasement of his wife.[15] This inexpressible abuse and degradation of woman went under the name of pastime, nor were the courts to be depended upon for defense.[16] Their sympathies and decisions were with the lord. Few except manorial courts existed. Even when freedom had been purchased for the bride, all feudal customs rendered it imperative upon her to bear the "wedding dish" to the castle. Accompanied by her husband, this ceremony ever drew upon the newly married couple a profusion of jeers and ribald jests from which they were powerless to protect themselves. While in ancient Babylon woman secured immunity by one service and payment to the temple, the claim of the lord to the peasant wife was not always confined to the marriage day, and refusal of the loan of his wife at later date brought most severe punishment upon the husband.[17]

Blessing the nuptial bed by the priest, often late at night, was also common, and accompanied by many abuses, until advancing civilization overpowered the darkness of the church and brought it to an end. When too poor to purchase the freedom of his bride, the husband was in one breath assailed by the most opprobrious names,[18] and in the next he was congratulated upon the honor to be done him in that perchance his oldest child would be the son of a baron.[19] So great finally became the reproach and infamy connected with the *droit de cuissage*, as this right was generally called in France,[20] and so recalcitrant became the peasants over its nefarious exactions, that ultimately both lords spiritual and lords temporal fearing for their own safety, commenced to lessen their demands.[21] This custom had its origin at the time the great body of the people were slaves bound either to the person or land of some lord. At this period personal rights no more existed for the lower classes than for the blacks of our own country during the time of slavery. Under feudalism, the property, family ties, and even the lives of the serfs were under control of the suzerain. It was a system of slavery without the name; the right of the lord to all first fruits was universally admitted;[22] the best in possession of the serf, by feudal custom belonged to the lord. The feudal period was especially notable for the wrongs of women. War, the pastime of nobles and kings, brought an immense number of men into enforced idleness. Its rapine and carnage were regarded as occupations superior to the tillage of the soil or the arts of peace. Large numbers of men, retainers of every kind, hung about the castle dependent upon its lord, obedient to his commands.[23] At an age when books were few and reading an accomplishment of still greater rarity, these men, apart from their families, or totally unbound by marriage, were in readiness for the grossest amusement. At an age when human life was valueless, and suffering of every kind was disregarded, we can readily surmise the fate likely to overtake unprotected peasant women. They were constantly ridiculed and insulted; deeds of violence were common and passed unreproved. For a woman of this class to be self-respecting was to become a target for the vilest abuse. Morality was scoffed at; to drag the wives and daughters of villeins and serfs into the mire of lechery was deemed a proper retribution for their attempted pure lives; they possessed no rights of person or morality against the feudal lord and his wild retainers. All Christian Europe was plunged into the grossest immorality.[24] A mistress was looked upon as a necessary part of a monarch's state.[25] Popes, cardinals, and priests of lesser degrees, down to the present century, still continued the unsavory reputation of their predecessors;[26] "nephews," "nieces," and "sacrilegious" children are yet supported by the revenues of the Church, or left to poverty, starvation and crime. It was long the custom of christian municipalities to welcome visiting kings by deputations of naked women,[27] and as late as the eighteenth century, a mistress whose support was drawn from the revenues of the kingdom, was recognized as part of the pageantry of the kingdom.

The heads of the Greek and Protestant Churches, no less than of the Catholic, appear before the world as men of scandalous lives. The history of the popes is familiar to all students. No less is that of the English Eighth Henry, the real father of the Reformation, in

England, and founder of the Anglican Church, whose adulteries and murders make him a historic Blue Beard. The heads of the Greek Church figure in a double sense as fathers of their people. The renowned Peter the Great, amused himself by numberless liasons, filling Russia with descendants whose inherited tendencies are those of discontent and turmoil. When he visited the Court of Prussia, 1717, he was accompanied by his czarina, son, daughter, and four hundred ladies in waiting, women of low condition, each of whom carried an elegantly dressed infant upon her arms. If asked in regard to the paternity of the child they invariably replied "my lord has done me the honor to make me its mother."[28]

In no country has a temporal monarch under guise of a spiritual ruler been more revered than in Russia. Even amidst nihilism a belief that the czar can do no wrong is the prevailing conviction among the Slavic peoples. This is both a great cause of, and a result of Russian degradation. If we except the proportionately few liberal thinkers, that conviction is as strong as it was in the time of Ivan the Terrible. In no civilized or half-civilized nation is ignorance as dense as among the peasantry of that vast empire embracing one-sixth of the habitable globe. Nor to the czar alone was such disregard of woman's right of person confined. The system of serfdom which existed until within the last half of the present century, was a system of feudalism in its oppression of women, although if possible even more gross. The sale of young peasant girls regularly took place, and the blood of the nobility of that country runs in the veins of its most degraded and ignorant population.[29] Although Italy the seat of the papal power is noted for the ignorance, squalor, and superstition of its people, we no less find such a condition of affairs existing in Russia. Amid the starvation of its people, accompanied by "hunger-typhus," that form of disease which in the Irish famine of 1848 was known as "ship-fever," the peasants will not accept aid from Count Tolstoi, whom they have been taught to regard as Anti-Christ, fearing that by so doing they will condemn themselves to eternal torment.[30] While the peasantry are thus suffering wrongs of every nature, the priesthood and churches are as thriving as before.

Having shown the results of power in the hands of a controlling class, upon women of low degree in both the Catholic and Greek divisions of christendom, we have but to look at our own country to find like condition under Protestantism. The state of the slave women of the South was that of serfs of the body under feudalism, or of the serf peasant women of Russia. Nor is other proof of this statement required than the hue of this race, no longer spoken of as the blacks, but as colored people. Let the condition of woman as to her rights of person, under the three great divisions of Christianity, be answer to all who without examination of history, or the customs of ancient and modern times, and with eyes closed to these most potent facts, so falsely assert that woman has been elevated by christianity, and is now holding a position never before in the world accorded her. But what has already been shown of her degradation under christian teachings and laws, is but a small portion of the wrongs woman has suffered during the christian centuries.

Under theory of the divine rights of man, society has everywhere been permeated with disregard for woman's rights of person. Monarchs not posing as spiritual heads of their people have yet equally made use of their place and power for woman's degradation, and an indefinite fatherhood outside of marriage. Augustus of Saxony, King of Poland, is chiefly renowned in history as the father of three hundred illegitimate children.[31] Of Charles II not alone King of England, but also head of the Anglican Church, one of his subjects declared him to be the father of many of his people in the literal as well as in the spiritual sense. Four English dukes of the present day trace their lineage to this monarch, who left no legitimate descendants.[32]

H. R. H. the present heir-apparent to the English throne bears an equally unsavory record.[33] To him and his aristocratic companions in guilt is due the support and protection of England's notorious and infamous purchase and sale, outrage, and expoliation of helpless young girls. An English clergyman writing the *New York Sun*, at the time of the disclosures made by the *Pall Mall Gazette*, declared he had in his possession a list of the names of the royal princes, dukes, nobles, and leading men who had been the principal patrons and supporters of the "gilded hells" devoted to the ruin of the merest children, girls from the ages of nine to thirteen.[34] The reputation of the male members of the Hanoverian dynasty has ever been bad. Trace as you will, the path of either ecclesiastical or temporal rulers claiming authority by "divine right," and you will find the way marked with the remains of women and children whose life has been wrecked by man under plea of created superiority. While Italy within the last forty years has escaped from the temporal control of the pope, its kings have no less copied the immorality of the "Vicar of God"; the predecessor of the late king of Italy having left thirty-three illegitimate children. An instance of the survival of the feudal idea as to the right of the lord to the person of his vassal women occured in Ireland within the past few years, graphically described in a letter upon landlords, from Mr. D. R. Locke, (Nasby), December, 1891, in which he says:

One was shot a few years ago and a great ado was made about it. In this case, as in most of the others it was not a question of rent. My Lord had visited his estates to see how much more money could be taken out of his tenants and his lecherous eye happened to rest upon a very beautiful girl, the eldest daughter of a widow with seven children. Now this beautiful girl was betrothed to a nice sort of a boy, who, having been in America, knew a thing or two. My Lord, through his agent, who is always a pimp as well as a brigand, ordered Kitty to come to the castle. Kitty knowing very well what that meant, refused.

"Very well," says the agent, "yer mother is in arrears for rent, and you had better see My Lord, or I shall be compelled to evict her."

Kitty knew what that meant also. It meant that her gray-haired mother, her six helpless brothers and sisters would be pitched out by the roadside to die of starvation and exposure, and so Kitty without saying a word to her mother or any one else, went to the castle and was kept there three days, till My Lord was tired of her, when she was permitted to go.

She went to her lover, like an honest girl as she was, and told him she would not marry him, but refused to give any reason.

Finally the truth was wrenched out of her, and Mike went and found a shot gun that had escaped the eye of the royal constabulary, and he got powder and shot and old nails, and he lay behind a hedge under a tree for several days. Finally one day My Lord came riding by all so gay and that gun went off, and, subsequent proceedings interested him no more. There was a hole, a blessed hole, clear through him, and he never was so good a man as before because there was less of him.

Then Mike went and told Kitty to be of good cheer and not be cast down, that the little difference between him and My Lord had been happily settled, and that they would be married as soon as possible. And they were married, and I had the pleasure of taking in my hand the very hand that fired the blessed shot and of seeing the wife, to avenge whose cruel wrongs the shot was fired.

Nor is this the only instance in modern Ireland. A certain lord Leitram was noted a few years since for his attempts to dishonor the wives and daughters of the peasantry upon his vast estate comprising 90,000 acres. His character was that of the worst feudal barons, and like those he used his power as magistrate and noble, in addition to that of landlord, to accomplish his purpose. After an assault upon a beautiful and intelligent girl, by a brutal retainer of his lordship, her character assailed, his tenantry finally declared it necessary to resort to the last means in their power to preserve the honor of their wives and daughters. Six men were chosen as the instruments of their rude justice, and among them the brother of this girl, upon whom the leadership fell. They took oath to be true to the end, in life or death, raised a sum of money, purchased arms, and seeking a convenient opportunity shot him to death. Nor were the perpetrators ever discovered; yet it is now known that two of them died in Australia, two in the Boer war in South Africa, and the leader who came to the United States, changing his name, passed away in the summer of 1892 in the State of Pennsylvania.

Under head of "A Story of Today," another tale is related of woman's oppression in Ireland aided by the Petty Sessions Bench in 1880.

Recently, a young girl named Catherine Cafferby, of Belmullet, in County Mayo—the pink of her father's family—fled from the "domestic service" of a landlord as absolute as Lord Leitrim, the moment the poor creature discovered what that "service" customarily involved. The great man had the audacity to invoke the law to compel her to return, as she had not given statuable notice of her flight. She clung to the doorpost of her father's cabin; she told aloud the story of her terror, and called on God and man to save her. Her tears, her shrieks, her piteous pleadings were all in vain. The Petty Sessions Bench ordered her back to the landlord's "service," or else to pay five pounds, or two weeks in jail. This is not a story of Bulgaria under Murad IV but of Ireland in the reign of the present sovereign. That peasant girl went to jail to save her chastity. If she did not spend a fortnight in the cells, it was only because friends of outraged virtue, justice, and humanity paid the fine when the story reached the outer world.

These iniquities have taken place in christian lands[35] and these nefarious outrages upon women have been enforced by the christian laws of both church and state. The degradation and unhappiness of the husband at the infringement of the lord's spiritual and temporal upon his marital rights, has been depicted by many writers, but history has been quite silent upon the despair and shame of the wife.[36] No hope appeared for woman anywhere. The Church which should have been the great conserver of morals dragged her to the lowest depths through the vileness of its teachings and its priestly customs. The State which should have defended her civil rights, followed the example of the church in crushing her to the earth. Christian laws were detrimental to woman in every relation of life.

The brilliant French author, Legouvé,[37] gives from among the popular songs of Brittany during the fourteenth century, a pathetic ballad, "The baron of Jauioz," which vividly depicts the condition of the peasant women of France at that date. In the power of the male members of her family over her, we also find an exact parallel in the condition of English women of the same

era. The moral disease thus represented being due to the same
religious teaching, the change of country and language but more
fully serves to depict the condition of woman everywhere in
christendom at this period.

Breton Ballad of the Fourteenth Century
The Baron of Jauioz
I.

As I was at the river washing,

I heard the sighing of the bird of death.

"Good little Jina, you do not know it, but you are sold to the
Baron of Jauioz."

Is this true, my mother, that I have heard?

Is it true that I was sold to old Jauioz?

"My poor little darling, I know nothing about it; ask your
father."

"My nice good father, tell me now—is it true that I am sold
to Loys de Jauioz?"

"My beloved child, I know nothing about it; ask your
brother."

Lannik, my brother, tell me now—is it true that I am sold to
that lord there?

"Yes you are sold to the Baron, and you must be off at once.
Your price is paid—fifty crowns of the white silver and as much
of the yellow gold."

II.

She had not gone far from the hamlet

when she beard the ringing of the bells; whereat she wept.

"Adieu Saint Ann! Adieu, bells of my fatherland;

Bells of my village church, adieu!"

III.

"Take a seat and rest thee till the repast is ready."

The lord sat near the fire; his beard and hair all white, and his eyes like living coals.

"Behold the young maiden whom I have desired this many a day!"

"Come my child, let me show thee, crown by crown, how rich I am; come, count with me, my beauty, my gold and my silver."

"I should like better to be with my mother counting the chips on the fire."

"Let us descend into the cellar and taste of the wine that is sweet as honey."

"I should like better to taste the meadow stream

Whereof my father's horses drink."

"Come with me from shop to shop to buy thee a holiday cloak."

"I should better like a linsey petticoat, that my mother has woven for me."

"Ah, that my tongue had been blistered when

I was such a fool as to buy thee!

Since nothing will comfort thee."

IV.

"Dear little birds as you fly, I pray you listen to me,

You are going to the village whither I cannot.

You are merry but I am sad."

"Remember me to my playmates,

To the good mother who brought me to light,

And to the father who reared me; and tell my brother

I forgive him."

V.

Two or three months have passed and gone when as the
family are sleeping,
A sweet voice is heard at the door.
"My father, my mother, for God's love pray for me;
Your daughter lies on her bier."

This ballad founded upon historic facts represents the social
life of christendom during the fourteenth century. The authority
of the son, the licentiousness of the lord, the powerlessness of the
mother, the despair of the daughter, the indifference of society,
are vividly depicted in this pathetic balled. It shows the young girl
regarded as a piece of merchandise, to be bought and sold at the
whim of her masters who are the men of her own household and
the lord of the manor. During the feudal period the power of the
son was nearly absolute. For his own aggrandisement he did not
hesitate to rob his sisters, or sell them into lechery.[38] Hopelessly
despairing in tone, this ballad gives us a clear picture of feudal
times when chivalry was at its height, and the church had reached
its ultimate of power. Woman's attitude today is the echo of that
despair. At this period the condition of a woman was not even
tolerable unless she was an heiress, with fiefs in possession.[39] Even
then she was deprived of her property in case of loss of chastity,
of which it was the constant aim to deprive her. Guardians, next
of kin, and if none such existed, the church threw constant temptations in her way. Ruffians were hired, or reckless profligates
induced to betray her under plea of love and sympathy, well paid
by the next heir for their treachery.

Although Sir William Blackstone in his Commentaries, said
that he discovered no traces of Marquette in England, a reminiscence of that custom is to be found in the "fine" or "permit"
known in that country as Redemption of Blood, and designated
as *Merchetum Sanguinis*, by Fleta.[40] This was a customary payment
made by a tenant to his lord for license to give his daughter in
marriage. Such redemption was considered a special mark of
tenure in villeinage.[41] It was not exacted from a free man, which

is corroborative proof of its origin in the *Jus Primæ Noctis*, of the feudal lord. Of the free man this fine was not permissible, because of the privilege of free blood. Raepsaet, M. Hoffman, Dr. Karl Schmidt, and other authors writing in the interest of the church and finding it impossible to deny the existence of some power over the bride, have questioned its character, declaring it not to be feudal, but a spiritual authority, to guard the bride by enforcing a penitence of marital abstinence of one to three days after the nuptials. It is not to be doubted that under the peculiar teachings of the church in regard to the uncleanliness of marriage that such continence was at a certain period part of church law.[42] Nevertheless this does not invalidate the fact that a widespread contrary custom existed in feudal times and at a still later period. The present usages of society point back to an age when right to the peasant's bride was enforced by the lord. A reminiscence[43] of this period is to be found in charavari and the buying off of a party of this character with refreshments from the house, or with money for the purchase of cigars and liquor. Such occurrences constantly fall within our knowledge, personally or through the press.[44] The very fact of such persecution of the bridal pair is a symbol of that custom under which the retainers of the feudal lord jeered and flouted the bridegroom, throwing him into foul water,[45] and other most unseemly practices. To others outside of the charavari party this practice still affords amusement, few persons inclining to interfere or prohibit such pastimes. Society no longer as sharply defined as in the feudal period, yet has preserved in this practice a symbol of the times when even the highborn dames in the castle equally as degraded as its lord, amused themselves while the bride was in the company of the lord by ridiculing and torturing the husband who in anxiety for his wife ventured too near the castle. The present nearly universal custom of a wedding journey must be referred in its origin to the same period, arising from an inherited tendency in the bride and groom to escape the jeers and ill treatment that in past ages invariably accompanied entrance into the married state.

In some European countries redemption was demanded from

all women, not alone the daughters of villeins and serfs, but also of those of noble birth who were freed by payment of a ransom in silver known as the "Maiden Rents." Lands were even held under Maiden Redemption.[46] In Scotland this ransom became known as "Marquette"; Margaret wife of Malcolm Canmore, generally spoken of for her goodness as Saint Margaret,[47] exercising her royal influence in 1057, against this degradation of her sex. Numberless seditions having arisen from this claim upon the bride the king more willingly established a release upon the payment of a piece of silver, a *demi-marc*, called marquette, (whence the name), and a certain number of cows. The piece of silver went to the king, the cows to the queen, and from that period cuissage was known as the droit de marquette. But this nefarious custom possessed such strength, appealing directly to man's basest passions, his love of power, his profligacy—the human beast within him—that it continued in existence nearly seven hundred years after the royal edict in Scotland against its practice.[48] This vile power extended over all ranks of women; the king holding it over the daughters of the grand seigneur, the suzurain over the daughters of his vassals; the seigneur over the daughters of his serfs, even the judge or ballie enforcing this right upon all women who passed upon his road.[49]

The Church has ever been the bulwark of this base claim. Holding the powers of penance and of excommunication, such custom could neither have originated nor been sustained without the sanction of the church.[50] At this date the privileges of the lower clergy were extraordinary. Even in England they were not amenable to the common law; they ruled the laity with iron hand, but the laity possessed no power over the priesthood.[51] All appointments were in priestly hands, the union of church and state complete.

God himself seemed to have forsaken woman, and the peasantry lost all belief in the justice of earth or heaven. The customs of feudalism which were akin to the customs of power wherever existing throughout Christendom did more to create what the church terms "infidelity" than all the reason of the philosophers. No human being is so degraded as not to possess an innate sense of justice; a wrong is as keenly felt by the most humble and ignorant as by the educated and refined, its effect more lasting because of the impossibility of redress. The power of the seigneur was nearly equal to that of the king himself. Manorial courts entirely local aided the seigneur in the enforcement of his traditional privileges[52] at the expense of the villeins. The crown possessed no jurisdiction over these courts. The lord held the right to make laws, render justice, lay imposts, declare war, coin money, dispose of the goods and lives of his subjects, and other prerogatives still more closely touching their personal rights, especially of the women living in his dominion.[53]

To persons not conversant with the history of feudalism and the church it will seem impossible that such foulness could ever have been part of Christian civilization. That the vices they have been taught to consider the outgrowth of paganism, and as the worst heathendom could have existed in Christian Europe upheld many hundred years by both church and state will strike most people with incredulity. Such however is the truth; we are compelled to admit well attested facts of history, however severe a blow they strike our preconceived beliefs.

The seigneural tenure of the feudal period was a law of Christian Europe more dishonorable than the worship of Astarte at Babylon.[54] In order to fully comprehend the vileness of marquette, we must remember that it did not originate in a pagan country, many thousand years since; that it was not a heathen custom transplanted to Europe with many others adopted by the church,[55] but that it arose in christian countries a thousand years after the origin of that religion, continuing in existence until within the last century.

The attempt made by some modern authors to deny that the claim of the feudal lord to the person of his female serf upon her marriage ever existed, on the ground that statutes sustaining such a right have not been discovered, is extremely weak.[56] The authority of custom or "unwritten law" is still almost absolute. A second objection that such customs are unchristian has been answered. The third plea in opposition, namely that those so outraged, so oppressed, left no record of resistance is false. Aside from the fact that education was everywhere limited, no peasant and but few of the nobility knowing how to read or write, and within the church learning very rare, we have indisputable evidence of strong character in the revolt of serfs at different periods, through which concessions were gained; the final refusal of the serfs to marry, and in the travesty upon religion known as the "Black Mass."

We can not measure the serf's power of resistance by the same standard as our own. The degradation of man with but a few exceptions was as great as that of woman. Civilly and educationally the peasant man was on a par with the peasant woman. No more than she had he a voice in making the laws; the serf was virtually a slave under the absolute dominion of his lord. No power existed for him higher than that of his feudal superior. It is nearly impossible to realize the hopeless degraded condition of the peasant serf of the middle ages. It has had no parallel in the present century, except in the slavery of the southern states. Free action, free speech, free thought was impossible. But our respect for humanity is increased when we know that these vassals, although under the life and death power of their lords, did not tamely submit to the indignities enforced upon their wives and daughters.

It must also be remembered that the historians of that period were generally priests by whom the fact of such usage or custom would pass unmentioned, especially as the church taught that woman was created to meet the special demands of man. Other important historical facts have been as lightly touched upon, or passed over entirely. The deification of Julius Cæsar while Emperor of Rome, is scarcely referred to in the more familiar literary sources of Roman history. And yet his worship was almost universal in the provinces, where he was adored as a god. The records of this worship are only to be found in scattered monuments and inscriptions but recently brought to light, and deciphered within the last few years. Through these it is proven that there was an organized worship of this emperor, and an order of consecrated priests devoted to him.[57] Higgins refers to this deification of Cæsar.[58] It is not alone proof of the low condition of morality at this period, but also of the universal disbelief in woman's authority over, or right to herself, that so few writers upon feudal subjects have treated of the libidinous powers of the lord over his female serfs. Even those presenting the evils of feudalism in other respects, have merely expressed a mild surprise that Christian people should have admitted that right of the lord over his feminine vassals. The various names under which this right was known as jus primæ noctis,[59] droit de seigneur,[60] droit de jambage,[61] droit de cuissage,[62] droit d'afforage,[63] droit de marquette,[64] and many other terms too indelicate for repetition, indicating this right of the lord over all the women in his domain, is still another incontestable proof of the universality of the custom.

The Mosaic teaching as to sacredness of "first fruits," under Judaism, dedicated to the Lord of Heaven, doubtless was in part the origin of the claim of the feudal lord. The law of primogeniture, or precedence of the first born son as the beginning of "his father's strength" is also a translation from Judaism into the customs of many nations, but nowhere under the law of primogeniture at the present day does even a first born daughter receive as high consideration as a first born son. This is especially noticeable in royal families. It is not therefore singular that men who took the literal sense of the bible in science, who believed that the world had been created in six days, this work having so greatly fatigued the Lord Almighty as to make rest on the seventh day necessary for him, should under example of that lord, claim the first fruits in all their possessions. No Christians of the present day, except the Mormons, so fully base their lives upon the teachings of the bible as the Catholics of the middle ages. If we accord divine authority to this book, accepting the literal word as infallible and sacred, we must admit that both Church and State were at this period in unison with its teachings, and even during the nineteenth century have not freed themselves from the stigma of sustaining woman's degradation; the theory of the feudal ages remains the same, although the practice is somewhat different. Legal bigamy or polygamy, nonmarital unions, are common in every large city of christendom. Government license has created a class in many European countries devoted to the most degraded lives under government sanction, protection, and control; in England known as "Queen's Women," "Government Women." Thus the State places itself before the world as a trafficer in women's bodies for the vilest purposes. The culmination of nearly two thousand years of christian teaching is the legalization of vice for women and the creation of a new crime. Previous to the enactment of this law the rules of modern jurisprudence held an accused person as innocent until proven guilty. Under this legalization of vice all women within a certain radius of recruiting, or other army stations, are "suspects," looked upon as immoral, and liable to arrest, examination, and registration upon government books as government women. It required seventeen years of arduous work to repeal this law in England. This legalization of prostitution in the nineteenth century by the State is its open approval of that doctrine of the Church that woman was created for man. It is an acknowledgment by men that vice is an inherent quality of their natures. It is in accord with man's repeated assertion that only through means of a class of women pursuing immorality as a business, is any woman safe from violence.

In a letter to the National Woman Suffrage Convention at St. Louis, May, 1879, Mrs. Josephine E. Butler, Honorable Secretary of the Federation and of the Ladies National Association for the Protection of Women, wrote:

> England holds a peculiar position in regard to the question. She was the last to adopt this system of slavery, and she adopted it in that thorough manner which characterizes the actions of the Anglo-Saxon race. In no other country has prostitution been registered by law. It has been understood by the Latin race, even when morally enervated, that the law could not without risk of losing its majesty and force sanction illegality and violate justice. In England alone the regulations are law.
>
> This legalization of vice, which is the endorsement of the "necessity" of impurity of man and the institution of the slavery of woman, is the most open denial which modern times have seen of the principle of the sacredness of the indi-

vidual human being. An English high-class journal dared to demand that women who are unchaste shall henceforth be dealt with "not as human beings, but as foul sewers," or some such "material nuisance" without souls, without rights, and without responsibility. When the leaders of public opinion in a country have arrived at such a point of combined skepticism and despotism as to recommend such a manner of dealing with human beings, there is no crime which that country may not presently legalize, there is no organization of murder, no conspiracy of abominable things that it may not, and in due time will not have been found to embrace in its guilty methods. Were it possible to secure the absolute physical health of a whole province or an entire continent by the destruction of one, only one poor and sinful woman, woe to that nation which should dare, by that single act of destruction, to purchase this advantage to the many! It will do it at its peril. God will take account of the deed not in eternity only, but in time, it may be in the next or even in the present generation.

Although a long and active work through seventeen years eventually brought about the repeal of this law in England, it still continues in the British colonies, being forced upon the people in opposition to their own action. After the Cape Parliament of the Colony of Good Hope, had repealed the law, Sir Bartle Frere reintroduced it by means of an edict.[65] When in London, 1882, Sir John Pope Hennessey, Govenor and Commander in Chief of British China, was waited upon by an influential deputation of members of parliament and others to whom he made known the practical workings of govermental regulation of prostitution introduced by England into that colony. He did not hesitate to characterize it as a system of slavery for the registered women and girls. He also declared that they detested the life they are thus compelled to enter having both a dread and an abhorrence of foreigners, especially foreign sailors and soldiers. He said such Chinese girls are the real slaves of Hong Kong.

Now to that statement I adhere. I give it to you on the full authority of the Governor of the colony. I have been five years

looking at the operation of this law in Hong Kong, and that is
the result to which I have arrived that, under the flag of England there is slavery there, but it is slavery created and protected
by these ordinances.

The relation of Christianity to this treatment of Chinese
women, and the contempt with which this religion is regarded by
these heathen, is most fully shown by Sir John's conversation with
the leading Chinese merchant of Canton, as given by himself, upon
the material progress of the colony. To this merchant Sir Pope said:
"Your people are making a large fortune here. Why not send down
your second son to enter the house of the Chinese merchant and
learn the business there?" The merchant replied, "I can not for this
reason; Hong Kong is a sink of iniquity." Sir Pope Hennessey
answered. "This is a Christian colony; we have been here now for
forty years, we are supposed to be doing the best we can to spread
civilization and christianity." The Chinaman repeated: "It is a sink
of iniquity in my mind. As Chinamen we think of domestic and
family life—we reverence such things—but how do I see the poor
Chinese treated in this colony?" And he related stories of the abuses
to which his country women were subjected.

In repeating this conversation to Her Majesty's government,
Sir Pope Hennessey declared the words that the merchant of
Canton who called Hong Kong a "sink of iniquity" have a wide
application, because the British colony at Hong Kong, is geo-
graphically a part of a great Empire, an empire where you have
missionaries of various churches. I have been asked to explain the
curious and distressing fact that christianity is declining in China.
I think it is declining mainly on account of the treaties we have
forced upon the Chinese; but I will frankly tell you, it is declining
also because they see these girls registered in such houses for
"Europeans" and made practically slaves under our flag.[66]

Nor are the Cape of Good Hope, and China, the sole foreign
countries in which this system of the legalized moral degradation
of women has been carried by England, nearly one hundred
places in India showing the same vice under license from the

British Government, even to bearing the same name.[67] Nor have innumberable petitions and protests from native and foreign ladies, from zenana workers, from missionaries, and even from all ranks of the resident English civil service for immediate repeal of this vilest of all laws, been of the least effect. So thoroughly imbued are English legislators with contempt for womanhood, as not only to maintain these outrageous laws but also to cause fear in the minds of those women who for twenty years wrought for the repeal of these acts in Great Britain and Ireland, of their again being introduced under more insidious and dangerous form.[68] A memorial signed by a number of native born and English ladies was presented to the Viceroy praying that the age of protection for young girls be raised. While in India a man's dog, horse, elephant, and even the plants of his garden are under the protection of English law, his daughter of ten years is outside this protection.[69] The penal code punishes with imprisonment or a fine, or both, the man who injures an animal valued at ten rupees; if the animal be worth fifty rupees his imprisonment may be for five years, while for dishonestly coaxing his neighbor's dog to follow him, the punishment is three years imprisonment, or a fine or both; while the man who induces "consent" from a girl-child of ten years escapes all punishment.

In deference to the bitter opposition these acts created, it was declared that legalized prostitution was abolished in British India, June 5th, 1888. A statement was made in the House of Commons that the contagious disease acts had been suspended in Bombay. But an investigation of these statements by the English Social Purity Society, proved them false, the *Sentinel*, its organ, stating, June 1890, that upon inquiry it was found that the licensing of prostitution systematically prevails in British India, and is always attended with results most disastrous to health of body as well as morals of the community. The most extraordinary course is taken towards the accomplishment of their ends, by the advocates of legalizing vice. In 1888 having failed to secure an act of the legislature of the state of New York, in its favor, a society to this end was formed in the city of New York, incorporated as a "Voluntary Association"; borrowing the name used in England at time its women were most degraded by the state.[70] This society grants certificates to women presenting themselves for examination. And thus step by step under many forms more extended than even under feudal law, is woman's moral degradation made the effort of the Christian civilization of today.

The "ten thousand licensed women of the town" of the City of Hamburg, are required by the State to show certificates that they regularly attended Church, and also partake of the sacrament. And even in Protestant Berlin, the capital of Protestant Prussia, the Church upon demand of the State furnishes certificates of their having partaken of holy communion to those women securing license to lead vicious lives; the very symbol and body of him, whom the Christian world worships as its saviour, thus becoming the key to unlock the doors of woman's moral degradation.[71]

The fact of governments lending their official aid to demoralization of woman by the registration system, shows an utter debasement of law. This system is directly opposed to the fundamental principle of right, that of holding of the accused innocent until proven guilty, which until now has been recognized as a part of modern law. Under the registration or license system, all women within the radius of its action are under suspicion; all women are held as morally guilty until they prove themselves innocent. Where this law is in force, all women are under an irresponsible police surveillance, liable to accusation, arrest, examination, imprisonment, and the entrance of their names upon the list of the lewd women of the town. Upon this frightful infraction of justice, we have the sentiments of the late Sheldon Amos, when Professor of Jurisprudence in the Law College of London University. In *The Science of Law*, he says, in reference to this very wrong:

> The loss of liberty to the extent to which it exists, implies a degradation of the State, and, if persisted in, can only lead to its dissolution. No person or class of persons must be under the the cringing fear of having imputed to them offenses of which they are innocent, and of being taken into custody in conse-

quence of such imputation. They must not be liable to be detained in custody without so much as a *prima facie* case being made out, such as in the opinion of a responsible judicial officer leaves a presumption of guilt. They must not be liable to be detained for an indefinite time without having the question of their guilt or innocence investigated by the best attainable methods. When the fact comes to be inquired into, the best attainable methods of eliciting the truth must be used. In default of any one of these securities, *public liberty* must be said to be proportionately at a very low ebb.

Great effort has been made to introduce this system into the United States, and a National Board of Health, created by Congress in 1879, is carefully watched lest its irresponsible powers lead to its encroachment upon the liberties and personal rights of women. A resolution adopted March 5, 1881, at a meeting of the New York committee appointed to thwart the effort to license vice in this country, shows the need of its watchful care.

> *Resolved*, That this committee has learned with much regret and apprehension of the action of the American Public Health Association, at its late annual meeting in New Orleans, in adopting a sensational report commending European governmental regulation of prostitution, and looking to the introduction in this country, with modifications, through the medium of State legislative enactments and municipal ordinances, of a kindred immoral system of State-regulated social vice.

Even the Latin races in their lowest degradation did not put the sanction of law upon the open sale of women to vice, says Mrs. Butler. This remained for the Anglo-Saxon and Teutonic races, under the highest christian civilization in a class of women licensed by the State, under protection and name of the head of the Anglican Church, as "Queen's Women," "Government Women," both Church and State here uniting in the nefarious business of making women, by law, the slaves of man's lowest nature. A system which openly declares "the necessity" for woman's foulest degradation, in order to protect man in his departure from the moral law, a system that annually sends its tens of thousands down to a death from which christian society grants no resurrection. Similar religious beliefs beget similar results. Times change, and with them methods, but as long as the foundation of the christian church of every name, rests upon the belief in woman's created inferiority to man, and that she brought sin into the world, so long will similar social, industrial, and moral results follow. The Catholic, Greek, and Protestant divisions, all degrade women but under different forms. That the women of every christian land fears to meet man in a secluded place by day or by night, is of itself sufficient proof of the low state of christian morality. Several states have at different times attempted the enactment of similar laws through bills introduced into their legislatures; requiring constant watchfulness on part of the friends of social purity lest this great wrong be consummated, a wrong primarily against woman. In certain cities, as St. Louis, where such registration and license was for sometime demanded, the foulest injuries were perpetrated upon entirely innocent and reputable women, injuries for which they had no redress.[72] Under the legalized vice system, woman are slaves, not possessing even the right of repudiating this kind of life.

A gentleman traveling in France, 1866, relates a most pathetic instance of the attempted escape and the forcible return to the house of infamy, of a young girl whose person there, was at the command of every brute who chose to pay the price of her master. The tram car in which this gentleman was riding, crowded with ladies and girls of refined appearance, was suddenly stopped on one of the principal streets of Havre, by a dense crowd swaying back and forth across the track. He said:

> I then became aware that two men, tall powerful fellows, were carrying or rather trying to carry, a young woman seemingly between sixteen and eighteen years of age, who occupied herself in violently clutching at everything and anything from a lamppost to a shop door handle, a railing, and the pavement itself.

As a matter of course, her body swayed between the two men, half dragging on the pavement, her clothing besmeared with mud and blood. For the rough handling had superadded crimson to other stains. This proved the case to be not one of accident, although the screams, shrieks and cries of the poor girl might well have led to the belief of her having been the victim of a run over, and of being in convulsions of acute agony. Her agonizing cries for "pity," "police," "protection," "help," "murder," "Oh! oh! oh!" were reiterated incessantly. At one particular moment her contortions, and the violence of her efforts to free herself, or even to bring her head into a more convenient position than hanging face downward, while a yard or so of long, bedraggled hair, all loose, was sweeping up the dirt from the pavement, were so violent that her two carriers had to let her slip from their grasp onto the flagstones.

All this time, unmoved by, and totally indifferent to her piercing cries, stood by, or strolled calmly onward with the crowd, a policeman in uniform and on duty. My enquiry of, "What is all this piece of work about? Is it an accident? Is the woman drunk, or what?" He smilingly answered: "Oh! not drunk, sir, not at all, not at all. It's only one of those young licensed girls, who has been trying to escape from her house, and that's her master, who has just caught her again, and is carrying her back to his place. That's all!"

"I was powerless to help." In many christian countries a traffic in girls exists under government protection and license.

Criminal vice chiefly finds its feminine prey among the poorest and most helpless class who are the victims of this new commercial business, its customers scattered in every christian land, and accepting their spoil only upon the certificate of some reputable physician as to their innocence and previous uncontamination. Crime, vice, and cruelty, were never before so closely united in one infamous system; the purchase of young innocence by old iniquity under protection of law.[73] A bill was introduced into the English parliament to check this business of girl destruction, accompanied by proof so direct, and proof of the necessity of immediate action so great, that it was not doubted that the bill would pass at once. Yet it encountered secret[74] and powerful opposition, was finally referred to a committee already so overburdened with work and so far behindhand that it was manifest that the bill could not be reached in years. Gilded vice laughed at this result, and the iniquitous business proceeded as before. At that period the *Pall Mall Gazette* entered into an investigation whose results roused the whole civilized world. Even clergymen, ignoring the fact that christian teaching had brought this vice into being, joined the press in scathing reproof of patrician London iniquity[75] Societies were formed for the protection of young girls from the vice of men who used the power of wealth and station to corrupt the daughters of the poor.[76]

Under English christian law it has never been a crime to morally destroy a girl of thirteen, because under that law she is held responsible for her own undoing. Girls of this tender age, infants, in all that pertains to the control of property, incapable of making a legal contract, because of immaturity of understanding, are yet held by that law as of age to protect themselves from a seducer; held to possess sufficient judgment to thwart all the wiles of men old in years and crime—of men protected in their iniquities by laws of their own making—men shielded by the legislation of their own sex—men who escape all punishment because men alone enact the laws. It is not alone the waifs of society who fall a prey to the seducer, but the children of reputable parents and good homes are waylaid on their way to and from school and lured to ruin.[77] To the modern ghoul it is of no moment upon whom he preys, provided his victim be but young and innocent. Lecky has portrayed the standard of morals of the present day as far higher than in pagan Rome, but we must be allowed to doubt this. Immoral sentiment is more deftly hidden, and law more dependent upon public opinion. As soon as the general consensus of public opinion rises in opposition to girl destruction, the law will regulate itself in accordance with this standard.

Lord Shaftsbury, upon this point, said:

> The *Pall Mall Gazette* has published to the world disclosures of a most horrible, and many would think of an incredible char-

acter. Not even the questionings of peace or war or most intricate foreign policy, ought to interfere with energetic measures to suppress these evils. But before we can make any great advance, there must be a considerable move of public opinion. It must be vigorous and determined, and I will tell you why. You may depend upon it that no government undertakes a question of a really important and social character until it has been forced upon it by the voice of public opinion. Consequently it is our duty to bring the voice of that public opinion to bear on this question. Law can be evaded in every possible way. The only thing that defies evasion is a wide spread and universally extended public opinion. I hope that we shall be able to create such a public opinion throughout the country that persons will be induced to come forward voluntarily and give evidence. The plague spot is too deep, too wide, and there are too many persons interested in the continuance of it, to enable us easily to wipe it out. Uncommon energy will be necessary, and I hope we shall raise such an amount of popular indignation that the effect will be irresistible.

But the public feeling, the public indignation against these enormities did not rise to the height of restrictive legislation. The policy of a portion both of the English and the American press was that of suppression, upon the plea that a knowledge of these crimes would be injurious to the morals of society. Suppression was also the aim of the "royal princes, dukes, nobles, and leading men," who were the principal patrons and supporters of this nefarious system. Suppression is the strongest opposing weapon against reform. To compel change needs light and discussion. "It is only when wrongs find a tongue that they become righted." Woman, legally powerless in the doing away with abuses, or the punishment of crime, must depend upon publicity for the creation of a public sentiment in her favor.

One of the most remarkable facts connected with disclosures of this crime against womankind was the extent to which men of all ages and character were found identified with it. The world of business and that of politics were equally as well known in the haunts of vice as in the outside world, but there were judged by a different standard and their relative importance was altogether changed.[78] It was a literal day of judgment, in which evil character, deftly hidden during public life, was there unveiled.

The most horribly striking fact connected with this investigation was the extreme youth of these victims. The report of the committee of the House of Lords, 1882, declared the evidence proved beyond doubt that juvenile vice from an almost incredibly early age was increasing at an appalling extent in England, and especially in London; ten thousand girls, thirteen, fourteen, and fifteen years of age, had been drawn into this vice, an English paper declaring the ignorance of these girls to be almost incredible. The condition of these girl-children is far more horrible than that of the victims of infant marriage in Syria, Egypt, India; the infant victims of christian lands are more fully destroyed, soon becoming mental, physical and moral wrecks; alternate imbecility and wild screaming being common among these child victims of vice.[79]

Christianity created the modern brothel, which as closely follows in the wake of evangelical work of the Moody and Sanky style, as did public women the ancient church councils.[80] While in the past the legal wrongs of woman in the marriage relation, in which she is robbed of name, personality, earnings, children, had a tendency to drive her to live with man outside of the authority of church or state, the occupations recently opened to her whereby she can gain a reputable livelihood by her own exertions, has greatly increased the ranks of single women.[81] No longer compelled to marry for a home or position, the number of young girls who voluntarily refrain from marriage, by choice living single, increases each year. No longer driven to immorality for bread, a great diminution has taken place in the ranks of "public women."[82] No longer forced by want into this life, the lessening number of such women not meeting the requirements of patrons of vice, resulted in the organization of a regular system for the abduction, imprisonment, sale, and exportation of young girls; England and Germany most largely controlling this business, although Belgium, Holland and France, Switzerland, several countries of South America, Canada, and the United States are to some extent also engaged in this most infamous traffic.[83]

Foreign traffic in young English girls was known to exist long before the revelation of the *Pall Mall Gazette* made English people aware of the extent of the same system under the home government. It was this widely extended and thoroughly organized commerce in girl-children which roused a few people to earnest effort against it, and secured the formation of a society called "Prevention of Traffic in English Girls." To the chairman of this society, Mr. Benjamin Scott, was the first official suggestion due that terminated in that investigation by Editor Stead, which for a moment shook the civilized world, and held christian England to light as a center of the vilest, most odious, most criminal slave traffic the world ever knew.

London, the great metropolis of christian England, the largest city of ancient or modern times, is acknowledged by statisticians and sociologists to be the point where crime, vice, despair, and misery are found in their deepest depth and greatest diversity. Not Babylon of old, whose name is the synonym of all that is vile; not Rome, "Mother of Harlots," not Corinth, in whose temple a thousand women were kept for prostitution in service of the god, not the most savage lands in all their barbarity have ever shown a thousandth part of the human woe to be found in the city of London, that culmination of modern christian civilization. The nameless crimes of Sodom and Gomorrah, the vileness of ancient Greece, which garnered its most heroic men, its most profound philosophers, are but amusements among young men of the highest rank in England; West End, the home of rank and wealth, of university education, being the central hell of this extended radius of vice. The destruction of girl-children by old men is paralleled by the self-destruction of boys and youth through vices that society hesitates to name. Yet each is the result of that system of teaching which declares woman a being divinely created for the use and sensual gratification of man.

Having for years tacitly consented to the destruction of the girl-children of its poor, at the rate of twenty thousand annually,

England was yet greatly shocked to find its boys of tender age and aristocratic lineage sunken in a mire of immorality. Eton, the highest institution of its kind in Great Britain, having in charge the education of boys connected with the most illustrious English families, recently became the source of a scandal which involved a great number of students. An extensive secret inquiry resulted in the suspension of nearly three hundred boys after full confession. Supplied with unlimited pocket money, they had bribed parkkeepers and the police to silence.

But a few years previous to these disclosures in reference to Eton, the civilized world was horrified at the discovery of the vice which destroyed Sodom, among some of the most wealthy, aristocratic young men of London. And yet with knowledge of the depravity into which this most christian city had sunk, the shocking character of the disclosures of the *Pall Mall Gazette* in reference to the traffic in young girls, involved details of vice so atrocious as to exceed belief had not the testimony been of the most convincing character. These mere children were lured by the most diabolical vices into traps, where by drugs, force, or cajoling, tens of thousands were brought to moral and physical ruin, innocent victims of a religious theory which through the christian ages has trained men into a belief that woman was but created as a plaything for their passions. That boys of the highest families, in the earliest years of their adolescence, should voluntarily associate with those vicious women who form a class created by the public sentiment of man as necessary to the safety of the feminine element in households, is not surprising to a philosophic observer. It was the direct result of an adequate cause. The wrong to woman passed so silently by, reached its culmination in the destruction of young boys. At Eton, suspension was tenderness, expulsion from that school ruining a boy's future.

Succeeding the revelation of London vice, came divulgence of similar shameless practices on the part of high government officials and men foremost in public life, in the Canadian Colonies. In Ottawa and other Canadian cities in which upon this side of the Atlantic the wholesale despolation of young girls but too closely paralleled London and other trans-Atlantic cities. These were closely followed by the revelations in regard to the north-western pineries of the United States, to whose camps women are decoyed, under pretense of good situations and high wages into a life whose horrors are not equaled in any other part of the christian world;—where the rawhide is used to compel drinking and dancing, and high stockades, bulldogs and pistols prevent escape, until death,—happily of quick occurence,— releases the victim. As elsewhere, men of wealth and high position, law-makers, are identified with this infamy.[84]

Among the notable facts due to an investigation of prostitution is that its support largely comes from married men, the "heads of families"; men of mature years, fathers of sons and daughters. To those seemingly least exposed to temptation is the sustaining of this vice due. Men of influence and position no less in this country than in England frequent disreputable houses. In 1878, the body of a woman buried in the principal cemetery of Syracuse, N. Y. was exhumed on suspicion of poison. One of the prominent city dailies said, "she commenced leading an abandoned life and went to Saratoga where she ran a large establishment of that character. Her place was the center for men of influence and position." A few years since the Rev. T. DeWitt Talmage accompanied by high police officials investigated such houses in person. In a sermon based upon knowledge there obtained Mr. Talmage declared those dens of infamy to be supported by married men, chiefly of the better classes.

> He found them to be judges of courts, distinguished lawyers, officers in churches, political orators that talk on the Republican, Democratic and Greenback platforms about God and good morals till you might almost take them for evangelists expecting a thousand converts in one night. On the night of our exploration I saw their carriages leaving these dignitaries at the shambles of death. Call the roll in the house of dissipation, and if the inmates will answer you will find stock-brokers from Wall street, large importers on Broadway, iron merchants, leather merchants, wholesale grocers and representatives from all the wealthy classes.

But I have something to tell you more astonishing than that the houses of iniquity are supported by wealthy people when I tell you that they are supported by the heads of families—fathers and husbands, with the awful perjury upon them of broken marriage vows; and while many of them keep their families on niggardly portions, with hardly enough to sustain life, have their thousands for the diamonds and the wardrobe and equipage of iniquity. In the name of high heaven I cry out against this popular iniquity. Such men must be cast out from social life and from business relations. If they will not reform, overboard with them from all decent circles. I lift one-half the burden of malediction from the tin-pitied head of woman and hurl it upon the blasted pate of offending man. What society wants is a new division of its anathema.

Without the support of the heads of families, in one month the most of the haunts of sin in New York, Philadelphia and Boston, would crumble into ruin.

That one-half of the children born into the world die before maturity, is acknowledged. Physiologists and philanthropists seek for the cause except where most likely to be found. To that mysterious interchange of germs and life principles, whose chemistry is still not understood, must we look for aid in solving this great problem. These questions woman is forced to consider; their investigation belong to her by right, as she and her children are the chief victims. She can no longer close her lips in silence, saying it does not concern me. No longer does the modern woman allow her husband to think for her; she is breaking from church bonds, from the laws of men alone, from all the restrictions the state has pressed upon her; she is no longer looking without, for guidance, but is heeding the commands of her own soul.

With such facts before us, we are not surprised that women are found who prefer the freedom and private respect accorded to a mistress, rather than the restrictions and tyranny of the marital household. Mr. Talmage but followed in the footsteps of Anna Dickinson, who took upon herself an acquaintance with this class of women. Asking one women living as mistress why she did not marry, the girl contemptuously ejaculated:

Marry; umph! I too well know what my mother suffered in the married state. She was my father's slave, cruelly treated, subject to all manner of abuse, neglected, half-starved, all her appeals and protests unheeded. How is it with me? I am free. I have all the money I want to use, a thing my mother never had. I come and go as I please, something my mother could never do, I am well treated, my mother was not. Should I be abused there is no law to hold me, no court to sit upon my right to my own child as there was with my mother. No, no, no, I am infinitely better off as a mistress than as a wife.

And yet so pronounced in difference are the moral codes by which men and women are judged, that while living together in unlegalized marital relations, the man is welcomed into society, is looked upon as fit for marriage with the most innocent young girl, while should he partially condone the wrong done the woman whose life under present condition of society he has ruined, by marriage with her, society for this one reputable act brands him as most unworthy. It is but a few years since a cavalry officer in Washington was court-marshalled, found guilty and sentenced to dismissal from the army on charge of conduct unbecoming an officer and a gentleman, because of his legally marrying a woman with whom he had been living unmarried. What a commentary upon christian civilization! While living in illicit relation with this woman, he was regarded as an officer and a gentleman; when taking upon himself a legal relation he was court-marshalled. Lecky says: "Much of our own feeling on this subject is due to laws and moral systems which were founded by men and were in the first instance deigned for their own protection." As far as he has examined this question, Lecky is correct, but he has failed to touch the primal cause of such laws and systems;—the church doctrine of woman's created inferiority to man. View these questions from any standpoint the cause remains the same. To this cause we trace the crime and criminals of society today. To this cause the darkness of an age which has not yet realized that civilization means a recognition of the rights of others at every point of contact.

To the honor of the pulpit the sins of men are occasionally made the subject of condemnation. Evangelist Davidson preaching in Syracuse, N. Y. 1887, said:

> I pray God to haste the day when vice in man will be marked by society the same as in woman. I know all the popular theories. You admit it is a fearful thing for a woman. There are poor women who are driven to it and you are the ones who drive them. You smile at the one thing in this sermon that ought to make a thinking man cry; the world is so depraved that it you laugh at the very idea of a man's saying he is a pure man.

Like Lecky, Mr. Davidson was correct as far as he went, but he, too, failed to reach the cause of this double code of morals. He did not touch it because in striking that, he would strike a blow at the very foundations of the church.

Christendom is percolated with immorality, large cities and small towns alike giving daily proof. Legislative and police investigations substantiate this statement; woman's protective agencies and private investigations alike proclaim the same fact. As under the same organic teachings results must continue the same, we find the United States no more free from immorality than European lands; Catholic countries no more vile than Protestant; although feudal law no longer exists, men still rule in church and state. Men's beliefs, their desires, their passions, create the laws under which the degradation of woman still continues. Evil consequences are not confined to the past, to days of comparative ignorance and tyranny; and in no country has the effects of belief in woman as a mere instrument for man's pleasure produced more horrible results than in our own. Not to speak of the effort made in Congress[85] a few years since to place all women of the country under suspect law, many cities, among them Washington, Philadelphia, Syracuse, have at different periods taken initial steps towards a prohibition of a woman's appearing in the street unaccompanied by male escort, during the evening, even its earliest hours. Such ordinances, primarily directed against working girls whose chief time for out-of-door exercise and recreation is during evening hours, and to that other rapidly increasing class of business women, physicans and others, whose vocation calls them out at all hours of day or night; places the liberty of woman at the option of every policeman, as though she were a criminal or a slave.[86] There is also proof of regularly organized kidnapping schemes and deportation of girls for the vilest purposes not only abroad, but to the pineries and lumber camps of Michigan and Wisconsin.

Bloodhounds kept for this purpose, or hunting down the girls with shotguns, prevents escape when attempted. In January, 1887, representative Breen appeared before the House Judiciary Committee of the Michigan legislature, confirming the charge that a regular trade in young girls existed between Milwaukee, Chicago and the mining regions of the upper peninsula of that state.[87] In case of conviction, the punishment is totally inadequate to the crime of those men; the law giving only one year of imprisonment. The freedom, innocence and lives of such women are of less account in law than the commonest larceny of property. If these girls were robbed of fifty cents the law would punish the theft, but robbed of themselves, enduring such brutal outrages that life continues only from two to twelve months, there have yet no laws of adequate punishment been passed. So little attention have legislators given, that policemen, judges and sheriffs are found aiding and abetting the proprietors of these dens.[88] Their emissaries find young girls between thirteen and sixteen the easiest to kidnap, and when once in power of these men, their hair is cut in order that they may be known. A regular system of transfer of the girls exists between the many hundred such dens, where clubs, whips, and irons are the instruments to hold them in subjection.[89] The *New York World* sent a representative disguised as a woodman in order to investigate the truth of these statements. He found these houses surrounded by stockades thirty feet in height, the one door guarded night and day by a man with a rifle, while within were a number of chained bulldogs that were let loose if a girl attempted escape. Certain men even in these forest depths are especially noted for their cruelty to these victims, who are compelled with club and whips to obey the master of the den. Suicide the only door of escape is frequent among these girls, who almost without exception were secured under promise of respectable employment at Green Bay, Duluth, or other points. From forty to seventy-five girls are found at the largest of such pinery dens.

The *World* reporter saw them strung up by the thumbs, beaten with clubs, kicked by drunken brutes and driven with switches over the snow. He afterwards interviewed a rescued girl who had engaged to work in a lumberman's hotel, supposing it to be a respectable place, but instead she was taken to a rough building, surrounded by a slab fence nearly twenty feet in height, within which was a cordon of thirteen bulldogs chained to iron stakes driven in the ground. Many of the details given by this girl are too horrible for relation. Three times she tried to escape and three times she was caught and beaten. The visitors by whom she tried to smuggle notes to the outer world would hand them to the proprietor, who liberally paid for such treason. Even county officers visited the place to drink and dance with the girls, who were not permitted to refuse any request of the visitors. A complaint of any kind, even of sickness, meant a whipping, frequently with a rawhide upon the naked body; some times with the butt of a revolver. Many denkeepers wield a powerful influence in the local elections; one of the worst of such after paying the constable twelve dollars for the return of a girl who had tried to escape, beat her with a revolver until tired and was then only prevented by a woodman from turning loose a bulldog upon her; but such was his political influence that he was elected justice of the peace the following spring.

Under the head of "White Slaves in Michigan" the *New York World* of January 24, 1887, published a special dispatch from Detroit, Mich., in regard to the case of a rescued girl.

Detroit, Jan. 23.—One of the infamous resorts maintained in the new iron region in the upper peninsulas, near the Wisconsin state line, was raided last September by the Sheriff's officers. Hers is the first word to reach the world direct from one of those dens. Many of the details she gave were too horrible to be even hinted. On the strength of inducements now familiar, she went to work in a lumberman's hotel in the North. She went, accompanied by another girl, both believing the situation to be respectable. She and her companion were taken to a rough two-story building, four-and-a-half miles from Iron Mountain, in Wisconsin. The house was surrounded by a slab fence nearly twenty feet high, within which about the building was a cordon of bulldogs, thirteen in number, chained to iron stakes driven into the ground. She said, "Scarcely a day passed that I was not knocked down and kicked. Several times when I was undressed for bed I was beaten with a rawhide on my bare back. There were always from eleven to thirty-two girls in the house and I did not fare a bit worse than the rest. A complaint of any kind, even of sickness, meant a whipping every time. When the log drives were going on there would be hundreds of men there night and day. They were not human beings, but fiends, and we were not allowed to refuse any request of them. Oh, it was awful, awful! I would rather stay in this prison until I die than to go back there for one day. I tried to escape three times and was caught. They unchained the dogs and let them get so near me that I cried out in terror and begged them to take the dogs away and I would go back. Then, of course, I was beaten. I tried, too, to smuggle out notes to the Sheriff by visitors, but they would take them to the proprietor instead and he would pay them. Once I did get a note to the deputy sheriff at Florence, Wis., and he came and inquired, but the proprietor gave him $50 and he went away. I was awfully beaten then. While I lived the life, from March until September, two inmates died, both from brutal treatment. They were as good as murdered. Nearly all the girls came without knowing the character of the house at first implored to get away. The county officers came to the places to drink and dance with the girls. They are controlled by a rich man in Iron Mountain, who owns the houses and rents them for $100 a month. I am twenty-four years old and was a healthy woman when I went into the first house, weighing 156 pounds. I was transferred to the house from which I was released by the officers in August last. When I left it I weighed 120. I now weigh

less. When I go home I will be a good woman, if I can only let
liquor alone. I was forced to drink that while there."

The traffic in girls from one part of the American continent
to another is under a well-organized plan that seldom meets discovery, although a trader of this character is now serving a sentence in Sing Sing prison, N.Y., for sending girls to Panama.
Three decoyed young girls found in Jamaica, were happily
returned uninjured, to their parents.[90] From Canada, girls are
imported to the large cities of the United States. The prices paid
to agents depend upon a girl's youth and beauty, varying from $20
to $200 each.[91] The traffic at Ottawa resembled that of London
in that prominent citizens, leading politicians, and members of
the government were implicated.[92]

The number of women and girls constantly reported
"missing" is startling in its great extent. Stepping out on some
household errand for a moment they vanish as though swallowed
by the earth. A few years ago the *Chicago Herald* sent one of its
reporters into the pineries of Wisconsin, to trace a little girl living
on State Street of that city who went one evening to get a pitcher
of milk and did not return. Not a month, scarcely a week passes,
that the disappearance of some woman, girl, or child, is not
chronicled through the press, besides the infinitely greater numbers of whom the world never hears. As it was abroad, so in our
own country, no energetic steps are taken to put an end to these
foul wrongs. Woman herself is needed in the seats of justice;
woman must become a responsible factor in government in order
to the enactment of laws which shall protect her own sex. The
spring of 1892, the *Chicago Herald* called attention to the continuance of this condition of things.

Marinette, Wis., April 17.—Four years ago when "The Herald"
exposed the pinery dens of Wisconsin, Marinette was known
as the wickedest city in the country. It was the rendezvous of
every species of bad men. Thugs, thieves and gamblers practically held possession of the town. Their influence was felt in all
municipal affairs. Certain officers of the law seemed in active

sympathy with them, and it was almost impossible to secure the arrest and conviction of men guilty of infamous crimes. Dives of the vilest character ran open on the outskirts of the town. Their inmates, recruited from all parts of the country by the subtle arts of well-known procurers, were kept in a state of abject slavery. Iron balls and chains, suffocating cords and the whistling lash were used on refractory girls and women. The dens were surrounded by stockades, and savage dogs were kept unmuzzled to scare those who might try to escape. Bodies of ill-starred victims were sometimes found in the woods, but the discovery was rarely followed by investigation. The dive keepers were wealthy and knew how to ease the conscience of any over-zealous officer.

The outburst of indignation which followed "The Herald's" exposure compelled certain reforms in the neighborhood. Sporadic efforts were made to clean out the criminal element; restrictions were placed on saloons and gambling houses; stockades and bloodhounds were removed from the dives near the woods, and gradually an air of semi-decency crept over the district. But the snake was scotched, not killed. For a time more attention was paid to the proprieties, vice and crime were not so open as formerly. By degrees, however, the old conditions assumed sway again. Games of every kind were run openly night and day, dives and dance halls have been thronged and the usual quota of men from the woods deliberately robbed of their winter's savings.

Man's assertion that he protects woman is false. Under laws solely enacted by men young girls in christian countries are held as assenting to their own degradation at an age so tender that their evidence would not be received in courts of law. Nor are these the laws of a remote age come down to the present time. As late as 1889, the Kansas State Senate voted 25 to 9 that a girl of twelve years was of sufficiently responsible age "to consent" to take the first step in immorality; the same senate afterwards unanimously voting that a boy of sixteen years was not old enough to decide for himself in regard to smoking cigarettes.[93] It should be remembered that youth is the most impressible season of life as

well as the most inexperienced. Young girls from thirteen to sixteen, mere children, are most easily decoyed, their youth and
innocence causing them to fall the readiest prey; and scarcely a
large city but proves the existence of men of mature years whose
aim is the destruction of such young girls.[94] The state of
Delaware yet more infamous, still retaining seven years as the "age
of consent." Seven short years of baby life in that state is legally
held to transform a girl-infant into a being with capacity to consent to an act of which she neither knows the name nor the consequences, her "consent" freeing from responsibility or punishment, the villain, youthful or aged, who chooses to assault such
baby victim of man-made laws.[95] While the doors of irresponsible vice are legally thrown open to men of all ages with girl victims as their prey, the restrictions against marriage with a minor
without the parents' consent are in most states very severe. That
the girl-wife herself has consented to the marriage ceremony is
of no weight. Where a legitimate union is under consideration
she is held as possessing no power to form a contract and can be
arrested under a writ of *habeas corpus*, and kept from her husband
at her father's pleasure. Instances have also occurred where the
wife has been punished by him for thus daring to marry.[96] Both
the husband and the officiating clergyman are also held amenable,
the former under charge of abduction, the latter as an accessory
in performing the marriage ceremony.

A significant fact is the rapid increase of child criminals
throughout christendom; Germany, France and England showing
one hundred percent within ten years, while in the United States
more than one-half the inmates of state prisons are under thirty
years of age. From criminals it is necessary to look back to crime-
making men sitting in earth's loftiest places, and note the fact that
crime germs are not alone generated with the child, but that
through the gestative period the mother, a religious and legal slave,
struggles between a newly awakened sense of that responsibility
which within the last four decades has come to woman, and the
crushing influence of religious, political and family despotism
which still overshadows her. Moralists have long striven for the sup-

pression of immorality by efforts directed to the reformation of corrupt women alone; for two reasons they have been unsuccessful.

First: the majority of women entering this life are found to have done so under the pressure of abject poverty, and as long as the conditions of society continue to foster poverty for woman it was impossible to create a marked change in morals.

Second: all efforts were directed towards the smallest and least culpable class, as it has been proven that ten men of immoral life are required for the support of one woman of like character. In London alone with its population of five millions, 100,000 women, one-fiftieth of its population are thus enumerated, requiring 1,000,000 men, one-fifth of its population, for their support. Recognizing the fact that men, not women, were most sunken in vice, the number leading vicious lives very much larger, the degradation of these men very much greater, an Italian lady, Madam Venturi, at the International Conference of the British Continental and General Federation for the abolition of governmental regulation of prostitution, while making a brief eloquent address upon the general subject of rescue work, referred to the great importance of reclaiming men as the fundamental work upon which others should be built up. Teach men, she said, to understand that he who degrades a fellow creature, commits a crime, the crime of high treason against humanity. In quick response to those fitly spoken words, the women of many countries combined in the work of man's reformation in an organization known as the "White Cross Society" founded in 1886, by Miss Ellice Hopkins of England, and now possessing branches in every part of the civilized world.[97] To this society, men alone belong; its work is of a still broader character than mere reformation of the vicious; it seeks to train young men and boys to a proper respect for woman and for themselves.

As to the world is indebted Christine of Pisa for the first public protest against the immorality of christendom, so to Mrs. Josephine Butler,[98] Madam Venturi, and Miss Ellice Hopkins are due the inauguration of a new moral standard for man whose results must be of incalculable value to the world. The "White

Cross" is a simply organized society without an admission fee, but requiring adherence to a fivefold obligation binding its members to purity of thought and action,[99] and maintaining that the law of chastity is equally binding on men and women. The International Federation, a union existing in several European countries, its chief object, work against state protection of vice, roused public thought in this direction as never before. People began to comprehend that a large vicious class was common to every community, a class whose reclamation had never been systematically attempted, never thought necessary or even deemed possible, because of the religious and social training that taught indulgence in vice to be a necessity of man's nature; and the coordinate statement, that protection to the majority of women was to be secured only through the debasement and moral degradation of the minority. For many hundreds of years this has been man's treatment of the question of vice in Christian lands.

But as soon as advancing civilization permitted woman's thought to be publicly heard, vice in man was declared to be upon the same basis as vice in woman. Had not man been trained by his religion into a belief that woman was created for him, had not the church for eighteen hundred and more years preached woman's moral debasement, the long course of legislation for them as slaves would never have taken place, nor the obstacles in way of change been so numerous and so persistent. For nine years the Criminal Reform Act was before Parliament. During that period, petitions, speeches and appeals of every kind in favor of its passage were made by those outside the halls of legislation aided by a few honest men within. But the vicious and immoral fought the act with energy, despite the fact that the women of their own families were exposed to destruction through government protected iniquity. The bitter opposition by legislators to this act, is an additional proof that woman cannot trust man in the state to any greater extent than in the church.

Until woman holds political power in her own hands, her efforts for protective legislation will be arduous and protracted. Among the customs of the early christian church, we are able to trace the inception of marquette, the mundium, the legalization of vice and crimes of kindred character. With exception of among some savage races, that woman should appear unclothed before man, has been regarded as evidence of the deepest sensuality, yet throughout the history of Christianity from its earliest years when women were required to divest themselves of clothing before baptism down to the Endowment House ceremonies of the Mormon Church, we constantly find proof of like sensual exactions by the "Fathers," priests and lay masculinity of the church. During the earliest days of christianity, women were baptized quite nude, in the presence of men, by men, their bodies being afterwards anointed with oil by the priest who had baptized them. One of the earliest schisms in the church arose from the protest of women against this indignity, their demand to be allowed to baptize those of their own sex, and the opposition of men to this demand.[100]

The early bishops of the church strenuously used their influence against the baptism of nude women by elders of their own sex. Women were sometimes brought entirely nude upon the stage at Rome, but it was in connection with religious representation, the theater at that period being an element of religious teaching. Lecky speaks of the undisguised sensuality of this practice.[101] What must be our conception of a Christian custom that placed nude maidens and wives in the very hands of men, not alone for baptism but also for anointing with oil? Nude baptism is still practiced when converts are received into the Greek church, no position or station in life excusing from it, Catharine, the first wife of Peter the Great being baptized in this primitive christian manner.[102] As late as the seventeenth century a work upon the "Seven Sacraments" set certain days in which female penitents were to appear entirely unclothed before the confessor in order that he might discipline them on account of their sins.

Notes

1. In the dominion of the Count de Foix, the lord had right once in his lifetime to take, without payment, a certain quantity of goods from the stores of each tenant. Cesar Cantu.—*Histoire Universelle.*

2. Two women seized by German soldiers were covered with tar, rolled in feathers, and exhibited in the camp as a new species of bird.

3. Among the privileges always claimed, and frequently enforced by the feudalry, was the custom of the lord of the manor to lie the first night with the bride of his tenant.—*Sketches of Feudalism*, p. 109.

By the law of "Marquette" under the feudal system (which rested on personal vassalage), to the "lord of the soil" belonged the privilege of first entering the nuptial couch unless the husband had previously paid a small sum of money, or its equivalent, for the ransom of his bride; and we read that these feudal lords thought it was no worse thus to levy on a young bride than to demand half the wool of each flock of sheep. *Article on Relation of the Sexes.—Westminster Review.*

4. The custom of Borough-English is said to have arisen out of the Marchetta or plebeian's firstborn son being considered his lord's progeny.—*Dr. Tusler.*

5. "It is not very likely that Louis XIV thought the time would ever come when the peasant's bride might not be claimed in the chamber of his seigneur on her bridal night. Those base laws, their revocation has been written in the blood of successive generations."

6. See *Feudal Dictionary.*

7. The interests of ecclesiastics as feudal nobles were in some respects identical with those of the barons, but the clergy also constituted a party with interests of its own.

8. M. Gérun, as quoted by Grimm, gives curious information upon this subject.

9. Par example, dans quelques seigneuries, on le seigneur passent trois nuits avec les nouvelles marriées, il fut convenu qu'il n'eu passant qu'une. Dans d'autres, ou le seigneur avant le premiere nuit seulment, ou ne lui accordes plus qu'une heure.

10. *Collins de Plancy.*

11. *Feudal Dictionary*, p. 179.

12. Claiming the right of the first night with each new spouse.—*Bœms Decisions* 297, 1–17.

13. *Raepsaet*, p. 179.

14. The popes anciently had universal power over the pleasures of marriage.—*Feudal Dictionary*, p. 174.

15. In the transaction the alternative was with the husband; it was he who might submit, or pay the fine, as he preferred or could afford. *Relation of the Sexes.*—*Westminster Review.*

16. These (courts) powerfully assisted the seigneur to enforce his traditional privileges at the expense of the villeins.—*H. S. Maine.*

The courts of Bearn openly maintained that this right grew up naturally.

17. Sometimes the contumacious husband was harnessed by the side of a horse or an ox, compelled to do a brute's work and to herd with the cattle.

18. He is followed by bursts of laughter, and the noisy rabble down to the lowest scullion give chase to the "cuckold."—*Michelet.*

19. The oldest born of the peasant is accounted the son of his lord, for he, perchance it was, that begat him. When the guests have retired, the newly wedded husband shall permit his lord to enter the bed of his wife, unless he shall have redeemed her for five shillings and four pence.—*Grimm.*

20. Droit de cuissage c'est le droit de mettre one cuisse dans le lit d'une autre, ou de coucher avec le femme d'une vassal ou d'une serf.

So much scandal was caused that finally the archbishop of Bourges abolished this right in his diocese.—*Feudal Dictionary.*

21. A yoke of cattle and a measure of wheat was afterwards substituted for a money ransom, but even this redemption was in most cases entirely beyond the power of the serf.

Under the feudal system the lord of the manor held unlimited sway over his serfs. He further possessed the so-called *Jus Primæ Noctis* (Right of the First Night), which he could, however, relinquish in virtue of a certain payment, the name of which betrayed its nature. It has been latterly asserted that this right never existed, an assertion which to me appears entirely unfounded. It is clear the right was not a written one, that it was not summed up in paragraphs; it was the natural consequence of the dependent relationship, and required no registration in any book of law. If the female serf pleased the lord he enjoyed her, if not he let her alone. In Hungary, Transylvania, and the Danubian principalities, there was no written *Jus Primæ Noctis* either, but one learns enough of this subject by inquiry of those who know the country and its inhabitants, as to the manners which prevail between the land owners and the female population. That imposts of this nature existed cannot be denied, and the names speak for themselves. August Babel.—*Woman in the Past, Present and Future.*

22. In a parish outside Bourges the parson as being a lord especially claimed the first fruits of the bride, but was willing to sell his rights to the husband.

23. The infamous noble who accompanied a certain notorious actress to this country in the fall of 1886, possessed forty livings in his gift.

24. No greater proof of this statement is needed than the rapidity with which the disease brought by the sailors of Columbus spread over Europe; infecting the king on his throne, the peasant in the field, the priest at the altar, the monk and nun in the cloister.

25. In deference to that public sentiment which required the ruler to pose before the world as a libertine, Friedrich Wilhelm I, of Prussia (1713-1740), although old and in feeble health, kept up the pretense of a liason with the wife of one of his generals, the intimacy consisting of an hour's daily walk in the castle yard.—*August Babel.*

26. Down to Pius IX. See *The Woman, the Priest and the Confessional.*

27. When the Emperor Charles II entered Bourges, he was saluted by a deputation of perfectly naked women. At the entrance of King Ladislaus into Vienna, 1452, the municipal government sent a deputation of public women to meet him the beauty of whose forms was rather enhanced than concealed by their covering of gauze. Such cases were by no means unusual.—*Woman in the Past, Present and Future.*

28. *Memoirs of the Princess of Bareith,* a sister of Frederick the Great.

29. In Russia the nobles have such rights by law over the women of their lands that the population scarcely resent the sale by auction of all the young peasants of their village. These nobles, a race once proud and mean, extravagant and covetous, full of vice and cunning, are said to be a class superior to the people. Yet they are working the ruin of their influence by multiplying in the masses the number of individuals, already very considerable, to whom they have transmitted their genius with their blood.—*A. R. Craig, M.A.*

30. London, February 1.—The Odessa correspondent of the *Daily News* says: Hunger typhus is spreading alarmingly. In large towns in this region all the hospitals are filled, and private buildings are being converted into hospitals. This is the state of affairs in Moskovskia and Viedomosti. A correspondent writing from Russia declares that the more fanatical and superstitious portion of the peasantry believe that Count Tolstoi is Antichrist and decline to accept his bounty for fear they will thus commit their souls to perdition.

31. Two celebrated women, Augusta, of Koningsmark, and

Madame Dudevant (George Sand), traced their descent to this king.—Letters to *New York Tribune*.

32. Adam Badeau.—*Aristocracy in England*.

33. The at one time famous "Alexandra Limp," affecting the princess of Wales, and copied in walk by ultrafashionable women, was said to be due to the effects of an infamous disease contracted by the princess from her husband.

34. Rev. Dr. Varley.—*New York Sun*, July, 1885.

35. At the beginning of the Christian era, Corinth possessed a thousand women who were devoted to the service of its idol, the Corinthian Venus. "To Corinthianize" came to express the utmost lewdness, but Corinth, as sunken as she was in sensual pleasure, was not under the pale of Christianity. She was a heathen city, outside of that light which, coming into the world, is held to enlighten every man that accepts it.

36. Les Cuisiniers et les marmitons de l'archeveques de Vienne avaient imposé un tribut sur les mariages; on croit que certains feudi-taires exigeaient un droit obscène de leur vassaux qui se mariaient, quel fut transformé ensuite en droit de *cuissage* consistant, de la part du seigneur, a mettre une jambe nue dans le lit des nouveaux époux. Dans d'autres pays l'homme ne pouvait coucher avec sa femme les trois pre-mières nuits sans le consentement de l'eveque on du seigneur du fief. Cesar Cantu.—*Histoire Universelle*, Vol. IX, pp. 202–203.

37. *Moral History of Women*.

38. There are those who to enrich themselves would not only rob their sisters of their portion, but would sell for money the honor of those who bear their name. The authority of the son during the feudal period was so absolute that the father and mother themselves often winked at this hideous traffic.—*Ibid.*, p. 46.

39. Unless an heiress, woman possessed no social importance; unless an inmate of a religious house, no religious position. There are some records of her in this last position, showing what constant effort and strength of intellect were demanded from her to thwart the machina-tions of abbotts and monks.—*Sketches of Fontervault*.

40. See p. 193.—*Fleta*.

41. Bracton, pp. 26, 195, 208. *Littleton's Tenures*, pp. 55, 174, 209.

42. Gratian, Canon for Spain in 633, says the nuptial robe was gar-nished with white and purple ribbons as a sign of the continence to which young married people devoted themselves for a time.

43. Eight young men, living in the vicinity of North Rose, Wayne

County, have been held to await the action of the grand jury for rioting.
A young married couple named Garlic were about to retire for the night
when they were startled by the appearance of a party of men in the yard.
The party immediately commenced beating on pans, discharging guns
and pistols, pounding with clubs, screaming and kicking at the doors of
the house. The bride and groom were terrified, but finally the groom
mustered enough courage to demand what the men wanted there.
Shouts of "Give us lots of cider or we'll horn you to death" were the
answers. An attempt was made to break in a rear door of the house. The
bride and groom and John Wager, who was also present in the house,
braced the doors from the inside to prevent a forcible entrance, and the
inmates had to defend the property nearly all night. The horning party,
at last weary of calling for cider, left the premises, giving an extra strong
fusillade of firearms and a series of yells as they departed. The eight
young men were arrested a few days later on suspicion of being in the
horning party.—*Press Report*, Jan. 14, 1887.

44. Whenever we discover symbolized forms, we are justified in
inferring that in the past life of the people employing them there were
corresponding realities. McLennon.—*Studies in Ancient History*, p. 6.

45. He was thrown into the moat to cool his ardor, pelted with
stones, derided as a proud and envious wretch.—*Michelet*.

46. The maids redeem their virginities with a certain piece of
money, and by that Terme their lands are held to this day. Heywoode.—
History of Women, London, 1624; *Lib.* 7, p. 339.

47. Margaret was canonized in 1251, and made the Patron Saint of
Scotland in 1673. Several of the Scotch feudalry, despite royal protesta-
tion, kept up the infamous practice until a late date. One of the earls of
Crawford, a truculent and lustful anarch, popularly known and dreaded
as "Earl Brant," in the sixteenth century, was probably among the last
who openly claimed leg-right, the literal translation of *droit de jambage*.—*Sketches of Feudalism*.

48. The feeling is common in the north that a laird, or chieftain,
getting a vassal's or clansmen's wife or daughter with child, is doing her
a great honor. Burke.—*Letters from an English Gentleman*, about 1730.

49. *Pres de cet étang, et devant sa maison.*

50. In days to come people will be slow to believe that the law
among Christian nations went beyond anything decreed concerning the
olden slavery; that it wrote down as an actual right the most grievous
outrage that could ever wound man's heart. The Lord Spiritual had this

right no less than the Lord Temporal. The parson being a lord, expressly claimed the first fruits of the bride, but was willing to sell his rights to the husband. The courts of Berne openly maintain that this right grew up naturally. Michelet.—*La Sorciere*, p. 62.

51. Among the rights asserted by the Protestant clergy in the middle ages, and which caused much dispute, was exemption from lay jurisdiction even in cases of felony.

From the throne downward every secular office was dependent upon the church. Froude.—*Times of Erasmus and Luther.*

52. Among these de coucher avec leur femmes, d'enlever les prémices de leurs filles.

53. *H. S. Maine.*

54. In Babylon every young woman was obliged once in her life to offer her person for sale, nor was she permitted to leave the temple, where she sat with a cord about her waist, until some stranger taking it in hand led her away. The money thus obtained passed into the treasury of the temple as her "purchase money, or redemption, releasing her from further prostitution, and permitting her marriage, which was forbidden until such sale had been consummated."

55. Although a similar custom is said to have prevailed in India under Brahaminical rule, it must be remembered that wherever found it is an accompaniment of the Patriarchate, and under some form of religion where the feminine is no longer considered a portion of the divinity, or woman allowed in the priesthood.

56. It has been too readily believed that the wrong was formal, not real. But the price laid down in certain countries exceeded the means of almost every peasant. In Scotland, for instance, the demand was for several cows, a price immense, impossible.

57. *Christian History, First Period*, by Joseph Henry Allen.

58. In the history of Julius Cæsar there is something peculiarly curious and mythical. Cæsar had all the honors paid to him as to a divine person. At the end of five years a festival was instituted to his honor, as to a person of divine extraction. A college of priests was established to perform the rights instituted for the occasion. A day was dedicated to him, and he had the title also of Julian Jove, and a temple was erected to him.—*Anacalypsis*, I, p. 611.

59. Law of the first night,

60. The lord's right.

61. Leg right—the right to place a naked leg in bed with the bride.

62. Droit de cuissage, c'est le droit de mettre une cuisse dans le lit d'une autre, ou de coucher avec le femme d'un vassal, ou d'un serf.

63. Droit d'afforge, the right to prey upon the bride.

64. Droit de marquette, took its name in Scotland from the redemption piece of money, a demi-mark, marquette, or little mark, a weight of gold or silver used in Great Britain and many other European countries.

65. *Mrs. Josephine Butler*, so stating.

66. A government license reads: "Chinese women for the use of Europeans only."

67. *Contagious Disease Acts.*

68. *The Emancipation of Women*, January, 1888.

69. The penal code provides for the punishment of a man who commits mischief by injuring an animal of the value of ten rupees or upwards, with imprisonment for a term which may extend to two years, or with fine, or with both. If the animal be worth fifty rupees, the punishment may be for five years. If a man induces his neighbor's dog, by bait or otherwise, to follow him with the intention of dishonestly taking the dog out of his neighbor's possession, he may be punished with imprisonment for three years, or with fine, or with both. But while a man's dog, his horse, his elephant are taken care of by legislation; while the very plants in his garden are protected; his young daughter, the light of his eyes and the joy of his home, may be ruined and her fair fame stolen with impunity, provided she has attained the age of ten years and is unmarried, and proof is wanting that she has resisted her seducer.

70. The New York Society for the "Prevention of Diseases."

71. Of Berlin, August Babel says: "Now things are neither better nor worse in Berlin than in any other large town. It would be difficult to decide which most resembled ancient Babylon; orthodox Greek St. Petersburg, Catholic Rome, Christian Germanic Berlin, heathen Paris, puritan London, or lively Vienna.—*Woman in the Past, Present and Future*.

72. The latest attempt for licensing vice in the United States was made in New Orleans, 1892, in the form of an ordinance proposing to grant to Dr. Wm. Harnon the privilege of levying an inspection tax upon those known as "Public Women" of $1.50 a week for fifteen years.

The *Louisiana Review* said of it:

"A more revolting proposition than this has never come under our notice, and we are amazed that the health committee failed to detect its character, however artfully it may have been screened by the pretext that it was intended to lessen the harm of the social evil."

The *New Delta*, in its issue of August 31, said:

"The queer and ill-favored monopoly which the ordinance for the regulation of houses of bad repute sought to establish has not been successful on the first effort. It goes back to a committee. Let us hope that it will remain buried there forever, and decent people be saved the infliction of a public discussion of the miserable scheme. Such systems of 'regulation' would disgrace the devil, and the proposition for the city to share in the plunder of these poor wretches would shame a Piute village."

The *Woman's Journal*, September 19, said:

"It is well that this measure has failed on the first attempt; but to refer a matter to a committee is not necessarily to kill it, and its fate in the committee should be closely watched. The laws establishing the state regulation of vice in England were smuggled through Parliament about 1 o'clock in the morning, when half the members were absent or asleep; but it took seventeen years of painful and distasteful agitation to repeal them. Prevention of bad legislation is better than cure."

This attempt was finally defeated through the energetic opposition and work of Mrs. Elizabeth Lyle Saxon.

73. The reporter, while the committee was still in session, went to a procuress and ordered a *pretty girl*, fourteen years of age, certified by a physician to be good, to be delivered to his order as "agent for *gentleman of sixty*." The madame accepted the order, and in a short time produced the girl certified. The reporter investigated the child's history, and ascertained that her father was dead and her mother was a poor working woman. The girl was dressed in an old black frock. Having completed the purchase of the girl, the reporter hastened to arrange for her delivery anywhere and to any person designated by the committee.

74. A committee composed of Cardinal Manning, the Archbishop of Canterbury, Bishop of London and two laymen, examined the evidence respecting criminal vice in London, becoming satisfied that the statements made by the *Pall Mall Gazette* were substantially true.

75. The Rev. Mr. Spurgeon preached a powerful sermon upon the patrician iniquity of London, comparing it to the worst sins of ancient nations, one sure, sooner or later, to bring destruction upon both individual and nation.

76. When you see a girl on the street you can never say without inquiry whether she is one of the most-to-be-condemned or the most-to-be-pitied of her sex. Many of them find themselves where they are because of a too trusting disposition; others are as much the innocent vic-

tims of crime as if they had been stabbed or maimed by the dagger of the assassin. . . . These women constitute a large standing army, whose numbers no one can calculate. Gen. Booth.—*Darkest England*, pp. 51–56.

77. Children as they go to and from school are waited for and watched until the time has come for running them down.—*Report of the Secret Commission*.

78. It seemed a strange inverted world, that in which I lived those terrible weeks, the world of the streets and brothel. It was the same, and yet not the same as the world of business and the world of politics. I heard of much the same people in the house of ill-fame as those of whom you hear in caucuses, in law courts and on 'change; but all were judged by a different standard, and their relative importance was altogether changed. Mr. Stead.—*Pall Mall Gazette*.

79. *Report of Secret Commission*.

80. An immense number of public women congregated at Nice during the time of its Historic Council, which settled the genuineness of the books of the Bible.

81. So fast has this class of pecuniarily independent single women increased within the past two and a half decades, women who prefer a single life with its personal independence, to a married life with its legal dependence and restrictions, as to call from the *London Times* the designation of "Third Sex."

82. The statistics of prostitution show that the great proportion of those who have fallen into it have been impelled by the most extreme poverty, in many instances verging upon starvation.—*Hist. European Morals*, 2, 203.

83. Belgium and Holland entered into an agreement a few years since for its suppression.

84. When Hon. Henry Blair presented a petition, asking for the better protection of girls, he said: "Our civilization seems to have developed an almost unknown phase of crime in the annals of the race, and today the traffic in girls and young women in this country, especially in our large cities, has come to be more disgraceful and worse than ever was that in the girls of Circassia."

This Christianity of ours has much to answer for.—*Woman's Tribune*.

85. It was at one time proposed to arrest all women out alone in the city of Syracuse, N. Y., after nine o'clock in the evening. Had the ordinance been enacted, a lady of mature years and position was prepared to test its legality.

86. Eighteen women were arrested on Monday night in the fif-

teenth and twenty-ninth police precincts, and after being held in confinement over night, were taken before Justice Duffy at the Jefferson Market Police Court Tuesday morning.

"What were these women doing?" asked the justice.

"Nothing," replied the officer.

"Then why did you arrest them?"

"We have to do it, sir. It is the order of the police superintendent when we find them loitering on the streets."—*New York Sunday Sun*, June 28, 1885.

87. Mr. Breen said the horrors of the camps into which these girls are inveigled cannot be adequately described. There is no escape for these poor creatures. In one case a girl escaped after being shot in the leg, and took refuge in a swamp. Dogs were started on her trail, and she was hunted down and taken back to her den. In another case a girl escaped while a dance was going on at the shanty into which she had been lured. After several days and nights of privation she made her way to an island near the shore in Lake Michigan, where a man named Stanley lived. But the dogs and human bloodhounds trailed her, Stanley was overcome, and the girl was taken back. The law now provides for imprisonment of only one year in case of conviction of any connection with this traffic, and it is proposed to amend it.—*Telegraphic Report*.

88. Tales of a horrible character reach us from Michigan and other northern lumber districts of the manner in which girls are enticed to these places on the promise of high wages, and then subjected to brutal outrages past description. Some three hundred of these dens are located. These girls are sold by the keepers, passing from one den to another, from one degree of hellish brutality to another (we beg pardon of all brutes), all escape guarded against by ferocious bloodhounds. The maximum of life is two months.—*Union Labor Journal*.

89. Tony Harden used to keep dives in Norway and Quinnesic, and it is said of him that after paying a constable twelve dollars to bring a girl back who had tried to escape, he beat her with a revolver until he was tired, and was about to turn a bulldog loose at her, when a woodsman appeared and stopped him. The next spring Harden was elected justice of the peace.—*Woman's Standard*.

90. The Rev. Mr. Kerr, of the Protestant Church, Colon, recently discovered three young girls brought to the Isthmus for improper purposes. He took the children away and with the assistance of others returned them to their parents in Jamaica.

91. Quebec, April 11.—Wholesale trading in young and innocent girls for purposes of prostitution has come to the notice of the authorities. Disreputable houses in Chicago, New York, Boston and other cities in the United States have agents here, who ingratiate themselves with young women and induce them to go to the states, where they are drawn into a life of infamy. The trade has been carried on to an alarming extent, sometimes fifteen girls being shipped in a week. The prices paid to agents depend on the looks of the girls, and vary from $20 to $200. It is stated that over fifty girls have been sent to one Chicago house within a year.—*Daily Press*.

92. The startling revelations within the past few days as to the traffic at Ottawa in young girls of from twelve to fourteen, in which a number of prominent citizens as well as several leading politicians are implicated, have caused the greatest indignation. Tuesday night a meeting was held under the auspices of the Society for the Prevention of Cruelty to Children, with a view to devising some means by which the great stain on the capital's good name might be removed. It was decided that the matter must become the subject of special legislation at the next session of Parliament, before the guilty scoundrels can be punished. Opposition is expected from the members of Parliament who are implicated in the outrages.—*Daily Press.*

93. *Topeka Leader.*

94. In Troy, N. Y., in the fall of 1891, discovery was made of an organized plan to ravish little girls. It numbered in its ranks married men, members of the police force, and men well known in business and church circles. With this discovery came the statement from other cities that like offenders were common.—*The Daily Press.*

95. Persistent effort has been made by women to stop these great wrongs, but having no power in legislation, her prayers and petitions have met with but scant success.

96. Married at Thirteen Years.—Maud Pearl Johnson, a thirteen-year-old girl of Fulton, who was married to Franklin Foster of that place on Monday, has been placed in the State Industrial School in Rochester under sentence by Police Justice Spencer of Fulton. Foster is a widower with three children. The minister at Fairdale who performed the ceremony is said to have been fined $3 for cruelty to children. The poor authorities arrested the young wife for vagrancy.

97. Africa, Australia, India, Canada, and the United States among the number.

98. Who gave seventeen years of her life to work for the overthrow of government legislation of vice in England.

99. 1. To treat all women with respect, and endeavor to protect them from wrong and degradation.

2. To endeavor to put down all indecent language and coarse jests.

3. To maintain the law of purity as equally binding upon men and women.

4. To endeavor to spread these principles among my companions, and try to help my younger brothers.

5. To use every possible means to fulfil the command: "Keep Thyself Pure."

100. The women claimed the right to baptize their own sex. But the bishops and presbyters did not care to be released from the pleasant duty of baptizing the female converts. Waite.—*Hist. of Christian Religion from A. D. to 200*, p. 23.

The Constitution of the Church of Alexandria, which is thought to have been established about the year 200, required the applicant for baptism to be divested of clothing, and after the ordinance had been administered, to be anointed with oil.—*Ibid.*, pp. 384–85.

The converts were first exorcised of the evil spirits that were supposed to inhabit them; then, after undressing and being baptized, they were anointed with oil.—*Bunsen's Christianity of Mankind*, Vol. VII, pp. 386–93; *3d Vol. Analecta.*

Women were baptized quite naked in the presence of these men.—*Philosophical Dictionary.*

Some learned men have enacted that in primitive churches the persons to be baptized, of whatever age or sex, should be quite naked. Pike.—*History of Crime in England*. See Joseph Vicecomes.—*De Ritibus Baptismi*. Varrius.—*Thesibus de Baptisme.*

101. Undisguised sensuality reached a point we can scarcely conceive. Women were sometimes brought naked upon the stage. By a curious association of ideas the theater was still intimately connected with religious observance. *Rationalism in Europe*, 2–288.

102. Catharine, the first wife of Peter the Great, was received into the Greek Church by a rite nearly approaching the primitive customs of the Christian Church. New converts to that church are plunged three times naked in a river or into a large tub of cold water. Whatever is the condition, age or sex of the convert, this indecent ceremony is never dis-

pensed with. The effrontery of a pope (priests of the Greek Church are thus called), sets at defiance all the reasons which decency and modesty never cease to use against the absurdity and impudence of this shameful ceremony. Count Segur.—*Woman's Condition and Influence in Society*.

CHAPTER V

WITCHCRAFT

Although toward the beginning of the fourth century, people began to speak of the nocturnal meeting of witches and sorcerers, under the name of "Assembly of Diana," or "Herodia," it was not until canon or church law had become quite engrafted upon the civil law that the full persecution for witch-craft arose. A witch was held to be a woman who had deliberately sold herself to the evil one; who delighted in injuring others, and who, for the purpose of enhancing the enormity of her evil acts, chose the Sabbath day for the performance of her most impious rites, and to whom all black animals had special relationship; the black cat in many countries being held as her principal familiar. "To go to the Sabbath" signified taking part in witch orgies. The possession of a pet of any kind at this period was dangerous to woman. One who had tamed a frog, was condemned to be burned in consequence, the harmless amphibian being looked upon as a familiar of Satan. The devil ever being depicted in

sermon or story as black, all black animals by an easy transition of
ideas, became associated with evil and witches.[1] Although I have
referred to witchcraft as having taken on a new phase soon after
the confirmation of celibacy as a dogma of the church by the Lateran Council of 1215, it yet requires a chapter by itself, in order
to show to what proportions this form of heresy arose, and the
method of the church in its treatment. This period was the age of
supreme despair for woman,[2] death by fire being the common
form of witch punishment. Black cats were frequently burned
with a witch at the stake;[3] during the reign of Louis XV of
France, sacks of condemned cats were burned upon the public
square devoted to witch torture. Cats and witches are found
depicted together in a curious cut on the title page of a book
printed in 1621. The proverbial "nine lives" of a cat were associated in the minds of people with the universally believed possible
metamorphosis of a witch into a cat.[4] So firmly did the diabolical
nature of the black cat impress itself upon the people, that its
effects are felt in business to this day, the skin of black cats being
less prized and of less value in the fur market than those of other
colors. A curious exemplification of this inherited belief is found
in Great Britain. An English taxidermist who exports thousands of
mounted kittens each year to the United States and other countries, finds the prejudice against black cats still so great that he will
not purchase kittens of this obnoxious color.[5] In the minds of
many people, black seems irradicably connected with sorcery.

In the *Folk Lore of Cats*, it is stated that as recently as 1867 a
woman was publicly accused of witchcraft in the state of Pennsylvania on account of her administering three drops of a black
cat's blood to a child as a remedy for the croup. She admitted the
fact but denied that witchcraft had anything to do with it, and
twenty witnesses were called to prove its success as a remedy.
From an early period the belief in metamorphosis by means of
magical power was common throughout christendom. St. Augustine relates[6] that "hostess or inkeepers sometimes put confections

into a kind of cheese made by them, and travelers eating thereof, were presently metamorphosed into laboring beasts, as horses, asses or oxen." It was also believed that the power of changing into various animals was possessed by witches themselves.[7] At the present day under certain forms of insanity persons imagine themselves to be animals, birds, and even inanimate things, as glass; but usually those hallucinations occur in isolated instances. But among the strange epidemics which have at various times affected christendom, none is more singular than that Lycanthropia, or wolf madness, which attacked such multitudes of inhabitants of the Jura in 1600, as to become a source of great public danger. The affected persons walked upon their feet and hands until their palms became hard and horny. They howled like wolves, and as wolves do they hunted in packs, murdering and devouring many children, nor could the most severe punishment put an end to this general madness. Six hundred persons were executed upon their own confessions, which included admissions of compact with the devil, attendance upon the Sabbath and cannibal feasting upon a mountain, the devil having used his power for their transmutation into wolves.[8] Witches were believed to ride through the air upon animals or bits of wood. The fact of their possession of such powers are asserted by many writers, the usual method of transportation being a goat, night crow or enchanted staff.[9] The rhyming Mother Goose question, "Old woman, old woman, A whither, oh whither so high?" And its rhyming answer, "To sweep the cobwebs from the sky, And I'll be back by and by," doubtless owes its origin to the witchcraft period.

A song said to be in use during witch dances ran:
"Har, Har, Diabole, Diabole, Sali huc,
Sali illuc; Lude hic, Lude illic;
Sabaoth, Sabaoth."

Although the confirmation by the church in the thirteenth century of the supreme holiness of celibacy, inaugurated a new era of persecution for witchcraft, a belief in its existence had from the earliest times been a doctrine of the church, Augustine, as shown, giving the weight of his authority in favor. But to the Christian

Emperor Charlemagne, in the eighth century, the first use of torture in accusation of witchcraft is due. This great emperor while defying the power of the pope, over whom he even claimed jurisdiction, was himself a religious autocrat whose severity exceeded even that of the papal throne. Torture was rapidly adopted over Europe, and soon became general in the church; the council of Salsburg, 799, publicly ordering its use in witch trials.

A new era of persecution and increased priestly power dates to the reign of Charlemagne, who although holding himself superior to the pope, as regarded independent action, greatly enlarged the dominion of the church and power of the priesthood. He forced Christianity upon the Saxons at immense sacrifice of life, added to the wealth and power of the clergy by tithe lands, recognized their judicial and canonical authority, made marriage illegal without priestly sanction and still further degraded womanhood through his own polygamy. Although himself of such wanton life, he yet caused a woman of the town to be dragged naked through the city streets, subject to all the cruel tortures of an accompanying mob.

> In the ninth century the power of the pope was again greatly increased. Up to this period he had been elected by the clergy and people of Rome, and the approbation of the emperor was necessary to confirm it. But Charles the Bald, 875, relinquished all right of jurisdiction over Rome, and thereafter the Roman Pontiff became an acknowledged if not sometimes a supreme power in the appointment of temporal princes. The power of bishops, clergy, and cardinals diminished as that of the pope increased.

Notwithstanding her claims of power through St. Peter, it has been by gradual steps that Rome has decided upon her policy and established her dogmas. It is but little over four decades, at the Ecumenical of 1849, that the dogma of the Immaculate Conception of the Virgin Mary was first authoritatively promulgated, although her worship had long existed, being traceable to the Egyptian doctrine of the trinity, with the substitution of Mary in place of Isis. It was not until 1085 that Hildebrand, Pope Gregory

VII, declared matrimony a sacrament of the church; and not until 1415, at the Council of Trent, that extreme unction was instituted and defined as a sacrament. Each of these dogmas threw more power into the hands of the church, and greater wealth into her coffers. Thus we see the degeneration of Christianity has had its epochs. One occurred when the Council of Nice allowed chance to dictate which should be considered the canonical books of the New Testament, accepting some theretofore regarded as of doubtful anthenticity and rejecting others that had been universally conceded genuine.[10] Another epoch of degeneration occurs when the State in person of the great emperor Charlemagne added to the power of the Church by the establishment of torture, whose extremest use fell upon that portion of humanity looked upon as the direct embodiment of evil. The peculiar character attributed to woman by the church, led to the adoption of torture as a necessary method of forcing her to speak the truth. The testimony of two, and in some countries, three women being held as only equal to that of one man. At first, young children and women expecting motherhood, were exempted, but afterwards neither age or condition freed from accusation and torture, and women even in the pangs of maternity were burned at the stake,[11] Christianity in this respect showing much more barbarity than pagan nations. In pagan Rome the expectant mother was held sacred; to vex or disturb her mind was punishable, to strike her was death. She even possessed a right pertaining to the Vestal Virgins; if meeting a condemned criminal on his way to execution, her word sufficed for his pardon. It scarcely seems possible, yet in some christian countries the most prominent class subjected to the torture, were women expecting motherhood. Christianity became the religion of Iceland A.D. 1000, and by the earliest extant law, the "Gragas," dating to 1119, we find that while torture was prescribed in but few instances yet the class principally subjected to it, were women about to become mothers. But generally throughout Europe, until about the fourteenth century, when priestly celibacy had become firmly established and the Inquisition connected with the state, a class consisting of nobles, doctors of the law, pregnant women, and children under fourteen, were exempt from torture except in case of high treason and a few other offenses. But at a later period when these institutions had greatly increased the irresponsible power of the church, we find neither sex, condition or age, freeing from its infliction, both state and church uniting in its use.

In Venitian folk lore, it is stated that Satan once became furious with the Lord because paradise contained more souls than hell, and he determined by fine promises to seduce human beings to his worship and thus fill his kingdom. He decided to always tempt women instead of men, because through ambition or a desire for revenge, they yield more easily. This legend recalls the biblical story of Satan taunting the Lord with the selfish nature of Job's goodness, and receiving from God the permission to try him. Witchcraft was regarded as a sin almost confined to women. The Witch Hammer declared the very word *femina* meant one wanting in faith. A wizard was rare; one writer declaring that to every hundred witches but one wizard was found. In time of Louis XV this difference was greatly increased; "To one wizard 10,000 witches"; another writer asserted there were 100,000 witches in France alone. The great inquisitor Sprenger, author of *The Witch Hammer* and through whose instrumentality many countries were filled with victims, largely promoted this belief. "Heresy of witches, not of wizards[12] must we call it, for these latter are of very small account." No class or condition of women escaped him; we read of young children, old people, infants, witches of fifteen years, and two "infernally beautiful" of seventeen years. Although the ordeal of the red hot iron fell into disuse in the secular courts early in the fourteenth century (1329),[13] ecclesiasticism preserved it in case of women accused of witchcraft for one hundred and fifty years longer.[14] One of the peculiarities of witchcraft accusations, was that protestations of innocence, and a submission to ordeals such as had always vindicated those taking part in them if passing through unharmed, did not clear a woman charged with witchcraft, who was then accused with having received direct help from Satan. The maxim of sec-

ular law that the torture which did not produce confession entitled the accused to full acquittal was not in force under ecclesiastical indictments, and the person accused of witchcraft was always
liable to be tried again for the same crime. Every safeguard of law
was violated in case of woman, even Magna Charta forbidding
appeal to her except in case of her husband.

Before the introduction of Christianity, no capital punishment existed, in the modern acceptation of the term, except for
witchcraft. But pagans, unlike christians, did not look upon
women as more given to this practice than men; witches and wizards were alike stoned to death. But as soon as a system of religion was adopted which taught the greater sinfulness of women,
over whom authority had been given to man by God himself, the
saying arose "one wizard to 10,000 witches," and the persecution
for witchcraft became chiefly directed against women. The
church degraded woman by destroying her self-respect, and
teaching her to feel consciousness of guilt in the very fact of her
existence.[15] The extreme wickedness of woman, taught as a cardinal doctrine of the church, created the belief that she was
desirous of destroying all religion, witchcraft being regarded as
her strongest weapon,[16] therefore no punishment for it was
thought too severe. The teaching of the church, as to the creation
of women and the origin of evil, embodied the ordinary belief of
the christian peoples, and that woman rather than man practiced
this sin, was attributed by the church to her original sinful nature,
which led her to disobey God's first command in Eden.[17]

Although witchcraft was treated as a crime against the state,
it was regarded as a greater sin against heaven, the bible having set
its seal of disapproval in the injunction "Thou shalt not suffer a
witch to live." The church therefore claimed its control. When
coming under ecclesiastical jurisdiction, witchcraft was much
more strenuously dealt with than when it fell under lay tribunals.
It soon proved a great source of emolument to the church, which
grew enormously rich by its confiscation to its own use of all
property of condemned. Sprenger, whose work (*The Witch
Hammer*), was devoted to methods of dealing with this sin, was

printed in size convenient for carrying in the pocket.[18] It based
its authority upon the bible, twenty-three pages were devoted to
proving that women were especially addicted to sorcery. This
work was sanctioned by the pope, but after the reformation
became equally authoritative in protestant as in catholic countries, not losing its power for evil until the eighteenth century. A
body of men known as "Traveling Witch Inquisitors," of whom
Sprenger was chief, journeyed from country to country
throughout christendom, in search of victims for torture and
death. Their entrance into a country or city was regarded with
more fear than famine or pestilence; especially by women, against
whom their malignity was chiefly directed, Sprenger, the great
authority, declaring that her name signified evil; "the very word
femina (woman), meaning one wanting in faith, for *fe* means faith,
and *minus* less."[19] The reformation caused no diminution in its
use, the protestant clergy equally with the catholic constantly
appealing to its pages. Still another class known as "Witch
Finders," or "Witch Persecutors" confined their work to their
own neighborhoods. Of these, Cardan, a famous Italian physician,
said: "In order to obtain forfeit property, the same persons act as
accusers and judges, and invent a thousand stories as proof."[20] The
love of power, and the love of money formed a most hideous
combination for evil in the church; not a christian country but
was full of the horrors of witch persecutions and violent deaths.
During the reign of Francis I more than 100,000 witches were
put to death, mostly by burning, in France alone. Christ was
invoked as authority, the square devoted to Auto de Fé being
known as, "The Burning Place of the Cross."

The Parliament of Toulouse burned four hundred witches at
one time. Four hundred women at one hour on the public
square, dying the horrid death of fire for a crime which never
existed save in the imagination of those persecutors and which
grew in their imagination from a false belief in woman's extraordinary wickedness, based upon a false theory as to original sin.
Remy, judge of Nancy, acknowledged to having burnt eight hundred in sixteen years, at the rate of two hundred a year. Many

women were driven to suicide in fear of the torture in store for them. In 1595 sixteen of those accused by Remy, destroyed themselves rather than fall into his terrible hands. Six hundred were burnt in one small bishopric in one year; nine hundred during the same period in another. Seven thousand lost their lives in Treves; a thousand in the province of Como, in Italy, in a single year; five hundred were executed at Geneva, in a single month.

While written history does not fail to give abundant record in regard to the number of such victims of the church, largely women whose lives were forfeited by accusation of witchcraft, hundreds at one time dying agonizingly by fire, a new and weird evidence as to the innumerable multitude of these martyrs was of late most unexpectedly brought to light in Spain. During a course of leveling and excavations for city improvement's in Madrid, recently, the workmen came upon the *Quemadero de la Cruz*.[21] The cutting of a new road through that part of the city laid bare like geological strata, long black layers superimposed one above the other at distances of one or two feet, in the sandstone and clay. Some of these layers extended 150 feet in a horizontal direction, and were at first supposed to be the actual discovery of new geological strata, which they closely resembled. They proved to be the remains of inquisitorial burnings, where thousands of human beings of all ages had perished by the torture of fire.[22] The layers consisted of coal coagulated with human fat, bones, the remains of singed hair, and the shreds of burnt garments. This discovery created great excitement, people visiting the spot by thousands to satisfy themselves of the fact, and to carry away some memento of that dark age of christian cruelty, a cruelty largely exercised against the most helpless and innocent, a cruelty having no parallel in the annals of paganism. Imagination fails to conceive the condensed torture this spot of earth knew under the watchword of "Christ and His Cross"; and that was but one of the hundreds, nay, thousands of similar "Burning Places of the Cross," with which every christian country, city, and town was provided for many hundreds of years. A most diabolical custom of the church made these burnings a holiday spectacle. People thus grew to look unmoved upon the most atrocious tortures, and excited crowds hung about witch burnings, eagerly listening as the priests exhorted to confession, or tormented the dying victims with pictures of an unending fire soon to be their fate.

An accusation of witchcraft struck all relatives of the accused with terror, destroying the ordinary virtues of humanity in the hearts of nearest friends. As it was maintained that devils possessed more than one in a family, each member sought safety by aiding the church in accumulating proof against the accused, in hopes thereby to escape similar charge. It is impossible for us at the present day to conceive the awful horror falling upon a family into which an accusation of witchcraft had come. Not alone the shame and disgrace of such a charge; the terrors of a violent death under the most painful form; the sudden hurling of the family from ease and affluence to the most abject poverty; but above all the belief that unending torment by fire pursued the lost soul throughout eternity, made a combination of terrors appalling to the stoutest heart. A Scotch woman convicted as a witch and sentenced to be burned alive could not be persuaded by either priest or sheriff to admit her guilt. Suffering the intensest agonies of thirst during her torture she espied her only son in the surrounding crowd. Imploring him in the name of her love for him she begged as her last request, that he should bring her a drink. He shook his head, not speaking; her fortitude her love, his own most certain conviction of her innocence not touching him; when she cried again, "Oh, my dear son, help me any drink, be it never so little, for I am most extremely drie, oh drie, drie." His answer to her agonizing entreaties could not be credited were it not a subject of history, and the date so recent. "By no means dear mother will I do you the wrong, for the drier you are no doubt you will burn the better."[23] Under Accadian law three thousand years before christianity, the son who denied his father was sentenced to a simple fine, but he who denied his mother was to be banished from the land and sea;[24] but in the sixteenth century of the christian era, we find a son under christian laws denying his mother a drink of water in her death agony by fire.

Erskine says:

> It was instituted in Scotland 1653, "that all who used witch-craft, sorcery, necromancy, or pretended skill therein, shall be punished capitally; upon which statute numberless innocent persons were tried and burnt to death, upon evidence which, in place of affording reasonable conviction to the judge, was fraught with absurdity and superstition."[25]

Thirty thousand persons accused of witchcraft were burned to death in Germany and Italy alone, and although neither age nor sex was spared, yet women and girls were the chief victims. Uncommon beauty was as dangerous to a woman as the possession of great wealth, which brought frequent accusations in order that the church might seize upon the witches' property for its own use.

Children of the most tender years did not escape accusation and death. During the height of witchcraft persecution, hundreds of little ones were condemned as witches. Little girls of ten, eight, and seven years are mentioned; blind girls, infants[26] and even young boys were among the numbers who thus perished. Everywhere the most helpless classes were the victims.

It was declared that witches looked no person steadily in the face, but allowed their eyes to wander from side to side, or kept them fixed upon the earth. To this assertion that a witch could not look any one in the face, the present belief of a connection between guilt and a downcast look, is due; although the church taught that a woman should preserve a downward look in shame for the sin she had brought into the world, and to this day, an open, confident look upon a woman's face is deprecated as evil. Attendance upon Sabbats[27] and control of the weather were among the accusations brought against the witch. In Scotland a woman accused of raising a storm by taking off her stockings was put to death. Sprenger tells of a Swiss farmer whose little daughter startled him by saying she could bring rain, immediately raising a storm.[28]

Whatever the pretext made for witchcraft persecution we

have abundant proof that the so-called "witch" was among the
most profoundly scientific persons of the age. The church having
forbidden its offices and all external methods of knowledge to
woman, was profoundly stirred with indignation at her having
through her own wisdom, penetrated into some of the most
deeply subtle secrets of nature: and it was a subject of debate
during the middle ages if learning for woman was not an additional capacity for evil, as owing to her, knowledge had first been
introduced in the world. In penetrating into these arcana, woman
trenched upon that mysterious hidden knowledge of the church
which it regarded as among its most potential methods of controlling mankind. Scholars have invariably attributed magical
knowledge and practices to the church, popes and prelates of
every degree having been thus accused. The word "magic" or
"wisdom" simply meaning superior science, was attributed in the
highest degree to King Solomon, who ruled even the Elementals
by means of his magic ring made in accord with certain natural
laws. He was said to have drawn his power directly from God.
Magi were known as late as the tenth century of this era. Among
their powers were casting out demons, the fearless use of poisons,
control of spirits and an acquaintance with many natural laws
unknown to the world at large. During the present century, the
Abbe Constant (Eliphas Levi), declared the Pentegram to be the
key of the two worlds, and if rightly understood, endowing man
with infinite power. The empire of THE WILL over the astral light
is symbolized in magic by the Pentegram, the growth of a personal will being the most important end to be attained in the history of man's evolution. The opposition of the church to this
growth of the human will in mankind, has ever been the most
marked feature in its history. Under WILL, man decides for himself, escaping from all control that hinders his personal development.

It is only an innate and natural tendency of the soul to go
beyond its body to find material with which to clothe the life
that it desires to give expression to. The soul can and must be

trained to do this consciously. You can easily see that this power possessed *consciously* will give its possessor power to work magic.

Ignorance and the anathemas of the church against knowledge to be gained through an investigation of the more abstruse laws of nature, have invested the word "magic" with terror. But magic simply means knowledge of the effect of certain natural, but generally unknown laws; the secret operation of natural causes, according to Bacon and other philosophers; consequences resulting from control of the invisible powers of nature, such as are shown in the electrical appliances of the day, which a few centuries since would have been termed witchcraft. Seeking to compel the aid of spirits was understood as magic at an early day. Lenormant says the object of magic in Chaldea was to conjure the spirits giving minute description of the ancient formula. Scientific knowledge in the hands of the church alone was a great element of spiritual and temporal power, aiding it in more fully subduing the human will. The testimony of the ages entirely destroys the assertion sometimes made that witchcraft was merely a species of hysteria. Every discovery of science is a nearer step towards knowledge of the laws governing "the Accursed Sciences," as everything connected with psychic power in possession of the laity was termed by the church. "Her seven evidences for possession" included nearly all forms of mesmerism. All modern investigations tend to prove what was called witchcraft, to have been in most instances the action of psychic laws not yet fully understood. An extremely suggestive article appeared in the January and February numbers of *The Path* 1887, by C. H. A. Bjerregaard entitled, "The Elementals and the Elementary Spirits." In it Mr. Bjerregaard referred to the Pacinian Corpuscles, the discovery of an Italian physician in 1830 and 1840. He said:

> Pacini found in all the sensible nerves of the fingers many elliptical whitish corpuscles. He compared them to the electrical organs of the torpedo and described them as animal magneto-motors, or organs of animal magnetism, and so did

Henle and Holliker, two German anatomists who have studied and described these corpuscles very minutely.

In the human body they are found in great numbers in connection with the nerves of the hand, also in those of the foot. . . . The ecstatic dances of the enthusiasts and the not-sinking of somnambulists in water, or their ability to use the soles of their feet as organs of perception, and the ancient art of healing by the soles of the feet—all these facts explain the mystery.

They are found sparingly on the spinal nerves, and on the plexuses of the sympathetic, but never on the nerves of motion. . . . Anatomists are interested in these Pacinian corpuscles because of the novel aspect in which they present the constituent parts of the nerve-tube, placed in the heart of a system of concentric membranous capsules with intervening fluid, and divested of that layer which they (the anatomists) regard as an isolator and protector of the more potential central axis within.

This apparatus—almost formed like a voltaic pile, is the instrument for that peculiar vital energy, known more or less to all students as Animal Magnetism.

Since the cat is somewhat famous in all witchcraft, let me state, that in the mesentary of the cat, they can be seen in large numbers with the naked eye, as small oval-shaded grains a little smaller than hemp-seeds. A few have been found in the ox (symbol of the priestly office) but they are wanting in all birds, amphibia and fishes.

"Magic" whether brought about by the aid of spirits or simply through an understanding of secret natural laws, is of two kinds, "white" and "black," according as its intent and consequences are evil or good, and in this respect does not differ from the use made of the well-known laws of nature, which are ever of good or evil character, in the hands of good or evil persons. To the church in its powerful control of the human will, must be attributed the use of "black magic," in its most injurious form. Proof that knowledge of the mysterious laws governing ordinary natural phenomena still exists even among civilized people, is undubitable. Our American Indians in various portions of the continent, according to authorities, also possess power to produce storms of thunder, lightning and rain.[29]

A vast amount of evidence exists, to show that the word "witch" formerly signified a woman of superior knowledge. Many of the persons called witches doubtless possessed a super-abundance of the Pacinian corpuscles in hands and feet, enabling them to swim when cast into water bound, to rise in the air against the ordinary action of gravity, to heal by a touch, and in some instances to sink into a condition of catalepsy, perfectly unconscious of torture when applied. Many were doubtless psychic sensitives of high powers similar perhaps to the "Seeress of Prevorst," whose peculiar characteristics were the subject of investigation by Dr. Kerner, about the end of the witch period, his report forming one of the most mysteriously interesting portions of psychic literature. The "Seeress" was able to perceive the hidden principles of all vegetable or mineral substances, whether beneficial or injurious. Dr. Kerner stated that her magnetic condition might be divided into four degrees.

> *First;* that in which she ordinarily was when she appeared to be awakened but on the contrary was the first stage of her inner life, in many persons of whom it was not expected and who was not aware of it themselves, being in this state.

> *Second;* the magnetic dream, which she believed to be the condition of many persons who were regarded as insane.

> *Third;* the half wakening state when she spoke and wrote the inner language, her spirit then being in intimate conjunction whith her soul.

> *Fourth;* her clairvoyant state.

With the investigation of Dr. Kerner, the discoveries of Galvani, Pacini, and those more recently connected with electricity, notably of Edison and Nikolas Testa, the world seems upon the eve of important knowledge which may throw full light upon the peculiar nerve action of the witch period, when a holocaust of women were sacrificed, victims of the ignorance and barbarity of the church, which thus retarded civilization and delayed spiritual progress for many hundred years. Besides the natural psychics who formed a large proportion of the victims of this period, other women with a natural spirit of investigation made scientific discoveries with equally baleful effect upon themselves; the one fact of a woman's possessing knowledge serving to bring her under the suspicion and accusation of the church. Henry More, a learned Cambridge graduate of the seventeenth century wrote a treatise on witchcraft explanatory of the term "witch" which he affirmed simply signified a wise, or learned woman. It meant "uncommon" but not unlawful knowledge or skill. It will assist in forming an opinion to know that the word "witch" is from wekken, to prophecy, a direct bearing upon the psychic powers of many such persons. The modern Slavonian or Russian name for witch, "vjédma," is from the verb "to know" signifying much the same as Veda.[30] Muller says "Veda" means the same as the wise, "wisdom." The Sanskrit word "Vidma" answers to the German "wir wissen," which literally means "we know." A Russian name for the witch, "Zaharku," is derived from the verb "Znat," to know.[31] A curious account of modern Russian belief in witch-craft is to be found in Madame Blavatsky's "Isis Unveiled." The German word "Heke," that is, witch, primarily signified priestess, a wise or superior woman who in a sylvan temple worshiped those gods and goddesses that together governed earth and heaven. Not alone but with thousands of the people for whom she officiated she was found there especially upon Walpurgis Night, the chief Hexen (witch) Sabbat of the north. A German scholar furnished this explantion.

> The German word Heke, (witch) is a compound word from "hag" and "idisan" or "disan." Hag means a beautiful landscape, woodland, meadow, field, altogether. Idisen means female deities, wise-women. Hexen-Sabbat, or Walpurgis Night is May twelfth. Perfume and avocation—originally the old gods—perverted by the priests. It is a remnant of the great gathering to worship the old deities, when Christianity had overshadowed them. A monument of the wedding of Woden or Odin with Freia—Sun and Earth at spring-time.

The Saxon festival "Eostre," the christian Easter, was celebrated in April, each of these festivals at a time when winter
having released its sway, smiling earth giving her life to healing
herbs and leaves, once more welcomed her worshipers. In the
South of Europe, the month of October peculiarly belonged to
the witches.[32] The first of May, May Day, was especially devoted
by those elementals known as fairies, whose special rites were
dances upon the green sward, leaving curious mementoes of their
visits in the circles known as "Faries Rings." In reality the original
meaning of "witch" was a wise woman. So also the word "Sab"
means sage or wise, and "Saba" a host or congregation;[33] while
"Bac," "Boc" and "Bacchus"[34] all originally signified book.[35]
"Sabs" was the name of the day when the Celtic Druids gave
instruction and is the origin of our words Sabbath and Sunday.
But the degradation of learning, its almost total loss among christian nations, an entire change in the signification of words, owing
to ignorance and superstition led to the strangest and most infamous results. The earliest doctors among the common people of
christian Europe were women[36] who had learned the virtues and
use of herbs. The famous works of Paracelsus were but compila-
tions of the knowledge of these "wise women" as he himself
stated. During the feudal ages women were excellent surgeons,
wounded warriors frequently falling under their care and to the
skill of these women were indebted for recovery from dangerous
wounds. Among the women of savage races to much greater
extent than among the men, a knowledge of the healing powers
of plants and herbs is to this day found. But while for many hundred years the knowledge of medicine, and its practice among the
poorer classes was almost entirely in the hands of women and
many discoveries in science are due to them, yet an acquaintance
of herbs soothing to pain, or healing in their qualities, was then
looked upon as having been acquired through diabolical agency.
Even those persons cured through the instrumentality of some
woman, were ready when the hour came to assert their belief in
her indebtedness to the devil for her knowledge. Not only were
the common people themselves ignorant of all science, but their

brains were filled with superstitious fears, and the belief that knowledge had been first introduced to the world through woman's obedience to the devil. In the fourteenth century the church decreed that any woman who healed others without having duly studied, was a witch and should suffer death; yet in that same century, 1527, at Balse, Paracelsus threw all his medical works, including those of Hippocrates and Galen into the fire, saying that he knew nothing except what he had learned from witches.[37] As late as 1736, the persecution of her male compeers cast Elizabeth Blackwell, an English woman physician, into prison for debt. Devoting herself even behind the bars to her loved science, she prepared the first medical botany given to the world. The modern discovery of anæsthetics by means of whose use human suffering can be so greatly ameliorated, is justly claimed as the greatest boon that science has conferred upon mankind, yet it must not be forgotten that this medical art of mitigating pain, is but an olden one rediscovered. Methods of causing insensibility to pain were known to the ancient world. During the middle ages these secrets were only understood by the persecuted women doctors of that period, subjected under church rule to torture, burning at the stake or drowning as witches. The use of pain-destroying medicaments by women can be traced back from five hundred to a thousand years. At the time that witchcraft became the great ogre against which the church expended all its terrific powers, women doctors employed anæsthetics to mitigate the pains and perils of motherhood,[38] throwing the sufferer into a deep sleep when the child entered the world. They made use of the Solanæ, especially Belladonna. But that woman should find relief at this hour of intense suffering and peril when a new being entered the world, provoked open hostility from the church. The use of mitigating herbs assailed that theory of the church which having placed the creation of sin upon woman, still further inculcated the doctrine that she must undergo continual penance, the greatest suffering being a punishment in nowise equal to her deserts. Its teachings that she had therefore been especially cursed by her Maker with suffering and sorrow at this period, rendered the use of mitigating remedies during childbirth dangerous alike to the "wise woman" and the mother for whose relief they were employed.[39] Although the present century has shown similar opposition by the church to the use of anaesthetics for women at this time, it is almost impossible to depict the sentiment against such relief, which made the witchcraft period one of especial terror to womankind—an age that looked upon the slightest attempt at such alleviation as proof of collusion with the devil. So strong was the power of the church, so universal the belief in the guilt of all women, that even those sufferers who had availed themselves of the knowledge of the "wise woman" did so in fear as calling in the aid of evil, and were ready to testify against her to whom they had been indebted for alleviation of pain, whenever required by the dread mandate of the church. A strong natural bias toward the study of medicine, together with deepest sympathy for suffering humanity, were required in order to sustain the "wise woman" amid the perils constantly surrounding her; many such women losing their lives as witches simply because of their superior medical and surgical knowledge. Death by torture was the method of the church for the repression of woman's intellect, knowledge being held as evil and dangerous in her hands. Ignorance was regarded as an especial virtue in woman, and fear held her in this condition. Few women dared be wise, after thousands of their sex had gone to death by drowning or burning because of their knowledge. The superior learning of witches was recognized in the widely extended belief of their ability to work miracles. The witch was in reality the profoundest thinker, the most advanced scientist of those ages. The persecution which for ages waged against witches was in reality an attack upon science at the hands of the church. As knowledge has ever been power, the church feared its use in woman's hands, and leveled its deadliest blows at her. Although the church in its myth of the fall attributes knowledge to woman's having eaten of its tree, yet while not scrupling to make use of the results of her disobedience for its own benefit, it has been most earnest in its endeavors to prevent her from like use. No less today than during the darkest period of its history, is the church the great opponent of woman's education, every advance step for her having found the church antagonistic.

Every kind of self-interest was brought into play in these accusations of witchcraft against women physicians: greed, malice, envy, hatred, fear, the desire of clearing one's self from suspicion, all became motives. Male physicians not skillful enough to cure disease would deliberately swear that there could be but one reason for their failure—the use of witchcraft against them. As the charge of witchcraft not only brought disrepute but death upon the "wise woman" at the hands of the church, she was soon compelled to abandon both the practice of medicine and surgery, and for many hundred years but few women doctors were to be found in christian countries. It is, however, a noticeable fact that Madam La Chapelle, an eminent woman accoucher of France, during the present century, and M. Chaussure revived the use of Belladonna[40] during parturition, thus acknowledging the scientific acquirements of serf women and "witches." Since the reentrance of woman into the medical profession within the past few years, the world has been indebted for a knowledge of the cause and cure of certain forms of disease peculiar to woman, to the skill of those physicians of her own sex whom the church so long banished from practice.

Through its opposition to the use of anaesthetics by the women physicians of the witch period, the church again interposed the weight of her mighty arm to crush science, leaving the load of preventable suffering of all kinds upon the world for many hundred years longer, or until the light of a scientific civilization threw discredit upon her authority. History proves that women were the earliest chemists. The witch period also shows us the germs of a medical system, the Homeopathic, supposed to be of modern origin, in *similia similibus curantor*. Among the strange epidemics of these ages, a dancing mania appeared; Belladonna among whose effects is the desire of dancing, was employed as a cure of the "Dancing Mania," and thus the theory of Hahnemann was forestalled. During the witch period these sages or wise-women were believed to be endowed with a supernatural or magical power of curing diseases. They were also regarded as prophets to whom the secrets of the future were known. The women of ancient Germany, of Gaul and among the Celts were especially famous for their healing powers,[41] possessing knowledge by which wounds and diseases that baffled the most expert male physicians were cured. The women of a still more ancient period, the fame of whose magical powers has descended to the present time, Circe, Medea and Thracia, were evidently physicians of the highest skill. The secret of compounding herbs and drugs left by Circe to her descendants, gave them power over the most poisonous serpents. Chief among the many herbs, plants and roots whose virtues were discovered by Medea, that of Aconite stands preeminent. The Thracian nation took its name from the famous Thracia whose medical skill and knowledge of herbs was so great that the country deemed it an honor to thus perpetuate her name.

Aside from women of superior intelligence who were almost invariably accused of witchcraft, the old, the insane, the bedridden, the idiotic,[42] also fell under condemnation. The first investigation by Rev. Cotten Mather in America resulted in the hanging of a half-witted Quaker woman. Later still, an Indian woman, an insane man, and another woman who was bedridden were also accused. Under the present theories regarding human rights, it seems scarcely possible that less than two hundred years ago such practices were not only common in England, but had also been brought into America by the Puritan Fathers. The humiliation and tortures of women increased in proportion to the spread of christianity,[43] and the broader area over which man's sole authority in church and state was disseminated. As the supreme extent of spiritual wrong grew out of the bondage of the church over free thought, so the extreme of physicial wrong rose from the growth of the inquisitional or paternal spirit, which assumed that one human being possessed divine authority over another human being. Paternalism, a species of condensed patriarchism, runs through ecclesiastical, civil, and common law. Down to the time of the American revolution, individuality was an uncomprehended word; many hundred crimes were punishable by death. That of pressing to death, *peine-fort-et-dure*, the strong and hard pain, was practiced upon both men and women in England for five hundred years and brought by the pilgrims to New England. The culprit was placed in the dark lower room of some prison, naked, upon the bare ground without clothing on rushes underneath or to cover him. The legs and arms were extended toward the four corners of the room and as great a weight placed upon the body as could be supported. "The first day he (or she) is to have three morsels of barley bread; upon the second day three draughts of water standing next to the door of the prison, without bread, and this to be his (or her) diet till he (or she) die."

It is computed from historical records that nine millions of persons were put to death for witchcraft after 1484, or during a period of three hundred years, and this estimate does not include the vast number who were sacrificed in the preceding centuries upon the same accusation. The greater number of this incredible multitude were women. Under catholicism, those condemned as sorcerers and witches, as "heretics," were in reality the most advanced thinkers of the christian ages. Under that protestant pope, the Eighth Henry, an Act of Parliament condemning witchcraft as felony was confirmed. Enacted under James, it had fallen into disuse, but numerous petitions setting forth that witches and sorcerers were "wonderful many," and his majesty's subjects persecuted to death by their devices, led to its reenactment. The methods used to extort confession without which it was impossible in many cases to convict for witchcraft, led to the grossest outrages upon woman. Searching the body of the suspected witch for the marks of Satan, and the practice of shaving the whole body before applying torture were occasions of atrocious indignities. It was asserted that all who consorted with devils had some secret mark about them, in some hidden place of their bodies; as the inside of the lip, the hair of the eyebrows, inside of the thigh, the hollow of the arm or still more private parts, from whence Satan drew nourishment. This originated a class of men known as "Witch Prickers" who divesting the supposed witch, whether maid, matron, or child, of all clothing minutely examined all parts of her body for the devil's sign. Woe to the woman possessing a mole or other blemish upon her person, it was immediately pointed to as Satan's seal and as undeniable proof of having sold herself to the devil. Belief in this sign existed among the most educated persons. Albertus Pictus, an advocate in the Parliament of Paris, declared he himself had seen a woman with the devil's mark on her shoulders, carried off the next day by the devil. Many authors affirmed the trustworthiness of witch-marks. It was supposed that upon touching the place the witch would be unable to speak. If under the torture of having every portion of her body punctured by a sharp instrument, the victim became no longer able to cry out, her silence was an accepted proof of finding the witch-mark and her condemnation was equally certain. So great was the number of accused, that these men found profitable employment. The depth of iniquity to which greed of money leads was never more forcibly shown than during witchcraft. One Kincaid, a New England Witch Pricker, after stripping his victims of all clothing, bound them hand and foot, then thrust pins into every part of their bodies until exhausted and rendered speechless by the torture, they were unable to scream, when he would triumphantly proclaim that he had found the witch-mark. Another confessed on the gallows, to which a just fate finally condemned him, that he had illegally caused the death of one hundred and twenty women whom he had thus tortured. No means were considered too severe in order to secure conviction. The Jesuit, Del Rio, said torture could scarcely be properly administered without more or less dislocation of the joints, and persons escaping conviction were frequently crippled for life.[44] The church declared the female sex had always been most concerned in the crime of christian witchcraft and as it was its aim to separate woman from all connection with its ordinances, it also asserted that the priestesses of antiquity held their high places by means of witchcraft.

Trials for witchcraft filled the coffers of the church, as whenever conviction took place, the property of the witch and her family was confiscated to that body. The clergy fattened upon the torture and burning of women. Books giving directions for the punishment to be inflicted upon them bore the significant titles of *Scourge, Hammer, Ant Hills, Floggings*, etc. During the middle ages the devil was a personal being to the church with power about equal to that of God, his kingdom maintaining its equilibrium with the Father, Son and Holy Ghost of Heaven, by means of three persons in Hell; Lucifer, Beelzebub and Leviathan. In this era of christian devil-worship the three in hell equipoised the three in the Godhead. Marriage with devils was one of the most ordinary accusation in witch trials. Such connections were sometimes regarded with pride; the celebrated marshall de Bassompierre boasting that the founder of his family was engendered from communion with a spirit. It was reported of the mother of Luther that she was familiar with an Incubus. During this period many nuns and married women confessed to having been visited by Incubi of whose visits no spiritual efforts could rid them. Church history also proves that young girls and boys, many under ten years of age were tried for intercourse with such spirits. Those infesting men were known as Succubi. Lady Frances Howard, daughter of the earl of Suffolk, obtained a divorce from her husband because of his connection with a Succubus.

One of the most notable things connected with such accusation was the frequent confession of its truthfulness. In 1459, a great number of witches and wizards were burned,[45] who publicly confessed to their use of ungents, to their dances, feasts, and their consort with devils. A Vicar General[46] among the Laodunenses, at his death left confession of his witch-rides, his copulation with devils, etc. Nor is the present age free from similar confessions. Tales of marriage with spirits; of dead lovers paying nightly visits to the living betrothed—of Incubi consorting with willing or unwilling victims;—all those mediæval statements regarding the intercourse of spirits of the dead with the living, all the customs of witchcraft and sorcery are paralleled in our midst today; and such statements do not come from the ignorant and superstitious, but are made by persons of intelligence as within their own personal experience. During the witchcraft period familiarity of this nature with Incubi or Succubi was punished with death. Occasionally a person was found of sufficient saintliness to exorcise them as Elementals are said to have been exorcised during the last half of the present century.[47] Devils were said to be very fond of women with beautiful hair and the direction of St. Paul in regard to woman's keeping her head covered was not always regarded as a sign of inferiority, but sometimes believed to be a precautionary admonition intended for the safety of christian women.[48] To this day the people of some eastern countries, men and women alike, will not expose the head uncovered, because of the danger of thus giving entrance to certain invisible beings of an injurious character; the Persians in particular, wearing a turban or cloth of peculiar appearance called Mathoomba. Confessions of magical and witchcraft practices were by no means rare even among the highest church dignitaries who implicated themselves by such avowals. It was customary to attribute the practice of magic to the most holy fathers of the church. The popes from Sylvester II to Gregory VII were all believed to have been magicians. Benedict IX was also thus accused. The difference between the practices of men and of women existed only in name. What was termed magic, among men, was called witchcraft in woman. The one was rarely, the other invariably, punished.

The practice of magic by the holy fathers was in furtherance of private or ecclesiastical advancement and therefore legitimate in the eye of the church. Yet, death-bed repentance was by no means infrequent. Of Pope Sylvester, it is said, that convinced of his sinfulness in having practiced magic, upon his deathbed he ordered his tongue to be torn out and his hands cut off because he had sacrificed to the devil; having learned the art when Bishop of Rheims. The significant question as to whether magnetism or hypnotism was not a custom of the church during the middle ages, as part of the "magic" practiced by illustrious ecclesiastical dignitaries, is one of importance in view of recent hypnotic experiments. The fact that by means of "suggestion" the responsibility for crime and the perpetration of overt criminal acts can be made to fall upon persons entirely innocent of criminal intention, who, at the time are in a condition of irresponsibility, while the actual felon, the person who incited the act remains unknown and unsuspected, exceeds in malign power all that christendom has taught regarding the evil one. Science trembles on the verge of important discoveries which may open the door for a full understanding of mediæval witchcraft. The Scotch woman who asked if a person could not be a witch without knowing it, had intuitive perception that by the action of one person upon another, consequences could be induced of which the perpetrator was entirely guiltless.[49] Doubtless the strange power which certain persons are capable of wielding over others, at present calling the attention of scientific investigators, was very common during the witchcraft period. Of this power the church as self-constituted guardian of the esoteric sciences was fully aware, frequently making it the method through which envy, greed and revenge, satisfied themselves while throwing the external appearance of guilt upon others. The most complete protection against such powers—a strong will—it has ever been the aim of the church to destroy. Freedom of the will has ever held place in clerical denunciation by side of "original sin," and punished as sorcery.[50]

A reminiscence of olden magic—far older than the witchcraft period—is found in the Masonic lamentation over the "lost word." This "lost word," the "supreme word," by whose use all things can be subdued, is still the quest of a certain portion of the world; and sorcerers are still mentioned, who cannot die until a certain mysterious word is passed from "mouth to ear." One of the latest occult societies extant, its membership widely extended, claims its origin from a mysterious word similarly passed. The Lord's Prayer demands the making whole (hallowed), of the Father's name, evidently in the esoteric sense referring to that loss which dwells in the minds of men through tradition, a species of unwritten history. With the restoration of the feminine in all its attributes to its rightful place everywhere, in realms seen and unseen, the lost power will have been restored, the "lost name" have been found. Numbers are closely connected with names, their early knowledge not only having preceded letters, but having been of much greater value, although after a time, letters and numbers became interchangeable. Certain persons devoted to the consideration of occult subjects therefore claim the lost power to abide in a number rather than in a word; sounds possessing great and peculiar influence in all magical formulas, their power largely depending upon inflection and tone or vibration; color and light are also called in aid during magical formulas.[51]

The three most distinguishing features of the history of witchcraft were its use for the enrichment of the church; for the advancement of political schemes; and for the gratification of private malice. Among these the most influential reason was the emolument it brought to the church. Although inquisitors and the clergy were the principal prosecutors, this period gave opportunity for the gratification of private malice, and persons imbued with secret enmity towards others, or who coveted their property, found ready occasion for the indulgence of that malice of covetousness; while the church always claimed one-half, it divided the remainder of the accused's possessions between the judge and the prosecutor. Under these circumstances accusation and conviction became convertible terms. The pretense under which the church confiscated to itself all property of the accused was in line with its other sophistical teaching. It declared that the taint of witchcraft hung to all that had belonged to the condemned, whose friends were not safe with such property in their possession. To make this claim more effective, it was also asserted that the very fact of one member of a family having fallen into the practice of this sin was virtual proof that all were likewise attainted. Under this allegation of the church, a protest against such robbery was held as proof of the witchcraft in the person so protesting. For the purpose of getting the property of the accused admission of the crime was strenuously pressed. In some countries the property was not forfeited unless such confession took place. Persecution for witchcraft was if possible more violent in the sixteenth and seventeenth centuries than at any previous date. By this period it had been introduced into America through the instrumentality of the Puritan Fathers. It was no less widespread in Calvanistic Scotland, while it reappeared with renewed vigor in Catholic countries. In the State of Venice it caused open rebellion against church authority, the Council forbidding the sentence of the Inquisition to be carried out.[52]

While only Venice in the whole of Europe defied the church upon this point, emphatically protesting against such robbery of her citizens, she ultimately succeeded in establishing a treaty with the pope whereby the inheritance of the condemned was retained in the family. The rebellion of Venice against the church upon the question of property belonging to its subjects, a question upon which the state held itself preeminent, soon effected a radical change and had remarkable effect in lessening the number of accusations in that state.[53] Theft by the church in that direction, no longer possible, accusations of witchcraft soon ceased; being no longer recognized as sin, after ceasing to bring money into the coffers of the church.

It is a fact noted by very many authorities that when witchcraft fell under control of the state, its penalties were greatly lessened while accusations grew fewer. Yet for a period, even the civil power aided in spreading this belief, offering rewards for conviction; and as the church had grown immensely rich by means of witch persecution, so the state increased its own power and wealth through similar means. The theory of Bishop Butler that whole communities at times become mad, seems proven by the experience of this period. Upon no other ground but that of universal insanity can excusable explanation be offered. But for the church no such exculpation is possible, her teachings and her acts having created this wholesale madness of communities. Experience of her course during preceding centuries show us that the persecution of the witchcraft period was but a continuation of her policy from the moment of her existence—that of universal dominion over the lives, the property, and the thoughts of mankind. Neither rank, nor learning, age, nor goodness freed a woman from accusation.[54] The mother of the great astronomer, Kepler, a woman of noble family, died in chains having been accused of witchcraft.[55] The council of Bourges tortured a reputed witch who was only known for her good works. A determined effort for the destruction of every virtue among women seemed made at this period. In the middle of the thirteenth century, the Emperor Theodore Lascarius caused a noble lady of his court to be entirely stripped of her clothing, and placed thus nude in a sack with cats, but even this torture failed to extort a confession from her innocent lips. Even in America, women of the purest lives, all of whose years had been given to good works, met with death from like accusation.

Soon after the confirmation of celibacy as a dogma of the church, at the time when the persecution for witchcraft so rapidly increased, which was also the period of the greatest oppression under feudalism—a peculiar and silent rebellion against both church and state took place among the peasantry of Europe, who assembled in the seclusion of night and the forest, their only place of safety in which to speak of their wrongs. Freedom for the peasant was found only at night. Known as "Birds of the Night," "Foxes," "Birds of Prey," it was only at night assemblages that they enjoyed the least happiness or freedom. Here with wives and daughters, they met to talk over the gross outrages perpetrated upon them. Out of their foul wrongs grew the sacrifice of the "Black Mass" with women as officiating priestess, in which the rites of the church were travestied in solemn mockery, and defiance cast at that heaven which permitted the priest and the lord alike to trample upon all the sacred rights of womanhood, in the name of religion and law. During this mocking service a true sacrifice of wheat was offered to the "Spirit of the Earth" who made wheat to grow, and loosened birds bore aloft to the "God of Freedom" the sighs and prayers of the serfs asking that their descendants might be free. We can but regard this sacrifice as the most acceptable offering made in that day of moral degradation; a sacrifice and a prayer more holy than all the ceremonials of the church. This service where woman by virtue of her greater despair acted both as altar and priest, opened with the following address and prayer. "I will come before Thine altar, but save me, O Lord, from the faithless and violent man!" (from the priest and the baron).[56] From these assemblages known as "Sabbat" or "the

Sabbath" from the old Pagan midsummer-day sacrifice to "Bacchus Sabiesa" rose the belief in the "Witches Sabbath," which for several hundred years formed a source of accusation against women, sending tens of thousands to most horrible deaths. The thirteenth century was about the central period of this rebellion of the serfs against God and the church when they drank each other's blood as a sacrament, while secretly speaking of their oppression.[57] The officiating priestess was usually about thirty years old, having experienced all the wrongs that woman suffered under church and state. She was entitled "The Elder" yet in defiance of that God to whom the serfs under church teaching ascribed all their wrongs, she was also called "The Devil's bride." This period was especially that of woman's rebellion against the existing order of religion and government in both church and state. While man was connected with her in these ceremonies as father, husband, brother, yet all accounts show that to woman as the most deeply wronged, was accorded all authority. Without her, no man was admitted to this celebration, which took place in the seclusion of the forest and under the utmost secrecy. Offerings were made to the latest dead and the most newly born of the district, and defiance hurled against that God to whose injustice the church had taught woman that all her wrongs were due.

Woman's knowledge of herbs was made use of in a preparation of Solanæ which mixed with mead, beer, cider, or farcy—the strong drink of the west—disposed the oppressed serfs to joyous dancing and partial forgetfulness of their wrongs during these popular night gatherings of the Sabbath.[58] It became "the comforter" throwing the friendly mantle of partial oblivion over the mental suffering of "him who had been so wronged" as it had done for the mother's physical pain. "The Sabbath" was evidently the secret protest of men and women whom church and state in combination had utterly oppressed and degraded. For centuries there seemed no hope for this class of humanity—for this degraded portion of christendom—yet, even then women held position of superiority in these night assemblages. Among the "Papers of the Bastile," a more extended account of woman officiating as her own altar, is to be found.[59]

The injustice of man towards woman under the laws of both Church and State engrafted upon society, have resulted in many evils unsuspected by the world, which if known would strike it with amazement and terror. Even Louis Lingg, one of the condemned Chicago anarchists, young, handsome, of vigorous intellect, who uncomplainingly accepted for himself that death he had decreed to the representatives to law; even he, who neither asked mercy nor accepted the death decreed him, was the outgrowth of woman's wrongs. His mother with whom his fate was thrown, a woman of the people in Hungary, belonging to a powerless class crushed for centuries, the plaything of those above them;—his father, a representative of the aristocracy descended from a long line of military ancestors, leaving him, as the church had taught him, to the sole care of the mother he had betrayed, it was impossible for this boy not to find in his breast a turmoil of conflicting emotions, but above all, ruling all, a hatred of entrenched oppression; nor did his father's military blood fail to play its part, leading to the final result which affrighted a city and closed his young life.

In looking at the history of witchcraft we see three striking points for consideration:

First; That women were chiefly accused.

Second; That men believing in woman's inherent wickedness, and understanding neither the mental nor the physical peculiarities of her being, ascribed all her idiosyncracies to witchcraft.

Third; That the clergy inculcated the idea that woman was in league with the devil, and that strong intellect, remarkable beauty, or unusual sickness were in themselves proof of this league.

Catholics and protestants yet agree in holding women as the chief accessory of the devil.[60]

The belief in witches indeed seemed intensified after the reformation. Luther said:"I would have no compassion for a witch, I would burn them all." He looked upon those who were afflicted with blindness, lameness, or idiocy from birth,[61] as possessed of demons and there is record of his attempt to drown an afflicted child in whom he declared no soul existed, its body being animated by the devil alone. But a magistrate more enlightened or more humane than the great reformer, interfered to save the child's life. Were Luther on earth again today with the sentiments of his lifetime, he would regard the whole community as mad. Asylums for the blind, the dumb and idiots, curative treatment for cripples and all persons naturally deformed, would be to him a direct intervention with the ways of providence. The belief of this great reformer proves the folly of considering a man wise, because he is pious. Religion and humanity were as far apart with him after the reformation as while he was yet a monk. The fruits of monasticism continued their effects, and his latter life showed slight intellectual or spiritual advancement. As late as 1768 John Wesley declared the giving up of witchcraft to be in effect giving up the Bible. Such was his low estimate of woman that he regarded his own wife as too sinful to conduct family prayers, although to Susannah, equally with John, is Methodism indebted for its existence. In Great Britain, the rapid increase of belief in witchcraft after the reformation was especially noticeable. The act of Parliament which declared witchcraft to be felony; confirmed under Henry VIII was again confirmed under Elizabeth. In England the reformation brought with it great increase of tyranny both civil and ecclesiastical. Under Henry VIII many new treasons were created. This king who sent the largest proportion of his six wives to the headsman's block, who neither hesitated at incest or at casting the taint of illegitimacy upon the daughter who succeeded him upon the throne, could not be expected to show justice or mercy to subject women. The penal laws of even celibate Elizabeth were largely the result of the change in religion of the realm.[62] The queen, absolute in Church as in State, who "bent priest and prelate to her fiery will," caused the laws to bear with equal severity upon protestant and catholic. Under her "A Statute of Uniformity for abolishing Diversity of Opinions" was enacted, and the clergy were continued in the enjoyment of secular power. Women received no favor. The restrictions of the catholic church in regard to the residence of a priest's mother or sister in his house were now extended to the laity. No man was permitted to give his widowed mother or orphan sister a home in his house without permission from the authorities, and then but for a limited time. Single women were allowed no control over their own actions. Twelve years was the legal marriageable age for a girl, after which period if still unmarried she could be bound out at the option of the court.[63] Nor did the Cromwellian period lessen woman's persecution. The number of witches executed under the Presbyterian domination of the Long Parliament according to a list[64] that has been preserved, amounted to between three and four thousand persons. The legal profession no less than the clerical asserted its belief in witchcraft, referring to the Bible in confirmation. Blackstone said:

> To deny the possibility, nay the actual existence of witchcraft and sorcery is at once flatly to contradict the revealed word of God, in various passages of the Old and New Testament; and the thing itself is a truth to which every nation in the world hath in its turn borne testimony, either by examples seemingly well attested, or by prohibiting laws.

The protestant clergy equally with the catholic priesthood were charged with fostering a belief in witchcraft for the purpose of gain. At no period of the world has a more diabolical system of robbery existed. For the sake of a few pounds or pence, the most helpless of human beings, made helpless through church teaching as to their unworthiness, were by the church daily brought under accusation, exposing them to a cruel death at the hand of irresponsible tyranny. The system of thuggery in India, shines white by side of this christian system of robbery, inaugurated by the church and sustained by the state. In the name of religion, the worst crimes against humanity have ever been perpetrated. On the accession of James I he ordered the learned work of Reginald Scott against witchcraft, to be burned.[65]

This was in accordance with the act of Parliament 1605–1609 which ratified a belief in witchcraft in the three kingdoms. At this date the tragedy of *Macbeth* appeared, deeply tinged with the belief of the times. A few persons maintaining possession of their senses, recognized the fact that fear, apprehension and melancholy gave birth to the wildest self-delusions; medical experience recording many instances of this character. In an age when ignorance and superstition prevailed among the people at large, while vice, ignorance, and cupidity were in equal force among those in power, the strangest beliefs became prevalent.

Sir George Mackenzie, the eminent king's advocate of Scotland, conducting many trials for witchcraft, became convinced it was largely a subject of fear and delusion. He said:

> Those poor persons who are ordinarily accused of this crime are poor ignorant creatures, and ofttimes women who understood not the nature of what they are accused of, and many mistake their own fears and apprehensions for witchcraft, of which I shall give you two instances; one of a poor man, who after he had confessed witchcraft being asked how he saw the devil, he answered "like flies dancing about a candle." Another of a woman who asked sincerely, when accused, "if a woman might be a witch and not know it?" And it is dangerous then. Those who of all others are the most simple should be tried for a crime which of all others is the most mysterious. Those poor creatures when defamed became so confused with fear and the close prison in which they were kept, and so starved for want of meals and sleep (either of which wants is enough to destroy the strongest reason), when men are confounded with fear and apprehension they will imagine things very ridiculous and absurd. Melancholy often makes men imagine they are horses. Most of these poor creatures are tortured by their keepers who are persuaded they do God good service. Most of all that were taken were tortured in this manner and this usage was the ground of their complaints.

To such an extent was this persecution carried even in protestant Scotland that accused women sometimes admitted their guilt that they might die and thus escape from a world where even if cleared, they would ever after be looked upon with suspicion. Sir George Mackenzie visiting some women who had confessed, one of them told him "under secrecie" that:

She had not confessed because she was guilty but being a poor creature who wrought for her meat and being defined for a witch, she knew she would starve, for no person thereafter would give her either meat or lodging, and that all men would beat her and hound dogs at her and therefore she desired to be out of the world, whereupon she wept bitterly and upon her knees called upon God to witness what she said.

Even under all the evidence of the persecution and cruel tortures that innocent women endured during the witchcraft period, no effort of the imagination can portray the sufferings of an accused woman. The death this poor woman chose, in voluntarily admitting a crime of which she was innocent, rather than to accept a chance of life with the name of "witch" clinging to her, was one of the most painful of which we can conceive, although in the diversity of torture inflicted upon the witch it is scarcely possible to say which one was the least agonizing. In no country has the devil ever been more fully regarded as a real personage, ever on the watch for souls, than in Christian Scotland. Sir George says:

Another told me she was afraid the devil would challenge a right to her soul as the minister said when he desired her to confess; and therefore she desired to die.[66]

The following is an account of the material used and the expenses attending the execution of two witches in Scotland.

For 10 loads of coal to burn the witches. £3 06.8
" A tar barrel 0 14.0
" towes 0 06.0
" hurdles to be jumps for them. 3 10.0
" making of them. 0 08.0
" one to go to Tinmouth for the lord to
     sit upon the assize as judge 0 06.0
" the executioner for his pains 8 14.0
" his expenses there. 0 16.4

What was the special office of the executioner does not appear; whether to drag the victims upon hurdles, to the places of burning, to light the fire, to keep it well blazing, is not mentioned although his office was important and a well-paid one; eight pounds and fourteen shillings above his expenses, sixteen shillings and four pence more; in all nine pounds, ten shillings and four pence, a sum equal to one hundred and fifty or two hundred dollars of the present day. At these rates it was easy to find men for the purpose desired. It is worthy of note that under the frequency of torture the payment lessened. Strange experiences sometimes befell those who were tortured: a cataleptic or hypnotic state coming on amid their most cruel sufferings causing an entire insensibility to pain. To the church this condition was sure evidence of help from Satan and caused a renewal of torture as soon as sensibility returned.

> In the year 1639 a poor widow called Lucken, who was accused of being a witch and sentenced to the rack at Helmstadt having been cruelly tortured by the screw, was seized with convulsions, spoke high German and a strange language and then fell asleep on the rack and appeared to be dead. The circumstance related to the juricounsul at Helmstadt she was ordered to be again submitted to the torture. Then protesting she was a good Christian while the executioner stretched her on the rack, whipt her with rods and sprinkled her with burning brimstone, she fell again fast asleep and could not by any means be awakened.[67]

Boiling heretics and malefactors alive, commonly in oil but occasionally in water, was practiced throughout Europe until a comparatively late period. In fact as a civil punishment in England it dates only to 1531 under Henry VII. The "Chronicle of the Gray Friars" mentioned a man let down by a chain into a kettle of hot water until dead. We have expense items of this form of torture, in the boiling of Friar Stone of Canterbury.

> Paid two men that sat by the kettle and boiled
> him. 1s

To three men that carried his quarters to the
      gate and set them up. 1s
For a woman that scoured the kettle. 2d

Boiling was a form of torture frequently used for women. The official records of Paris show the price paid for torture in France was larger than in England; boiling in oil in the former country costing forty-eight francs as against one shilling in the latter. It must be remembered these official prices for torture are not taken from the records of China or Persia, two thousand years ago, nor from among the savages of Patagonia, Australia or Guinea, but two European countries of highest Christian civilization within the last three hundred years.

The following list of prices for dealing with criminals is taken from the official records in Paris:

For boiling a criminal in oil, francs 48
For tearing a living man in four quarters with horses 30
Execution with the sword 20
Breaking on the wheel 10
Mounting the head on a pole 10
Quartering a man 36
Hanging a man 29
Burying a man 2
Impaling a man alive 14
Burning a witch alive 28
Flaying a man alive 28
Drowning an infanticide in a sack 24
Throwing a suicide's body among the offal 20
Putting to the torture 4
For applying the thumb-screw 2
For applying the boot 4
Torture by fire 10
Putting a man in the pillory 2
Whipping a man 4
Branding with a red-hot iron 10
Cutting off the tongue, the ears and the nose 10

Burning a witch, probably because of its greater frequency, cost but little over one-half as much as boiling in oil. The battle of gladiators with wild beasts in the Coliseum at Rome in reign of Nero, had in it an element of hope. Not the priesthood but the populace were the arbiters of the gladiator's destiny, giving always a chance for life in cases of great personal bravery. But in France and England the ecclesiastical code was so closely united with the civil as to be one with it; compassion equally with justice was forgotten, despair taking their place. Implements of torture were of frequent invention, the thought of the age turning in the direction of human suffering, new methods were continually devised. Many of these instruments are now on exhibition in foreign museums. One called "The Spider" a diabolical iron machine with curved claws, for tearing out a woman's breasts was shown in the United States but a few years since. In Protestant Calvanistic Scotland, where hatred of "popery" was most pronounced, the persecution of witches raged with the greatest violence, and multitudes of women died shrieking to heaven for that mercy denied them by Christian men upon earth. It was in Scotland after the reformation that the most atrocious tortures for the witch were invented, one of most diabolical being known as "the Witches' Bridle." By means of a loop passed about the head, this instrument of four iron prongs was fastened in the mouth. One of the prongs pressed down the tongue, one touched the palate, the other two doing their barbarous work upon the inner side of the cheeks. As this instrument prevented speech thus allowing no complaint upon the part of the victim, it was preferred to many other methods of torture.[68] The woman upon whom it was used was suspended against a wall by a loop at the back, barely touching the floor with her toes. The iron band around her neck rendered her powerless to move, she was unable to speak or scarcely to breathe. Every muscle was strained in order to sustain herself and prevent entire suffocation, the least movement causing cruel wounds by means of the prongs in her mouth.

The victims were mostly aged women who having reared a family, spending their youth and beauty in this self-denying work, had lived until time threading their hair with silver had also robbed cheek and lip of their rosy hue, dimmed the brilliancy of the eye and left wrinkles in place of youthful dimples. Such victims were left for hours, until the malignity of their persecutors was satisfied, or until death after long torture released them from a world where under the laws of both Church and State they found their sex to be a crime. Old women for no other reason than that they were old, were held to be the most susceptible to the assaults of the devil, and the persons most especially endowed with supernatural powers for evil. Blackstone refers to this persecution of aged women in his reference to a statute of the Eight Henry.[69] We discover a reason for this intense hatred of old women in the fact that woman has chiefly been looked upon from a sensual view by christian men, the church teaching that she was created solely for man's sensual use. Thus when by reason of declining years she no longer attracted the sensual admiration of man, he regarded her as having forfeited all right to life. England's most learned judge, Sir Mathew Hale, declared his belief in the agency of the devil in producing diseases through the aid of old women. The prosecution against this class raged with unusual violence in Scotland under the covenanters.

To deny the existence of especially evil supernatural powers, in old women, was held as an evidence of skepticism exposing the doubting person to like suspicion. Great numbers of women were put to death at a time; so common indeed was the sight as to cause but little comment. A Scotch traveler casually mentioned having seen nine women burning together at Bath in 1664. Knox himself suffered a woman to be burned at St. Andrews, whom one word from him would have saved. Father Tanner speaks of "the multitude" of witches who were daily brought under the torture that was constantly practiced by the church.

The reformers were more cruel than those from whose superstitious teachings they professed to have escaped. All the tortures of the old church were repeated and an unusual number of new and diabolical ones invented to induce confession. Nor were these tortures applied to the suspected witch alone; her young and tender children against whom no accusation has been brought, were sometimes tortured in her presence in order to wring confession from the mother. Towards the end of the sixteenth century, a woman accused of witchcraft endured the most intense torture, constantly asserting her innocence. Failing to secure confession, her husband, her son, and finally her young daughter of seven short years were tortured in her presence, the latter being subjected to a species of thumb-screw called "the pinniwinkies" which brought blood from under the finger nails with a pain terribly severe. When these were applied to the baby hands, to spare her innocent child, the mother confessed herself a witch; but after enduring all the agonies of torture upon herself and all she was made to suffer in the persons of her innocent family, confession having been obtained through this diabolical means, she was still condemned to the flames, undergoing death at the stake a blazing torch of fire, and died calling upon God for that mercy she could not find at the hands of Christian men.[70] In protestant Scotland as in catholic countries, witchcraft was under control of the clergy. When a woman fell under suspicion of being a witch, the minister denounced her from the pulpit, forbade anyone to harbor or shelter her and exhorted his parishoners to give evidence against her.[71] She was under ban similar to the excommunicate of the catholic church, a being outside of human help or sympathy. In protestant as in catholic countries the woman accused was virtually dead. She was excommunicated from humanity; designated and denounced as one whom all must shun, to whom no one must give food or lodging or speech or shelter; life was not worth the living. To afford such a one aid was to hazard accusation as a confederate. The first complaint was made to the clergy and Kirk Sessions.[72]

Notwithstanding two hundred years of such experience, when by an act of parliament in 1784, the burning and hanging of witches was abolished, the General Assembly of the Calvinistic Church of Scotland "confessed" this act "as a great national sin." Not only were the courts and the church alert for the detection of alleged witches, but the populace persecuted many to death.[73]

Deserted by her friends, the suspected witch was beaten, worried by dogs, denied food and prevented from sleeping.[74] Contrary to equity and the principles of modern law, the church sought in every way to entrap victims into giving evidence against themselves. Once a person was accused, no effort was spared to induce confession. Holding control over the soul as well as the body, enquiry into these crimes was pushed by every method that human ingenuity could devise. The kirk became the stronghold of superstition; both rewards and punishments were used as inducements towards ferreting out witches. All ties of natural affection were ignored, the kirk preaching it to be a matter of greater duty to inform against one's nearest relatives than against strangers. Unlike the theory of Roman civil law which held the accused innocent until proven guilty, ecclesiastical law everywhere produced a condition under which the accused was held guilty from the moment of accusation. During the witchcraft period the minds of people were trained in a single direction. The chief lesson of the church that betrayal of friends was necessary to one's own salvation, created an intense selfishness. All humanitarian feeling was lost in the effort to secure heaven at the expense of others, even those most closely bound by ties of nature and affection. Mercy, tenderness, compassion were all obliterated. Truthfulness escaped from the Christian world; fear, sorrow and cruelty reigned preeminent. All regard that existed for others grew up outside of church teaching and was shown at the hazard of life. Contempt and hatred of woman was inculcated with greater intensity; love of power and treachery were parts of the selfish lessons of the church. All reverence for length of years was lost. The sorrows and sufferings of a long life appealed to no sympathetic cord in the heart. Instead of the tenderness and care due to aged women, they were so frequently accused of witchcraft that for years it was an unusual thing for an old woman in the north of Europe to die in her bed. Besides the thousands of accused who committed suicide in order to escape the horrors incident upon trial, many others tired of life amid so much humiliation and suffering, falsely accused themselves, preferring a death by the torture of fire to a life of endless isolation and persecution. An English woman on her way to the stake, with a greatness of soul born of despair, freed her judges from responsibility, by saying to the people, "Do not blame my judges. I wished to put an end to my own self. My parents keep aloof from me; my own husband has denied me. I could not live on without disgrace. I longed for death and so I told a lie." The most eminent legal minds became incompetent to form correct judgment. Having received the church as of divine origin, and its priesthood as the representatives of the divinity, they were no longer capable of justice. Old and ignorant women upon the most frivolous testimony of young children were condemned to death. One of the most notable examples of the power of superstitious belief to darken the understanding, is that of Sir Matthew Hale, living in the seventeenth century. He was spoken of by his contemporaries as one of the most eminent jurists of the world, whose integrity, learning and knowledge of law were scarcely to be paralleled in any age, and yet he became so entirely convinced of the diabolism of two women as to condemn them to death while sitting at Bury St. Edmunds, without even summing up the evidence. The learned and famous Sir Thomas Browne, who was present, coincided in the justice of this decision, although but a short time previously he had published a work against superstition. The testimony upon which these women were condemned was of the most petty and worthless character, yet among all the persons present at the trial, but one or two seemed inclined to doubt the sufficiency of the evidence.

The records of this remarkable trial were preserved to the world by a gentleman who privately took a report for his own use, which was published in pamphlet form a number of years afterwards. This extremely rare book is not to be found even in the Congressional Library at Washington, but the Supreme Court Library owns a copy from which this report is taken:

Trial March 10, 1664 by Sir Matthew Hale, Knight, Lord Chief Baron of his Majesty's Court of Exchequer held before a judge who for his integrity, learning and wisdom hardly any age before or since could parallel; he not only took a great deal of pains and spent much time in this trial himself, but had the assistance and opinion of several other very eminent and learned persons; so that this was the most perfect narrative of anything of this nature hitherto extant.

The persons tried were Ann Durant, or Drury, Susan Chander, Elizabeth Pacy. The celebrated Dr. Brown of Norwich who had written a work against witchcraft, was present and after hearing the evidence expressed himself as clearly of the opinion the persons were bewitched, and said in Denmark lately there had been a great discovery of witches who used the same way of afflicting persons by the agency of pins. This trial took place in the sixteenth year of Charles II. The witnesses were two children of eleven and nine years who fell into fits, vomiting pins and nails. Sargeant Keeling asserted deception on part of the witnesses. The Court appointed Lord Cornwallis, Sir Edmund Bacon and Sargeant Keeling as committee to examine the girl alone, when they became fully satisfied of her imposture but without convincing the learned judge who contrary to all justice and law did not sum up the evidence, but gave the great weight of his opinion in favor of their guilt saying: "That there are such creatures as witches, I have no doubt at all. For First, Scripture has offered so much. Second, the wisdom of all nations has propounded laws against such persons, which is an argument of their confidence of such a crime." And such has been the judgment of this kingdom as appears by that Act of Parliament which hath provided punishments proportionate to the guilt of this offense, and desired them strictly to observe the evidence; and desired the great God of Heaven to direct their hearts in the weighty things they had so heard. For to condemn the innocent and to let the guilty go free, were both an abomination to the Lord. Within half an hour the jury returned a verdict of guilty on thirteen counts. The judge and all the court were fully satisfied with the verdict and therefore gave judgment against the witches that they should be hanged.

The evidence was of the most paltry character; as when out of door a little thing like a bee flew upon the witness face, putting a ten penny nail with a broad head into her mouth. Lath nails and pins said to have been vomited by the children were produced in court. When arraigned the accused pleaded not guilty nor did they ever change this plea. Great pressure was upon them to induce confession, but they could not be prevailed upon to thus criminate themselves and were executed the seventeenth of March, just one week after trial, confessing nothing.

This trial is the more remarkable that confessions usually deemed the best of evidence, were not obtained, these poor illiterate, persecuted women braving all the learning of the great judge and power of the kingdom in maintaining to the last the assertion of their innocence. The minutes of this trial were taken by a gentleman in attendance upon the court and were not published until 1716 when the record fell into the hands of a person who saw its value "so that," he says, "being the most complete minutes of anything of this nature hitherto extant, made me unwilling to deprive the world of it; which is the sole motive that induced me to publish it."

Not alone the clergy and the legal fraternity wrought in unison, but the medical as well, gave the weight of their authority in favor of witchcraft; and many persons needing the wisest medical appliance for their relief from disease were executed as witches. Half-witted and insane persons met with the same persecution as old women. It was an era of the strong against the weak, the powerful against the helpless. Even Sir Thomas Browne, himself a physician, regarded the fainting fits to which one of the accused women had long been subject as fuller evidence of her guilt. In his character of medical examiner he asserted that the devil had taken opportunity of her natural fits, to operate with her malice.

An almost equally notable trial as that of Bury St. Edmunds before Sir Matthew Hale, was known as the Sommers Trial, or that of the "Lancashire Witches," in 1612. Among the accused were two extremely aged women decrepit and nearly blind, tottering into second childhood, incapable of understanding wherof they were accused, or the evidence against them which, as in the case argued before Sir Matthew Hale, was of the most worthless character. One needs but refer to the records in order to learn the extreme age, ignorance and many infirmities of these women. But as was the case in Scotland, these weaknesses were used as evidences of guilt. The feeble mental and physical condition of "the Lancashire witches," their great age and failing power were used as evidence for their condemnation. From published accounts of this trial, we learn that:

> This Annie Whittle, alias Chattox, was a very old withered and decrepid creature, her sight almost gone, a dangerous witch of very long continuance, her lips ever chattering and walking (talking)? but no one knew what. She was next in order to that wicked, fierce bird of mischief, old Demdike.

This poor old creature "confessed" that Robert Mutter had offered insult to her married daughter; and the court decreed this was a fair proof of her having bewitched him to his death. No condemnation of the man who had thus insulted her daughter, but death for the aged mother who had resented this insult. Designated as "Old Demdike, a fierce bird of mischief" this woman of four score years of age, had not only brought up a large family of her own, but her grandchildren had fallen to her care. She had lived a blameless life of over eighty years, much of it devoted to the care of children and children's children. But when decrepit and almost blind she fell under suspicion of a crime held by Church and State as of the most baleful character, her blameless and industrious life proved of no avail against this accusation. She seems to have originally been a woman of great force of character and executive ability, but frightened at an accusation she could not understand and overpowered by all the dread majesty of the law into whose merciless power she had fallen, she "confessed" to communion with a demon spirit which appeared to her in the form of a brown dog.[75] From a work entitled *The Sommer's Trials*, the form of indictment is learned.[76]

Indictment

This Annie Whittle, alias Chattox, of the Forest of Pendle, in the countie of Lancaster, widow, being indicted for that she feloniously had practiced, used and exercised divers wicked and divelish artes, called witchcraftes, inchantments, charms and sorceries, in and upon one Robert Mutter of Greenhead, in the Forest of Pendle, in the countie of Lane; and by force of the same witchcraft, feloniously the sayed Robert Mutter had killed, contra pacem, etc. Being at the barre was arraigned. To this indictment, upon her arraignment, she pleaded, not guiltie; and for the tryall of her life put herself upon God and her country.

One of the chief witnesses at this trial was a child of nine years.[77] Upon seeing her own daughter arraigned against her, the mother broke into shrieks and lamentations pleading with the girl not to falsify the truth and thus condemn her own mother to death. The judges instead of seeing in this agony a proof of the mother's innocence looked upon it as an attempt to thwart the ends of justice by demoniac influence, and the child having declared that she could not confess in her mother's presence, the latter was removed from the room, and as under the Inquisition, the testimony was given in the absence of the accused. The child then said that her mother had been a witch for three or four years, the devil appearing in the form of a brown dog, Bill. These trials taking place in protestant England, two hundred years after the reformation, prove the worthless nature of witchcraft testimony, as well as the superstition, ignorance and entire unfitness for the bench of those men called the highest judicial minds in England. The church having almost entirely destroyed freedom of will and the expression of individual thought, men came to look upon authority and right as synonymous. Works bearing the stamp of the legal fraternity soon appeared. In 1618 a volume entitled, "The County Justice," by Michal Dalton, Gentleman of Lincoln Inn, was published in London, its chief object to give directions, based upon this trial, for the discovery of witches.

Now against these witches the justice of the peace may not always expect direct evidence, seeing all their works are works of darkness and no witness permitted with them to accuse them, and therefore for their better discovery I thought good here to set down certain observations out of the methods of discovery of the witches that were arraigned at Lancaster, A.D. 1612 before Sir James Altham and Sir Edward Bromley, judges of Assize there.

1. They have ordinarily a familiar or spirit which appeareth to them.

2. The said familiar hath some bigg or place upon their body where he sucketh them.

3. They have often pictures of clay or wax (like a man, etc.) found in their house.

4. If the dead body bleed upon the witches touching it.

5. The testimony of the person hurt upon his death.

6. The examination and confession of the children or servants of the witch.

7. Their own voluntary confession which exceeds all other evidence.

At this period many persons either in hope of a reward[78] or because they believed they were thus aiding the cause of justice, kept private notebooks of instruction in the examination of witches, and new varieties were constantly discovered. When witchcraft by Act of Parliament was decreed felony this statute gave the legal fraternity double authority for a belief in its existence. Even Sir George Mackenzie although convinced by his own experience that many persons were wrongfully accused of witchcraft, still declared that its existence could not be doubted, "seeing that our law ordains it to be punished with death." The most fatal record the world possesses of the plague is that of the fourteenth century, known as the "Black Death," when whole villages were depopulated and more than half the inhabitants of Europe were destroyed. It will aid in forming our judgment as to the extent of woman's persecution for witchcraft, to remember it has been estimated that the number of deaths from this cause equalled those of the plague.

The American Colonies adopted all the unjust previsions of European christianity as parts of their own religion and government. Fleeing from persecution, the Puritans yet brought with them the spirit of persecution in the belief of woman's inferiority and wickedness, as taught by the church from whence they had fled. The "Ducking Stool" for women who too vigorously protested against their wrongs, and the "Scarlet Letter" of shame for the woman who had transgressed the moral law, her companion in sin going free, or as in England, sitting as juror in the box, or judge upon the bench. With them also came a belief in witchcraft, which soon caused Massachusetts Colony to enact a law ordering suspected women to be stripped naked their bodies to be carefully examined by a male "witch pricker" to see if there was not the devil's mark upon them. The public whipping of half-naked women at the cart's tail for the crime of religious free thought soon followed, a union of both religious and judicial punishment; together with banishment of women from the Colony for daring to preach Christ as they understood his doctrines. These customs more barbarous than those of the savages whose home they had invaded, were the pleasing welcome given to the pioneer woman settlers of America by the husbands and fathers, judges and ministers of that period, with which the words "Plymouth Rock," "May Flower" and "Pilgrim Fathers" are so intimately associated. The same persecution of aged women took place in New England as in old England, while children of even more tender years were used as witnesses against their mothers if accused of witchcraft, or were themselves imprisoned upon like suspicion. The village of Salem, Massachusetts, is undissolubly connected with witchcraft, for there the persecution raged most fiercely, involving its best women in ruin. One of the oldest buildings still extant in the United States is "The Witch House" of that place, erected in 1631, although it was sixty-one years later before this persecution reached its height.

A terrible summer for Salem village and its vicinity was that of 1692—a year of worse than pestilence or famine. Bridget

Bishop was hanged in June; Sarah Good, Sarah Wilder, Elizabeth Howe, Susanna Martin and Rebecca Nurse in July; George Burroughs, John Proctor, George Jacobs, John Willard and Martha Carrier in August; Martha Corey, Mary Easty, Alice Parker, Ann Pudeator, Margaret Scott, Wilmit Reed, Samuel Wordwell, and Mary Baker in September; in which last month Giles Corey eighty-one years of age, was pressed to death under a board loaded with heavy stones, not heavy enough however to crush out life until a day or two of lingering torture had intervened. Sarah Good's daughter Dorcas between three and four years old, orphaned by her mother's execution, was one of a number of children who with several hundred other persons were imprisoned on suspicion of witchcraft; many of these sufferers remained in a wretched condition, often heavily ironed for months, some upwards of a year; and several dying during this time, A child of seven, Sarah Carrier, was called upon to testify as witness against her mother. Some of the condemned, especially Rebecca Nurse, Martha Corey, and Mary Easty, were aged women who had led unblemished lives and were conspicuous for their prudence, their charities and all domestic virtues.[79]

So extended became the persecution for witchcraft that the king was at last aroused to the necessity of putting a stop to such wholesale massacre of his subjects, issued a mandate forbidding the putting of any more persons to death on account of witchcraft.[80] A remarkable family gathering took place at Salem, July 18, 1883, of two hundred persons who met to celebrate their descent from Mrs. Rebecca Nurse, who was executed as a witch at that place in 1692. The character and life of Mrs. Nurse were unimpeachable. She was a woman seventy years of age, the mother of eight children, a church member of unsullied reputation and devout habit; but all these considerations did not prevent her accusation, trial, conviction and death, although she solemnly asserted her innocence to the last. A reprieve granted by the governor was withdrawn through the influence of the church, and she was hung by the neck till she was dead. In order to give her body burial, her sons were obliged to steal it away by night, depositing it in a secret place known but to the family. Forty persons at the hazard of their own lives testified to the goodness and piety of Mrs. Nurse. Their names were inscribed upon the monument erected by her descendants, in 1892, to her memory.[81] The Rev. Cotton Mather and the Rev. Samuel Parrish are indissolubly connected with this period, as both were extremely active in fomenting a belief in witchcraft. Richard Baxter, known as the "greatest of the Puritans," condemned those who expressed a disbelief in witchcraft as "wicked Sadbucees." Increase Mather, president of Harvard College, was one of the most bitter persecutors of witches in New England. The dangerous spirit of a religious autocracy like the priesthood, was forcibly shown by a paper read by Rev. Dr. George E. Ellis, a few years since, before the Massachusetts Historical Society, in which he excused the act of stripping women naked in order to search for a witch-mark, upon the ground of its being a judicial one by commissioned officers and universally practiced in christendom.

Boston as "The Bloody Town" rivalled Salem in its persecution of women who dared express thoughts upon religious matters in contradiction to the Puritanic belief; women were whipped because of independent religious belief, New England showing itself as strenuous for "conformity" of religious opinion as Old England under Queen Elizabeth. The cruelties of this method of punishing free thought, culminated in the Vagabond Law of Massachusetts Colony, passed May 1661.

The first ecclesiastical convocation in America was a synod especially convened to sit in judgment upon the religious views of Mistress Anne Hutchinson, who demanded that the same rights of individual judgment upon religious questions should be accorded to woman which the reformation had already secured to man. Of the eighty-two errors canvassed by the synod, twenty-nine were charged to Mistress Hutchinson, and retraction of them was ordered by the church. The State united with the Church in opposition to Mistress Hutchinson, and the first real struggle for woman's religious liberty, (not yet at an end), began upon this side of the Atlantic. The principal charge brought against Mistress Hutchinson was that she had presumed to instruct men. Possessed of a fine intellect and strong religious fervor, she had inaugurated private meetings for the instruction of her own sex; from sixty to a hundred women regularly gathering at her house to hear her criticism upon the Sunday sermon and Thursday lectures. These meetings proved so interesting that men were soon found also in attendance and for these reasons she was arbitrarily tried in November 1637, before the Massachusetts General Court upon a joint charge of sedition and heresy. In May of the same year a change had taken place in the civil government of the colony. Sir Henry Vane, who like herself, believed in the supreme authority of the in-dwelling spirit, having been superceded by John Winthrop as governor, the latter sustaining the power of the clergy and himself taking part against her. Two days were spent by him and prominent clergymen in her examination, resulting in a sentence of imprisonment and banishment from the colony for having "traduced the ministers" and taught men against the direct authority of the Apostle Paul, who declared "I suffer not a woman to teach."

Thus the old world restrictions upon woman, and their persecutions, were soon duplicated in the new world. Liberty of opinion became as serious a crime in America as in England, and here as in Europe, the most saintly virtue and the purest life among women were not proof against priestly attack. While Mistress Hutchinson was the first woman thus to suffer many others were also persecuted. When Mary Fisher and Anne Austin, two Quaker women who had become famous for their promulgation of this heretical doctrine in many parts of the world, arrived in Boston harbor, July 1656, they were not at first permitted to land, but were ultimately transferred to the Boston jail, where they were closely confined, and notwithstanding the heat of the weather their one window was boarded up. Their persons were also stripped and examined for signs of witchcraft, but fortunately not a mole or a spot could be found. Boston—"The Bloody Town"—was the center of this persecuting spirit and every species of wanton cruelty upon woman was enacted. Stripped nude to the waist they were tied to a whipping-post on the south side of King Street and flogged on account of their religious opinions; but it was upon the famous "Common" that for the crime of free speech, a half-nude woman with a newborn babe at her breast was thus publicly whipped; and it was upon the "Common" that Mary Dyer, another Quaker woman, was hung in 1659. Both she and Anne Hutchinson prophesied calamity to the colony for its unjust course, which was fulfilled, when in 1684 it lost its charter in punishment for its intolerance. No Christian country offered a refuge for woman, as did Canada the colored slave. But the evils of woman's persecution by the church, did not end with the wrongs inflicted upon her; they were widely extended, affecting the most common interests of the world. While famines were unknown among the ancient Romans in the first period of their history, yet Christendom was early and frequently afflicted with them. While the operations of nature were sometimes the cause, the majority of famines were the result of persecutions, or of christian wars, especially the crusades which took such immense numbers of men from the duties of agriculture at home, making them a prey upon the scanty resources of the countries through which these hordes passed. As was seen in the Irish famine of 1847–48 and at the present moment as result of a scanty food supply in Russia, pestilence of various kinds followed famine years. But the crusades in which the church attempted to wrest the holy sepulchre from Turkish hands, were scarcely more productive of famines than its persecuting periods when mankind lost hope in themselves and the future. Our own country has shown the effect of fear and persecution upon both business and religion, as during the witchcraft period of New England, scarcely two hundred years since, all business of whatever nature in country and in town was neglected, and even the meeting house was allowed to fall out of repair. Nor was this ruin of a temporary nature, as many people left the Colony and its effects descended to those yet unborn. Both Bancroft's *History of the United States*, and Lapham's *History of the Salem Witchcraft*, paint vivid pictures of the effects following the different church persecutions of woman. Of the Hutchinson trial, Bancroft says:

> This dispute infused its spirit into everything. It interferred with the levy of troops for the Pequot war; it influenced the respect shown to magistrates; the distribution of town lots; the assessment of rates and at last the continued existence of the two parties was considered inconsistent with public peace.

Of the witchcraft period, Upham says:

> It cast its shadows over a broad surface and they darkened the condition of generations. . . . The fields were neglected fences, roads, barns, even the meeting house went into disrepair. . . . A scarcity of provisions nearly amounting to a famine continued for some time. Farms were brought under mortgage, or sacrificed, and large numbers of people were dispersed. The worst results were not confined to the village but spread more or less over the country.

Massachusetts was not the only colony that treated witchcraft as a crime. Maryland, New Jersey and Virginia possessed similar enactments. Witchcraft was considered and treated as a capital offense by the laws of both Pennsylvania and New York, trials taking place in both colonies not long before the Salem tragedy. The peaceful Quaker, William Penn, presided upon the bench in Pennsylvania at the trial of two Swedish women accused of witchcraft. The Grand Jury acting under instruction given in his charge, found true bills against these women, and Penn's skirts were only saved from the guilt of their blood by some technical irregularity in the indictment.

Virginia, Delaware, Maryland, South Carolina, Pennsylvania, New Jersey, Massachusetts and New York, eight of the thirteen colonies recognized witchcraft as a capital crime. Margaret M—— was indicted for witchcraft in Pennsylvania in 1683, the law against it continuing in force until September 23, 1794. By law of the Province of East New Jersey, 1668, any person found to be a witch, either male or female, was to suffer death. In that state the right of complaining against a child who should smite or curse either parent, pertained to both father and mother; the penalty was death. As late as 1756, Connecticut recognized the right of parents to dispose of children in marriage. In Maryland 1666 the commission given to magistrates for Somerset county directed them under oath to make enquiries in regard to witchcraft, sorcery, and magic arts. In 1706 Grace Sherwood of Princess Anne County, Virginia, was tried for witchcraft. The records of the trial show that the court after a consideration of the charges, ordered the sheriff to take the said Grace into his custody and to commit her body to the common jail, there to secure her with irons or otherwise, until brought to trial.[82]

In 1692, the Grand Jury brought a bill against Mary Osgood of the Province of Massachusetts Bay, as follows:

> The powers for our sovereign lord and lady, the king and queen, present that Mary Osgood, wife of Captain John Osgood in the county of Essex, about eleven years ago in the town of Andover aforesaid, wickedly, maliciously and feloniously a covenant with the devil did make and signed the devil's book, and took the devil to be her God, and consented to serve and worship him and was baptized by the devil and renounced her former Christian baptism and promised to the devil both body and soul, forever, and to serve him; by which diabolical covenant by her made with the devil; she, the said Mary Osgood is become a detestable witch against the peace of our sovereign lord and lady, the king and queen, their crown and dignity and the laws in that case made and provided. A true bill.[83]

When for "witches" we read "women," we gain fuller comprehension of the cruelties inflicted by the church upon this portion of humanity. Friends were encouraged to cast accusation upon their nearest and dearest, rewards being offered for conviction. Husbands who had ceased to care for their wives or who by reason of their sickness or for any cause found them a burden, or for reasons of any nature desired to break the indissoluble bonds of the church, now found an easy method. They had but to accuse the wife of witchcraft and the marriage was dissolved by her death at the stake. Church history is not silent upon such instances, and mention is made of a husband who by a rope about the neck dragged his wife before that Arch-Inquisitor, Sprenger, making accusation of witchcraft against her. No less from protestant than from catholic pulpits were people exhorted to bring the witch, even if of one's own family, to justice.

In 1736, the statute against witchcraft was repealed by the English Parliament, yet a belief in witchcraft is still largely prevalent even among educated people. Dr. F. G. Lee the vicar of an English church, that of All Saints in Lambeth, a few years since publicly deprecated the abolition of its penalties in a work entitled *Glimpses of the Twilight*, complaining that the laws against witchcraft had been "foolishly and short-sightedly repealed." A remarkable case occurred in Prussia 1883 when the father of a bedridden girl, having become persuaded that his daughter was bewitched by a woman who had occasionally given her apples and pears, was advised the child would be cured if she drank some of the blood of the supposed witch. The woman was therefore entrapped into a place where some of the chief men of the commune had assembled to receive her. She was seized, one of her fingers pricked with a needle and her blood given to the sick child. In 1885 a case of slander based upon alleged witchcraft came before Justice Randolphs, District Court of Jersey City. The justice listened to the evidence for several hours before recalling the fact that there was no law upon which he could base his decision, the latest legislation being the law of 1668 repealed 1775 (twenty years after our Declaration of Independence), the crime was no longer officially recognized.[84] It is curious to note the close parallel between accusations during the witchcraft period and those against the New Jersey suspect of 1885. It was said of her that during the night she accomplished such feats by supernatural power as jumping from a third-story window, alighting upon a gate post as gently as a falling feather. It was also asserted that people whom she was known to dislike became gradually ill, wasting away until they died. The accused woman declared it was her superior knowledge that was feared, and thus again the middle ages are paralleled, as the witches of that period were usually women of superior knowledge. In 1882, a Wisconsin farmer was put under bonds to keep the peace, on account of his attempts to assault an old lady whom he averred was a witch, who injured his cattle, and entered his house through the chimney or keyhole, to his great terror and distress. The state of Indiana about sixty years ago possessed a neighborhood where the people believed in witchcraft. If the butter failed to come, or the eggs to hatch, or a calf got choked, or even if the rail fences fell down when covered with sleet and snow, the whole trouble was attributed to the witches, who were also believed to have the remarkable power of saddling and bridling a man and with sharp spurs riding him over the worst roads imaginable, to his great harm and fatigue. Even the great Empire State, as late as January 1892, had within its borders a case of murder where an inoffensive old man lost his life because he was believed to be a wizard; and this occurred in the center of a prosperous farming country where money is liberally expended for educational purposes, this being one of the rare instances where a man fell under suspicion.

It is but a few years since the great and enlightened city of Paris caused the arrest, under police authority, of fourteen women upon charge of sorcery; and it is but little more than twenty years since a woman in the state of Puebla, Mexico, was hung and burned as a witch, because unable to reveal the whereabouts of a lost animal. She was seized, hung to a tree shot at and then plunged into fire until she expired.[85] The body at first buried in the cemetery, was exhumed the following day by order of the priest, who refused to allow the remains of a witch to be buried in consecrated ground. The state, in person of the mayor of the city, authorized the proceedings by taking part in them as principal persecutor. In the same province another woman was severely flogged as a witch, by four men, one of them her own son. Thus now, as in its earlier ages, wherever the light of civilization has not overcome the darkness of the church, we find woman still a sufferer from that ignorance and superstition which under Christianity teaches that she brought sin into the world.

Notes

1. Black was hated as the colors of the devil. In the same manner red was hated in Egypt as the color of Typhon.

2. At what date then did the witch appear? In the age of despair, of that deep despair which the guilt of the church engendered. Unfalteringly I say, the witch is a crime of their own making.—*Michelet.*

3. "It is not a little remarkable, though perfectly natural, that the introduction of the cat gave a new impulse to tales and fears of ghosts and enchantments. The sly, creeping, nocturnal grimalkin took rank at once with owls and bats, and soon surpassed them both as an exponent of all that is weird and supernatural. Entirely new conceptions of witchcraft were gained for the world when the black cat appeared upon the scene with her swollen tail, glistening eyes and unearthly yell."—*Ex.*

4. Steevens says it was permitted to a witch to take on a cat's body nine times.—*Brand* 3, pp. 89–90.

5. Mr. E. F. Spicer, a taxidermist of Birmingham, whose great specialty is the artistic preparation of kittens for sale, will not purchase black ones, as he finds the superstition against black cats interferes with their sale.—*Pall Mall Gazette*, Nov. 13, 1886. But the United States, less superstitious, has recently witnessed the formation of a "Consolidated Cat Company" upon Puget Sound for the special propagation of black cats to be raised for their fur.

6. *City of God*, Lib. XVIII. Charles F. Lummis, in a recent work, *Some Strange Corners of Our Country, the Wonderland of the Southwest*, refers to the power of the shamans to turn themselves at will into any animal shape, as a wolf, bear or dog.

7. Italian women usually became cats. The Witch Hammer mentioned a belief in Lycanthropy and Metamorphosis. It gave the story of a countryman who was assaulted by three cats. He wounded them, after which three infamous witches were found wounded and bleeding.

8. For a full account of this madness, and other forms that sometimes attacked whole communities during the middle Christian ages, see Hecker.—*Epidemics of the Middle Ages.*

9. The conventicle of witches was said to be held on Mt. Atlas, "to which they rode upon a goat, a night crow, or an enchanted staff, or bestriding a broom staff. Sundry speeches belonged to these witches, the words whereof were neither Hebrew, Greek, Latin, French, Spanish, Italian, nor indeed deriving their Etymology from any known language."

10. *St. Gregory, of Nyassa*, a canonized saint, the only theologian to whom the church (except St. John) has ever allowed the title of "The Divine," was a member of that council, aiding in the preparation of the Nicene Creed. It is a significant fact that a great number of public women, "an immense number," congregated at Nice during the sessions of this council.

11. In Guernsey a mother and her two daughters were brought to the stake; one of the latter, a married woman with child, was delivered in the midst of her torments, and the infant, just rescued, was tossed back into the flames by a priest with the cry, "One heretic the less."

12. "Old writers declared that women have been more addicted to these devilish arts than men, was manifest by 'many grave authors,' among whom Diodorus, Sindas, Pliny and St. Augustine were mentioned. Quintillian declared theft more prevalent among men, but witchcraft especially a sin of women."

13. Lea.—*Superstition and Force.*

14. Certain forms of ordeal, such as the ordinary ones of fire and water, seem to have owed their origin to the trials passed by the candidate for admission into the ancient mysteries, as Lea has also conjectured. During the mysteries of Isis, the candidate was compelled to descend into dark dungeons of unknown depth, to cross bars of red-hot iron, to plunge into a rapid stream at seeming hazard of life, to hang suspended in mid-air; while the entrance into other mysteries confronted the candidate with howling wild beasts and frightful serpents. All who passed the ancient ordeals in safety, were regarded as holy and acceptable to the Deity, but not so under Christian ordeal, its intention being conviction of the accused. Those who proved their innocence by carrying red-hot iron uninjured for three paces and the court was thus forced to acquit, or who passed through other forms of torture without confession were still regarded with suspicion as having been aided by Satan, and the sparing of their lives was to the scandal of the faithful.

15. Woman was represented as the door of hell, as the mother of all human ill. She should be ashamed at the very thought she is a woman. She should live in continual penance on account of the curses

she has brought upon the world. She should be ashamed of her dress, for it is the memorial of her fall. She should be especially ashamed of her beauty, for it is the most potent instrument of the demon.—*Hist. European Morals*, Vol. 2, p. 358.

16. Witchcraft was supposed to have power of subverting religion.—*Montesquieu*.

17. The question why the immense majority of those who were accused should be women, early attracted attention; it was answered by the inherent wickedness of the sex, which had its influence in predisposing men to believe in witches, and also in producing the extreme callousness with which the sufferings of the victims were contemplated.—*Rationalism in Europe* I, p. 88.

18. 18 mo. An unusually small size for that period.

19. *Witch Hammer*.

20. The Court of Rome was fully apprized that power cannot be maintained without property, and thereupon its attention began very early to be riveted upon every method that promised pecuniary advantage. All the wealth of Christendom was gradually drawn by a thousand channels into the coffers of the Holy See. Blackstone.—*Commentaries* 4, 106. "The church forfeited the wizard's property to the judge and the prosecutor. Wherever the church law was enforced, the trials for witchcraft waxed numerous and brought much wealth to the clergy. Wherever the lay tribunal claimed the management of those trials, they grew scarce and disappeared."

21. Burning Place of the Cross.

22. An *MS* upholding the burning of witches as heretics, written in 1450 by the *Dominican Brother Hieronymes Visconti,* of Milan, is among the treasures of the *White Library*, recently presented to Cornell University.

23. It shall not be amiss to insert among these what I have heard concerning a witch of Scotland: One of that countrie (as by report there are too many) being for no goodness of the judges of Assize, arrayed, convicted and condemned to be burnt, and the next day, according to her judgment, brought and tied to the stake, the reeds and fagots placed round about her, and the executioner ready to give fire (for by no persuasion of her ghostly fathers, nor importunities of the sheriff, she could be wrought to confess anything) she now at the last cast to take her farewell of the world, casting her eye at one side upon her only sonne, and calls to him, desiring him verie earnestly as his last dutie to her to bring her any water, or the least quantity of licuor (be it never so small), to comfort her, for

she was so extremely athirst, at which he, shaking his head, said nothing; she still importuned him in these words: "Oh, my deere sonne helpe me to any drinke, be it never so little, for I am most extremely drie, oh drie, drie"; to which the young fellow answered, "by no means, deere mother will I do you that wrong; *for the drier you are (no doubt) you will burne the better.*" Heywoode.—*History of Women*, Lib. 8, p. 406.

24. Lenormant.—*Chaldean Magic and Sorcery*, p. 385.

25. *Institutes of Scotland*.

26. At *Bamburg, Germany*, an original record of twenty-nine burnings in nineteen months, 162 persons in all, mentions the infant daughter of Dr. Schutz as a victim of the twenty-eighth burning. Hauber.—*Bibliotheca Magica*.

27. In those terrible trials presided over by Pierre de Lancre, it was asserted that hundreds of girls and boys flocked to the indescribable Sabbats of Labourd. The Venitians record the story of a little girl of nine years who raised a great tempest, and who like her mother was a witch. Signor Bernoni.—*Folk Lore*.

28. Some very strange stories of such power at the present time have become known to the author, one from the lips of a literary gentleman in New York City, this man of undoubted veracity declaring that he had seen his own father extend his hand under a cloudless sky and produce rain. A physician of prominence in a western city asserts that a most destructive cyclone, known to the Signal Service Bureau as "The Great Cyclone," was brought about by means of magical formulæ, made use of by a schoolgirl in a spirit of ignorant bravado.

29. These and similar powers known as magical, are given as pertaining to the Pueblo Indians, by Charles F. Lummis, in *Some Strange Corners of Our Country*, pub. 1892. A friend of the author witnessed rain thus produced by a very aged Iowa Indian a few years since.

30. A *Hindoo Scripture* whose name signifies knowledge.—Max Muller.

31. *Isis Unveiled*, I, p. 354.

32. Of which the tricks of Halloween may be a memento.

33. *Anacalypsis*, Vol. I, p. 35.

34. Bacchus was not originally the god of wine, but signified books. Instruction of old, when learning was a secret science, was given by means of leaves. "Bacchus Sabiesa" really signified "book wise" or learned, and the midsummer-day festival was celebrated in honor of learning. In the *Anacalypsis* Higgins says: "From Celland I learn that in

Celtic, Sab means wise, whence Saba and Sabasius, no doubt wise in the stars. From this comes the Sab-bath day, or day dedicated to wisdom, and the Sabbat, a species of French masonry, an account of which may be seen in *Dulane's History of Paris*. Sunday was the day of instruction of the Druids, whence it was called Sabs.—*Ibid.*, I, p. 716.

35. From the preachment of the Sabs, or Sages, or wise Segent Sarcedos.—*Ibid.*, I, p. 716.

36. The only physician of the people for a thousand years was the witch. The emperors, kings, popes and richer barons had indeed the doctors of Salermo, then Moors and Jews, but the bulk of the people in every state, the world, it might as well be called, consulted none but the *Sages* or wise women. Michelet.—*La Sorcière*.

37. I make no doubt that his (Paracelsus) admirable and masterly work on the Diseases of Women, the first written on this theme, so large, so deep, so tender, came forth from his special experience of those women to whom others went for aid, the witches, who acted as midwives, for never in those days was a male physician admitted to the women.—*Ibid*.

38. Within the past fifty years the death rate in childbirth was forty in a thousand, an enormous mortality, and although the advances in medical knowledge have somewhat lessened the rate, more women still lose their lives during childbirth than soldiers in battle.

39. In childbirth a motherly hand instilled the gentle poison, casting the mother herself into a sleep, and soothing the infant's passage, after the manner of modern chloroform, into the world.—*Michelet*.

40. *Poruchet Solenaees.*

41. Alexander.—*History of Women*.

42. You will hardly believe it, but I saw a real witch's skull, the other evening, at a supper party I had the pleasure of attending. It was at the house of Dr. Dow, a medical gentleman of culture and great skill in his profession here. You will admit that a skull is not a pleasant thing to exhibit in a parlor, and some of the ladies did not care about seeing it; but the majority did, and you know one cannot see a witch's skull every day. So, after a little hesitation and persuasion on the part of the doctor, he produced the uncanny thing and gave us its history, or rather that of the witch. She lived at Terryburn, a little place near here. One day it came to the ears of the kirk session of the parish that she had had several interviews with his Satanic Majesty. Strange enough, when the woman was brought before that body—which seems to have been all-powerful in the

several parishes in those days—and accused of it, she at once admitted the charge to be true. The poor soul, who could have been nothing else than an idiot, as the doctor pointed out from the very low forehead and small brain cavity, was sentenced to be prevented from going to sleep; or in other words, tortured to death, and the desired end was attained in about five days, her body being buried below high-water mark.

Her name was Lilias Adie, and there is no doubt that she was only a harmless imbecile. The skull, and also a piece of the coffin, were presented to the doctor by a friend who had read in the kirk session records an account of the trial, and went to the spot stated as being the place of burial. The remains were found by him exactly as indicated, although there was nothing to mark their resting place. One would have thought that after the lapse of so many years it would be exceedingly difficult to find them, but you know things do not undergo such radical changes in this country as they do in America.—From a traveler's letter in the *Syracuse Journal*, August 22, 1881.

Almost indistinguished from the belief in witchcraft was the belief that persons subject to epilepsy, mania or any form of mental weakness, were possessed of a devil who could be expelled by certain religious ceremonies. Pike.—*History of Crime in England*, pp. 7–8.

43. The mysteries of the human conscience and of human motives are well nigh inscrutable, and it may be shocking to assert that these customs of unmitigated wrong are indirectly traceable to that religion of which the two great commandments were that man should love his neighbor as himself. Lea.—*Superstition and Force*, p. 53.

44. Fox's *Book of Martyrs* gives account of persons brought into court upon litters six months after having been subjected to the rack.

45. In this case both men and women says Johannus Megerus, author of *A History of Flanders*.

46. Adrianus Ferrens.

47. St. Bernard exorcised a demon Incubus, who for six years maintained commerce with a woman, who could not get rid of him. Lea.—*Studies in Church History*.

48. It was observed they (devils) had a peculiar attachment to women with beautiful hair, and it was an old Catholic belief that St. Paul alluded to this in that somewhat obscure passage in which he exhorts women to cover their heads because of the angels.—*Sprangler*.

49. The attention of scientific men and governments has recently been directed to what are now called "The Accursed Sciences," under whose action certain crimes have been committed from "suggestion,"

the hand which executed being only that of an irresponsible automaton, whose memory preserves no traces of it. The French Academy has just been debating the question—how far a hypnotized subject from a mere victim can become a regular tool of crime.—*Lucifer*, October 1887.

Merck's Bulletin, New York medical journal, in an editorial entitled "Modern Witchcraft," December, 1892, relates some astonishing experiments recently made at the *Hopital de la Charité*, Paris, in which the power to "exteriorize sensibility" has been discovered reproducable at will; suggestion through means of simulated pinching producing suffering; photographs sensitive to their originals even having produced. Thus modern science stamps with truthfulness the power asserted as pertaining to black magicians, of causing suffering or death through means of a waxen image of a person. "The Accursed Sciences," although brought to the bar of modern investigating knowledge, seems not yet to have yielded the secrets of the law under which they are rendered possible.

50. In 1609 six hundred sorcerers were convicted in the Province of Bordeaux, France, most of whom were burned.—*Dr. Priestly*. Within the last year fourteen women have been tried in France for sorcery.

51. The supreme end of magic is to conjure the spirits. The highest and most inscrutable of all the powers dwells in the divine and mysterious name, "The Supreme Name," with which Hea alone is acquainted. Before this name everything bows in heaven and earth, and in hades, and it alone can conquer the Maskim and stop their ravages. The great name remained the secret of Hea; if any man succeeded in divining it, that alone would invest him with a power superior to the gods.—*Chaldean Magic and Sorcery*.

52. Venetians concluded not unreasonably that the latter ran no more risk from the taint of witchcraft attached to their inheritance than did the clergy or the church. Where profits were all spiritual their ardor soon cooled. Thus it happened as the inevitable result of the people's attitude in religious matters, that while in Venice there were representatives of the vast sisterhood, which extended from the Blockula of Sweden to the walnut tree of Beneveuto, sorcery there never became the terrible scourge that it was in other lands where its victims at times threatened to outnumber those of the Black Death.—*The Witches of Venice*.

53. One of the most powerful features of the belief in witchcraft was the power that greed had in producing belief and causing persecution. The church had grown rich from such trials, and the state was now to take its turn. By the public offering of a reward for the finding of witches, their numbers greatly increased.

54. The most exceptional conduct, the purest morals in constant practice of everyday life, are not sufficient security against the suspicion of errors like these.—*Montesquieu.*

55. For a number of years her celebrated son struggled amid his scientific studies for the preservation of her life.

56. Michelet.—*La Sorcière*, p. 151. See *Papers on the Bastile.*

57. In its earliest phase the Black Mass seemed to betoken the redemption of Eve, so long accused by Christianity. The woman filled every place in the Sabbath. Following its celebration was the denial of Jesus, by whose authority the priests and barons robbed the serf of human hope—the paying of homage to the new master—the feudal kiss. To the closing ceremonies, "The Feast of Peace," no man was admitted unaccompanied by a woman.—*La Sorcière.*

58. "This word at different times clearly meant quite different things. In the fourteenth century, under the Avignon popes, during the great schism when the church with two heads seems no longer a church, the Sabbath took the horrible form of the Black Mass."

59. This important part of the woman being her own altar, is known to us by the trial of La Voisin, which M. Revanna *Sen* published with other *Papers of the Bastile.*—*Ibid.*

60. That women have been more addicted to this devilish art than man is manifest by the approbation of many grave authority. Diodorus, in his fifth book, speaks of Hecate. Heywood.—*History of Women*, London, 1624. St. Augustine, in his *City of God*, declared that women are more prone to these unlawful acts, for so we read of Medea, Cyrce and others. Suidas, speaking of witches, cites an old proverb, declaring witchcraft peculiar to woman and not to man. Quintillian, referring to this statement, says: Theft is more common with man, but witchcraft with woman.

61. Idiots, the lame, the blind and the dumb, are men in whom devils have established themselves, and all the physicians who heal these infirmities as though they preceded from natural causes are ignorant blockheads, who know nothing about the power of the demons.—*Tishreden*, p. 202.

62. See *Reeves*, and *Hume.*

63. *The Statute of Labourers* (5 Eliz. c. 4) enacted that unmarried women between twelve and forty years old may be appointed by two justices to serve by the year, week, or day, for such wages and in such reasonable sort and manners they shall think meet.—*Reeves* 3, pp. 591–98.

64. Seen by *Dr. Gray.*

65. James believing in their (witches) influence, and Bacon partly

sharing in the belief. *Macbeth* appeared in this year mixed up with Bacon's inquiries into witchcraft. Ignatius Donnelly.—*The Cryptogram*. From the accession of James I, witchcraft became the master superstition of the age. The woman accused of witchcraft was practically beyond the pale of the law; the mere fact of accusation was equal to condemnation.

66. *Laws and Customs of Scotland*, 2, p. 56.

67. *The Seeress of Prevorst*.

68. Iron collars, or Witches' Bridles, are still preserved in various parts of Scotland, which had been used for such iniquitous purposes. These instruments were so constructed that by means of a loop which passed over the head, a piece of iron having four points or prongs, was forcibly thrust into the mouth, two of these being directed to the tongue and palate, the others pointing outward to each cheek. This infernal machine was secured by a padlock. At the back of the collar was fixed a ring, by which to attach the witch to a staple in the wall of her cell. Thus equipped, and day and night waked and watched by some skillful person appointed by her inquisitors, the unhappy creature, after a few days of such discipline, maddened by the misery of her forlorn and helpless state, would be rendered fit for confessing anything in order to be rid of the dregs of her life. At intervals fresh examinations took place, and they were repeated from time to time until her "contumacy," as it was termed, was subdued. The clergy and Kirk Sessions appear to have been the unwearied instruments of "purging the land of witchcraft," and *to them, in the first instance, all the complaints and informations were made.—Pitcairn*, Vol. I, Part 2, p. 50.

"Who has not heard of the Langholm witches, and 'the branks' to subdue them? This was a simple instrument formed so as to fit firmly on the head, and to project into the mouth a sharp spike for subjugating the tongue. It was much preferred to the ducking-stool, 'which not only endangered the health of the patient, but also gave the tongue liberty betwixt every dip!' Scores of these 'patients' were burned alongside Langholm castle; and the spot is fully as interesting as our own reminder of the gentle days, Gallows Hill, at Salem."

69. By statute 33 of Henry VIII, C. 8, all witchcraft and sorcery was to be felony without benefit of clergy. This act continued in force till lately to the terror of all ancient females in the kingdom.—*Commentaries*. As bad as the Georges are depicted, thanks are due to two of them from women. By statute of George II, C. 5, no future prosecution was to be carried on against any person for conjuration, witchcraft, sorcery or enchantment.

70. Towards the end of 1593 there was trouble in the family of the Earl of Orkney. His brother laid a plot to murder him, and was said to have sought the help of a notorious witch called "Allison Balfour." No evidence could be found connecting her with this particular offense or with witchcraft in general, but it was enough in these matters to be a woman and to be accused. She swore she was innocent, but she was looked upon as a pagan who thus aggravated her guilt. She was tortured again and again, but being innocent she constantly declared her innocence. Her legs were put into the Casctulars—an iron which was gradually heated until it burned into the flesh—but no confession could be wrung from her. The Casctulars having utterly failed to make her tell a lie, "the powers that be," whom Paul tells us "are of God," tortured her husband, her son and her daughter, a little child of only seven years. The "powers" knew the tenderness and love of a wife and mother, so they first brought her husband into court and placed by her side. He was placed in the "long irons," some accursed instrument. She did not yield. Then her son was tortured; the poor boy's legs were set in "the boot," the iron boot, and wedges were driven in, which forced home crushed the very bone and marrow. Fifty-seven mallet strokes were delivered upon the wedges, yet this failed. This innocent tortured heroic woman would not confess to a lie. So last of all her baby daughter was brought in, the fair child of seven short years. There was a machine called the pinniwinkies, a kind of thumbscrew which brought blood from under the fingernails with a pain terribly severe. These tortures were applied to the baby hands, and the mother's fortitude broke down and she would admit anything they wished. She confessed the witchcraft. So tried she would have confessed the seven deadly sins, but this suffering did not save her to her family. She was burned alive, with her last suffering breath protesting her innocence. This account is perfectly well authenticated and taken from the official report of the proceedings. Froude.— *Short Stories on Great Subjects.*

71. The same dark superstition shared the civil councils of Scotland as late as the beginning of the eighteenth century, and the convictions which then took place are chiefly to be ascribed to the ignorance and fanaticism of the clergy.

72. Excommunication was both of temporal and spiritual effect, the person under ban not only being deprived of absolution, extreme unction, consecrated burial, etc., but all persons were forbidden to deal with the recalcitrant. Under the strictest protestantism in Scotland, the clergy

held almost entire control. When a woman fell under suspicion of being a witch, the minister denounced her from the pulpit, forbade anyone harboring or sheltering her, and exhorted his parishioners to give evidence against her. To the clergy and Kirk Sessions were the first complaints made. It is scarcely more than 150 years since the last witch was burned in Scotland, having been accused of raising a thunderstorm by pulling off her stockings.—*Witchcraft Under Protestantism.*

73. Many witches lost their lives in every part of England, without being brought to trial at all, from injuries received at the hands of the populace. Mackay.—*Memoirs of Extraordinary Popular Delusions.*

74. One of the most powerful incentives to confession was to systematically deprive the suspected witch of her natural sleep. It was said who but witches can be present and so witness of the doings of witches, since all their meetings and conspiracies are the habits of darkness. "The voluntarie confession of a witch doth exceede all other evidence. How long she has been a witch the devil and she knows best."

75. Among the Lancashire witches was Old Demedike, four score years old, who had been a witch fifty years, and confessed to possessing a demon which appeared to her in the form of a brown dog.—*Sommer's Trials.*

76. *Ibid.*

77. Which examination, although she was but very young, yet it was wonderful to the Court in so great a presence and audience.—*Ibid.* Ties of the tenderest nature did not restrain the inquisitors. Young girls were regarded as the best witnesses against their mothers, and the oaths of children of irresponsible age were received as evidence against a parent.—*Superstition and Force*, p. 93.

78. When a reward was publicly offered there seemed to be no end of finding witches, and many kept with great care their notebook of "Examination of Witches," and were discovering "hellish kinds of them."

79. *Salem Witchcraft* I, 393-94; 2, 373.

80. I seemed to have stepped back to Puritan time, when an old gentleman said to me, "I am descended from that line of witches; my grandmother and 120 others were under condemnation of death at New Bedford, when an order came from the king prohibiting farther executions."

81. Salem, Mass., July 30, 1892.—The 200th anniversary of the hanging of Rebecca Nurse of Salem village for witchcraft, was commemorated in Danvers Centre, old Salem village, by the Nurse Monu-

ment Association. The distinct feature of the occasion was the dedication of a granite tablet to commemorate the courage of forty men and women, who at the risk of their lives gave written testimony in favor of Rebecca Nurse in 1692.

82. Howes.—*Historical Collection of Virginia*, p. 438.

83. *Collection Massachusetts Historical Society* for the year 1800, p. 241.

84. No prosecution, suit or proceedings shall be commenced or carried on in any court of this state against any person for conjuration or witchcraft, sorcery or enchantment or for charging another with such offense.

85. Under the church theory that all members of the witch's family are tainted, the husband of this unfortunate woman hid himself, fearing the same fate.—*Telegram*.

CHAPTER VI

WIVES

U nder Roman law before Christianity had gained control of the empire, a form of marriage existed known as "Usus," which secured much freedom to wives. It was entered into without the terrifying religious ceremonies which made "Confarreatio" practically indissoluble and the wife the veritable slave of the husband, who held power even over her life. Neither did it possess the civil formality of "Coemptio" under which the bride purchased entrance into the marriage duties and her husband's household by the payment of three pieces of copper.[1] "Coemptio" like "Confarreatio" gave the husband entire power over the person and property of the wife, while "Usus," a form of simple consent, left the wife practically free, keeping her own name and property. The real origin of this form of marriage is not fully known. Maine declared it to be as old as or even older than the Twelve Tables, under which woman possessed the right to repudiation in marriage. These laws, a compilation of still older ones, were afterwards incorporated into statutes by a woman of Athens, and were received by the Romans as extremely pure natural laws.[2] Plato refers to an early Athens entirely ruled by women, its laws of preeminently just character. Tradition, whose basis is half-forgotten, half-remembered history, attributes the origin of Athens to the ancient Atlantians. The former existence of this submerged continent is daily becoming more fully recognized. The explorations of the "Challenger," the "Dolphin," the "Gazelle," and the discoveries of Le Plongeon in Yucatan, at later date, confirming olden tradition. Maine thus ascribes a much older origin to "Usus" than Gibbon, who attributes it to the effect of the Punic triumphs.[3] In reality "Usus" seems to have been a reminiscence of the Matriarchate, incorporated into the law of the Twelve Tables, and accepted by Rome as a more just form of the marriage relation for women than the religious "Confarraetio" or the civil form of "Coemptio." But as Rome increased in wealth and luxurious modes of living, the influence of the Patriarchate correspondingly extended, the perception of justice at the same time diminishing. Pomp and ceremony were associated with the marriage rite among patricians, while "Usus" was regarded as a plebeian form especially suited to the populace. But at later date when Rome rebelling against the tyranny of her rulers tended towards a republican form of government, "Usus" again became general. It was impossible for patrician women not to see the greater freedom of plebeian wives under "Usus," a form that while equally binding in the essentials of the union did not make the wife a marital slave,[4] and "Usus" eventually became the basis of Roman legal conception of marriage, against which Christianity from the first waged a warfare of ever increasing fierceness,[5] the very foundation of that religion being the subordination of woman in every relation of life. Under "Usus" the mere fact of two persons living together as husband and wife was regarded as a marriage. If during each year the wife remained away from the home for three days, she kept herself from under her husband's power. She remained a part of her father's family; her husband could not mortgage or in any way alienate her property. This was absolutely contrary to the laws of the christian form of marriage, under which the wife surrendered her person, her property, and her conscience into the indisputable control of the husband. Under "Usus" a large proportion of Roman property fell into woman's hands. She became the real estate holder of the Eternal City and its provinces, and in consequence was treated with great respect; the holding of property, especially of real estate conducing to that end. Under "Usus" the cruelties sanctioned by "Confarraetio" were rended impossible; a wife could no longer be put to death, as was formerly the custom, for having tasted wine, a treacherous kiss from her husband upon his return home, betraying her, nor could her infant daughter be exposed or murdered at the pleasure of her husband who as inexorable master was frequently wont to refuse her pleadings for the life of her babe, calling her prayers naught but the scruples of a foolish woman.[6]

Thus under "Usus" human life became more sacred, and woman endowed with a greater sense of personal security. It affected an entire change for the better in the moral sentiments of the Roman empire.[7] A complete revolution had thus passed over the constitution of the family. This must have been the period, says Maine, when a juriconsulist of the empire defined marriage as a lifelong fellowship of all divine and human rights.

Not alone Maine, but also Reeves, failed not to see that the disruption of the Roman Empire was very unfavorable to the personal and proprietory rights of woman.[8] The practical effect of the common Roman form of marriage being the absolute legal independence of the wife, under which a large proportion of Roman property fell into the hands of women, the wife retaining her family name and family inheritance. All this was changed as soon as Christianity obtained the rule. Under Christian forms of marriage a wife was taken from her own family and transferred into that of her husband the same as a piece of property. She assumed his name, the same as the slave took that of the new master to whom he was transferred. That this idea of the wife as a slave did not belong alone to the earlier christian period, but is a part of christian doctrine of today is clearly shown by the continued custom of a woman's dropping her family name upon marriage and assuming that of the husband–master.

For this middle Roman period carried its blessings to wives no longer than until the empire became christianized, when the tyranny of ecclesiastical marriage again fell to womans' lot. While under the influence of "Usus," Roman jurists of the middle period had declared the ownership of property by married women to be a principle of equity this drew forth opposing legislation from the christians, and under christian law, the husband again became master of his wife's person, and property, her children also falling under his entire control, the mother possessing no authority over them. From that period down to the twentieth century of christianity, under all changing civil laws, woman has ever felt the oppressions of ecclesiasticism in this relation.[9]

Guizot strangely declares that woman's present, and what he terms, superior, position in the household today, is due to feudalism.[10] The isolation and strife under which the nobility lived during the feudal period, warring against each other when not engaged in foreign aggression, compelled to certain forms of social life within each castle, thus creating the modern family, or the family under its present social form. At that period the feudal wife with her retinue of household serfs and a vast number of her husband's retainers in charge, held a more responsible position than that of woman under primitive christian habits of life. But the knights and lords of these feudal castles were lecherous robbers, rather than men of kindly regard for womankind. Their inclination was not towards justice or family life, but the despoiling of all beneath them, and even of their equals with whom they were not upon terms of amity. The ruins of such castles, like the nest of the eagle, perched upon some inaccessible rock, add today an element of picturesque beauty to the Rhine and other rivers of Europe, but owe their elevated and isolated positions to the evil character of their owners, the banditti of the middle ages.[11] When not engaged with their king in warfare, they made the despoiling of serfs and the betrayal of wives and daughters their chief diversion, the robbery of burghers and travelers their business; churchmen equally with laymen living by the same means.

During the year 1268, Rudolph of Germany, destroyed sixty-six castles of these christian robber nobility in Thuringia alone, and hung twenty-nine of these "family builders" at one time in Erfurt. He compared Rome to the lion's den in fable; the footsteps of many animals to be found going thither, but none coming back. At this period the soldiers of Christian Europe found pleasure in torture for its own sake, chiefly selecting women as their victims. In mediæval England the condition of woman was one of deep degradation. Wives were bought and daughters sold for many hundred years after the introduction of Christianity.[12] Although England was christianized in the fourth century, it was not until the tenth that the christian wife of a christian husband acquired the right of eating at table with him, nor until the same century did a daughter gain the right of rejecting the husband her father might have selected for her. While the sale of daughters was practiced in England for seven hundred years after the introduction of Christianity, we note that by the ancient law of India, a father was forbidden to sell his daughter in marriage, or receive the smallest present therefor. In mediæval England the daughter was held as a portion of the father's property to be sold to the highest bidder. The Mundium[13] recognized the father's right to sell his daughter to the husband he might select for her, usually the highest bidder in point of wealth or political influence. While Marquette pertained to kings, feudal lords, and men of no family relationship to the victim, Mundium inherred in the father himself. Through it he sacrificed his own daughter for money or power.

The practice of buying wives with cattle or money was regulated both in the laws of King Æthelbert and King Ine. In event of the woman who had been thus bought, becoming a widow, half of the sum paid for her seems to have been set aside for her support, provided her husband had not died without issue. The other half remained absolutely the property of her father, brother, or guardian by whom she had been sold. At a somewhat later period the church doctrine of celibacy influenced all ranks of men, while at the same time an unmarried woman because of her maiden-hood was regarded as disreputable. A bachelor held honorable place, even though all celibate men were looked upon as libertines of especially impure life. Warnings against matrimony were the ordinary topics of conversation, while virtue in women was held so little sacred that no nearness of relationship was security for either a married or a single woman.[14] Husbands trafficked in the honor of their wives, fathers sold their daughters,[15] yet if under temptation, a woman fell, outside of such sale, her punishment was most severe. To a husband was accorded the power of life and death over his household, and either personally or by means of a hired assassin he not unfrequently assigned his wife to death or to a punishment more atrocious and barbarous.[16] Disraeli says:

> If in these ages of romance and romances the fair sex were scarcely approached without the devotion of idolatry, when-ever "the course of true love" altered; when the frail spirit loved too late, and should not have loved, the punishment became more criminal than the crime, for there was more selfish revenge and terrific malignity than of justice when autocratical man became the executioner of his own decree.

The English christian husband of that age is paralleled by cer-tain North American Indians of the present day.[17] The horizon of woman's life was bounded by the wishes of her father or husband. Single, she was regarded as a more or less valuable piece of prop-erty[18] for whose sale the owner was entitled to make as good a bargain as possible. It was as a bride that the greatest sum was secured.[19] Prominent among the laws of the first Christian king of Kent, were provisions for the transfer of money or cattle in exchange for the bride.[20] The theory of woman's ownership by man was everywhere carried into practice, and with great severity in case the wife proved unfaithful to her enforced vows. The facts that her consent to the marriage had not been asked, that mayhap the man she was forced to wed was utterly repugnant to her, that her affections might already have been bestowed, that she was transferred like a piece of goods with no voice upon the question, were not taken into consideration, and did the husband not choose to kill his derelict spouse, the question still remained continued one of property[21] and a new bride was demanded of the lover in place of the wife whose love he had gained.

A husband, attracted by a new face, more wealth, greater political influence, or for any reason desiring to be rid of his wife, was regarded as justifiable in hiring an assassin to strangle her, or if walking by a river-brink, of himself pushing her into the water where her cries for help were disregarded. Those in whose hearts pity, rose, were prevented from giving aid, by such remarks as, "It is nothing, only a woman being drowned."[22] A horse or other domestic animal received more consideration than the women of a household. Notwithstanding this period, the early part of the fourteenth century, before the days of printing or rapid intercourse between nations, yet the evil fame of christendom reached distant lands. Its hypocrisy and baseness were known by those very Saracens from whom the Crusaders attempted to wrest the Holy Sepulchre. To Sir John Mandeville the Sultan of Egypt mercilessly criticized the christianity of England[23] and the christian method of serving God; the total disregard of chastity, the sale of daughters, sisters and wives. We cannot agree with Disraeli in his doubts if there was a single christian in all christendom at this period. To the contrary, it may be regarded as an epoch when the doctrines of christianity were most fully sustained, the church at that time carrying out the principles of both the Old and the New Testament regarding women. From Moses to Paul, the Bible everywhere speaks of her as a being made for man, secondary to man, and under his authority by direct command of the Almighty; the state, as coadjutor and servant of the church, basing her codes of law[24] upon its teachings. Under these codes woman has not only been looked upon as naturally unchaste, but also regarded as a liar, the state demanding the testimony of two or three, and in some instances of seven women to invalidate that of one man; the man even then in extreme cases clearing himself by his single oath. Condemned as having brought evil into the world, woman's every step was looked upon with suspicion, and the most brutal treatment as far short of her just deserts. To speak well of her was to cause misgivings of one's self. The system of defamation inaugurated by the church in reference to women, was later recognized by the Jesuits as a most effective plan for the personal subjugation of men. Busenbaum, an influential writer of this order, directing:

> Whenever you would ruin a person you must begin by spreading calumnies to defame them. Repetition and perseverance will at length give the consistency of probability, and the calumnies will stick to a distant day.

The astute Jesuits learned their lesson from church treatment of women. Its practical results were ever before their eyes in the contempt with which woman was regarded, and her own consequent loss of self-respect. Under early and mediæval christian law, as in most states today, the father alone had right to the disposal of his children. He possessed the sole power of giving away his daughter in marriage; if he died, this right devolved upon the eldest son; only in case there were no sons was the right of the mother in any way recognized. If neither father or brother were living, the mother gave her daughter away in marriage, and this was the only instance in which one woman possessed control over another woman, the law allowing the mother no voice in the marriage of her daughter unless she was a widow without sons. So greatly enslaved were daughters, that nonconsent of the victim in no way impaired the validity of the marriage.[25] A girl was simply a piece of family property to be disposed of as the family thought best. Although wives were simply the slaves of husbands, yet the condition of an unmarried woman was even more deplorable. Deprived of the society of young persons of her own sex, not allowed speech with any man outside of her own family, she was fortunate if she escaped personal[26] ill-treatment in her father's house. Not permitted to sit in the presence of either her father or her mother, continually found fault with, the laws constraining her to marry while giving her no preference as to a husband, and marriage still more fully taking from her the control of her own person, yet it was anxiously looked forward to as at least a change of masters, and the constant hope that in the husband she might find a lover who for dear love's sake would treat her with common humanity.

Such was the condition of women during eighteen hundred years of christianity. Legislated for as slaves, imprisoned for crimes that if committed by a man were only punished by branding the hand; buried alive for other crimes that committed by men were atoned for by the payment of a fine; denied a share in the government of the family or the church, their very sex deemed a curse, the twentieth century is now about to open showing no truly enlightened nation upon the face of the earth. From the barbarism of inhumanity the world is slowly awakening to the fact that every human being stands upon the plane of equal natural rights. The church has not taught the world this great truth, the State has not conceded it; its acknowledgment thus far, has been due to the teachings of individual men and women, that self-constituted authority over others is a crime against humanity. Under christian teaching regarding woman, the daughter was looked upon as a more remote relative and heir than the son, and this upon the ground of her inferiority. Blackstone, although admitting that such views did not pertain in Rome, yet speaks of males as "the worthier of blood." Such views were not held by pre-christian Britain. Under common law, before that country accepted christianity, property was equally divided between sisters, and only by special custom, between brothers.[27] But as early as Henry II it was the general rule that a woman could not share an inheritance with a man. An exception sometimes existed in a particular city where such custom had long prevailed.

Until quite recently, English women have not been permitted

to express an opinion upon political questions, although the Primrose League and other similar organizations have effected a great change within a few years. Yet it is but little more than two hundred years, in 1664, at Henley-upon-Thames, a woman having spoken against the taxation imposed by Parliament, was condemned for this freedom of political criticism, to have her tongue nailed to the body of a tree at the highway side upon a market day, and a paper fastened to her back detailing the heinousness of her offense. It was thus the state deterred similar politically minded women from the expression of their views, and in line with the church used its most stringent measures to retain woman in the "sphere" to which both church and state assigned her. Many savage tribes of Africa exhibit the same grade of civilization that was extant in christian England from the fourth to the eighteenth centuries.

> A father will sell his daughter among Unyamwazi, Africa, for one up to ten cows. A Lomali asks of a poor wooer from ten to twenty horses, of a wealthy one from one hundred upward, together with fifty camels and three hundred sheep. On the other hand, in Uganda, four oxen are sufficient to buy the most perfectly formed village belle, provided six needles and a box of cartridges are thrown in.

The sale is the same, the payment alone of different character. An African girl in case of a wealthy wooer, bringing even more than was ordinarily received during the middle ages for an English christian maiden. The patriarchal spirit wherever cropping out exhibiting the same characteristics, whether among Jews, Christians, or African savages. This is the more notable as among civilized or savage races yet governed by the principles of the Matriarchate, the position of woman is very high. In Samoa, no woman is compelled to work, all labor of whatever character being performed by the men. The celebrated traveler, Prof. Carl Lumholz, in his work *Among the Cannibals*, makes some interesting statements in regard to the course adopted by the natives of

Georgia River, Australia, to save women from giving birth to undesired children, and to prevent the needless suffering and infant mortality so common in christian lands.

Among the methods adopted in christian countries for a continuance of the crimes common in the marriage relation, have been more or less stringent laws against divorce, ever falling with heaviest force upon her whom christian marriage laws have made a slave. The *Christian Union* declares as a significant act of evil import, that "in Wyoming, where the power of woman in affairs of government is greatest, one divorce takes place in every six marriages, the proportion being greater than in any other state." But if this assertion of the *Christian Union* is true, it is proof that a share in making the laws which govern her is wisely used by the women of that state; and it marks a new era in civilization, when woman holding political power in her own hands, refuses longer to degrade herself by living in a relation that has lost the binding power of love. The laws of church and of state during the christian ages originated with man, and it is a promising sign of woman's growth in self-reliance, independent thought, and purity of character, that she thus protests against the bondage of a relation which virtually holds the wife as slave of the husband; for despite the changes of the last four and a half decades, we still find the general tone of legislation in line with the church teaching of woman's created inferiority to man. We still find belief in the wife's duty of obedience to the husband; we still discover the church, the state, the world, all regarding the exercise of her own judgment even upon the questions most closely related to herself as woman's greatest sin. As free as woman is called today, she has not yet as daughter secured perfect liberty of choice in marriage, the power of the family too often compelling her into a hated relation. Money still leads parents to prefer one suitor above another, even in the United States; while in many European countries, marriages are arranged by friends, or through a broker, entirely without the girl's consent, who is frequently taken from a convent or school to be thus sold to some wealthy and perhaps octogenarian wooer, who covets the youth or beauty of the victim.[28]

The burning of twenty missionaries in a portion of savage Africa, a few years since, filled the civilized world with horror. But for several hundred years after the introduction of christianity into Great Britian, the penalty for simple theft by a woman slave was burning alive, and all the other women slaves were compelled to assist at her *auto-de-fé*. Upon such an occasion mentioned by Pike, eighty other women each brought a log of wood for the burning.[29] By the old Roman Code, burning alive as a punishment was forbidden because of its barbarity, but christianity reintroduced it, and for long centuries after the destruction of the Roman Empire, that other land aspiring to control of the sea, which proudly boasts that the sun never sets on her possessions, kept it in her criminal code for the punishment of helpless women.[30] So rigorous was woman's slavery that the friendships of women with each other, or with men, were strictly prohibited; yet the deep affection of one man for another to whom he consecrated his life and fortune, and of whom he spoke with that deep tenderness, was highly commended.[31] The despotic, irresponsible power of husbands in christian England at this period is shown by the diverse manner in which the murder of a wife by a husband, or a husband by a wife, was regarded. For a husband to murder a wife either by his own hands or those of a hired assassin, was of frequent occurrence, but as she was his slave over whom he had power of life and death, this was looked upon as a trivial affair. But under the laws of both church and state, the murder of a husband by a wife was regarded as petty treason, to be punished with the utmost severity, burning alive being a not uncommon form.[32]

Under christian legislation not alone the wife's person but her property so fully became her husband's that her use of any portion of it thereafter without his consent was regarded as theft; and such is still the law in the majority of christian countries; it is less than sixty years since a change in this respect took place in any part of the christian world. While a wife may steal from her husband it is still the law that a husband cannot steal from his wife. If she allows him to transact business for her, or in any way obtain possession of her property even for a moment, he has acquired legal ownership. Since the passage of the Married Woman's Property Act, the courts of England have decided that a husband cannot steal from his wife while she is living with him. A case before Baron Huddleston, 1888, commented upon by the *Pall Mall Gazette*, under head of "Stealing from a Wife," called attention to the superior position of the mistress in respect to property rights over that of the wife.

> Can a husband rob his wife? Baron Huddleston yesterday answered this by saying he can not rob her at all under the common law, which regards all the wife's property as the husband's; and, theft is only robbery under the Married Women's Property Act, when the wife is living apart from her husband, or when he is preparing to desert her. It is really quite amazing how many advantages a mistress has over a wife in all matters relating to property and to person. It almost seems as if the object of the law was to inflict such disabilities on wives in order to induce the fair sex to prefer concubinage to matrimony.

The separate moral codes for man and woman in all christian lands, show their evil aspect in many ways. Adultery, in all christian countries is held to be less sinful for men than for women. In England, while the husband can easily obtain a divorce from the wife upon the ground of adultery, it is almost impossible for the wife to obtain a divorce from the husband upon the same ground. Nothing short of the husband's bringing another woman into the house to sustain wifely relations to him, at all justifies her in proceedings for a separation; and even then, the husband retains a right to all the wife's property of which he was in possession, or which may have fallen into his hands. Less than a dozen years since, an English husband willed his wife's property to his mistress and her children of whom he was the father. The wife (in what is known as "The Birchall Case") contested the will, but the courts not only decided in its favor, but added insult to that legal robbery, by telling the wife that a part of her money was enough for her, and that she ought to be willing that her husband's mistress and illegitimate children should share it with her.

Woman's disobedience to man is regarded by both the church and the state as disobedience to God. As late as the first half of the present century it was held as constructive treason, in England, punishable by the state, for a wife to refuse obedience to her husband's commands or in any way to question his authority. She was required to be under submission to him as the direct representative of the deity. For the woman who protested against this annihilation of her individuality, a flogging was the customary form of punishment and so common was the use of the whip that its size was regulated by law.[33] The punishment of petit treason[34] was more severe for woman than for man because her crime was regarded as of a more heinous character. She was dragged on the ground or pavement to the place of execution then burned alive; a man was drawn and hanged. It was long after the conquest before even a man convicted of treason secured the right of being carried to execution on a sledge or hurdle. Blackstone comments upon the extreme torment of being dragged on the ground or pavement. In case of a woman the wounds and lacerations thus received must have greatly added to her intensity of suffering, yet so blinded was he through those laws, that he calls her punishment of burning, a tribute to the decency due to the sex.[35]

During a portion of the christian era the wife has not been looked upon as related to her husband. The residium of this disbelief in the relationship of husband and wife, occasionally shows itself to the present day.[36] She was his slave under both religious and civil law, holding the same relations to him as the subject did to the king, and liable to punishments similar to those inflicted upon unruly slaves, or disloyal subjects. Rebellion against the husband's authority was treason punishable by law, similarly as treason to the king. The difference was but in name. Down to the end of the eighteenth century in England, the wife who had murdered her husband was burned alive; if the husband murdered his wife he suffered simple decapitation, "the same as if he had murdered any other stranger." For the wife's crime of petit treason the penalty was that of the slave who had killed her master. It is scarcely a hundred years since the punishment of burning the wife alive for the murder of her husband, or the female slave for the murder of her master, as petit treason, passed out of the English penal code; the last instance occurring in 1784, eight years after our declaration of independence. This same code was operative in the colonies; the last woman thus punished in this country, being a slave in 1755, who had murdered her master, America having twenty-nine years precedence in the abolition of this penalty.[37]

A cablegram from Europe, September 1892, proves the continued existence in this last decade of the nineteenth century of the crime of petit treason, and also the barbarous punishment still inflicted under christian law, upon the wife who murders her husband. This case, occurring in Finland, was carried up to the Court of Appeals, which not only affirmed the decision of the lower court but decreed additional punishment. Because the wife had also forged her husband's name for small sums of money, having, under law, first been robbed by him of her earnings, the judgment of having her right hand cut off, was added to the original sentence. She was then decapitated, her body fastened to a stake, covered with inflammable material and burned to ashes. Although this wife was not burned alive, the barbarity of her punishment was most atrocious, and took place under the christian laws of the church and the state, in a Protestant country in the "year of our Lord," 1892. That the punishment was infinitely more severe than would have been inflicted upon the husband in case he had murdered his wife, was due to christian teaching of woman's inferiority and subordination to man; thus making the wife's crime that of petit treason, under law only a trifle less heinous than murdering a king, or attempting destruction of the government. Had the husband murdered the wife it would have been, according to legal prevision, the same as if he had killed "*any other stranger.*" The marriage ceremony robbed her of her property and earnings, but in equity the money she was accused of stealing from him belonged to her. Under the laws of most christian states, a woman is robbed of herself and all of her possessions by the simple fact of her marriage. Under christian law, the services of the wife in the marital relation are all due to the husband,[38] her earnings all belong to him; she is a slave owning nothing and with no rights in the property her husband calls his own. This wife's crime was provoked by preexisting criminal legislation of the christian church and state. Possessing no legal right to the control of her own person, property or conscience, the wife was held to have sinned against a divinely appointed master to whom she owed more than human allegiance: she was a criminal so great that the punishment of severing her hand and head were deemed entirely inadequate, and her body fastened to a stake was covered with inflammable material and burned to ashes.[39]

While the external government of Finland, as declarations of war, peace, treaties, etc., is under control of the Czar, or Grand Duke, yet in the internal administration of affairs this country is an Independent State, under a Constitution dating 1772, and confirmed by three successive czars. It became christianized in the twelfth century but is not under the Greek church; its established religion is Evangelical and Lutheran, under control of the archbishop of Abo, and the bishops of Bogia and Knopo; an ecclesiastical assembly meeting every ten years; and the Diet, composed of representatives of the clergy, nobility, citizens and peasants, every five years. Without consent of these bodies no laws are enacted or repealed; but woman possesses no representation either in ecclesiastical or civil affairs.

The old law of marriage instituted by the church, which held the wife as belonging body and soul to the husband who not alone possessed control over her actions but decided her religion, is still extant. In but few countries do we see a tendency towards it abolition, even those that have somewhat favorably legislated upon the question, still retaining the general principle of a wife's subserviency to her husband. A few years since an English lady desirous of uniting with the Catholic church was refused consent by her husband, "a staunch churchman." Unknown to him she was received into that body, which proved occasion of an animated controversy between the husband and the late Cardinal Manning, the former basing his opposition and his letter of remonstrance to the cardinal upon the ground of the admitted legal right of a hus-

band, under English law, to ordain the form of his wife's religion.[40] Nor do we find material difference in the United States.
In Virginia, in the winter of 1891, a wife, despite the opposition
of her husband, caused her infant to be baptized by an Episcopal
clergyman into that church, the husband openly expressing his
disapproval while the ceremony was in progress, and afterwards
suing the clergyman for an interference with his vested rights over
wife and child. This supreme authority of the husband in christian countries is shown in many strange ways. Among the Hindoos the naming of the child belongs to the mother. If the father
expresses desire for a different name, each one is written upon a
paper over which lighted lamps are set, the one   burning the
longest deciding the choice of name. But in Rhode Island as late
as 1892, a controversy between the parents as to the naming of a
child was settled by law. The father and mother each filed a certificate with the registrar; the father employing a lawyer who to
the satisfaction of the city solicitor proved his client's prior right,
and an order was issued to the registrar in favor of the father's
choice of name.[41] The claim of the christian husband in each of
these instances was that of his supreme and prior right, on the
church theory incorporated into law, that both wife and child
belong to the husband. The celebrated Agar-Ellis case in England
during the latter part of the seventies, was brought by a wife to
compel the keeping by a husband of his pledges in regard to the
religious education of his children. The decision was against the
wife, upon the general ground that a wife had no rights in law as
against a husband. A man's pledged word broken at the gaming
table renders him infamous and subjects him to dishonor through
life. But a husband's pledged word broken to his wife, under ruling
of the highest court and the profoundest legal talent of England,
the Court of Appeals, and the Vice-Chancellor, is just, implying no
dishonor, but rather entitling him to respect as a man who in a
befitting manner has maintained his marital rights and authority.
The judge instructed the wife that she had no right to teach her
children what her husband did not believe, even though she herself most fully believed what she taught. He impressed upon her

that she was not rearing her children for herself, but as her husband's property, over which she possessed no control only in so far as the husband made her his agent. In affirming the order of the Vice-Chancellor, the court of appeals declared that the father had the legal right to bring up the children in his own faith, and in pledging his word to the contrary he had in no way forfeited or abandoned his authority. This decision of the English Court of Appeals, is in accord with the laws of the United States. The Albany, N.Y., *Law Journal* in commenting upon this case under the head of "Curious Question," declared the decision to be in harmony with the general rule as to religious education; the child is to be educated in the religion of the father.

The *English Women's Suffrage Journal* in its comments, declared English law to be based upon the Koran, quoting, in proof, from a writer in the *Contemporary Review*:

> The East has long been noted for the subordination of its women, and this subjection is not only preached by Musselmen and Buddhists but even by Christian Churches. Woman is not regarded as a person but as a field, cultivable or not, as the possessor desires. As a field can neither have faith, nor intellect, nor a will of its own, it would be absurd for a man to occupy himself about what a woman believes, thinks, or wishes. She is absolutely nothing but her husband's domain. He cultivates it and reaps the harvest, for the harvest belongs to the proprietor.

According to the *Women's Suffrage Journal*, this condition accurately depicted the spirit of the injunction laid upon Mrs. Agar-Ellis, by Lord Justice James.

> To the wife and mother he declared that she had no right to teach her children what she believed, but must, to the contrary, teach them what her husband believed, whether she believed it or not; the law not concerning itself with what a woman believes, or wishes, as she is in law absolutely nothing but her husband's domain.

The mistake of the *Journal* lies in ascribing this law to the teachings of the Koran, instead of the teachings of the Bible, which in general tone, and through particular instruction, places woman upon the same level as a man's "flocks and herds, oxen and cattle." We do not find the personal rights of women in the United States differing from those of the women of England. A famous suit was tried in Ohio, 1879, known as the "Lucy Walker Case," a former wife suing the present wife for alienating her husband's affections. Great attention was called to this suit from the high position of the parties; Judge Seney, former husband of one, and present husband[42] of the other wife, being widely known as author of a "Civil Code," bearing his name. The suit gained still greater notoriety from the principle enunciated in his decision rendered against the plantiff, by Judge Dodge, before whom the case came to trial; he dismissed it upon the ground that a wife had no rights as against her husband. All testimony upon part of the injured first wife was excluded upon the same ground. He decided:

> *First:* That the husband has a property interest in his wife which the wife does not possess in the husband.
>
> *Second:* That the law protects him in this right of property in her.
>
> *Third:* Upon the ground that he holds her and dares the world to meddle with him in the holding.
>
> *Fourth:* But on the contrary the wife looks alone to the husband, the law compelling her to do so.

Thus less than fifteen years since, the legal decision was rendered in the United States, that a wife is a husband's property; that the husband has a pecuniary interest in the wife, the law protecting his right of property in her, while the wife possesses no reciprocal right of property in the husband.

The *Toledo Bee* gave the full text of Judge Dodge's decision:

> The question submitted is this: Has a wife such a property in her husband, has she such a legal pecuniary interest in him, that she can bring an action at law against one who injures him, against

one who imprisons him, and, finally, can a wife recover damages at law against a woman who has carnal intercourse with her husband without her consent? It will be at once admitted that the question is a novel one. Our courts adjudicate primarily upon property interests. A husband has a pecuniary, a property interest in his wife. The law protects this right of property.

A father can recover damages against a man who seduces his daughter, but a mother can not recover for the seduction of a daughter. Why not? Is she not as dear to the mother as the father? Nay, dearer, by as much as a mother's love exceeds a father's. But she has not property in her, is not entitled to her wages; neither is a mother bound to support her children. The father is the head of the family, not the mother. He, by virtue of his headship, is legally entitled to the services of his family. The husband is head of the wife; not the wife of the husband.

But can a husband sue his wife if she refuses to support him out of her property, to give him her earnings, or keep her marriage contract? Not at all. Can a father sue his minor child that refuses him obedience and service? Not at all. And why is this? For the same reason that he cannot sue his flocks or his herds, his oxen and his cattle—they are his. His to command. He is reponsible for and to them. He cannot sue his own. He can sue any one who takes them away; any one who keeps or harbors them; any one who injures them; because they are his own. But the wife does not own her husband; the child does not own the father, and, therefore, I hold that the child cannot sue for an injury to the father, nor the wife for an injury to the husband. There is in her no property right upon which to found the action. My conviction is that the wife looks to her husband alone for the fulfillment of his marriage vows. If he refuses her the support, protection and love which he pledged her, she applies to a court to enforce the claim against him. Every dollar he has, every penny of his earnings, all his arm can gain or his intellect can attain are subject to her right. But she looks to her husband alone, the law compels her to do so. The husband enforces his claim to his wife by striking down every one who interferes with his right to her. He holds her and dares the world to meddle with her. The law protects him in holding. The law gives courage to his heart, strength to his arm in defending his position. But the wife looks to the husband. She relies upon his pledge and his promise, which the law will enforce, and she looks to that alone. The law does not permit her to go forth to smite the seducer of her husband, nor the man or woman who entices him away.

But as showing the rapid growth of public opinion in favor of the wife's equality of right with the husband, through the persistent rebellion of woman against established laws and usages of Church and States, thus forcing an advancing civilization upon the world, was a decision rendered 1891, twelve years later, in the state of Indiana. The case was that of Leah Haynes, plaintiff, against Flora Knowles, defendant; a suit similar in character to the "Lucy Walker Case." Judge Elliot in Supreme Court of that State, on appeal from the decision of the Circuit Court of Dearborn County, reversed the finding of the lower court, deciding in favor of the right of a wife to sue for the alienation of her husband's affections. This decision, so contrary to common law, and to ordinary christian legislation for woman, is proof of an advancing civilization which does not look to the church for approval. Court decisions of this character establishing a precedent, are of far greater value in demonstrating the growth of a purer public sentiment, than are simple legislative victories upon school or municipal questions. They speak even more clearly than do the host of newly opened industries, freer opportunities for education, married woman's property laws and similar legislation, of a growing recognition of woman's personal rights, and of a civilization founded upon the common rights of humanity, and no longer upon church authority.

The general spirit and letter of the christian laws of husband and wife was most fully carried out by a husband of the state of Missouri a few years since. Mrs. Olive Davenport of St. Louis, suing for a divorce, upon the ground that her husband required her to obey him in all things. "Davenport's rules for his Wife" were offered in evidence.

Rules for the Government of my Wife's Conduct while away from me, June 1, 1879:

First: Not to speak to any person or allow any person to speak to her on the car except the conductor and porter in the discharge of their duty.

Second: Go directly from depot in New York, to Mrs. Haight's house, and occupy room with mother and sleep only in room.

Third: Speak kindly and politely to Mrs. Haight, but not in a friendly or familiar manner. Say to her you do not wish to meet anyone in the house. Ask for a table to yourself, with only your family or go somewhere else.

Fourth: Never sing in the parlor or sing in your room when any person except your immediate family be present.

Fifth: Never leave mother day or night for five minutes at a time for any reason whatsoever. Do not walk, ride, or go anywhere without her, even with your own brother.

Sixth: Do not call on any person whatsoever, and allow no one who may call on you to see you unless they be your brothers or their wives. Do not speak to any person you may meet whom you have not known in the past.

Seventh: Write every night to me a full, truthful and exact account of everything you have done, where you have been, to whom you have spoken, and whom you have seen. This must be done every night.

Let nothing but sickness or death prevent your keeping these rules, for I will excuse no breach on any account.

Do not leave New York even for one hour without my permission, except to Brooklyn or Harlem.

If my wife cannot keep these rules in word and spirit, I desire never to see her again.

—Benjamin R. Davenport

The divorce suit showed the married pair to have been separated once before, Mrs. Davenport, unable to bear her husband's tyranny, returning to her mother's house. At that time her husband required her to eat only what he directed and to wear only those clothes he bade her wear, selecting even the color of her ribbons. The only fault he had to find with her was that she "talked back," which has always been deemed an unpardonable crime in woman; one for which the Ducking Stool and Scold's Bridle were invented. After she left him, Mr. Davenport wrote affectionate letters to his wife, calling her the sweetest and best of women, imploring her to return. She relented and lived with him once more, but her husband again put his rules in force. She then sued for a divorce, which the court granted. Mr. Davenport's treatment of his wife is by no means exceptional. The following excerpt is from a letter in the Terra Haute, Ind., *Mail*, 1884.

An individual who considers himself a representative man in the city, and perhaps he is, said in the presence of several persons, "I went home at three o'clock this morning and found my wife sitting up. She burst into tears and asked me where I had been and why I treated her in that manner? I just told her if she said another word I would leave the house; that as long as she had a comfortable home where she could spend her evenings it was none of her business where I spent mine. Now, if I did not provide for my family, it would be a different thing but so long as my wife is well provided for, she has no right to complain and I don't propose to allow it." These are the man's own words, and there are a great many men who hold the same opinions. If their wives protest because they drink, gamble and spend their nights away, they say, "You have a good home and enough to eat and wear; what more do you want?"

A lady of Richmond, Va., anxious to know from a legal source just what her rights as a wife were, consulted a lawyer of that city.

"Well, Madam," he replied, head thrown back, thumbs in armholes: "Well, Madam, you have a right to comfortable food, a fire to keep you warm, and two calico dresses a year. These are your legal rights; all beyond these are the gifts of your husband. Luxuries of food and clothing, journies and books, these are not yours by law; it remains with your husband to decide whether he will furnish them to you or not."

And this is Christian civilization for woman at the close of the nineteenth century of this era.

Although married women of the State of New York have enjoyed certain property rights since 1848, subsequent legislation in various ways increasing that power, it was not until 1882, that the Court of Appeals decided them to be the rightful owners of articles of personal adornment and convenience coming from their husbands, possessing power to bequeath them at death to their heirs. The same year the Supreme Court of that state decided that a wife may sue her husband for damages for assault and battery. The influence of these decisions in recognizing woman's rights of person, especially that of the Supreme Court in deciding the right of the wife to punish the husband through the courts for brutal treatment, can scarcely be overestimated. It opened a new era for woman:

First: A recognition of the wife's personality.

Second: Holding the husband responsible for his treatment of the wife.

Third: An acknowledgment of the wife's right to protection as against the husband. It destroyed, in this state the old *femme covert* teaching of Christianity, and recognized a wife as possessing the common rights of a human being.

The United States, making pretense of the greatest governmental freedom in the world, and in reality according it to men of every color and degree of intelligence or property, still denies such liberty to woman. In many of the states, the old restrictions of modern common law still prevail. There are states where the property of the wife upon marriage falls into the control of the husband, to do with as he alone pleases, the wife not retaining the right to its use or its management in anyway whatsoever. There are other states where the separate property of the husband and the wife is made communal, but in those states the control of this communal property is in the husband's hands. In most states the old restrictions still exist, and a woman cannot make a will; cannot act as executrix or administratix; can neither sue nor be sued. In the largest proportion of the states in which the separate property of the wife is recognized, the husband still has the advantage in heirship. In less than one-fifth of the states has the wife the same control over the children of the marriage as the husband. In the remaining four-fifths and over, the father is assumed to be sole owner of the children, who can be bound out, willed or given away without the consent or even knowledge of the mother. Can barbarism go farther than this?

So that even in this year 1892, within eight years of the twentieth Christian century, we find the largest proportion of the United States, still giving to the husband custody of the wife's person; the exclusive control of the children of the marriage, of the wife's personal and real estate; the absolute right to her labor and all products of her industry. In no state does the law recognize the legal existence of the wife, unless she relinquishes her own name, upon marriage, taking that of her husband, thus sinking her identity in his; the old *femme covert*—or covered woman—idea of the law books under state and church. That woman is an individual with the right to her own separate existence, has not yet permeated the thought of church, state or society. A letter to the American press from Rev. Robert Laird Collyer, while revisiting his native country a few years since, gives the unbiased views of a native-born English clergyman as to woman's position in that land of christian civilization, the husband being represented as king of the household, the wife as his dutiful subject. The letter was headed:

Marriage Customs in England

The Man King of the House, the Woman His Dutiful Subject

The man is the king of the English household, and the wife is only the prime minister. There is no confusion or overlapping of authority. The will of the husband is law. He has not only the place of honor but of ease. The arrangements of the house, the company entertained, and the service employed, all have respect to his wishes and to his convenience. The wife conducts the affairs of state for the king. She has her household and, more than likely, her personal allowance, and she renders a strict account of stewardship either weekly or monthly.

The wife's personal expenditures are less, much less than the husband's. In many instances he will spend more on his dress as a man than she does as a woman, for the rule is, the Englishman is the best-dressed man and the English woman is the worst dressed in the civilized world.

"The will of the husband is law," the wife possessing no freedom, but renders "a strict account of her stewardship, either weekly or monthly." Kicks, blows, wounds inflicted upon the wife under the countenance of the civil law; the will of the husband as undisputed law; her person, her property, her children under his sole control; what is the condition of the wife in England today but one of degraded slavery? That every woman does not endure all these wrongs is simply because she has a lenient master. Like Adolph under St. Clair, in *Uncle Tom's Cabin*, she has freedom because a good master allows her to take it; under a bad master she suffers as Adolph when falling into the hands of Legree. Personal rights are the basis of all other rights; personal slavery is the root of all other wrongs. Neither freedom of the intellect or conscience can exist without freedom of person. Thus civilization has not yet existed, that which has borne the name having been but the thought of the few; the civilization of the present is not enlightened, it belongs to the barbarous ages; authority and not justice is the rule. To the present time the lenient sentence imposed upon the English husband who beats his wife is such as to invite a repetition of the offense; knocking a wife down, beating and bruising her with a poker are rights secured to the husband under present English law.

A man named Hefferon, at Rotherham, finding his wife had gone to some place of which he disapproved, knocked her down and beat her violently with a poker. She bled from both ears, her throat was scratched, and she was badly bruised on her back and arms. Mr. Justice Day practically told the jury to acquit. He said the case ought not to have come before them, and he suggested that the prisoner had been merely exercising that control over his wife which was still sanctioned by the law of England.[43] The jury acquitted promptly, as directed.[44]

To such extent is this abuse of woman under law as to have called forth a vigorous article in the *Westminster Review*,[45] under head of "The Law in Relation to Woman."

There is another cruel injustice to woman, which is so notorious as to have become a mere truism. It is referred to almost daily, yet familiarity has bred such contempt, that it goes on unchecked and unabated. We refer to the monstrously lenient sentences passed upon husbands who assault and beat their wives. In one of our criminals courts recently, two men and a woman were sentenced to six years years penal servitude for stealing a watch by force, while a man who assaulted and greviously wounded his wife and mother-in-law with a reaping hook, got eighteen months' imprisonment. An instance occured the other day in a small municipal court. A man pleaded guilty to assaulting and kicking his wife and another woman with effusion of blood and injury to their persons. He was fined a pound for each female. Shortly after two men were convicted of injuring public seats belonging to the municipality, by knocking them about, etc., they were fined two pounds each. Clearly, therefore, in the eyes of this magistrate a muncipal seat is worth exactly twice the value of a woman. Parallel sentences to these may be seen almost daily in the newspapers in any part of the United Kingdom. In the police courts, wife-beaters often get off with a few days imprisonment, sometimes with an admonition. If it be argued that theft is such a common offense that it is necessary that it should be punished with greater severity than cruelty, we rejoice that the argument applies quite as forcibly to wife-beating, which, unfortunately is as common an offense as can be found among a certain class of society.[46]

The comparison here shown between the penalty of criminally assaulting and wounding women, not alone the man's wife but also her aged mother, most forcibly shows the entire disregard of Christian England in the last half of the nineteenth century, for the personal rights of all women. No proof is needed other than such decisions; nor is the United States far in advance. Within ten months from the formation of the "Protective Agency for Women and Children," organized in Chicago, April 1886, it had investigated nearly one hundred complaints. Although in a majority of these cases the agency was successful in securing redress, it yet found there was not legal remedy where the husband and father failed to provide for his family; and that in cases of crimes against women, its efforts were crippled by the disposition of police justices to regard such crimes as venial offenses, either dismissing such cases upon frivolous pretexts or imposing light sentences. Nothing could more clearly demonstrate woman's degraded condition in the nineteenth century of christian civilization, than the almost universal demand for laws securing better protection to women and children. These two classes, unrecognized by church or state, are still largely without that pale of protection man has reared for himself. January 23, 1886, the *Inter Ocean* gave more than six columns to an account of the dreadful crimes committed against women and children in Chicago alone, within the short period of the preceding four months. It also showed the ease with which criminals of that class escaped punishment, not alone from laxity of protective legislation for their victims but still more from the tendency of magistrates to ignore crimes perpetrated by men against women; this condition being the natural result of the teaching of the church in regard to woman. In the city of Boston, 1884, the Chief of Police testified that there were at least fifteen cases of brutal wife-beating in that city every week, and this is but one type of the injuries perpetrated upon women for which the teachings of christianity are directly responsible. So common this crime and so ineffective all efforts to stop it, that the State of Delaware has reestablished the long abolished whipping-post, for offenders of this character, thus acknowledging christian civilization to be a failure, and resorting to the retributive punishment common among barbarians. But the remedy for crimes against women, and for the indifference of magistrates, does not lie in the punishment of the offenders, but in different sentiments in regard to woman in both church and state. Their teachings are the real foundations of the evil. Within the past ten years, the judge of an English Court decided that the flogging of a wife in the presence of her son did not constitute cruelty, sustaining his decision by reference to Blackstone and other learned christian jurists. It was during that same year (1884) that the chief of the Boston police testified to the many cases of brutal wife beating in that "Athens of America," every week. So common this form of assault that a bill was introduced in the Massachusetts lower House for the punishment of wife beaters, by a public whipping of not less than ten or more than thirty lashes.[47] For those refractory wives of mediæval christian England, whom whippings failed to subdue, other punishments were invented; such as the "Ducking Stool," the "Scold's Bridle," etc.[48] The Scold's Bridle, also known as the Witches Bridle and the Brank, was an extremely painful method of torture, although not as absolutely dangerous to life as the Ducking Stool, yet fastened in the mouth, its sharp edges pressing down upon the tongue, if the "Brawling Woman" attempted to speak her tongue was cut and the torture great.[49] An American clergyman describing in a public lecture an ancient machine" seen by him in christian England, "for curing a scolding wife," accompanied his description by the very clerical intimation that it could now be made by an ordinary blacksmith. Two curved plates of bronze conformed to the shape of the head, were delicately hinged and provided with hooks to place in the corners of the mouth. When adjusted, the machine was buckled back of the head.[50]

The Ducking Stool[51] consisted of a chair securely fastened upon a long plank balanced upon upright standards, and so arranged that the victim could be launched sixteen or eighteen feet into the pond or stream, while the executioner of the sentence stood upon dry ground. The back and arms of the chair were engraved with representations of devils torturing scolds. The culprit securely fastened in this chair, so confined as to be entirely helpless, was sometimes drowned; the chair being plunged once, twice, or thrice in some muddy stream or slimy pond. The suggestive and usual place of storing the Ducking Stool, when not in use, was the church-yard. Almost every English town of importance possessed one; their use was continued until the present century. The Leominster Ducking Stool, still preserved, was used in 1809, by order of the magistrates, upon a woman named Jane Corran, who received her punishment near Kenwater, Bridge. As late as 1817 Sarah Leeke was wheeled around town in this chair, although the lowness of the stream prevented the ducking[52] she would otherwise have received. Railing and scolding or "answering back," were deemed crimes on the part of the wife, who, "commanded to be under obedience," was expected silently to submit to oppression of every kind. That she did not—that she dared revolt by words—that women in sufficient number to cause the invention of such an instrument were rebellious in midst of the horrid oppression created by the church, speaks well for the womanly nature and thrills the heart with admiration the same as when old Margaret Pole, Countess of Salisbury, refused to lay her head on the block at the executioner's mandate, declaring that as she was innocent, she would not voluntarily place herself in position for death. While England has the shame of originating the Ducking Stool, the "Pilgrim Fathers," fleeing from religious persecution, failed not to take with them the implements of cruelty used in the domestic oppression of woman. The Ducking Stool, and the "Stool of Penitence" figure in the early annals of New England. Upon the latter, the Scarlet Letter of shame affixed upon her breast, the unmarried mother was forcibly seated beneath the pulpit, under public gaze, while her companion in sin protected by church and state, perchance held his place among the elders in the jury box, or upon the bench as the judge who had condemned her. Old Colonial legislation makes us acquainted with the various methods in use for punishing the free speech of women in this country two hundred years since.

"A Law to Punish Babbling Women" enacted by the General Assembly, of Virginia, 1662.

> Whereas, many babbling women slander and scandalize their neighbors, for which their poor husbands are often involved in chargable and vexatious suits and cost in great damages. Be it therefore enacted by the authority aforesaid, that in actions of slander caused by the wife, after judgment passed for damages, the wife shall be punished by ducking; and if the slander be so enormous as to be judged at greater damages than 500 lbs. of tobacco, then the wife to suffer ducking for each 500 pounds of tobacco adjudged against the husband, if he refuses to pay the tobacco.

As this was the state in which wives were bought in exchange for tobacco, it is not surprising to find the penalty of her free speech to be paid in tobacco, the wife to suffer ducking for each 500 pounds penalty in excess of the first. Massachusetts was not long in following the example of Virginia, and in 1672 ten years later, passed:

A Law for the Punishment of Scolds in Massachusetts

> Whereas, there is no express punishment (by law hitherto established) affixed to the evil practice of sundry persons by exhorbitancy of tongue in reviling and scolding; it is therefore ordered that all such persons convicted before any court or magistrate that hath proper cognizance of the case, shall be gagged, set in a ducking stool and dipped over head and ears three times, in some convenient place of fresh or salt water, as the court or magistrate shall judge meet.[53]

Nor must we believe that the punishment of women for use of the tongue, is of past ages. Even in the United States, women are to this day sometimes arraigned for free speaking. Laws to punish "babbling women" enacted in colonial days are still in force. It is but a few years since a women of St. Louis was arrested and brought before a magistrate as a common scold.[54] In the State of New Jersey, 1884, a woman was brought before the courts, convicted, on the old grounds of being a "common scold" and fined twenty-five dollars, and costs. Death not infrequently accompanied the use of the ducking stool, the poor gagged victim, her hands securely fastened, being utterly unable to help herself. But we do not learn that either the magistrate or the husband were held responsible to the law for such death. The sufferers, like those under the catholic inquisition of the fourteenth century, were deemed outside of the pale of sympathy or human rights, and the devils depicted upon the back of ducking stools as laying hold of their victims were conceded to have but taken their rightful prey.

Such has been part of Christian legislation for women in America, and yet she is told to see how much Christianity has done for her. To such extent has this church doctrine of man's superiority to woman, and the right of the husband to control of the wife proceeded, that many husbands believe they possess the right to sell their wives. Since the reformation her sale in the marketplace as an animal, held by a halter about her waist, has been recognized by English law even as late as the present century. Although now forbidden, the practice of wife-sale is still occasionally found both in England and in America. But when the law takes cognizance of such a sale its penalty is visited upon the innocent wife and not upon the guilty husband. The *English Women's Suffrage Journal* of December 1, 1883, reported such a case.

> November 13th, 1883, Betsy Wardle, was indicted for having on the 4th of September, 1882, married George Chusmall, her former husband being alive. The prisoner pleaded guilty, but said her former husband gave her no peace and sold her for a quart of beer. She imagined this was a legal transaction and that she could marry again. The second husband was asked how he came to marry the prisoner. He answered "Well, I bout her." The judge said, "You are not fool enough to suppose you can buy another man's wife?" on which he replied, "I was."
>
> Mr. Swift asked his lordship not to pass a severe sentence. The prisoner imagined that because she had been sold for sixpence

there was nothing criminal in marrying again. His lordship said it was absolutely necessary to pass some punishment on *her* to teach her that a *man* had no more right to sell his own wife than his neighbor's wife, or cow, or ox, or ass, or anything that was his.

The reason given by the judge for punishing the woman is extremely suggestive of woman's condition under the law. The wife who had been sold, the innocent victim of this masculine transaction, was sentenced to a week's imprisonment with hard labor, while the man who sold her and the man who bought her escaped without punishment or censure. The judge in quoting the tenth commandment graded the wife with the ox and the ass in the belongings of a man; the decision thus ranking her with the cattle of the stable.[55] To add to the infamy of this trial, it was the occasion of much unseemly jesting and laughter. It took place at the Liverpool Assizes before Justice Denham. His judgment paralleled the decision of the "Seney Trial" in Ohio, 1879. The selling a wife as a cow[56] in the marketplace was by no means uncommon during the early part of the century in England. Ashton[57] gives numerous instances of such sales.

The laws of England are those of Christianity based upon the theological teaching of man's superiority over woman; she is his servant, subordinate to him in all things, a condition except where removed by special statute, existing today.[58] Returned missionaries who refer to the wife as waiting upon the husband at table in heathen countries not eating until he is satisfied, as proof of the different customs brought about by christianity, should inform themselves of the condition of the christian wife for nearly a thousand years in what is regarded as the foremost christian country in the world. He will then have learned that circumstances quite contradictory to ecclesiasticism finally permitted the English wife to assume a seat at the table with her husband, a place she was not allowed to take for many hundred years after the introduction of christianity into that island. In every country where christianity exists, women now are, and during all the years of its civil power have been, legislated for as slaves. They have been imprisoned for crimes which if committed by a man were punished by simply branding on the hand; they have been condemned to be buried alive for other crimes which if committed by a man, were atoned-for by the payment of a fine. Having first robbed woman of her property and denied her the control of her own earnings, the christian religion allowed her to suffer the most agonizing form of death, a living burial, for lack of that very money of which she had been civilly and ecclesiastically robbed. The law so far controlled family life that for many hundred years it bound to servile labor, all unmarried women between the ages of eleven and forty. The father possessed absolute control over the marital destiny of his daughter.

Instances of wife sale are not uncommon in the United States, and although the price is usually higher than that given for English wives, reaching from three hundred to four thousand dollars, still, as low a sum as five cents has been recorded. A prosperous resident of Black Hills, Dakota, is said to have begun his business start in life through sale of his wife. If a wife is a husband's property the same as a cow, it is manifestly unjust that legal punishment of any kind should fall upon her because of her master's action. She is irresponsible. The right of sale logically goes with the right of beating, of taking the wife's property and holding her earnings, of owning her children, and she should be exempt from punishment for her own sale. In a much larger measure we find the same rule of punishing wives for the crimes of husbands enforced in the United States, in the penalty of disfranchisement of the women of Utah for the polygamy of the men of Utah. And this penalty was extended not alone to the wives of polygamous husbands—themselves possessing but one husband—victims alike of church and state, but the non-Mormon, or "Gentile Women" of that territory, were also disfranchised by the Forty-ninth Congress of the United States because of the polygamy of a portion of the Mormen men; all women of that territory were deprived of their vested rights, rights that had been in existence for seventeen years, because of the crimes of men.[59] Against this injustice, the Woman Suffragists of the country protested through means of a committee in a

Memorial

To the President of the United States:

The National Woman Suffrage Association, through this committee, respectfully present to you a protest against that clause of the anti-polygamy measure passed by congress, which, whether in the Edmunds bill of the senate or the Tucker substitute of the house, disfranchises the non-polygamous women of Utah.

The clause relating to the disfranchisement of women has no bearing on the general merits of the end sought to be attained by the measure, since Mormon men are the majority of the voters of the territory.

The non-polygamous women of Utah have committed no crime. Dis-franchisement is reserved by the United States government for arch traitors. Justice forbids that such a penalty should be inflicted on innocent women.

Non-polygamous Mormon women and the Christian women of Utah being thus disfranchised—the former for their opinions and the latter for the opinions of the former—a precedent is established subversive of the fundamental principles of our government, and threatening the security of all citizens.

If congress deems it necessary to disfranchise citizens because of injurious beliefs, discrimination between sexes is manifestly unjust.

It has been held by the foremost statesmen of the nation that the right of suffrage once exercised, becomes a vested right which cannot be taken away. Gratz Brown once said, in the senate of the United States, that if the idea that suffrage could be taken away at pleasure once crystallized in the minds of the people, it would "ring the death knell of American liberty." Mr. Vest, of Missouri, on the 25th, day of this month, said, on the floor of the senate: "Suffrage once given can never be taken away. Legislatures and conventions may do everything else; they never can do that. When any particular class or fraction of the community is once invested with this privilege it is fixed, accomplished and eternal."

Thus every argument for justice, equal legislation and the

safety of our republican form of government calls for the defeat of this clause.

We, therefore, respectfully urge you, as guardian of the rights of all American citizens, to veto any measure coming before you which disfranchises the women of Utah.

> Lillie Devereux Blake,
> Matilda Joslyn Gage,
> Caroline Gilkey Rogers,
> Mary Seymour Howell,
> Clara B. Colby,
> Sarah Miller,
> Elizabeth Boynton Harbert,
> Harriette R. Shattuck,
> Louisa Southworth,
> Committee

This memorial, supplemented by personal argument from the committee demonstrating the political dangers connected with such a denial of vested rights, together with the greater injustice of punishing women for the crimes of men, was met by reply of the President that as great changes were frequently made in bills before their final passage, he had as yet not given the subject much thought; promising, however to give it his fullest attention whenever brought before him. The method taken by the President to avoid responsibility of decision, is notable as he neither signed nor vetoed the bill, but allowed it to become law through such non-action. Crimes of omission being parallel with those of commission, the women of the United States can but hold Grover Cleveland equally guilty with the Forty-ninth Congress in punishing women for the crimes of men.

The Code of England, from which that of the United States is largely borrowed, was the outgrowth of Christianity, based upon a belief in man's superiority and woman's subordination to him as entering every relation of life. All legislation was class; the line was sex. During the early and middle ages man exhibited an antagonism towards woman,[60] which if not wholly created by religious belief was strenuously fostered by the church. Man's basest passion, love of power, was appealed to and he was assured by what he had been trained to regard as indisputable authority, that God had ordained his rule over woman. A quick response met all such priestly teaching. Christianity has ever been a religion of the emotions rather than of the reason. The former was cultivated; the latter bitterly condemned. The church has ever found its most powerful enemy in reason, hence the exercise of reason has ever been a crime in her eyes.

During the Christian ages the different code of morals for man and woman has created infinite wrong. Open and notorious vice among both churchmen and laymen passed unreproved, but an heiress forfeited her possessions by unchastity, and wily plans were laid to thus gain possession of her property, the betrayer receiving payment from the guardian, whose tool he was, for his perfidy.[61] To this moral code we trace the present legal condition of girls, daughters having no status in the courts in case of betrayal. The father alone, as master and owner, can sue for loss of her services, while the injury to herself is passed by, even upon so momentous a question as the paternity of a child born out of wedlock.

Many of the most flagrant wrongs perpetrated against woman can be traced to a denial of a right of ownership, beginning with the denial of her right to herself. Even the Salic law which in France was used to bar the succession of woman to the throne, was not specifically or primarily in favor of males; it was a property law growing out of the patriarchal idea of property in woman. Under Christian form of marriage, woman was transferred to another family whose name she took. She not only became the property of her husband but all real or personal estate which she possessed, also became his. Thus her property went to the enrichment of another family. Her home was no longer with her own people, but where her husband chose to make it. Salic law derived its name from Sala, a house. Salic land, said Montesquieu, was the land belonging to the house.[62] At time of its adoption the line of descent was male. Under it during the middle ages when a daughter married, she received merely a chaplet of roses. Thenceforth, her interests were elsewhere, and her children became part of another family; she was entirely lost to the family of her birth. As she was no longer a part of it she did not receive inheritance. "It was not a subject of affection but gens."

Guizot with a fine sense of irony, termed Salic law essentially a penal code. Its application to woman was incontestibly penal. In France its action has been most pronounced. Robertson speaks of the Salic law as the most venerable monument of French jurisprudence, although the real period of its birth has never yet been fully acknowledged. While during the struggle of Phillippa de Valours, and Edward III for the crown of France, this law was invoked to prevent the succession of Phillippa, yet we know that in Gaul during the time of Cæser, mothers had sole authority over their children, even boys remaining in entire charge of the mother until old enough for instruction in arms. Wives also possessed property rights, upon marriage the husband adding the same amount of property he had received with his wife. This was kept as a separate fund, the survivor taking the whole. Hallum designated the contest between Phillippa and Edward as in every way remarkable, but especially on account of its result in the exclusion of woman from the succession,[63] then first suggested. It was the Latin races rather than the Scandinavian or Teutonic that first essentially degraded woman. The Riparian Franks, preeminent as lovers of liberty, were the first who broke away from the rule of this law. Both the Scandinavians and Teutons possessed prophetic women or priestesses to whom the highest deference was shown. The Teutonic races were early noted for the high respect in which they held women, a respect closely bordering upon veneration. The greatest deference was shown to their opinions even upon war, the chief business of men's lives. Victoria received the title of "Mother of Camps" and was an especially venerated person. Veleda by superior genius directed the counsels of the nation and for nine years prevented the progress of the imperial armies of Rome. The most momentous questions of state and of religion were submitted to woman's divine judgment.

The relation between the wrongs of woman and her non-ownership of property, and of herself, are very complicated. The custom of Marquette originated from the theory of property in woman; the Suzerain or lord possessing not only a certain property right in his male vassals, but a double right to the woman who as a bride became the property of his vassal. Thus Marquette was the outgrowth of the husband's property right in his wife, and a secondary result of man's assumed right of property in woman. In France, where the Salic law possessed greatest strength we find the custom of marquette most prevalent. Next to marquette, the law known as "Mund" or "Mundium" offered the greatest indignity to woman, and in some respects may be called more vile. While the baseness of marquette took its victims from a class beneath the lord in social standing, Mundium entered the family, the father selling his daughter to such wooer as he chose, or from whom he received the greatest payment, entirely regardless of the wishes of the daughter herself. The Salic law seemed to have been founded on the principle of the Mund, as under it a sum was paid by the husband to the family of the bride in consideration of the transference of the authority they possessed over her, to the husband, and this payment was known as "Mundium" and the bride as a "Mund" bought woman. In Denmark, to which country the custom of mundium extended, her appellation was "mundi-keypt-krom," signifying a mund bought woman. At that period descent was reckoned from the father, to whom alone the children were held to be related, and his relinquishment of authority by sale of his daughter, transferred her relationship from her father to her husband, and she thus became a component part of another family. She no longer belonged to the family of her birth, but to that of her purchaser. The Franks were the first to break Salle customs and to permit a father to settle an estate upon his daughter and her children.[64] Under the law of Gavelkind as it existed in Great Britain, daughters never inherited, although the rights of even an illegitimate son were recognized as equal to those of legitimate sons. By the laws of gavelkind, property could not descend to women, but the County of Kent possessed more freedom than in any other part of England. There was a custom of privilege annexed to all lands of this kind in Kent, among them, that the wife should be endowed with a moiety; gavelkind land was devisable by will. Ordinarily in gavelkind, property was kept in male hands, descending from father to son. The very name gavelkind is said to bear this signification, the word *kynd* in dutch signifying a male child, thus *gife eal cyn*, means give all to the son. Its modern signification is the custom of partition of property among males alone, or the greatest share to the oldest son.

Lord Coke looked upon the practice of gavelkind among the Irish as a mark of their descent from the ancient Britons. At this period wives were not entitled to dower, thus in respect to property, all women of the family were equally disinherited. But it was the opinion of Lord Holt that by the Common Law, both before and after the conquest, all the children, both male and female, inherited both the real and the personal estate, and in like proportion. But in the reign of Henry I daughters, in case there were sons, began to be excluded from the real estate. These laws, so essentially Salic, it can readily be seen, originated in the mundium. Passing as a mund woman into another family, the succession of property to her under this slave[65] condition was contrary to sound domestic policy. To bestow property upon a daughter was to enrich another family at the expense of the one from whom the slave-wife was purchased, and her disinheritance was but a logical result of her legal condition. If we admit the premises we must admit the wisdom of her exclusion from succession.

It is curious to note the difference in woman's position which possession of property has ever made. This difference, especially noticeable during Feudalism in case of an heiress with fiefs, is no less so at the present day. It is a mark of an unripe civilization that the rights of property have ever been regarded before those of person. Walker[66] over sixty years since, recognized the power of property in ameliorating woman's condition, then declaring that the first step toward an acknowledgment of her equality, must be a recognition of her rights of property; his broad knowledge of ancient law having taught him the close connection of property rights and personal rights. During many ages battle was done for possessions and the protection of what a man owned. Even the war of the American Revolution was begun for property rights rather than for those of person. The Stamp Act and the tax on tea roused the Colonies to resistance. A woman first spoke the words "inherent rights," and by the time nationality was proclaimed the colonists had learned far enough to say that "governments derive their just powers from the consent of the governed." Consent is an important consideration in all questions affecting humanity and is one in which woman is most deeply concerned. At close of the civil war Frederick Douglass advised colored men to get property. He had not failed to learn the connection between property and personal rights. Since Mississippi, in 1839,[67] Pennsylvania and New York in 1848, and Rhode Island about the same period secured property rights to married women, there has been a great and rapidly increasing change in woman's position, and as she constantly enters new industries, earning and controlling money, we find her as constantly more free and respected. When the English "Married Women's Property Bill," based upon that of New York, became a law a few years since, the *London Times*, with the perspicuity of our great thinker, Walker, said:

> It probably portends indirect social effects much greater than the disposition of property, and it may in the end pulverize some ideas which have been at the basis of English life. Measures which affect the family economy are apt to be "epoch making"; and probably when the most talked of bills of the session are clean forgotten this obscure measure may be bearing fruit.

The exception of married women in the demand for political rights by the women of England owes its origin to the old monkish theory that marriage is debasement, and celibate life in either man or woman a much higher condition. After the passage of the Emancipation Proclamation during the civil war, John Stuart Mill declared that married women were the only class of slaves remaining on earth. As long as a condition of religious or political subjection continues for her, a belief in the sanctity of womanhood cannot exist and crimes against her will be lightly punished. The most debased men of England and the United States, if arrested for cruelty to wives, agree in the indignant questioning protest: "Is she not my own that I should punish her as I please?"

Such has been the power of the priesthood over the consciences and lives of men, that we find whatever is bad in the laws either directly or indirectly traceable to their influence.[68] Our Anglo Saxon forefathers were early amenable to religious authority and for a period of many hundred years clerical influence was exceedingly powerful over them.[69] The church is responsible for the severity with which the simplest infraction of law was visited upon the most humble and helpless classes, and the greater penalty awarded to, those least capable of resistance. It was for the free man of low estate, for the slave, and for woman that the greatest atrocities were reserved. If a free woman stole she was to be thrown down a precipice or drowned, which Pike regards as the origin of dragging witches through a pond. If the thief was a slave and stole from any but her own master, she was condemned to be burnt alive, and her fellow slaves were compelled to assist at the incineration.[70] None dared to speak a good word for women in opposition to church teachings. All her instincts were held as evil. As the law and the father robbed the daughter, so the law and the church alike robbed the family. By ancient English law, as before noted, every person who made a will was bound to remember his lord with the best thing he possessed, and afterwards the church with the next best thing, but as the church gained power it took supreme place in the testament.[71] The peasant was looked upon as but slightly above the cattle he cared for. A certain degree of sameness in material and intellectual conditions everywhere existed. The masses over christendom were alike under bondage of thought and modes of action; social life showed no marked change for many hundred years. Freedom was an unknown word, or if by chance spoken, found itself under the ban of the church and the state. Justice was unthought of; the only question being, "has the church ordered it?" A complete system of espionage existed under both church and state. As late as the time of Alfred, in England, every nine men were under charge of a tenth. No man could work outside of his father's employment to which he was bound; at nine o'clock curfew bell, all fires and lights were extinguished. A mechanic could not find work outside of his own village; monastaries and castles contained all there was of power and comfort. As late as the reformation we find the condition of English society lax and immoral. Henry the VIII was a fair type of the nation; the court, the camp, the church were all in line moulding the sentiment of community. Although Henry had declared the church to be an entire and perfect body within itself, possessing authority to regulate and decide all things without dependence upon any foreign power—meaning the pope—he did not fail to generally define the supremacy of the church as united with and dependent upon the temporal government of the realm; the king, instead of the pope, becoming its spiritual head. Many new and restrictive canons were promulgated. Under Henry the prohibitory laws regarding nearness of relationship in marriage exceeded those of the Catholic Church. It is but a few decades since these prohibitions commencing with "a man shall not marry his grandmother";"a woman shall not marry her grandfather"; and extending down to remote cousinship, were to be found printed upon the fly leaves of every New Testament.[72]

For a long period after the reformation, English women were not permitted to read the Bible, a statute of the Eighth Henry prohibiting "women and others of low degree" from its use.[73] Apparently for the purpose of preventing conversation among women regarding the tyranny under which they were kept, a law was passed forbiding the residence of more than one woman in a cottage, and this after the Protestant religion had been confirmed as that of the realm. As late as Elizabeth, 31–32, it was held a "heinous offence" for a cottager to give a home to his own widowed mother or homeless sister. The especial criminality of thus "harboring" one's female relatives lay in the fact of their being "masterless." As late as the sixteenth century the law still entered houses, and magistrates bound out to servile labor all women between eleven and forty years of age.[74] The degradation of women under the reformation was still more gross than under catholicism. The worship of the Virgin Mary, and the canonization of many women as saints in the Romish Calendar, threw a certain halo about womankind that is impossible to discover in the Protestant Church, or since the reformation.

The church of whatever name taught woman's innate depravity was so great that forcible restraint alone prevented her from plunging into vice. While Christian women outside the Levant were not confined in a harem under watch and ward, yet various methods of restraint have been used in christian lands within the past few centuries. Among the most noted of these, the "Chastity Belt," three are yet known to be in existence. One is preserved in the museum at Cluny, France, another is in keeping of the Castle of Rosenburg, Copenhagen, the third was exhibited in the United States, 1884, by Dr. Heidmann's traveling museum. According to tradition the one preserved at Cluny was in use during the sixteenth century, in reign of Francis I, who ascended the throne January 1, 1515; the remaining two in Denmark under Christian IV in the seventeenth century. At this period Denmark was greatly agitated by a religious war, which, however, did not include woman's freedom in its demands. These belts are hideous proofs of the low estimate in which woman's moral character was held, and equally striking evidence of man's freedom and immorality.

The disrespect shown by the clergy towards marriage as compared with the celibate condition has influenced thought in many singular directions. England's married women under the combined influence of church and state, deprecate the claim of suffrage for themselves, although asking it for single women and widows.[75]

The bill referred to in the Memorial, 49 Vic, extended Parliamentary franchise to single women alone.

> Second Sec. For all purposes of and incidental to the voting for members to serve in Parliament, women shall have the same rights as men, and all enactments relating to, or concerned in such election shall be construed accordingly. Provided that nothing in this Act contained shall enable women under coverture to be registered or to vote at such elections.

The word "coverture" expresses a married woman's subordinate condition, both civilly and religiously.[76] It means, under the power of the husband; controlled by the husband; possessing neither personal nor individual rights; a being not allowed to use her own judgment unless such judgment is ratified by the husband. Under coverture, the wife can make no contract without the husband's consent, the law holding her incompetent. A woman under coverture is an irresponsible being except in case of crime. When married women refuse to seek the same freedom for themselves they ask for single women, they practically endorse the judgment of church and state in favor of celibacy. When married women thus ignore their equality with single women, they practically condemn that relation, practically affirm the superior purity of a celibate condition.[77] The low estimate of women in England as late as the seventeenth and eighteenth centuries is shown in its literature, especially that emanating from its great universities. The betrayal of women formed the basis of story and song; not content with portraying their own vices, these men did not hesitate to put a plea against chastity in the mouths of mere children. Of such character is "A Ballad" emanating from this source, but professing to have been "composed by Miss Nelly Pentwenzle, a young lady of fifteen," to be sung to the tune of "Scraps of Pudding."

A periodical entitled *The Old Woman's Magazine* printed in London, without date, but from internal evidence shown to belong to the latter part of the eighteenth century, forcibly protests against the destruction of innocence, which was the chief amusement of the men of this period. It asks:

> Why should it be less a crime to deceive an inexperienced girl whose youth renders it impossible that she should know the world, than it would be to lead a blind man to the brink of a precipice?

Thus the laws and customs of family and social life, the literature of different periods, the habits of thought, the entire civilization of christian centuries, has tended to the debasement of woman and the consequent destruction of moral life. The world stands where it does today upon all these great questions, biased by a nonrecognition through the ages of the sanctity of womanhood, and a disbelief in her rights of person within the marriage relation, or without; taught, as this lesson has been, by the church, and emphasized by the laws of the state.

There have ever been many severities connected with dower in England. By old law if a widow married within a year from the death of her husband she forfeited her dower.[78] This law accounts for the superstitious sentiment as to ill-luck following the woman who remarries within a year and a day. Like the freedom of the Roman "Usus" kept up by a three days' absence in each year, this extra day of the widow's mourning seems to have been added as security for the dower; while under the most ancient law of christian Europe, the widow lost her dower if she married again, the Turks recognizing the greater freedom of a widow, pay her who remarries, a sum for parting with her liberty.

The general rule of dower[79] held that when arranged at time of marriage, although the husband then possessed but a small portion of freehold and afterwards made great acquisitions, if no mention of new purchases was made at time of such arrangement, the widow could not claim more than the third part of the land possessed by the husband at time of marriage. In like manner if a husband had no land and endowed his wife with chattels, money, or other things, afterwards making great acquisitions in land, she could not claim dower in such acquisition. Neither could a woman dispose of her dower during her husband's life. This was quite unlike the freedom enjoyed by a wife in ancient Wales where the dower became absolutely her own, to dispose of as she pleased. Under English law the husband during the lifetime of his wife could give or sell or alien her dower in any way that it pleased him to do, and the wife in this, as in all other things, was obliged to conform to the husband's will. The wife's dower right in personal property can be aliened by the husband in the United States. During the wife's lifetime he may give, sell, or in any way dispose of the whole of his personal property absolutely, and the wife has no redress; she is not held as having any right, title or interest in it as long as her husband lives.[80] The husband can also alien his real estate, subject only to his wife's dower right in case she survive him; should she decease before him she has no power over it. The law in England as laid down by Glanville was that in case the wife withheld her consent to the sale of property she might claim her dower after her husband's death, but this could only have had reference to real property, and is the same in the United States. If the wife withholds her consent to the sale of real estate, it still can be sold away from her and she thus be deprived of a home. It is merely subject to her dower right in the value of the property at time of sale, and in case she survives her husband; should she die first, she has no redress. Sales of this character are constantly made, at a small discount, upon chance of the wife's nonsurvival. As dower right in real estate does not invest the wife with its ownership in fee, but merely the use of one-third during her natural life, it will readily be seen how very small is the wife's protection in dower-right even in this last half of the nineteenth century. Bracton gives two reasons why the English husband could sell the dower assigned to the wife without her consent:

> *First*, Because a wife has no freehold in a dower previous to its being assigned to her. *Second*, because she cannot gainsay her husband.

As late as the last quarter of the present century, the learned Professor of Jurisprudence of Cambridge University, attempted to prove that it was no reproach against woman's intellect that she was prohibited from making a contract during marriage; although failing in this attempt, he clearly succeeded in proving woman's condition of pecuniary and personal slavery in the marriage relation. He said:

> It is not an imputation on the wife's experience or strength of mind, but is solely grounded on her not being assumed by common law to have sufficient command of her purse or of her future actions where with to procure materials for making a contract. The legal presumption then is, that she did not

intend to make one, and therefore the allegation that she did make a contract would imply on the face of it a fraud.[81]

The legal presumption that the wife has neither sufficient command of her purse or of her future actions to guarantee an intent of making a contract needs no further assertion to prove her enslavement. The person neither possessing control of property or of their own actions is a slave, regardless of or under what verbiage of law or custom that condition is represented. Attempts are constantly made both in the United States and England to take from woman the dower right now accruing to them. During 1883, an act was passed taking from English wives all dower right, giving the husband power to bar the wife in all cases; and scarcely a legislature convenes in the United States that has not a similar bill introduced before it. As dower rights increase the complication of land transfer, just as soon as the law which gave the husband the power to bar this right became operative in England, conveyancers began to insert a debaring clause in every deed of conveyance, thus systematically despoiling the wife even when the husband might not otherwise have been so disposed.

As "masterless women," widows in England have received similar contemptuous treatment as accorded single women, to whom that country long showed such barbarity. It is curiously noted by Alexander[82] that Moses placed widows in the same rank as harlots and profane women.[83] The law of tenancy by courtesy, which gives a husband rights in the separate property of a wife, is very unjust when compared with the dower rights of a wife. In such case, provided she has borne a living child, even should such child breathe but once, the husband in case of the death of his wife, holds the entire real estate during his life, as "tenant by courtesy." He also takes the whole of her personal property absolutely, to dispose of as he chooses. In a few of the United States, the wife can defeat this by will, but in the large majority of christian lands, the full rights "of tenancy by the courtesy," still prevail. Where right of dower still prevails, the wife, if there are children, takes but one-third of the personal property absolutely, one-half if there are no children, the rest passing to collateral heirs, who may be the husband's most distant relatives. In case no such relative can be found, the balance escheats to the state, although in the State of New York the widow, under such circumstances, receives two thousand dollars over one-half. Of the real property she has the use of but one-third, in contradistinction to the use of the whole of her real property, which goes to the husband by "tenancy of courtesy." In tenancy by courtesy the children are robbed of the mother's real estate during the life of the father, and of her personal property, forever. In enacting property laws, man, under tenancy by courtesy robs his own children. The law of inheritance in Spain, that country distinguished among European nations as "Most Christian land," compels a man to leave four-fifths of his property to his children, but does not make it obligatory upon him to endow his wife with the remaining fifth. Neither has the wife a dower right in property owned by her husband at time of the marriage. The suit of a Spanish widow for dower right, in an estate of several millions left by her deceased husband, was fully reported by the New York daily papers within the past few years. Suddenly reduced from affluence as the wife of this man, to the most abject poverty as his widow, this wife and mother brought suit against the estate and her children, who receiving all the property by the husband's will, left her absolutely beggared.

In ancient Ireland, the condition of woman was far superior to that of the christian women of England or Scotland. Two forms of marriage existed. Under that of "Equal Dignity," the rights of the contracting parties were the same, and took place when the man and woman possessed the same amount of land, cattle, or household goods. No force or sale accompanied it, the woman giving free consent equally with the man. This marriage was looked upon as a contract between equals. The property of the wife did not revert to the husband. She retained its control, loaning it and receiving interest entirely free from the interference of her husband.[84] Ancient Irish law also secured to the mother equal authority with the father over the children of the marriage. There is no trace of that arbitrary control over both wife and children with which Christianity endowed the father.[85] The daughter was held to be more closely related to the father; a son to the mother, this belief contributing an equality of right between the sexes. These laws were authoritative over the whole of Ireland until the invasion of the Danes, in the eighth century (A.D. 792).

It is remarkable what effect the ownership of property by woman has ever had in ameliorating her legal condition. Even in ancient Ireland the wife without possessions became the slave of her husband. Although the son was held as more nearly related to his mother, this ancient code provided that in case his parents were poor and he had not wealth enough to support both father and mother, he was to leave the latter to die in the ditch, but was to carry his father back to his own home.[86] Tradition ascribes this code to St. Patrick in the fifth century. Under modern Christian law, the legal obligation of a son to support his father is greater than it is to support his mother, quite in opposition to the old Scandinavian (pagan) law, which provided for the support of the mother, if but one parent could be cared for. Not the least among the wrongs inflicted upon Ireland by English usurpation has been the destruction of the wife's rights of property. The right of the Irish wife to deal with her own property as she chose, irrespective of her husband's consent, was expressly declared illegal by English judges at the beginning of the seventeenth century.

There are traces of separate property rights for woman early among Aryan peoples. By the old laws of Wales, a wife became legal owner of part of her husband's effects immediately upon marrying him, and had the sole disposal of this portion even during her husband's life. Debt owed by a husband to a wife was as binding on him and his heirs and executors as a debt to any other person. After the English laws were introduced into Wales, innumerable disputes arose upon this ground, the Welsh woman being persistent in her determination to cling to her old rights, and for nearly two hundred years her will upon this subject was stronger than the will of English legislators, as proven by legal records.[87] In other respects the ancient law of Wales favored woman. A husband's fetid breath was held as good cause for divorce on part of the wife, who in such case took with her the whole of her property. While still living with her husband, the Welsh wife possessed the right to three kinds of property, cowyll, gowyn, and sarand, known as her three peculiars.[88] Old Welsh law was unique in that it forbade both satisfaction and vengeance for the same wrong. Even if detecting his wife in adultery, for which he should chastise her, the husband was forbidden any satisfaction besides that. In case of an illegitimate birth the law provided that the man should wholly maintain the child,[89] a species of justice not found under Christianity. The laws of "Howell the Good," enacted at a later date under the supervision of the church[90] favored the man at the woman's expense. Under these laws if a husband and wife separated, the father took two-thirds of the children, the oldest and the youngest falling to his share, while the middle one fell to the mother. A woman was not admitted as surety, or as a witness in matters concerning a man.[91] In the division of property the daughters received only one-half the amount given to the sons.

Under the christian laws of England, by which the property of a married woman passed entirely into the control of her husband, the abduction of heiresses in that country was very common for many hundred years, no punishment following such a theft, although the most compulsory measures were used, even to forcibly bending the bride's head in affirmative response during the marriage ceremony. She was a woman; the law furnished her no redress. It regarded her as the legal wife of her abductor, to whom she thereafter under this christian law, owed service and obedience. The sole right to her person, her property, her children then becoming legally invested in the robber husband. As noted in the opening chapter, the abduction of a woman, or even an immodest proposal to her, was punished in older un-christianized Scandinavia, by greater or lesser outlawry; rape being a capital crime, placing the culprit's life in the hands of any man. He was outside the pale of law.

France under frequent changing names and forms of government, and with a broader general recognition each year of human rights, is yet very closely allied to the barbarism of the middle ages in its treatment of woman, and its conception of her natural rights. This was shown even during the revolution of 1787, of which Madame Roland and Charlotte Corday were such central heroic figures. Although this revolution established an equal succession between sons and daughters, yet it did not tolerate the proposition of Sieyes and Condorcet that woman should be endowed with the suffrage. One hundred years later, in 1887, a bill was introduced during the legislative session, to secure to woman the same political rights accorded man. This bill was lost; *Le Gaulois*, commenting upon it, declared that in whatever manner the question was discussed, it appeared grotesque and ridiculous. In the Legislative Assembly of 1851, M. Chapot proposed the prohibition of the right of petition to women upon all subjects of a political nature. During the same session, Athenase Coquerel, the most distinguished member of a Protestant family of clergymen, presented a bill to the Chambers excluding women from political clubs. Woman's testimony is not accepted in regard to civil acts. They cannot attest to a birth or a death, nor is their testimony admitted in the identification of persons. Neither can they become members of the family council, nor are they accepted as guardians of their own children. It is only since 1886 that their condition has been in any way ameliorated. The remarriage of widows is forbidden under ten months after the husband's death, and until within the last decade, divorces were of great rarity. The oppressed condition of woman in the marriage relation was notably shown by the vast number of applications for release from the hated bond upon the passage of the new law; a number so great—eleven thousand—that two years scarcely sufficed to reach them all. No stronger argument against the evils of an indissoluble marriage is required, and as the greater number of applicants were women, it is further evidence of woman's degradation under christian marriage laws.

According to the famous Code Napoleon, accepted by France as her modern system of jurisprudence and declared (by man) to be nearly perfect in its provisions, every child born outside of wedlock is deemed to be fatherless unless such father of his own free will formally acknowledges his offspring. While fifty percent of all children born in Paris are illegitimate, statistics prove that such acknowledgment takes place but once in fifty births. Thus forty-nine percent of Parisian children under the Code Napoleon, theoretically come into the world without fathers—they are born fatherless. A still more heinous provision of this Code, forbids all research into paternity.[92] The father of an illegitimate child—rendered illegitimate by church canons—is held as both morally and legally irresponsible for his fatherhood. Under this Code, upon the mother falls all the contumely associated with such birth, together with the care and expense of rearing the child. We cannot be surprised at the prevalence of infanticide, a crime resulting from such unjust legislation, and for which the church is directly responsible. In the whole history of French jurisprudence, not a single case can be found where the father of an illegitimate child has been compelled to acknowledge his offspring.[93] Under French law, woman is a perpetual minor under the guardianship of her own, or that of her husband's family. Only in case of the birth of an illegitimate child is she treated as a responsible being, and then only that discomfort and punishment may fall upon her. The same legal degradation of the unmarried mother, the same protection accorded the unmarried father, the same enticement of the law for man to assume a fatherhood freeing him from accountability, the same covert contempt of womanhood and of motherhood, also exists in Italy, its penal code forbidding all research into paternity. And this is not the legislation of the middle ages but of the nineteenth century.

But French disregard for the rights of woman, as already shown, far preceded the Code Napoleon; that system but legally emphasized the low estimate of the feminine we have traced through the Salic, Feudal, and Witchcraft periods. Louis VII, referring to the number of girls born in his dominions, requested his subjects to pray unto God that he should accord them children of the better sex. Upon the birth of his first child, Margaret, who afterwards married Henry Courtmantel of England, his anger was so great that he would not look at her; he even refused to see his wife. He afterwards accorded an annual pension of three livres to the woman who first announced to him the birth of a son. Although five hundred years have passed since the graphic portrayal of woman's condition, in the ballad of the Baron of Jauioz, we find the Breton farmer whose wife has given birth to a daughter, still saying, "My wife has had a miscarriage." Question an ordinary French peasant in regard to his family and if the father of girls alone, he will reply, "I have no children, sir, I have only daughters."[94]

During the feudal period parents gave themselves up to merrymaking and rejoicing upon the marriage of the last of their daughters.[95] Even yet, in some countries, the birth of a boy is announced by a servant wearing a white apron and carrying two bouquets in her hand; if a girl she carries but one; in some countries the father of a boy annually received the gift of two loads of wood from the state; but a single one if the child was a girl. Even in the United States we yet see this contempt of the feminine variously manifested, although the kindness and affection of girls to their parents is usually more notable than that of boys.[96] Family regard is usually manifested in the descending, rather than the ascending line, yet Herbert Spencer declares that full civilization is dependant upon the respect and affection shown to parents. France is not the only christian land that invalidates a woman's testimony, receiving the assertion of the woman with less authority than the denial of the man. In Scotland in case of an illegitimate birth, the accused man is allowed to clear himself upon oath, in opposition to that of the woman. Under Scottish law the child born outside of marriage was formerly compelled to do penance in church for the sins of his parents. Such has been the justice of christianity to women and children during the ages. These methods of christianity were in great contrast to those of heathendom. The early Anglo-Saxon (pagan) laws contained provisions for the punishment of assaults upon women. Crimes against her were punished by greater or less outlawry according to the attendant circumstances. Old Scandinavia possessed many laws for the protection of woman. It has sometimes been asserted that these laws were a dead letter, so many instances of loose connections are recorded in the Iceland Sagas. It is, however, a question of fact that these illegal relations, according to the same Sagas were much more frequent after the introduction of christianity than before.[97] Roman law presumed that no woman went astray without the seduction and arts of the other sex, upon whom alone the punishment fell. Under old Saxon, Gothic and Scandinavian law, rape was punished by death. Under the Conqueror, its punishment was castration and loss of the eyes, which continued English law until after Bracton wrote in time of Henry III. A lighter punishment then superceded it, but the effects of this leniency was so evil, the old penalty was restored. While forbidding woman control of her own property, common law, under one of those anomalous renderings which mark the constant injustice of Church and State towards woman, held twelve years as the age of female discretion or consent, rape after that age not being regarded as criminal.

Germany, with sudden strides has coalesced from a number of independent principalities through the management of him of the iron hand, into a magnificent empire, based upon the destruction of human life. In this empire, where war underlies all, we find woman much more deeply degraded than during the old pagan days, when as chieftain and prophetess, her voice was heeded even upon the battlefield. Now, while men are preparing to kill other men, the agriculture of the country and the lowest forms of mechanical labor fall into her hands. But it is not as responsible owner we thus find her; she cultivates the fields as a drudge, upon whom falls all the most severe portion of work. Equally in Germany as in other christian lands is the wife looked upon as the servant of the husband, to whom she bears children that are his alone, and to whom greater deference is paid by the mother, when a large number of little ones call him father.[98] It has been the custom to reward a husband in proportion to the number of children borne him by his wife, and it is but a year since a Parisian journalist suggested that for each additional child borne by his wife, the husband should be allowed half a vote. In

Germany as under the common law of England, the wife is subject to chastisement by her husband, its severity being left to his discretion. But the height of barbaric absurdity and wickedness is found in that provision of the Prussian common law which decrees that a husband can determine the length of time his wife must nurse her child. As might be expected, at his death the wife is not regarded capable of caring for the children, and must accept a guardian for them; the law going so far as to declare her underage, similarly to that French law which makes woman a perpetual minor. It matters not if the family property all came through the wife, or was accumulated by her labor, she is still held as not of sufficient judgment for its control. In Prussia, woman is still forbidden to take part in political or other public meetings.[99]

Morganatic or left-hand marriage still continues the custom in Germany. Under its provisions the wife does not take the husband's rank, nor do the children inherit the father's property, as they are not regarded as of full legitimacy. This form of marriage is recognized by the civil law of Germany, and is sustained by the church. The custom, at first confined to princes, gradually extended to the higher aristocracy, and as the moral perceptions of a nation bends itself to unison with civil law, the inferior gentry began to contract marriages of this kind. Under a morganatic union woman is still more debased than in the ordinary marriage relation. Aside from the ceremony, the wife is scarcely other than a concubine. The children of the morganatic marriage do not bear the father's name, nor inherit from him, under the law of the state. Neither they nor the wife have more lasting claim upon him in these respects than had the concubines known as "the Honored Ones" upon the priestly destroyers of the thirteenth, fourteenth and fifteenth centuries.

Several notable instances of morganatic marriages have occurred within the present century. It is but a few years since the Grand Duke, Louis IV of Hesse Darmstadt, son-in-law of Queen Victoria, made a morganatic marriage with Madame de Kalamine, whose lover he was long known to have been, and with whom he had previously lived outside of his relation, she having borne him several children. From the high position of the morganatic husband, and because of the previous relationship of the parties, this marriage became the talk of all Europe, and to some extent of the United States. Queen Victoria herself did not escape criticism, notwithstanding the prudery for which she is famed, because of her entertaining the Grand Duke at Windsor soon after this marriage unaccompanied by his wife,[100] for the purpose, it was intimated, of placing him under the influence of Princess Beatrice. The very fact of such suggestion, whether true or not, as well as the fact that Queen Victoria universally conceded a prude in reference to infractions of the moral law by those of her own sex, received the Grand Duke at her especial home of Windsor soon after his morganatic marriage, is a vivid commentary upon the two codes of morals extant in christendom and their influence even upon woman herself. Morganatic marriage degrades the wife of the right hand ceremony equally with her of the left hand, as it is a recognition by the law of a christian country today of man's right to become a bigamist, provided he but gives his left hand instead of his right, to the bride during the marriage ceremony. It is a system of legalized concubinage under protestantism, which throws the shield of protection around man in illicit relations, and like all other forms of woman's degradation, it reaches back for authority to that religious teaching which proclaims woman to have been created inferior and subordinate to man. Because of woman's former superior position there, no country but Germany can as fully show the degradation of woman under Christianity. Not from pagan Greece can more vivid illustration of her moral degradation be shown, while pagan Rome shines clear and bright beside the Germanic races of today. While even left-handed marriages among the higher classes are encouraged and protected, yet among the lower orders in Germany the ordinary marriage is cumbered with so many restrictions as to have become almost an impossibility, and no disgrace or loss of character falls upon the girl of this class who becomes a mother outside of legal prevision, but such motherhood upon the contrary is looked upon as the means of a higher position and greater wages as nurse. As *amme* in a rich or noble family she becomes a person of arrogance, part of the pomp and show of the house.[101]

Despite these wrongs of the ages towards woman, of late so vividly presented, we still find both Church and State opposing a free discussion of the question. Within the last decade two northern European countries have strangely exhibited such hostility, the opposition coming upon ground of woman's surpassing sinfulness.[102]

But the most notable opposition has been against the works of two eminent literary men. *Ghosts*[103] by Ibsen, the dramatic poet of Norway, attacking the irresponsible position of the wife under present marriage law, brought about the social ostracism of its author.[104] Sweden's supremely great thinker of the present century, August Strindberg, recently published a work entitled *Giftas* (to marry), which incidentally treated of the influence of religion upon this relation.[105] The State authorities at once ordered its confiscation.[106] Instead of a Papal *Librorum Prohibitorum*, it fell under the censure and prohibition of a Protestant State. But no more ready method for increasing its circulation could have been devised; so rapidly was the first edition of four thousand sold that only four hundred fell into the grasp of the censorious government. In order to escape the further penalty of imprisonment that had been pronounced against him, the author was compelled to temporarily leave the country. But his work was not without effect upon the minds of his countrymen, and upon his return a few months later, a great demonstration in his honor took place. Strindberg defined the rights of woman as those which came to her by nature but of which, through a perverted social order she had been deprived. He declared that woman's desire for deliverance was the same as man's restless desire for deliverance. Let us, said he, therefore emancipate man from his prejudice and then woman will certainly be freed. To that end it is necessary to work together as friends not as enemies.

That a work of this moderate character, should fall under the ban of a protestant government, in the last half of the nineteenth century, should be confiscated and its author banished, is a striking

proof of the degraded condition of woman in the marriage relation and of the power still exerted for the continuance of this
subjection. Opposition to discussion of this question in Sweden
is more strange in view of the excess of women in the population, as they outnumber the men some 40,000; while of single
women over fifteen, there are 259,000. Despite the fact of this
excess, impossible to provide for by marriage even were that condition one of equity and equality, all effort towards opening occupations to them, or the avenues of education, still meets with
resistance from the church. The only opponent of Mr. Berner's
Bill, 1882, for permitting women to take the first two degrees in
the University, those of Arts and Philosophy, was from a clergyman. The bill passed the Odelstling, one of the two Chambers
of the Strothing, with only his dissentent voice.[107] It received the
unanimous vote of the other house, the Sagthing, April 21,
becoming a law June 15 of that year.

Russia, which we are accustomed to regard as less than a half-
civilized country, gives evidence of an early civilization which in
the field of morals reached a high place. Samokversof, a Russian
author, has made a rich collection relating to prehistoric times,
proving that as early as the first centuries of this era, the Slavo-
nians lived in large societies, possessed fortified towns with treasures of gold and silver, silk, embroidered tissues, iron weapons,
ornaments of gold, silver, bronze and bone; while sickles, and the
grasses of wheat, oats, and barley, found in the graves of South
Russia, show this people even to have been devoted to agriculture. The early history of Russia proves that women then held
influential positions in the family, in the church, in the state; as was
the case under the ancient common law of England, so woman
among the ancient Slavs possessed the right of inheritance and
the power of dividing such inheritance with her brothers. In the
State we find woman's wisdom at early date still continuing to
shape the policy of the Russian empire; to the wise statesmanship
of the Czarina Olga is the unchanging plan of that country for
the ultimate possession of Constantinople due. Visiting the Patri-
arch of the East, during the tenth century, she at once perceived

the vast importance of Constantinople to the power desiring universal dominion; the possession of that city giving control of the Dardanelles, of Asia Minor, and Europe itself. Thenceforth she sought its annexation or seizure and her policy became that of the Russian nation, which for more than eight hundred years has made the ultimate possession of Constantinople the great object of its ambition. Nor has Olga's statesmanship less influenced the entire European continent, the allied powers constantly struggling to defeat Russia's aggressive plan, through maintenance of the "sick man" upon his throne.

From the advent of christianity, forced upon the Slav peoples a thousand years since by Vladimir, their baptism taking place by tens of thousands as driven into the rivers and streams mid-deep, priests upon the banks recited the baptism formula, a change was noticeable. As soon as the thorough establishment of the Byzantine church in Russia, which took no inconsiderable period, it being brought about by force rather than free will, its priests, like those of the Western Church, directed their principal efforts towards control of the marriage relation, and, through that, of the family. Nor are we to regard this as strange inasmuch as every form of christianity regards woman as an inferior being, the creator of original sin, rendering the sacrifice of a God necessary in order to reestablish the equilibrium overthrown by her.[108] Edmond Noble, in tracing the cause of the present social upheaval in that empire, says:[109]

> Scarcely had the priests of the Greek Church begun their teaching of the new faith when change began to unsettle the position of woman and burden her relationship to the family with a sense of inferiority . . . her status falling with the natural extension of the ecclesiastical policy. The Russian woman at last became the slave of her Christian husband; as much his chattel as if she had been purchased at market or captured in war.

An examination of history proves that in Christian Russia as in Christian England the husband could release himself from the marriage bond by killing his wife, over whom, under christian law he had power of life and death. Her children, as today in Christian England and America, are not under her control; she is to bear children but not to educate them, for, as under Catholic and Protestant Christianity, women are looked upon as a lower order of beings, of an unclean nature. The assertion of Agathes, the Sophist that he detected the smell of her whose hands had milked the cow, is more than paralleled under Greek Christianity, woman not even being allowed to kill a fowl under assertion that should she so do, the meat would become poisonous. Wife beating enjoined as a religious duty, became so common, says Noble, that love was measured by it, "The more whippings the more love." "The Domstrol," a household guide, compiled by a dignitary of the Greek Church in time of Ivan the Terrible, counseled use of the rod to keep wives, children, and servants in subjection. By it, husbands were given almost unlimited power over wives, who were not even permitted to attend church without the husband's consent. The prominent ideas regarding woman under Byzantine Christianity, have been her uncleanliness, her sinfulness and the small value of her life.[110] She is regarded as a being of lower order than man, and as looked upon in a different light by God.

Where marriage is wholly or partly under church control, its very form degrades woman, her promise of obedience not yet having passed away. In the old Covenanter period of Scotland, the records give a still more debased form, in which the man as head was declared united to an ignoble part, represented by the woman. But in modern times, both in Catholic and Protestant countries a more decent veil is thrown over this sacrifice of woman than in the Greek Church, where the wife is sometimes delivered to the husband under this formula, "Here wolf, take thy lamb!" and the bridegroom is presented with a whip by his bride giving her a few blows as part of the ceremony, and bidding her draw off his boots as a sign of her subjection to him. With such an entrance ceremony it may well be surmised that the marriage relation permits the most revolting tyranny. And this condition can be directly traced to the period since Christianity was adopted under Vladimir, a thousand years since, as the religion of that nation. The old Slavs recognized the equality of woman in household, political, and religious matters, and not until Byzantine Christianity became incorporated with, and a part of, the civil polity of its rulers, did Russia present such a picture of domestic degradation as it shows today. The chastisement of wives is directly taught as part of the husband's domestic duty. Until recently, the wife who killed her husband while he was thus punishing her was buried alive, her head only being left above ground. Many lingered for days before death reached them.

Ivan Panim, a Russian exile, while a student at Harvard College, 1881, made the following statement at a Convention of the Massachusetts Woman Suffrage Society:

> A short time ago the wife of a well-to-do peasant came to the justice of one of the district courts in Russia and demanded protection from the cruelty of her husband. She proved conclusively by the aid of competent witnesses that he had bound her naked to a stake during the cold weather on the street, and asked the passers-by to strike her; and whenever they refused he struck her himself. He fastened her moreover to the ground, put many stones and weights on her and broke one of her arms. The court declared the husband "not guilty." "It cannot afford," it said, "to teach woman to disobey the commands of her husband."

Mr. Panim declared this to be by no means an extreme or isolated case, and that few became known to the public through the courts or the press. While the above incident illustrates the cruelty of the state towards woman under the Greek form of christianity, others with equal pertinence prove the cruelty of the church.

> A peasant in the village of Zelovia Baltic, having reason to doubt the fidelity of his spouse, deliberately harnessed her to a cart in company with a mare—a species of double harness for which the lady was doubtless unprepared when she took the nuptial vow. He then got into the cart in company with a friend, and drove the ill-assorted team some sixteen versts

(nearly eleven English miles,) without sparing the whip-cord. When he returned from his excursion he sheared the unlucky woman's head, tarred and feathered her and turned her out of doors. She naturally sought refuge and consolation from her parish priest; but he sent her back to her lord and master, pre-scribing further flaggellations. An appeal to justice by the poor woman and her relatives, resulted in a non-suit, and recourse to a higher court will probably terminate in the same manner.

Popular Russian songs allude to woman's wrongs in the mar-riage relation. The wife of a son living with his father, is looked upon as an additional animal to be urged to the utmost exertion. She is treated almost like a slave and with less consideration than a horse or cow. Lady Varney[111] gives the chorus of a song in the "Lament of a Young Russian Bride," which portrays the father-in-law's part.

Chorus

"Thumping, scolding, never lets his daughter sleep,"
"Up you slattern! up you sloven sluggish slut!"

The wife also entreats her husband for mercy.

"Oh husband, only for good cause beat thou thy wife
Not for little things."
"Far away is my father dear, and farther still my mother."

While demanding marital fidelity from wives, Russian hus-bands do not bind themselves to the same purity; and aside from wife beating, the husband's infidelities form the general subject of songs. Peter the Great, head of the Greek Church, not only beat his Empress Catherine, but while demanding marital fidelity from her, was notorious for his liasons with women of low rank.[112] Women were not counted in the census of Russia until the reign of this monarch. So many "souls," no woman named. So long continued has been this treatment of woman, that the poet, Nekrasof says:

> Ages have rolled away, the whole face of the earth has brightened;
> only the somber lot of the Mowguk's wife God forgets to change.

Man's opinion of woman is shown in the proverb, "A hen is not a bird, neither is a woman a human being." Nekrasof makes one of his village heroines say: "God has forgotten the nook where he hid the keys of woman's emancipation," which woman's despair has changed to the proverb "God remembers everything but the Slavonian woman; he has forgotten where he hid the keys of her emancipation." The system of indulgence is as marked in the Greek as in the Catholic Church, but under slightly different aspects. The worship of saints is an important part of the Byzantine religion. There are two saints, to whom if a person prays as he goes out to commit a crime, however heinous, he takes his pardon with him.[113] The present condition of Russian affairs is ascribed by Edmond Noble to a long-felt revolt in the minds of the people, against the social, political and religious system of that country. While the peasant implicitly obeys the czar, regarding his position as divine and all his commands as just, there is an element that recalls the former period of freedom, with intensity of desire for its reestablishment. To this class, permeated as it must be with the spirit of the age, the efforts for constitutional change, and what the world knows as Nihilism, is attributable. It is in reality a mighty protest against that christianity which in destroying political freedom, instituted a monstrous spiritual and material tyranny in its place. Nihilism is not wholly nor even chiefly a form of political change; it has a depth and a power much beyond mere social or governmental change; it looks to an entire overthrow of that religious system which permeates and underlies all moral and political tyranny in Russia.

Class legislation of extreme character is still constantly met in all christian lands. The English Bill of 1887, for extending Parliamentary Franchise to woman, as shown, having as its last clause, "Provided that nothing in this Act contained shall enable women under coverture to be registered or to vote at such elections." In this Bill, the State recognized the marital subordination of woman, held by law as under her husband's control not possessing freedom of thought, judgment, or action upon questions of vital importance to herself. Walter Besant declares:

> That it is only by searching and poking among unknown pamphlets and forgotten books that one finds out the actual depth of the English savagery of the last century . . . that for drunkenness, brutality and ignorance the Englishmen of the baser kind, reached the lowest depth ever reached by civilized men . . . a drunkard, a brawler, a torturer of dumb beasts, a wifebeater, a profligate.

It is not necessary to search "unknown pamphlets and forgotten books," in order to find out the depths of English or other christian savagery of the present century. Every newspaper report, every court decision, every Act of Parliament or Legislature, every decree of king, or czar, or other potentate; every canon, decree or decision of the church, proclaims the ignorance, brutality and savagery of Christendom. Nor is it among men of the baser kind with their infliction of corporal punishment upon wives, but in the subtler and more refined methods of torture made use of by men of the highest position that we most truly find out the depths of the savagery of the nineteenth century. Profligacy among men of the highest position never flourished more luxuriantly than at the present time; drunkenness has by no means passed away; wife beating is still a common amusement; the law still fails to extend a protecting arm around those most needing its defence; the church yet fails to recognize a common humanity in all classes of people. Old traditional customs of thought and action still prevail, and the men of a hundred years hence will look upon the present time with the same criticizing astonishment that the historian of today looks upon the last century. Savagery instead of civilization is still the predominant power in christendom. In comparison with the treatment many wives receive in christian lands, that of women among the American Indians, or the most savage races of the old world, is far more humane than shown in England, America and other christian lands, where even maternity does not free woman from the coarsest brutality upon the part of husbands, nor the illness incident upon bringing a new being into the world, from writs of "contempt," even though the death of mother or babe result. In 1890, the Press of New York City reported the case of Mrs. R. Bassman, who was summoned to appear before the Surrogate Court, for a funeral debt. Being in confinement she was unable to appear. Thereupon an order for her arrest for Contempt of Court was issued, and while still unrecovered from her illness, she was arrested and incarcerated in Ludlow Street jail. Her newly born babe deprived of its mother's care sickened and died; and this is part of Christian civilization for woman, in nearly the two thousandth year of its existence.

Booth's *Darkest England*[114] relates a somewhat parallel case, parallel in so far as it shows the enslaved condition of the English wife under present christian laws.

> A woman who lived just opposite had been cruelly kicked and cursed by her husband, who had finally bolted the door against her, and she had turned to Barbie, as the only hope. Barbie took her in with her rough and ready kindness, got her to bed and was both nurse and doctor for the poor woman till her child was born and laid in the mother's arms. Not daring to be absent longer she got up as best she could and crawled on hands and knees down the little steep steps, across the street, and back to her own door; . . . it might have cost the woman her life to be absent from her home more than a couple of hours.

That brutal men exist everywhere, that women and children are in all lands abused, that prizefighting with its concomitants of broken jaws, noses, heads, takes place in christian lands are undeniable facts, usually although in defiance of law and subjecting their perpetrators to punishment. But the peculiarity of the cases noted and of ten thousand others, is that they are done under the authority of the law, to a being whom the law seems not bound to protect. No husbands in the world are more brutal than lower-class Englishmen into whose hands the wife is given by law, and he protected by the law in his ill-usage of her. It is Christian law of which complaint is made; it is the effect of Christian civilization, in its treatment of woman, to which attention is called. *Darkest England* furnishes still fuller statements of woman's degraded condition in that country. In the opening pages of that work it is said:

> Hard it is, no doubt, to read in Stanley's pages of the slave-traders coldly arranging for the surprise of a village, the capture of the inhabitants, the massacre of those who resist, and the violation of all the women; but the stony streets of London, if they could but speak, would tell of tragedies as awful, of ruin as complete, of ravishments as horrible, as if we were in Central Africa; only the ghostly devastation is covered, corpse-like, with the artificialities of modern civilization.
>
> The lot of a negress in the Equatorial Forest is not, perhaps, a very happy one but is it so much worse than that of many a pretty orphan girl's in our christian capital? We talk about the brutalities of the dark ages and we profess to shudder as we read in the books of the shameful exactions of the rights of feudal superiors. And yet here, beneath our very eyes, in our theaters, in our restaurants, and in many other places unspeakable, it be enough but to name it, the same hideous abuse flourishes unchecked. A young penniless girl, if she be pretty, is often hunted from pillar to post by her employers, confronted always by the alternative—starve or sin. Darkest England, like Darkest Africa, reeks with malaria.

It should be impressed upon the mind that the difference between "Darkest Africa," and "Darkest England," lies in the two facts, that one is the darkness of ignorant and savage races who are in the very night of barbarism; while the other is the moral darkness of christian civilization, in the very center of Christendom, after two thousand years of church teaching and priestly influence. A few years since, in Massachusetts, an action for cruelty on part of a husband came before a court, the charge being that he came home one night in February, when the thermometer was ten degrees below zero, and turned his wife and little child, with his wife's mother of eighty, out of the house.[115] While the wife was giving testimony, the judge interrupted, saying:

> The husband had a right to do so, there was a quarrel between the husband and wife, and he had a legal right to turn her out and take possession of the house, that was not cruelty.

From the newspapers of April, 1886, we learn that:

> At Salem, W. Va., Thomas True drove his wife out of doors and swore he would kill any one who would give her shelter. Robert Miller took her into his house, and was killed by True.

The system of marriage recognized by the church has ever been that of ownership and power by the husband and father, over the wife and children, and during the Middle Ages the ban of the church fell with equal force upon the woman, who for any cause left her husband, as upon the witch. The two were under the same ban as the excommunicated, denounced as one whom all others must shun, whom no one must succor or harbor, and with whom it was unlawful to hold any species of intercourse.

The "boycott" is not an invention of the present century, but was in use many hundred years since against a recalcitrant wife, under sanction of both church and state. The advertisements of absconding wives seen at the present day, whom the husband sets forth as having left his bed and board and whom all persons are thereafter forbidden to trust upon his account, are but a reminiscence of the wife-boycott of former years, when all persons, were forbidden to "harbor her" under penalty, unless it could be proven that her life was in danger without such aid. The husband was held to possess vested rights in the wife, not only as against herself, but as against the world, and it is not half a decade since the notice below, appeared in a Kansas paper,[116] accompanied by the cut of a fleeing woman.

A $50 Capture

A woman who ran away from her husband at Lawrence some time ago, was found at Fort Leavenworth yesterday by a Lawrence detective and taken back to her home. The officer received a reward of $50 for her capture. *Leavenworth Standard*, Kans., Dec. 21, 1886.

This advertisement and others of a similar character to be seen in the daily and weekly press of the country are undeniable proofs of the low condition under the law, of woman in the marriage relation, and read very much like the notices in regard to absconding slaves a few years since. Kansas was one of the very first states which recognized the right of a married mother to her own child, that provision having been incorporated in its constitution at early date as an enticement for bringing women emigrants into that state at a period when the antislavery and proslavery contests within its borders had made it bloody ground. Although the married woman's property law and the spirit of free thought has rendered such action less frequent than formerly, it is less than forty years, as before noted, since the New York Court of Common Pleas rendered a judgment of $10,000 in favor of a husband against the relatives of his wife, who at her own request "harbored and sheltered" her. The Christian principle of man's ownership of woman, for many hundred years under English law, rendered the party giving shelter to a fleeing wife liable to the husband in money damages, upon the ground of having aided a runaway servant to the master's injury. Under but one circumstance was such shelter admissable. In case the wife was in danger of perishing, she could be harbored until morning, when she must be returned to her master by the person who had thus temporarily taken care of his perishable property. In England as late as 1876, the case of a Mrs. Cochrane, who had lived apart from her husband for years, and showing another phase of property law in the wife, came up before Judge Coleridge. Her character was not at all impeached, but she indulged in amusements which her husband considered reprehensible, and through stratagem she was brought to his lodgings and there kept a prisoner. A writ of *habeas corpus* being sued out, the husband was compelled to bring her before the court of the Queen's Bench. The decision of the judge rendered in favor of the husband's right of forcible detention was declared by him to be upon ground that English law virtually considered the wife as being under the guardianship of the husband, not a person in her own right, and this distinctly upon the ground of her perpetual infancy;[117] she must be restored to her husband. As late as 1886, the *Personal Rights Journal* of England called attention to the suit of a clergyman for the "restitution of conjugal rights" and custody of child. The wife not being able to live in agreement with the husband, had taken her child and left him. A decree for such restitution having been pronounced by court, the husband, Rev. Joseph Wallis, advertised for his absconding wife, Caroline Wallis, offering one hundred pounds reward for such information as should lead to her discovery.

£100 REWARD

WHEREAS, A Decree was pronounced in the Probate, Divorce, and Admiralty Division of the High Court of Justice, on the 5th day of June, 1886, in the suit of Samuel Joseph Wallis *versus* Caroline Wallis, for restitution of conjugal rights, and for custody of the child, May Wallis, to the petitioner, the said Samuel Joseph Wallis. And WHEREAS it has been ascertained that the said Caroline Wallis has lately been seen at Whitstable and the Neighborhood,

NOTICE IS HEREBY GIVEN,

That the above Reward will be paid to any Person or Persons who shall give such information as will lead to the discovery of the whereabouts of the said Caroline Wallis, and the recovery by the said S. J. Wallis of the custody of the said Child.

Information to be sent to me, Richard Howe Brightman, of Sheerness, Kent, Solicitor to the said Samuel Joseph Wallis.

This brutal advertisement in the dying hours of the nine-teenth century had the effect of rousing public attention to woman's enslaved condition in the marital relation, and a rapid growth of public sentiment in recognition of a wife's individual and distinct personality, took place between 1886 and 1890, a period of four years. During the latter year another English hus-band, one Jackson, forcibly abducted his wife who lived apart from him, holding her prisoner with gun and bayonet, threat-ening her friends with death—as was his legal right—in case of her attemped rescue. When this was known, hundreds of letters poured into the press, upholding the right of a wife to the con-trol of her own person, and writ of *habeas corpus* compelled her production in court. Under the pressure of a public sentiment he found it wise to conciliate, the judge decided in favor of her right to live away from her husband, who was also restrained from fur-ther molesting her. The Supreme Court of Georgia recently ren-dered a decision in regard to the rights of husbands as related to the wife's rights of property's, in which the church theory of her subordination was maintained.

> The wife has been much advanced by the general tenor of leg-islation of late years in respect to her property. She has acquired a pretty independent position as to title, control and disposition, but this relates to her own property, not to his. The law has not yet raised her to the station of superintendent of her husband's contracts and probably never will. In taking a wife a man does not put himself under an overseer. He is not a subordinate in his own family but the head of it. A subjugated husband is a less energetic member of society than one who keeps his true place, yet knows how to temper authority with affection.

During the famous Beecher trial, Hon. Wm. M. Evarts defined woman's legal position as one of subordination to man, declaring "that notwithstanding changing customs and the amenities of modern life, women were not free, but were held in the hollow of man's hand, to be crushed at his will." In exemplification of this statement he referred to a recent decision of the New York Court of Appeals, and to the highest tribunals of England. He gave his own sanction to these principles of law, all of which owe their foundation to church teaching regarding woman, enforced by the peculiar forms of marriage ceremony it has instituted.

The church everywhere strenuously opposes civil marriage. The Plenary Council of 1884, and the celebration of the hundredth anniversary of the Catholic hierarchy in the United States, each making church marriage a prominent part of their discussions. Different parts of Europe and of South America have recently been shaken by church action in regard to it. Prussia, Belgium, Italy, France, have fallen under the odium of the church in consequence of the civil laws declaring marriage valid without the aid of the church. The celebrated M. Godin, founder of the cooperative Familistere, at Guise, was married in 1886 under civil form, to a lady member of the French League for the Rights of Women, and thus announced the marriage to their friends:

> M. Godin, manufacturer, founder of Familistere, and Madame Marie Godin, nee Moret, his secretary and co-laborer in the work of the Familistere, and in the propagation of social reform, have the honor of announcing to you the purely civil marriage which they contracted at Guise, the 14th day of July, 1886, that they might manifest to all their union, and the common purpose of all the efforts of their lives.

Civil marriage, where the church is supreme, is followed by excommunication and odious insults. In 1885 a remarkable instance of this kind occurred in the city of Concepcion, Chili. A young couple were married, with consent of their parents, according to the civil law. Their social and political prominence made the occasion conspicuous, as it was the first wedding among the aristocracy in that country dispensing with the aid of a priest. The church paper, edited by a Jesuit priest, thus commented,

> The *Libertad* calls this "a happy union," but it should remember that "happy unions" of this sort have hitherto existed only in the animal kingdom.

The bride, groom, and all their families suffered excommunication from the church. But it is not alone the Catholic church which desires to retain its bold upon marriage. Less than two years since certain clergymen of the Anglican church agreed to officiate at marriages without a fee, for the purpose of retaining control of this relation; and so strong has been the influence of the church during the ages, that few people look upon a ceremony under the civil law with the same respect as one performed by a priest, even of a Protestant denomination. The control of marriage by the church while throwing wealth into its own coffers, has ever had a prejudicial effect upon morals, as impediments to marriage of whatever character increase immorality. In the city of Concepcion referred to, of 200,000 inhabitants, there are two thousand children of unknown parentage. In 1884, statistics showed sixty-two percent of the children to be illegitimate. The parents of those little ones were mostly known, being persons too poor to pay the cost of a church marriage, twenty-five dollars, its price, being quite beyond the means of the humbler classes. The Liberal party, in establishing civil marriage as legitimate, authorized any magistrate to perform the ceremony, and furnish a certificate for twenty-five cents. This assault upon the ancient prerogative of the church depriving priests of the largest source of their revenue, at once made a religious-political issue of the question, the church taking strenuous action against all connected with framing the law, and its repeal became the prominent political issue, to aid which, all the faithful were called. Using its old weapons, the church through the Archbishop, issued an edict excommunicating the president of the republic, the members of his cabinet and the members of congress who voted for the statute; directing that a similar penalty should fall upon every communicant who obeyed it and neglected to recognize the church as the only authority competent to solemnize the marriage rite.

A correspondent of the *New York Sun*, in Chili, wrote:

This brought matters to a crisis. On the one hand, the State declared all marriages not under the civil law illegal, and their issue illegitimate, refusing to recognize rites performed by the priests. On the other, those who obey the law are excommunicated from the church, and their cohabitation forbidden by the highest ecclesiastical authority. Thus matrimony is practically forbidden, and those who choose to enter it have their choice between arrest and excommunication. A young member of Congress, a man of gifts and influence, who stands as one of the leaders of the Liberal party, and who voted and argued for civil marriage, is engaged to the daughter of a wealthy merchant with proud lineage and aristocratic connections. He is willing to accept the civil authority, which he helped to create, and she and her father are also willing, but her mother is a devout church woman and cannot regard marriage as sacred without the blessing of a priest. She favors the alliance, but insists that the Church shall be recognized. The bishop declines to permit the ceremony unless the young man shall go to the confessional and retract his political record, with a vow to hereafter remain steadfast to the church. This he refuses to do. The couple will go to Europe or the States and there have the ceremony performed.

This action of the Chilian republic in substituting a civil for a religious ceremony in marriage and declaring the latter to be illegal, is a most important step in civilization, of which freedom for woman is such an essential factor; and its results in that country must be felt in woman's every relation of life, promoting self-respect, self-reliance and security in place of the degradation, self-distrust and fear to which its church has so long condemned her.

Notes

1. He bought his bride of her parents according to the custom of antiquity, and she followed the coemption by purchasing with *three* pieces of copper a just introduction to his treasury and household duties. Gibbon.—*Rome*, 4; 395.

2. By the law of the *Twelve Tables* woman possessed the right of repudiation in marriage. These tables were a compilation of still older

laws or customs, a species of common law incorporated into statutes by Lachis of Athens, daughter of one Majestes; and were so wise and of such benefit to the people of Attica that the Romans received them as natural laws in which there was more of patriotism and purity than in all the volumes of Popinanus. H. S. Maine.—*Ancient Law*.

3. After the Punic triumphs the matrons of Rome aspired to the common benefits of a free and opulent republic. . . . They declined the solemnities of the old nuptials; defeated the annual prescription by an absence of three days, and without losing their name or independence subscribed the liberal and definite terms of a marriage contract. Of their private fortunes they commuted the use and secured the property; the estate of a wife could neither be alienated or mortgaged by a prodigal husband. Religious and civil rites were no longer essential, and between persons of similar rank, the apparent community of life was allowed as sufficient evidence of their nuptials. . . . When the Roman matrons became the equal and voluntary companions of their lords, their marriage like other partnerships might be dissolved. Gibbon.—*Rome*, 4; 347.

4. Uses or Usucapion, was a form of civil marriage securing the wife more freedom than the form which held her "under his thumb" as his daughter. It was as old or even older than the Twelve Tables, and although for many centuries not considered quite as respectable a form of marriage as that in which the wife became the husband's slave with divorce impossible, it eventually grew to be the customary form of Roman marriage. Maine.—*Early History of Ancient Institutions*, p. 517.

5. It was with the state of conjugal relations thus produced that the growing Christianity of the Roman world waged a war ever increasing in fierceness, yet it remained to the last the basis of the Roman legal conception of marriage.—*Ibid*.

6. When the Chremes of Terence reproaches his wife for not obeying his orders and exposing their infant, he speaks like a father and master, and silences the scruples of a foolish woman. Milman.—*Note to Gibbon's Rome*.

7. " 'Usus' had the very important consequence that the woman so married remained in the eye of the law in the family of her father, and was under his guardianship and not that of her husband. A complete revolution had thus passed over the constitution of the family. This must have been the period when a juriconsulist of the empire defined marriage as a life-long fellowship of all divine and human rights."

8. Reeves.—*Hist. Eng. Law*, p. 337.

9. Maine says: "No society which preserves any tincture of Christian Institutions is likely to restore to married women the personal liberty conferred on them by middle Roman laws."—*Ancient Law.*

10. Reeves says, while many great minds, as Lord Chief Justice Hale, Lord John Somers, Henry Spellman, Dr. Brady and Sir Martin Wright think feudalism came in with the conqueror, others, as Coke, Seldon, Bacon and Sir Roger Owen are of opinion that tenures were common among the Saxons. Blackstone, Dalrymple and Sullivan endeavor to compromise the dispute by admitting an imperfect system of feuds to have been instituted before the conquest.—*History of English Law,* Vol. I, pp. 18–19.

11. A certain bishop, wishing a person to take charge of his castle during his absence, the latter asked how he should support himself. For answer *the bishop* pointed to a procession of tradesmen with their goods then crossing the valley at their feet.

12. Wives were bought in England from the fifth to the eleventh century. Herbert Spencer.—*Descriptive Sociology of England.*

13. There was another law even more odious than Marquette; the father's right to the price of mundium, in other words, the price of his daughter. Legouvè.—*Hist. Morales des Femmes,* p. 104.

14. Murder under the name of war, the ruin of women under the name of gallantry, were the chief occupations of the nobility. Pike.—*Hist. of Crime in England.*

The chief qualification for success at courts was the power of making and appreciating mirth. The infidelities of women were commonly the narrator's theme, and an exhortation to avoid matrimony was the most common form of advice given by a man to his friend. War and intrigue were regarded as the principal amusements of life; the acquisition of wealth the only object worth serious consideration. A consequence of this creed was that the husband frequently set a price upon his wife's virtue, and made a profit out of his own dishonor. Fathers were ready to sell their daughters.—*Ibid.*

15. Both married and single found their worst foes in their nearest friends. The traffic in women was none the less real in Christian England than it is now in the slave marts of Stamboul or Constantinople.—*Ibid.*

One of the most recent illustrations of the general regard in which woman is held throughout Christendom is the experience of the young California heiress, Florence Blythe, who although but fifteen years old, was in constant receipt of proposals of marriage both at home and from abroad. Her attorney, General Hunt, said: "I do not think there is a woman living who has had the number of written proposals that Florence has received, but in all the letters woman is regarded as a chattel, a thing to be bought and sold." The constant receipt of letters of this character, and the equally constant attempt of adventurers to gain a personal interview with the child, at last became unendurable, and to escape such insulting persecution, Florence suddenly married a young man of her acquaintance living near her. These letters, among them, from sixty titled Europeans, lords, counts, dukes, barons, viscounts, marquises and even one prince, confirm the statement of August Bebel, that marriage sales of women are still as common as in the middle ages, and are expected in most Christian countries.

16. A husband upon his return from the Crusades, finding his wife had been untrue, imprisoned her in a room so small she could neither stand erect nor lie at full length; her only window looking out upon the dead body of her lover swinging in chains.

17. The Shoshone Indian who hires his wife out as a harlot, inflicts capital punishment on her if she goes with another without his knowledge. Bancroft.—*Native Races*, I; 436.

18. Therefore a single woman for whom no bid was offered, an "old maid," was looked upon with contempt as a being of no value in the eyes of men.

19. *Hist. of Crime in England,* Vol. I, p. 90.

20. By the laws of the king of Wessex, who lived at the end of the eighteenth century, the purchase of wives is deliberately sanctioned; in the preface it is stated that the compilation was drawn up with the assistance of the Bishop of Winchester and a large assemblage of God's servants.—*Ibid*.

21. Nothing, says Pike, was considered but the market value of the woman, and the adulterer was compelled to expend the equivalent of her original price on the purchase of a new bride, whom he formally delivered to the injured husband. Nor were these laws merely secular, they were enacted and enforced by all the dread power of the church.

22. In the fourteenth century, either the female character was utterly dissolute, or the tyranny of husbands utterly reckless, when we find that it was no uncommon circumstance that women were strangled by masked assassins, or walking by the river side were plunged into it. This drowning of women gave rise to a popular proverb: "It is nothing, only a woman being drowned." And this condition constituted the

domestic life of England from the twelfth century to the first civil war, when the taste of men for bloodshed found wider scope, and from the murder of women they advanced to the practice of cutting one another's throats. Disraeli.—*Amenities of Literature*, Vol. I, p. 95.

23. "And they were so covetous that for a little silver they sellen 'ein daughters, 'ein sisters and 'ein own wives, to putten 'ein to lechery."

24. The Church from the earliest period furnished its full portion to the codes of our simple forefathers, that of the first Christian king being that for the property of God and the Church (if stolen) twelve-fold compensation was to be made. Thorpe.—*Ancient Laws and Institutions of England*.

25. *Journal of Jurisprudence*, Vol. XVI, Edinburg, 1872.

26. Until the maiden was wedded she was kept strictly under control, and the kind of discipline which was enforced is well illustrated by a letter written late in the reign of Henry VI. The writer was the widow of a landholder, and she was corresponding with the brother of the young lady whose case she describes and whom she is anxious to serve by finding a husband. This young lady was under the care of her mother, and the following was her condition: She might not speak with any man, not even her mother's servants; and she had since Easter the most part been beaten once in the week, or twice, and sometimes thrice in a day, and her hand was broken in two or three places. Pike.—*History of Crime in England*.

27. Britton.—*Introduction*, p. 39. Glanville.—*De Legibius Anglica*, p. 158.

28. Doubtless in all ages marriages were by far oftener determined by pecuniary considerations than by love or affection, but proofs are wanting to show that marriage was formerly made an object of speculation and exchange in the open market with anything like the same effrontery as today. In our time among the propertied classes—the poor have no need of it—marriage barter is frequently carried on with a shamelessness which makes the phrases about the sacredness of marriage, that some people never tire of repeating, the emptiest mockery. August Bebel.—*Woman in the Past, Present and Future*.

29. To make women the special objects of this torture, to teach them hardness of heart in the office of executioners, was refinement of atrocity. . . . It was for slaves and women that the greatest atrocities were reserved.—*Hist. of Crime in England*.

30. Women in England had burned women to death in the tenth century; they had been set on the stool of filth to be mocked as brewers

of bad ale in the eleventh; on the stool of filth they had been jeered as common scolds from time immemorial; they were legally beaten by their husbands down to a comparatively recent period. In the fourteenth century they were such as circumstances had made them; strong of muscle but hard of heart, more fit to be mothers of brigands than to rear gentle daughters or honest sons.—*Ibid.*

31. The elder Disraeli says: "Warton, too, has observed that the style of friendship between males in the reign of Elizabeth would not be tolerated at the present day." Disraeli himself declares that "a male friend, whose life and fortunes were consecrated to another male, who looks upon him with adoration and talks of him with excessive tenderness, appears to us nothing less than a chimerical and monstrous lover."—*Amenities of Literature*, Vol. II, p. 105.

32. Poisoning or otherwise murdering husbands was a crime visited with peculiar severity in almost all codes. Lea.—*Superstition and Force.*

33. Blackstone says it was to be no thicker than a man's thumb, thus an instrument of ever varying size. According to palmistry the thumb of a self-willed or obstinate man, a cruel man, or of a murderer, is very large at the upper portion or ball.

34. Petit treason may happen in three ways: By a servant killing his master; a wife her husband, or an ecclesiastical person (either secular or regular) his superior, to whom he owes faith and obedience. The punishment of petit treason in a man is to be drawn and hanged, and in a woman to be drawn and burnt.—*Commentaries*, Vol. IV, pp. 203–204.

35. But in treason of every kind the punishment of women is the same and different from men. For as the decency due to the sex forbids the exposing and publicly mangling their bodies, their sentence is to be drawn (dragged) to the gallows and there be burnt alive.—*Ibid.*, IV, p. 92.

36. The daily press, in its minute record of events, all unwittingly furnishes many a little item, whose primal reason only the student of history can read. The Syracuse, N.Y., *Daily Standard*, of February 22, 1884, published from its exchanges the following incident:

"An eccentric old man in New Hampshire surprised his neighbors and friends the other day by shouldering his gun and starting for the woods on the morning of his wife's funeral. On being urged to come back, he refused, saying: 'She warn't no blood relation of mine.' "

37. But now by the statute 30, George 3 c., forty-eight women convicted in all cases of treason shall receive judgment to be drawn to the place of execution, and there to be hanged by the neck till dead. Before

this humane statute women were sentenced to be burnt alive for every species of treason.—*Commentaries*, p. 92.

38. See decision *New York Court of Appeals*, January, 1892.

39. St. Petersburg, September 22—In April last Mrs. Aina Sainio, wife of a professor in the State College at Travasteheuse, Finland, was found guilty of poisoning her husband, and in accordance with the mediæval law, which is still in force there, she was sentenced to be beheaded, and her body to be affixed to a beacon and burned. It was charged that Mrs. Sainio had been unfaithful to her husband, carrying on a liaison with one of the students at the college. She strenuously denied this, and said her motive in killing her husband was to get the insurance of $2,500 on his life as she was deeply in debt. The case was carried to the Court of Appeals and today a decision was handed down affirming the judgment of the trial court and adding to the punishment. It transpired during the trial that Mrs. Sainio had forged her husband's name to checks for small sums some time before his death, and for this offense the Court of Appeals ordered that her right hand be cut off. Then she will be decapitated, her body fastened to a stake covered with inflammable material and set on fire.

40. Reported in the *London Telegraph*.

41. *Telegraphic Report* from Providence, R.I., September 24, 1892.

42. Mrs. Judge Seney's trouble.—A deserted wife suing the woman who enticed her husband away from her.

Tiffin, Ohio, February 14.—Judge Dodge gave his decision yesterday in the novel case of the former Mrs. George E. Seney against the present Mrs. George E. Seney. Judge Seney is one of the well-known lawyers of Ohio, and author of a "Civil Code" that bears his name. He married his first wife, Mrs. Anna Seney, in 1858, and for fourteen years they lived happily together. At about that time Mrs. Seney and Miss Walker became very intimate friends, and continued to be so until, as is alleged, Mrs. Seney ascertained that Miss Walker was undermining the affections of her husband. A separation between Mr. and Mrs. Seney soon followed, and subsequently the judge married Miss Walker. Mrs. Seney, therefore, instituted a suit against her successor, claiming damages to the amount of $10,000 for the seduction of her husband.—*New York Sun*.

43. James Howard, thirty-five years old, was taken from jail at Texarkana, Ark., on Wednesday night by a mob and lynched. He was under arrest for horrible cruelty to his fourteen-year-old wife. The woman says that he frequently tied her feet together while she was in a

state of nudity, and hanging her up by the feet beat her unmercifully and threatened to kill her if she told anyone of his cruelties. On the first of November, Howard took a common branding iron, used to brand live-stock, and heating it red hot branded a large letter "H" on his wife's person in two places while she was tied to a bed.

44. *Pall Mall Gazette*, 1888.

45. *Westminster Review*, September, 1887.

46. Cato, the Roman (pagan) censor three centuries before the Christian era, said: "They who beat their wives or children lay sacrilegious hands on the most sacred things in the world. For myself, I prefer the character of a good husband to that of a great senator."

47. The bill failed of passing upon the ground that the lash belonged to the dark ages, degrading a man by its infliction.

48. An English lady, *Mrs. Margaret Bright Lucus*, in writing a description of this implement said: "This country has even now but little to boast in her laws regarding woman, and your country is burdened with similar evil laws; the Franchise is most important."

49. The Museum at Reading, England, contains among its curiosities a bridle formerly used to stop the mouths of scolding women in that town.

50. Sometimes called Timbrel, or Gum Stole.

51. "It would seem that almost every English town of any importance had its ducking stool for scolds. In 1741 old Rugby paid 2s 4d for a chair for the ducking stool. The parish of Southam, in Warwickshire, got a beautiful stool built in 1718 at an expense of £2 11s 4d. Ancient Coventry had two stools."

The most noteworthy of all the instruments designed for the correction of Eve's offending daughters was the ducking stool, known as the tumbrel and the trebuchet. A post, across which was a transverse beam turning on a swivel and with a chair at one end, was set up on the edge of a pond. Into the chair the woman was chained, turned toward the water—a muddy or filthy pond was usually chosen for this purpose when available—and ducked half a dozen times; or, if the water inflamed her instead of acting as a damper, she was let down times innumerable, until she was exhausted and well nigh drowned.

From the frequency with which we find it mentioned in old local and county histories, in church wardens' and chamberlains' accounts, and by the poets, we shall probably not be wrong in concluding that at one time this institution was kept up all over the country.—*London Graphic.*

52. John Dillon.—*Colonial Legislation of America.*

53. *Ibid.*

54. Jersey City, N.J., July 23, 1887—Mrs. Mary Brody, convicted a few days ago of being a common scold, was today sentenced to pay a fine of twenty-five dollars and costs.

Only the other day a woman in this city, under some ancient unrepealed law of this state, was arrested and brought before a magistrate on the charge of being a common scold. A too free use of the tongue was reckoned a public offense in all the American colonies, and in England the lawful punishment of common scolds was continued until a recent day. It was for these that the "ducking stool" was invented, which usually consists of a heavy chair fastened to the end of a large piece of timber, which was hung by the middle to a post on the river side. The offender was tied into the chair, and then soused into the water until it was judged that her shrewishness had departed from her. Sometimes she was dipped so thoroughly that her breath departed for good, as happened to a certain elderly lady at Ratcliffe Highway. The ducking stool was constantly hanging in its place, and on the back of it were engraved devils laying hold of scolds, etc.—*St. Louis Republican.*

55. If it is a crime to buy and sell wives, let the men who do such things be punished; if there is no crime in the transaction, why should the wife who is sold be punished. Unfortunately this is not a solitary instance of law made or administered to punish women in order to teach men.—*English Women's Suffrage Journal.*

Before Mr. Justice Denman, at the Liverpool Assizes, Betsy Wardle was charged with marrying George Chisnal at Eccleston, bigamously, her former husband being alive. It was stated by the woman that as her first husband had sold her for a quart of beer, she thought she was at liberty to marry again.

George Chisnal, the second husband, apparently just out of his teens was called.

His Lordship—"How did you come to marry this woman?"

Witness (in the Lancashire vernacular)—"Hoo did a what?" [Laughter.]

Question repeated—"A bowt her." [Laughter.]

His Lordship—"You are not fool enough to suppose you can buy another man's wife? Oi?" [Laughter.]

His Lordship—"How much did you give for her?" Six pence. [Great laughter.]

His Lordship asked him how long he had lived with the prisoner.

Witness—"Going on for three years."

His Lordship—"Do you want to take her back again?"

"Awl keep her if you loike." [Laughter.]

His Lordship (addressing the prisoner)—It is absolutely necessary that I should pass some punishment upon you in order that people may understand that men have no more right to sell their wives than they have to sell other people's wives, or to sell other people's horses or cows, or anything of the kind. You cannot make that a legal transaction. So many of you seem to be ignorant of that, that it is necessary to give you some punishment in order that you may understand it. It is not necessary it should be long, but you must be imprisoned and kept to hard labor for one week.—*News of the World*, 1883.

A peculiar case came up in the mayor's office at Vincennes, Ind., in 1887. A man named Bolin sold his wife to another man named Burch for $300, and held Burch's note therefor. The sale was a reality, but the note was never paid, hence the difficulty.

"We know a man in the Black Hills—a man who is well-to-do and respected—the foundation of whose fortune was $4,000, the sum for which he sold his wife to a neighbor. The sale was purely a matter of business all around, and the parties to it were highly satisfied." 1889.— *The Times*, Bismarck, N.Dak.

56. In the *Doncaster Gazette* of March 25, 1803, a sale is thus described: "A fellow sold his wife, as a cow, in Sheffield marketplace a few days ago. The lady was put into the hands of a butcher, who held her by a halter fastened around her waist. 'What do you ask for your cow?' said a bystander. 'A guinea,' replied the husband. 'Done,' cried the other, and immediately led away his bargain. We understand that the purchaser and his 'cow' live very happily together." Ashton.—*The Progress of Women*.

57. *Morning Herald*, March 11, 1802.—On the eleventh of last month a person sold, at the market cross, in Chapel en la Frith, a wife, a child, and as much furniture as would set up a beggar, for eleven shillings.

Morning Herald, April 16, 1802.—A butcher sold his wife by auction at the last market day at Hereford. The lot brought £1 4s and a bowl of punch.

Annual Register, February 14, 1806.—A man named John Garsthorpe exposed his wife for sale in the market at Hall about one o'clock, but owing to the crowd, which such an extraordinary occurrence had brought together, he was obliged to defer the sale, and take her away, about 4 o'clock. However, he again brought her out, and she was sold for twenty guineas, and delivered with a halter, to a person named Houseman, who had lodged with them for four or five years.

Morning Post, October 10, 1808.—One of those disgraceful scenes which have of late become too common took place on Friday se'nnight at Knaresborough. Owing to some jealousy, or other family difference, a man brought his wife, equipped in the usual style, and sold her at the market cross for 6d and a quid of tobacco.—*Ibid.*

58. Our laws are based on the all-sufficiency of man's rights; society exists for men only; for women, merely in so far as they are represented by some man, are in the *mundt*, or keeping of some man. Herbert Spencer.—*Descriptive Sociology, England.*

59. A committee appointed by the National Woman Suffrage Association, at that time in convention assembled in Washington, waited upon President Cleveland with the memorial.

60. Mediæval Christian husbands imprisoned erring wives in cages so small they could neither stand upright nor lie down at full length. Mediæval Christian priests boiled living infants in osier baskets in presence of helpless heretical mothers. In mediæval times the public scourging of women was one of the amusements of the carnival; even as late as the eighteenth century English gentlemen, according to *Herbert Spencer*, made up parties of pleasure to see women whipped at Bridewell.

61. Seduction was connived at that the guardian might secure the estate of the ward.—*Ibid.*

62. The Salic law had not preference to one sex over the other—purely economical law which gave houses and lands to males who should dwell there, and consequently to whom it would be of most service.—*Spirit of the Laws.*

63. In order to give color to the usurpation (for it was nothing better), the lawyers cited an obscure article from the code of the barbarous Salians, which, as they pretended had always been the acknowledged law of the French monarchy. . . . Since that time the Salic law, as it is called, has been regarded as an essential constitutional principle in France.—*Student's History of France*, p. 19.

64. Montesquieu.—*Spirit of the Laws.*

65. Women in England were for more than a thousand years legislated for as slaves. Crimes committed by men which could be atoned for by a fine were by women punished with burning alive. The period is not

very distant when she was distinctly legislated for as a servant, and but on a level with chattel slaves.—*Hist. Crime in England*.

66. *American Law*, 1829.

67. Through the influence of *Governor M'nutt*, who instituted many reforms.

68. There was no distinction between offenses against the church on one hand, and offenses against the state or individual on the other. Cases of theft and sorcery, like those of witchcraft, could be tried in the church. From the position of the clergy as lawgivers, it follows not only that the secular laws had the sanction of religion, but that religious observance were enforced by the secular arm.

69. From 499 to 1066. Herbert Spencer.—*Descriptive Sociology*.

70. To women were still applied those punishments, which had been instituted by the men whose practice it was to buy their wives and sell their daughters. Pike.—*Hist. Crime in Eng.*

71. Bracton.—*De Legibus Angliæ* I., 479.

72. The reformation altered, but did not better the condition of woman. Socially it rescued her from the priest to make her the chattel of the husband, and doctrinally it expunged her altogether. Martin Luther declared that the two sacred books, which especially point to woman as the agent of man's final redemption—the books of Esther and Revelations—that in "so far as I esteem them, it would be no loss if they were thrown into the river."

73. "The forefathers of *Benjamin Franklin* used a Bible kept fastened under the seat of a four-legged stool, the leaves held in place by pack-threads. When the family assembled to hear it read, one of the number was posted as sentinel some distance from the house to give warning of any stranger's approach, in which case the stool was hurriedly replaced upon its legs, and someone seated upon it for more effectual concealment of the book."

74. Herbert Spencer.—*Descriptive Sociology, England*.

75. The *English Women's Suffrage Journal*, November, 1886, reported: "Mrs. ——— rose to move a resolution. After reading a memorial, she said: 'Now, when I was asked to add a few words of support to the memorial I have just read, my first feeling was that I was very far from the right person to do so, inasmuch as being a married woman—and therefore disqualified—and rightly disqualified,'" etc.

76. The coverture of a woman disables her from making contracts to the prejudice of herself or her husband without his allowance or confirmation.

77. "I have arrived at conclusions which I keep to myself as yet, and only utter as Greek *phogagta sunetotsi*, the principle of which is, that there will never be a good world for women till the last monk, and therewith the last remnant of the monastic idea of, and legislation for, woman, i.e. the Canon Law is civilized off the face of the earth. Meanwhile all the most pure and high-minded women in England and Europe have been brought up under the shadows of the Canon Law, and have accepted it with their usual divine self-sacrifice, as their destiny by law of God, and nature, and consider their own womanhood outraged when it, their tyrant, is meddled with." Canon Charles Kingsley.—*Letter to John Stuart Mill,* June 17, 1849, in *Life and Letters.*

78. Dowers were first introduced into England by the Danish king, Cnut or Canute, and into Denmark by Swein, father of Canute, who bestowed it upon Danish ladies in grateful acknowledgment of their having parted with their jewels to ransom him from the Vandals. For account of Dowers, see *History of Dowers;* Grote.—*History of Greece* 2, 112–13; Alexander.—*History of Women*; Lord Kames.—*Sketch of the History of Man; Histoire des Morales des Femmes.* In Denmark, King Sweinn Forkbeard was the first to give woman a share in her parents' property. Saxo Grammaticus says, "The king was taken prisoner by the Vinds who demanded so large a sum of money for his ransom, the men of Denmark would not pay it, so their king remained a prisoner. The women of Denmark sold their ornaments and ransomed him. From gratitude the king decreed that afterwards daughters should inherit one-third of their father's property." *Journal of Jurisprudence.* One especial right belonged to wives among the Northmen; this was the custody of her husband's keys, and if he refused them the wife could compel him by law to give her their possession. These were the keys of the storeroom, chest, and cupboard.

79. The law of dower was less favorable to the wife in the thirteenth century than it became later.

80. See, *Reeves*, p. 156.

81. Sheldon Amos.—*Science of Law.*

82. *History of Women,* 1779.

83. Higgins says the word *widow* comes from Vidya, to know.

84. *Ancient Laws of Ireland, Sanchus Mor,* pp. 347–51.

85. At a time when the English law of husband and wife, which now for three centuries has been substituted for the Irish law in this country, has been condemned by a committee of the House of Com-

mons as unjust towards the wife, and when the most advanced of modern thinkers are trying to devise some plan by which wives may be placed in a position more nearly approaching to equality with the husband, it is interesting to discover in the much despised laws of the ancient Irish, the recognition of the principle on which efforts are being made to base our legislation on this subject. Preface to *Sanchus Mor*, Vol. 2.

86. Vol. 3, p. 35.—*Ibid.*

87. *Rambles and Studies in Old South Wales.*—Wirt Sikes.

88. The three peculiars of a woman are her cowyll, her gowyn, and her sarand; the reason these three are called three peculiars is because they are the three properties of a woman and cannot be taken from her for any cause; her cowyll is what she receives for her maidenhood; her sarand is for every beating given her by her husband, except for three things; and those three for which she may be beaten are, for giving anything she ought not to give; for being detected with another man in a covert; and for wishing drivel on her husband's beard; and if for being found with another man he chastises her, he is not to have any satisfaction beside that, for there ought not to be both satisfaction and vengeance for the same crime; her gowyn is, if she detect her husband with another woman, let him pay her six score pence for the first offense, for the second, one pound; if she detect him a third time she can separate from him without leaving anything that belongs to her. *Aneurin Owen*, Professor of Welsh Law.

89. The law enacts that she ought not to suffer loss on account of the man, since she received no benefit from him, and therefore he is to rear the child. *Ancient Laws and Institutions of Wales.*

90. The Welsh laws of Howell the Good were enacted by four laics and two clerks who were summoned lest the laws should ordain anything contrary to scripture. *Ibid.*

91. A woman cannot be admitted as surety or as a witness concerning man. *Ibid.*

92. *Civil Code*, Art. 340.

93. *The Woman Question in Europe.*—T. Stanton. This law of France differs greatly from the old Welsh pre-christian law, which threw the support of an illegitimate child upon the father. Notwithstanding the responsibility thus thrown upon her, a French proverb declares that "the most reasonable woman never attains the sense of a boy of fourteen."

94. It was no mere accident that the French language only possessed one word, *l'homme*, for man, and human being. French law only recognizes man as a human being.—*August Bebel.*

95. Legouvè.—*History of Morals of Women.*

96. The baby was born in the next house, and of course I was interested. How can one not be interested when one of these little angels becomes imprisoned in the earth form and begins a career that makes one tremble to think of? Meeting the father a few hours later I ask the customary question.

"Another no account girl to be supported," he said gloomily, and passed on.—*Woman's World.* A father of experience spoke differently: "My gals never forget me. They married and went away to their own homes: and though they were none of them well-to-do, yet not one of them ever saw the time she wouldn't steal a dollar from her husband to give to father or mother; but it isn't so with the boys. They never knew they owed me anything; they never put their hands in their pockets for me: they never laid awake o' nights thinking how to scrimp household expenses to get me or mother a present like the gals did. And yet when I was araisin' 'em I thought one boy was worth a dozen gals."

97. See *Scandinavian Jurisprudence.*

98. A story is told by an American traveller, of a party met upon the cars, the mother a delicate little personage, the father stout and strong. Upon leaving the train he walked off incommoded by a single traveling impedimenta, while the wife was almost hidden under the pack she was carrying. With indignation the American asked, "Why do you not let the man take some of these things?" "What! and he the father of a family?" was the surprised answer.

99. It is unnecessary to let the whole many-colored map of German common law pass in review; a few specimens will suffice. According to German common law woman is everywhere in the position of a minor with regard to man; her husband is her lord and master, to whom she owes obedience in marriage. If she be disobedient, Prussian law allows a husband of "low estate" to inflict moderate bodily chastisement. As no provision is made for the number or severity of the blows, the amount of such chastisement is left to the sovereign discretion of the man. In the communal law of Hamburg the regulation runs as follows: "The moderate chastisement of a wife by her husband is just and permissible." Similar enactments exist in many parts of Germany. The Prussian common law further decrees that the husband can determine the length of time during which a woman must suckle her child. All decisions with regard to the children rest with the father. When he dies the wife is everywhere under the obligation of accepting a guardian for the children; she is

decided to be underage, and incapable of conducting the education of children alone, even when their means of support are derived entirely from her property or her labor. Her fortune is managed by her husband and in cases of bankruptcy is regarded in most states as his and disposed of accordingly, unless a special contract has been made before marriage. When landed property is entailed on the eldest child, a daughter has no rights, as long as husband or brothers are alive; she cannot succeed unless she has no brothers or has lost them by death. She cannot exercise the political rights which are as a rule connected with landed property, unless in some exceptional cases, as for instance in Saxony, where communal regulations in the country allow her to vote, but deny her the right of being elected. But even this right is transferred to her husband if she marry. In most states she is not free to conclude agreements without the consent of her husband, unless she be engaged in business on her own account, which recent legislation permits her to do. She is excluded from every kind of public activity. The Prussian law concerning societies, forbids schoolboys and apprentices under eighteen, and women to take part in political associations and public meetings. Until within the last few years women were forbidden by various German codes to attend the public law courts as listeners. If a woman becomes pregnant of an illegitimate child she has no claim on support if she accepted any present from the father at the time of their intimacy. If a woman is divorced from her husband, she continues to bear his name in eternal memory of him, unless she happens to marry again.

August Bebel.—*Women in the Past, Present and Future.*

100. Who, indeed, would not have been received by the queen.

101. A German girl continues to be a maid-of-all-work until circumstances elevate her to a higher position. She becomes a mother, and this opens a fresh career to her as an *amme* or wet nurse. Her lines thenceforward fall in pleasant places. An *amme* is a person of consideration. No disgrace or loss of character is attached to the irregularity of conduct which often is the origin of her promotion to a higher sphere. Her wages are quadrupled; her fare by comparison is sumptuous; she can never be scolded; she is called upon to fulfill but one duty. The occupation is so much more remunerative than ordinary service that one can scarcely be surprised if plenty of women are found ready and willing to follow the trade. With them the child is only a means to an end. Marriage among the lower orders in Germany is cumbered about with so many restrictions and conditions, that it has come to be looked upon as almost an impossibility.

102. When *Miss Aarta Hansteen*, a Norwegian lady, announced her purpose of lecturing on woman's natural equality with man, she met little or no support, the church strenuously opposing on ground of woman's original curse.

103. Translated into English under title of "Nora," by *Miss Frances Lord*.

104. So profound was its effect that visiting invitations were coupled with the request not to speak of the work.

105. *Marian Brown Shipley*, an American lady, long a resident of Sweden and thoroughly conversant with its literature and tone of thought, said of it, "A more glorious thing has not been done in Sweden for centuries. Strindberg has defied church and state, striking both to their foundations with his merciless satire, and rallied the Swedish people at a single stroke."

106. Bjornsen said, "The confiscating of August Strindberg's book *Giftas*, is the greatest literary scandal in the North in my time. It is worse than when one wished to put me in the house of correction on account of the King; or thrust out Ibsen from the society of honorable people for *gjengungerd* (Ghosts)."

107. March 30, 1882.

108. *Russian Revolt.*

109. A Russian writer of the seventeenth century said: "As Eve did wrong, so the whole race of women become sinful and the cause of evil."

110. She was spoken of as a "Vanity itself," "A storm in the home," "A flood that swells everything," "A serpent nourished in the bosom," "A spear penetrating the heart," "A constantly flying arrow."

111. *Rural Life in Russia.—The Nineteenth Century.*

112. See chap. 4, p. 161.

113. I myself am the happy possessor of a little rude wooden bas-relief, framed and glazed, of two saints, whose names I have ungratefully forgotten, to whom if you pray as you go out to commit a crime, however heinous, you take your pardon with you.—*Rural Life in Russia.*

114. See chap. 4, p. 182.

115. Reported by *Mrs. Livermore*.

116. *Leavenworth Standard*, Dec. 21, 1866.

117. Under common law a woman is classified with lunatics, idiots, infants and minors.

CHAPTER VII

POLYGAMY

It is of indisputed historic record that both the Christian Church and the Christian State in different centuries and under a number of differing circumstances gave their influence in favor of polygamy. The Roman emperor, Valentinian I, in the fourth century, authorized christians to take two wives; in the eighth century the great Charlemagne holding power over both church and state in his own person practiced polygamy, having six, or according to some authorities, nine wives. With the Reformation this system entered Protestantism. As the first synod in North America was called for the purpose of trying a woman for heresy, so the first synod of the reformation was assembled for the purpose of sustaining polygamy, thus further debasing woman in the marital relation. The great German reformer, Luther, although perhaps himself free from the lasciviousness of the old priesthood was not strictly monogamic in principle. When applied to by Philip, Landgrave, of Hesse Cassel, for permission to marry a second wife while his first wife, Margaret of Savoy, was still living, he called together a synod of six of the principal reformers—Melancthon and Bucer among them—who in joint consultation decided "that as the Bible nowhere condemns polygamy, and as it has been invariably practiced by the highest dignitaries of the church," such marriage was legitimate, and the required permission was given. Luther himself with both the Old and the New Testaments in hand, saying, "I confess for my part that if a man wishes to marry two or more wives, I cannot forbid him, nor is his conduct repugnant to the Holy Scriptures." Thus we have the degrading proof that the doctrine of polygamy was brought into reformation by its earliest promoters under assertion that it was not inconsistent with the Bible or the principles of the Gospel. The whole course of Luther during the reformation proved his disbelief in the equality of woman with man; when he left the Catholic church he took with him the old theory of her created subordination. It was his maxim that "No gown or garment worse becomes a woman than that she will be wise," thus giving the weight of his influence against woman's intellectual freedom and independent thought. Although he opposed monastic life, the home for woman under the reformation was governed by many of its rules.

First: She was to be under obedience to man as head of the house.

Second: She was to be constantly employed for his benefit.

Third: Her society was strictly chosen for her by this master and head.

Fourth: This "head" was a general-father confessor, to whom she was held accountable in word and deed.

Fifth: Neither genius nor talent could free her from his control without his consent.

Luther's views regarding polygamy have been endorsed and sanctioned since that period by men eminent in church and state. Lord Seldon, known as "The Light of England" in the seventeenth century, published a work under title of *Uxor Haebraica* for the purpose of proving that polygamy was permitted to the Hebrews. His arguments were accepted by the church as indisputable. Bishop Burnet, who while holding the great Protestant Episcopal See of Sailsbury, so successfully opposed the plan inaugurated by Queen Anne for the establishment of a woman's college in England, added to his infamy by writing a tract entitled "Is a Plurality of Wives in any case Lawful under the Gospel." This question he answered in the affirmative sustaining the rightfulness of polygamy under the Christian dispensation. Quoting the words of Christ upon divorce, he said:

> We must not by a consequence condemn a plurality of wives since it seems not to have fallen within the scope of what our Lord does there disapprove. Therefore I see nothing so strong against a plurality of wives as to balance the great and visible imminent hazards that hang over so many thousands if it be not allowed.

The famous Puritan Poet of England, John Milton, known in the University as "The Lady of Christ College," writing upon "The Special Government of Man" says:

> I have not said the marriage of one man with one woman lest I should by implication charge the "holy patriarchs and pillars of our faith, Abraham and others who had more than one wife, at the same time, with habitual sin; and lest I should be forced to exclude from the sanctuary of God as spurious, the whole offspring which sprang from them, yea, the whole of the sons of Israel, for whom the sanctuary itself was made. For it is said in Deuteronomy (xxii. 2), "A bastard shall not enter into the congregation of Jehovah even to the tenth generation." Either, therefore polygamy is a true marriage, or all children born in that state are spurious, which would include the whole race of Jacob, the twelve tribes chosen by God. But as such an assertion would be absurd in the extreme, not to say impious, and as it is the height of injustice as well as an example of the most dangerous tendency in religion, to account as sins what is not such in reality it appears to me that so far from the question

respecting the lawfulness of polygamy being trivial, it is of the highest importance that it should be decided. Not a trace appears of the interdiction of polygamy throughout the whole law, not even in any of the prophets.

The *Paradise Lost* of Milton, is responsible among English-speaking people for many existing views that are inimical to woman, and while his essays upon liberty have been of general beneficial influence upon the world, his particular teachings in regard to woman have seriously injured civilization. This man of polygamous beliefs, this tyrant over his own household who could not gain the love of either wives—of whom he had three—or of daughters, did much to popularize the idea of woman's subordination to man. "He for God; she for God in him" as expressed by the lips of Eve and so often quoted as proclaiming the true relationship between husband and wife in the line, "God thy law; thou mine." While the record of Milton's life shows him to have been an intolerable domestic tyrant, yet for the wife who could not live with him, the daughters whom social conditions and lack of education deprived of the necessary means for their support, thus compelling them to remain his victims looking forward to his death as their only means of release, the world has as yet exhibited but little sympathy. His genius, undisputed as its record must be in many directions, has made his views of overpowering influence upon the world since his day. But above all, more than all, that created and sustained this influence were his views as to the polygamous rights of man, his depictment of Eve as looking upward to Adam as her God, and his general maintainance of the teaching of the church in regard to woman. Although it has been affirmed that after his blindness he dictated his great epic to his daughter and a Scotch artist has painted a scene (a picture owned by the Lenox Library), yet this is one of the myths men call history and amuse themselves in believing. Voltaire declared history to be only a parcel of tricks we play with the dead; and this tale of blind Milton dictating *Paradise Lost* to his daughters is a trick designed to play upon our sympathies. Old Dr. Johnson is authority for the statement that Milton would not allow his daughters to learn to write and it is quite certain that he did not permit them a knowledge of any language except the English, saying "one tongue is enough for a woman." Between Milton and his family it is known there was tyranny upon one side, hatred upon the other.[1]

The number of eminent Protestants both lay and clerical who have sanctioned polygamy has not been small. In the sixteenth century a former Capuchin monk, a general of that order who had been converted to the Protestant faith, published a work entitled "Dialogues in favor of Polygamy." In the latter part of the seventeenth century, John Lyser, another divine of the reformed church strongly defended it in a work entitled "Polygamia Triumphatrix" or the triumphant defense of polygamy. Rev. Dr. Madden, still another Protestant divine, in a treatise called "Thalypthora," maintained that Paul's injunction that bishops should be the husbands of one wife, signified that laymen were permitted to marry more than one. The scholarly William Ellery Channing could find no prohibition of polygamy in the New Testament. In his "Remarks on the Character and Writings of John Milton," he says, "We believe it to be an indisputable fact, that although Christianity was first preached in Asia which had been from the earliest days the seat of polygamy, the apostles never denounced it as a crime and never required their converts to put away all wives but one. No express prohibition of polygamy is found in the New Testament." That eminent American divine, Henry Ward Beecher, the influence of whose opinions over all classes was for many years so great as to constitute him a veritable Protestant pope in the United States, a few years before his death was selected to reply at a New England dinner to a toast upon the Mormon question, the subject of polygamy then being under discussion by Congress. He not only deprecated the use of force in its suppression, but quoted Milton in seeming approval. We can therefore consistently rank Mr. Beecher as among the number of Protestant divines who believed there was scriptural warrant for this degradation of woman.

But it is not alone to the action of Christian monarchs or the opinion of jurists and ministers that we must solely look, but also to the action of the church as a body during different periods of its history. In the year 1846, the question of polygamy came up before the American Board of Commissioners for Foreign Missions in the United States. Through a committee of which the eminent Chancellor Walworth, of New York, was chairman, this body reported against instructing missionaries to exclude polygamists from the church. This report was adopted without a dissenting voice.[2] This discussion brought out some interesting facts having especial bearing upon the views of those churches which numbered polygamists among their communicants. It was shown that the secretaries of the board appeared to consider the existence of polygamy in the churches as so entirely a frivolous question that even after it was especially brought to their notice they forbore to make inquiries, and even when polygamists had actually been admitted into the Mission churches, no taint of disapproval had been made by the Prudential Committee.[3] The whole subject was left to the decision of the missionaries themselves, one of whom published his views in the *Boston Recorder*. After prevising that the Bible was their rule of faith, he asks:

> Is it not evident from Paul's instruction respecting the qualifications of a bishop, viz., that he "should be the husband of one wife" that polygamy was permited in the primitive Church under the apostles, and that too in circumstances precisely similar to those in which churches are gathered among the heathen at the present day. If so, why should a different standard be set up than that set up by the apostles?

That polygamy is not regarded as contrary to the principles of Christianity was again most forcibly shown in its endorsement by missionaries located in those countries where this custom prevails. One of the most notable instances of recent church action in recognizing polygamy as sustained by Christianity, occurred a few years since in Calcutta during a Conference upon the question. This body was convened by the missionaries of England and America located in India. Its immediate cause was the application of Indian converts, the husbands of several wives, for admission to the church. A missionary conference of the several Christian denominations was therefore called for the purpose of deciding upon this grave request. It included representatives of the Episcopal, Baptist, Presbyterian and Congregationalist churches. Taking the Bible as authority full consideration was given to the subject. Quotations from that "holy book" proved to the satisfaction of the conference that not alone did the Bible favor polygamy, but that God himself endorsed, regulated and sustained the institution.

In addition it was declared that these converted polygamists "had given credible evidence of their personal piety." The conference therefore unanimously rendered favorable decision for retention of the polygamous members within the respective churches to which they belonged, upon the ground that as both the Jews and the early Christians had practiced polygamy, it was allowable to the new converts.

If a convert before becoming a Christian has married more wives than one, in accordance with the practice of the Jewish and primitive Christian churches, he shall be permitted to keep them all.

Yet apparently as a concession to the somewhat altruistic civilization of the present age, which outside of the church does not look upon polygamous marriages with favor, such persons were declared ineligible to any office in the church. Rev. David O. Allen, D.D., missionary of the American Board in India for twenty-five years and from whose report of the action of the missionary conference the above facts were gained, said:

> If polygamy was unlawful, then Leah was the only wife of Jacob and none but her children were legitimate. Rachel as well as Bilhah and Zilpah were merely mistresses and their children, six in number, were bastards, the offspring of adulterous connection. And yet there is no intimation of any such views and feelings in Laban's family, or in Jacob's family or in Jewish history. Bilhah and Zilpah are called Jacob's wives, (Genesis xxxvii: 2.). God honored the sons of Rachael, Bilhah and Zilpah equally with the sons of Leah, made them patriarchs of seven of the tribes of the nation and gave them equal inheritances in Canaan.

Thus the endorsement of polygamy as not contrary to the Bible, or to Christianity, is shown by action of Christian churches both in the United States and India within the present century; and we can readily understand why a gentleman from the New England states traveling in Utah said: "Mormonism seems a very devout sect of the Christian church, differing but little from the great body of Christian people."[4] Nor is this judgment at all strange as we find polygamy endorsed by the majority of Christian sects. Nor can we be surprised that the Mormons of Utah and the adjoining states should look upon the opposition of the United States to their practice of polygamy, as an unjust interference with an established custom of the Christian church, recognized and indorsed through the ages, as not alone part of the Jewish and early christian practice, but permitted as allowable at the present day. President Eliot, of Harvard, speaking in Salt Lake City, compared the Mormons to the Puritans, thus throwing the weight of his statement as to the harmony between Mormonism and other christian sects.

The Rochester, N.Y., *Herald*, in forgetfulness of early puritan history, says, "It would be interesting to know from what point of view President Eliot took his observation, and refers to 'Mormon Contempt and debasement of Womanhood; Mormon discouragement of intelligence and education among its dupes and victims, etc.'" The *Herald* has apparently forgotten the trial of women for heresy by the Puritans; their imprisonment, heavily ironed in airless jails, for the crime of religious free thought; the flogging of naked women on Boston Common by the Puritans for free speech and their being executed as witches, in the Puritan colony of Massachusetts. The *Herald* has apparently forgotten that although the first money given for the foundation of Harvard itself was by a woman, her sex, "dupe and victim," is still denied the full advantage of education in that institution. It forgets that although the first plot of ground for a free school in the Puritan colony of Massachusetts was given by a woman, girls were denied education even in common schools until it became necessary to permit their attendance during the summer months while the

boys were engaged in fishing, in order to retain possession of
school monies. The *Herald* seems unaware of the vigorous letter
of Mrs. [Abigail] Adams, wife of the second president of the
United States, to her husband, John Adams, when he was a
member of the first Congress, in reference to the need of education for women. Should the *Herald* pursue its investigations still
further, it will find the Puritans connected with the most serious
"crimes" against humanity; it will discover priestly and governmental "usurpation," Puritan "fanaticism and bigotry"; even
Puritan "disloyalty." When President Eliott favorably compared
the Christian Puritans and the Christian Mormons, he spoke both
as a close reader of Puritan history and a close observer of
Mormon history; his declaration of their similarity to each other
cannot be denied by the candid historian. Building upon the
same common foundation, acknowledging the same common
origin, the doctrines of the two systems necessarily bear close
resemblance to each other.[5] Under the Christian theory regarding
woman, her origin and her duties, it should not be regarded as at
all strange that polygamy should find defenders in the christian
world. Nor is it to be looked upon as at all as surprising that the
Mormons, the most recent Protestant sect, should teach polygamy
as a divinely organized institution, nor that their arguments in its
favor should be drawn from the Bible and not from the book of
Mormon. That polygamy was not an original Mormon tenet is
well known; it was derived from a professed revelation to Joseph
Smith, sustained by biblical authority. The polygamous
Mahommedans regard Christ as a prophet, the same as the Mormons respect the authority of the Bible. The Mormon marriage
formula directs the man to look to God, but enjoins the woman
to look toward her husband as God, rendering him the same
unquestioning obedience that has been demanded from all Christian wives through the ages; the priest, as customary with the
hierarchal class, declaring himself endowed with an authority
from on high to bind or to loose on earth, seals the union of the
pair for time and eternity. Although the marriage ceremony of
the Mormon church is more complex, in many respects it paral-

lels that of the Presbyterians of Scotland during the early day of
the Reformation, authority for woman's degradation in each case
being derived from the Bible, the language in each instance being
unfit for publication.[6]

An epistle of the First Presidency to the Church of Jesus
Christ of Latter Day Saints, in General Conference, said:

> The Gospel of the Son of God, brings life and immortality to
> light. "We believe in Jerusalems, such as the one which John
> saw when banished as a slave to the Isle of Patmos because of
> his religion, where promises made to Abraham, Isaac and Jacob
> are to be fulfilled; "which had a wall great and high, and had
> twelve gates, and at the gates twelve angels—and the twelve
> gates were twelve pearls; every several gate was one pearl." Its
> walls were of jasper, its streets and the city were pure gold. The
> foundations of the wall were garnished with all manner of pre-
> cious stones, and the glory of God did lighten it, "and the
> Lamb is the light thereof." Its pearly gates had written upon
> them the names of the twelve tribes of the children of Israel
> and the foundations of its walls, "the names of the Twelve
> Apostles of the Lamb." "The throne of God and of the Lamb
> shall be in it, and His servants shall serve Him; and they shall
> see His face; and His name shall be in their foreheads. The
> porters of its gates were angels and its light the glory of God."
> What was written on those pearly gates? The names of the
> twelve tribes of Israel. Who was Israel? Jacob. From whom did
> the twelve tribes descend? From Jacob. What were their names?
> The names of the sons of Jacob, which he had by four wives.
> Jacob, then, was a polygamist? Yes; he was one of those barbar-
> ians of which the judge of the Third Judicial District says:
> "These practices might have been proper in a barbarous and
> primitive time—in crude times—but they won't do now. Civ-
> ilization has thrown them away. It won't do to gather up these
> old customs and practices out of the by-gone barbarism and
> by-gone ages, and attempt to palm them upon a free and intel-
> ligent and civilized people in these days."
>
> How free the people are in Utah today needs no discus-
> sion. If the judge cannot stand these things it would seem God

and the Lamb can, for He is the light of the city, on the gates
of which are written the names of twelve men, the sons of one
man by four women—a polygamist. Had Jacob lived now, the
judges would have sent spies, spotters and deputy marshals after
him, and if caught would have sent him to the penitentiary.

This epistle boldly challenges christian belief in the New
Jerusalem as based upon polygamy; upon its gates the names of
twelve polygamous children are inscribed, sons of one man, children of four mothers, two wives and two concubines. Of
Solomon, this epistle could likewise have spoken, whom the Bible
represents as the wisest man that lived; his wives numbering three
hundred, his concubines seven hundred. Nor are Jacob and
Solomon two isolated instances of Jewish polygamy; Mormons, in
common with the lay and clerical authorities previously referred
to, find abundant proof for their sanction of polygamy both in the
revelations of the Old and the New Testaments. But each human
being entering the world is a revelation to himself, to herself, and
the revelation inherently abiding in all women, declares against
such degradation of herself and her sex.

Brigham Young, the first Mormon president, husband of
nineteen wives, father of forty-two children, possessed great natural fascination; was a man of wonderful magnetism. Of him a
daughter said: "his slightest touch was a caress." His seventh wife,
an elegant and fashionable woman, was said by her daughter to
worship the ground that he walked upon and never to have been
herself since his death. From this favorite daughter of Young who
after his death apostacized from the Mormon religion, much has
been learned in regard to the real feeling of these polygamous
wives toward each other, which she characterized as "an outward
semblance of good will, but in reality a condition of deadly
hatred." Such outward semblance of good will, such real condition of deadly hatred is the result of all forms of religion which
subjugate the many to the caprice of the few, even though done
under assumption of divine authority. That envy, jealousy and
hatred should be among the dire results of woman's religious

degradation, cannot be a subject of surprise to the student of human nature; and it is supreme proof of the bondage of the human will under fancied authority from God, that such minds as those of Luther, Milton, Seldon, Beecher, Walworth and others like them should uphold a system so degrading in character alike to the men and the women who practice it. Young's daughter Dora with five of her sisters were expelled a few years since from the Mormon church for having gone to law with certain of the Mormon brethren who attempted to rob them of their patrimony. The elders realizing the injury these women might do for the church, sent a couple of teachers to interview Dora, invoking her father's name to influence her dropping the suit[7] and return to the church. Dora had been aroused by a sense of the iniquity of the church, through hearing its elders declare upon oath that they knew nothing of polygamous marriage ceremonies being performed, while the same day of this denial no less than fourteen such marriages had taken place at the Endowment House. Referring to the conscientious belief held by many women of the necessity of polygamous marriage in order to secure the sanctification requisite for their salvation, Dora said:

> Since my eyes have been opened I sometimes ask myself how I could ever possibly have regarded the horrible and licentious practices of which I was aware, and the terrible things I have witnessed with anything but horror? And yet I was brought up to consider these things right and I thought nothing about them—just as I suppose children brought up where human sacrifices are offered, learn to regard such sacrifice as right and to look upon them with indifference.

Experience taught Dora that the natural character of the human mind soon accomodates itself to circumstances, becomes in accord with its environment, and regards as right whatever law or custom teaches is right. This, called the conservative tendency of the human mind, is merely the result of habitude of thought induced by authoritative teaching. Both church and state have availed themselves of the influence of authoritative custom for the perpetuation of power. In this way despotism has gained its chief victories. The beliefs to which persons have been habituated from childhood are, without investigation, deemed truths by the majority of the world. No step so great in its far-reaching results as that of independent thought; none so greatly feared by priestly and civil power and among women during the Christian ages, none has met with such swift rebuke, no sin has been characterized as its equal in malignancy. Therefore while the world has possessed full knowledge of man's opinions regarding polygamy, not until the present century and in the United States have the views of women been attainable. Until the present age there has been no escape from bondage for the polygamous wife, no opportunity for learning its effects upon her own inner self. From the daughter of its chief prophet, the man whose fame in connection with polygamy has gone throughout the world, we have learned something of its evils as seen and felt by woman. Yet other and still stronger testimony is not lacking. A private letter written in Salt Lake City a few years since, published in the *Boston Transcript* under head of "The Silent Woes of Mormonism," depicts one phase in its influence upon the unborn.

> A few years ago an educated young journalist came to Salt Lake City from Europe with his young wife. Both became sincere believers in Mormonism. Then strong pressure was brought to bear by the priesthood upon the husband to force him into polygamy. The wife finding opposition in vain, at last gave her nominal consent. A second bride was brought into the house. In a short time the first wife became a mother, but the infant never cried aloud. It came voiceless into the world. But it wept in secret all the time. Sleeping or waking the tears flowed from its closed eyes, and in a few weeks it died. The mother said that it died of a broken heart. Every day of its life it shed the tears that its mother had repressed before its birth.

The experience of Caroline Owens, whose suit for bigamy against her polygamous husband, John D. Miles, appealed from the Supreme Court of Utah to the Supreme Court of the United

States—a suit implicating Delegate Cannon, of the Congress of the United States, in its tale of wrong, presents another phase. Miss Owens was an English girl acquainted with Miles from her childhood. He had emigrated to Utah, but in England on a visit he urged her to return with him, promising her marriage when they reached Salt Lake City. She questioned him as to polygamy. He replied that a few old men were allowed more than one wife, but that young men like himself had but one, although he spoke of one Emily Spencer who had expressed affection for him but whom he had no intention of marrying. Upon reaching Salt Lake City, Miss Owens staid at the house of United States Delegate George Q. Cannon, where but one wife resided. When the day of the wedding arrived she went through the ceremonies of the Endowment House, lasting from ten o'clock in the morning until three in the afternoon, and had been wedded to John D. Miles. She says:

> I can never tell the horrors of the next few hours. Before that day was over my love had turned to burning hated. When we started to go home, Miles told me that he had invited Emily Spencer to our wedding reception. I said if she came to the house I should leave. He replied he was now master. I went to my room and dressed for the reception, which took place at Cannon's other house, where he kept his three wives. When I went down there was a crowd there, among the rest a plain-looking girl in a calico dress, to whom I was introduced. It was Emily Spencer.
>
> I did not speak to her. After a while they wanted to dance, and asked me to play. Emily Spencer sat on a piano stool. I told her to get up. Miles came forward and said, "Sit still, Emily Spencer, my wife." I felt as though I had been shot. I said, "Your wife! then what am I?" He said, "You are both my wives." All at once my shame flashed over me. Here I was dishonored, the polygamous wife of a Mormon. I ran out of the house, bent only on escape, I did not think where; I could not do it, though, for Miles and young Cannon, a son of the delegate, ran after me and dragged me back. We had been intending to stay in that house all night, but I stole away and returned to the other house, where I had been living the three weeks since my

arrival from England. I noticed there was no key in the lock, but shot a little bolt and piled up chairs against the door. I cried myself to sleep. The next thing I knew I don't know what time it was, Miles stood in the room and was locking the door on the inside. I screamed, because Mrs. Cannon and Miles' stepmother had been living in the house with me. Miles said I need not take on, for brother Cannon had anticipated that I would make trouble and had had the house cleared of everyone else. I found out that it was so. He told me that I might as well submit; there was no law here to control the saints; there was no power on earth that would save me.

She was subjected to great brutality, again and again beaten and exhorted to bear her condition patiently as a sister to be exalted; because of her rebellious spirit she was hectored and threatened, stoned, jeered at and abused in many ways, all under pretense of religion, until after three weeks of such matrimonial life she escaped and among the "Gentiles" found rest and help. She speaks of polygamous wives as half-clad, poorly fed, toiling like serfs without hope under the chains of a religious despotism.[8] Mormon polygamy possesses the peculiar feature of tracing the system of plural marriage to the gods; a father and mother god and goddess; a grandfather and grandmother god and goddess, and thus in constantly ascending scale; from these they claim the origin of their own polygamous system. Every Mormon man, however depraved, is taught that if he lives up to the plural marriage system, upon his death he will become a god, holding power and procreating children to all eternity. But should any Mormon, however pure his life, die unmarried, he has forever lost his opportunity of becoming a god, but remains simply an angel, a servant of the polygamous gods.[9] The belief is inculcated in woman, that to her marriage is even more necessary than to man. Without marriage there is no resurrection for her, and thus believing polygamy a requisite for eternal salvation, thousands silently endure the woes of this condition. This latest christian sect, this final outgrowth of centuries of barbarous teaching, is the most determined effort against the integrity of womanhood since the days of the Jewish patriarchs. The duty of giving birth to numerous children in order to save waiting spirits and to swell the glory of the polygamous father in his after-death godship, is as thoroughly taught as when in mediæval days monk and priest preached woman's duty to constantly add numbers to the church. The late Helen H. Jackson who had thoroughly investigated the Mormon question, writing of polygamy in the *Century*, said:

> The doctrine, to be completely studied, must be considered both from the man's point of view and the woman's, the two being, for many reasons, not identical.
>
> But it is the woman's view of it, her belief and position in regard to it, which are most misrepresented and misunderstood by the world. If the truth were known, there would be few persons in whose minds would be any sentiment except profound pity for the Mormon woman—pity, moreover, intensified by admiration. There has never been a class or sect of women since the world began who have endured for religion's sake a tithe of what has been, and is, and forever must be, endured by the women of the Mormon church. It has become customary to hold them as disreputable women, light and loose, unfit to associate with the virtuous, undeserving of any esteem. Never was greater injustice committed.
>
> The two doctrines which most help the Mormon woman to endure the suffering of living in plural marriage are the doctrines of preexistence and of the eternal continuance of the patriarchal order. The mere revelation from Joseph Smith, to the effect that polygamy was to be permitted and was praiseworthy and desirable, would never, alone, have brought the Mormon women to hearty acceptance of the institution.
>
> They are taught and most unquestioningly believe that the universe is full of spirits waiting, and waiting impatiently, to be born on this earth. These spirits have already passed through one stage of discipline and probation and are to enter upon a second one here. The Rev. Edward Beecher once published a book setting forth a similar doctrine. The Mormon doctrine goes farther than Dr. Beecher's, inasmuch as it teaches that these spirits may select of their own free will where and how

they will be born into their earthly probation, and that they are, one and all, anxious to be born in the Mormon church, as the one true Zion, where alone are to be found safety and salvation. They also believe that the time is limited during which these spirits can avail themselves of this privilege of being born into Zion. They look for the return of Jesus Christ to the earth before long and for the establishment then of the millennial dispensation, after which no more of the spirits can be reborn and reclaimed. Hence the obligation resting upon every faithful Mormon woman to bring into the world, in the course of her life, as many children as possible. Not only does she thus contribute to the building up and strengthening of the true church but she rescues souls already existing and in danger of eternal death. It is easy to sneer at this doctrine as inconceivable rubbish; and, in truth, it must be admitted that it is hard to conceive of an educated mind receiving it; but it is no more absurd or unprovable than hundreds of kindred speculations and notions which have been devised, preached and passionately believed in times past. Neither has the absurdity or nonabsurdity, falsity or truth of the belief, anything to do with our judgment of its believers.

In furtherance of its plan for temporal power, the astuteness of the Mormon theocracy is shown in this doctrine of preexistent spirits[10] continually waiting birth upon the earth. This together with its other theory of the superior power and godhood in a future life, of the father of numerous children, imposes the condition of continual motherhood upon Mormon wives.

But during the christian ages this theory of woman's duty to constantly bear children in order to the upholding of the church has ever been taught. Even Philip Melancthon, the great associate of Luther in the Reformation, saying: "If a woman becomes weary of bearing children, that matters not. Let her only die from bearing, she is there to do it." So little does the church yet understand the right of woman to an existence for herself alone, that not five years have passed since a minister of the Methodist church in the state of New York, publicly declared he saw no reason for woman's creation but the bearing of children. In a lecture upon Mormonism in Boston, Prof. Conyear, of the Salt Lake City Collegiate Institute, speaking of the sufferings endured by Mormon women in order thus to secure personal salvation, said:

> Hate the system as you hate Satan, but have mercy on the people who are there in such a bondage—a bondage worse than that in which the negro in the South was ever held.

But these doctrines accepted as truth by devout Mormon women are not more degrading to them, not more injurious to civilization, than is the belief of orthodox Christian women in regard to the frailty and primal sin of her sex and the curse of her Creator upon her in consequence. To this belief she has been trained from her childhood as her mother before her and her feminine relatives for innumerable centuries, and without investigation she has accepted these doctrines of the church as true. Yet all these theories so degrading to woman are of purely human masculine origin, their object, power for man, and the subordination of woman to him in every relation of life. The eternal continuance of the patriarchal order, a doctrine of the Mormons, is paralleled among orthodox christians by the teaching of an eternal continuance of the male priestly order, woman forever excluded. The Mormon woman no more fully places herself in position of servant to her husband, whom at the Endowment House marriage ceremony, she promises to "obey," than has the orthodox christian woman through the ages, when she has promised obedience to her husband at the marriage altar. Nor is the general religious training of the two, very different. The Mormon woman is taught that her salvation depends upon polygamous marriage and her subjection to her husband in all things; the orthodox christian woman is taught that her salvation depends upon her belief that woman brought sin into the world, in punishment whereof God placed her in subjection to man; and during the ages her promise of obedience to man has been held as an integral part of the marriage ceremony. Nor did a change begin to take place until after the inauguration of the woman suffrage reform. Not until woman herself rebelled against such annihilation of her own conscience and responsibility, did a few sects in some instances omit this promise from their forms of marriage, although it still remains a portion of the Greek, Catholic and Anglican ceremony as well as of other Protestant sects. The shock of finding educated women of New England birth, members of the Mormon church as polygamous wives, is lessened upon a careful analysis of the Mormon doctrine in comparison with those of orthodox Christianity regarding women: all alike rest upon the same foundation; all teach that sin entered the world through woman; all alike darken the understanding through such false teaching. The women of the Mormon church received their training under orthodox Christianity, which laid the foundation of their self-contempt.[11] With the professed revelation of the Book of Mormon, a class of priests arose who no less positively and authoritatively asserted its doctrines to be of God than the priesthood of other divisions of christianity assert the Bible to be of God; and alike each declare themselves and their followers to be his chosen people. "By authority of the priesthood of God," has carried weight in all ages, and no greater weight among the Mormons of the present day than among Christians of all ages. Under the christian theory regarding the origin and duties of woman it is not surprising that polygamy should ever have found defenders in the christian world, nor is it at all singular that Mormonism as "the latest founded christian sect" should teach polygamy as a divinely organized institution, drawing its arguments from the Bible. Bishop Lunt of that church defending polygamy as of divine origin, said:

> God revealed to Joseph Smith the polygamous system. It is quite true that his widow declared that no such revelation was ever made, but that was because she had lost the spirit. God commanded the human race to multiply and replenish the earth. Abraham had two wives, and the Almighty honored the second one by a direct communication. Jacob had Leah and

Zilpah. David had a plurality of wives, and was a man after God's own heart. God gave him Saul's two wives, and only condemned his adulteries. Moses, Gideon and Joshua had each a plurality of wives. Solomon had wives and concubines by hundreds, though we do not believe in the concubine system. We leave that to the Gentiles. Virtue and chastity wither beneath the monogamic institution, which was borrowed from the pagan nations by the early Christians. It was prophesied that in the latter days seven women would lay hold of one man and demand to bear his name, that they might not be held in dishonor. The Protestants and Catholics assail us with very poor grace when it is remembered that the first pillars of the religion they claim to profess were men like the saints of Utah—polygamists. The fact cannot be denied. Polygamy is virtually encouraged and taught by example by the Old Testament. It may appear shocking and blasphemous to Gentiles for us to say so, but we hold that Jesus Christ himself was a polygamist. He was surrounded by women constantly, as the Scriptures attest, and those women were his polygamous wives. The vast disparity between the sexes in all settled communities is another argument in favor of polygamy, to say nothing of the disinclination among young male Gentiles to marrying. The monogamic system condemns millions of women to celibacy. A large proportion of them stray from the path of right, and these unfortunates induce millions of men to forego marriage. As I have said, virtue and chastity wither under the monogamic system.

There are no illegitimate children in Utah; there are no libertines; there are no brothels, excepting where the presence of Gentiles creates the demand for them. Even then our people do what they can to root out such places. There is a positive advantage in having more than one wife. It is impossible to find a Gentile home, where comforts and plenty prevail, in which there is only one woman. No one woman can manage a household. She must have assistance. Hence we claim that when a man marries a second wife, he actually benefits the first one, and contributes to her ease, and relieves her of a large burden of care. The duties of the household are divided between the two women, and everything moves on harmoniously and peacefully. The whole thing is a matter of education. A girl reared under the monogamic system may look with abhorrence on ours; our young women do not do so. They expect, when they marry a man, that he will some day take another wife, and they consider it quite natural that he should do so. In wealthy Gentile communities the concubine system largely takes the place of the polygamous system. Any man of intelligence, observation and travel, knows that such is the case. The fact is ignored by general consent, and little is said about it and nothing is written about it. It is not regarded as a proper subject of conversation or of publication. How much better to give lonely women a home while they are uncontaminated, and honor them with your name, and perpetually provide for them, and before the world recognize your own offspring! The polygamous system is the only natural one, and the time rapidly approaches when it will be the most conspicuous and beneficent of American institutions. It will be the grand characteristic feature of American society. Our women are contented with it—more, they are the most ardent defenders of it to be found in Utah. If the question were put to a vote tomorrow, nine-tenths of the women of Utah would vote to perpetuate polygamy.

In line with other Christian sects Mormons claim that polygamy is countenanced by the New Testament as well as by the Old. They interpret Paul's teaching in regard to bishops, while commanding them to marry one wife, as also not prohibiting them from marrying more than one; their interpretation of this passage but slightly varying from that of Rev. Mr. Madan. Rev. C. P. Lyford, of the Methodist church, long a resident of Utah, does not fail to see the degradation of the people as in proportion to the despotism of the hierarchy. He says:

It took the Methodist church forty years to get a membership of 38,000. Mormonism in forty-four years counted 250,000. It seems incredible, nevertheless it is a fact. In this brief space of time it has also been able to nullify our laws, oppose our institutions, openly perpetrate crimes, be represented in Congress, boast of the helplessness of the nation to prevent these things, and give the church supremacy over the state and the people. Bills introduced in Congress adequate to their over-throw have been year after year allowed to fall to the ground without action upon them.

Our public men can only pronounce against the crime of polygamy; the press can see only polygamy in Utah; the public mind is impressed with only the heinousness of polygamy. Back of polygamy is the tree that produces it and many kindred evils more dear to the Mormon rulers. They do not care for all the sentiment or law against this one fruit of the tree, if the tree itself is left to stand. The tree—the prolific cause of so many and so great evils in Utah, the greatest curse of the territory, the strength of Mormonism, and its impregnable wall of defense against Christianity and civilization, is that arbitrary, despotic, and absolute hierarchy known as the Mormon Priesthood.

Mr. Lyford has partial insight into the truth when he says "back of polygamy is the tree that produces it and many kindred evils"; but in defining that tree as the hierarchy—the priest-hood—he has not reached the entire truth. He does not touch the ground which supports the tree. Polygamy is but one devel-opment of the doctrine of woman's created inferiority, the con-stant tendency of which is to make her a mere slave under every form of religion extant, and of which the complex marriage of the Christian sect of Perfectionists at Oneida Community was but another logical result.

When woman interprets the Bible for herself, it will be in the interest of a higher morality, a purer home. Monogamy is woman's doctrine, as polygamy is man's. Backofen, the Swiss jurist, says that the regulation of marriage by which, in primitive times, it became possible for a woman to belong only to one man, came about by a religious reformation, wherein the women in armed conflict, obtained a victory over men.

While the greatest number of converts to the Mormon church are from among the ignorant peasantry of foreign coun-tries, still no less than in orthodox christianity do we find people of culture and education upholding its doctrines, an irrefragable proof that the power of religious despotism lies in two condi-

tions; *First*, ignorance; *Second*, fear. To fear must ever be attributed
the great victories of religious despotism. Fear of punishment
after death from which obedience to priestly teaching is believed
to free. Such slavery of the human mind has ever been the
greatest obstacle to advancing civilization. Men and women of
the Christian church not daring to use their own free thought
upon such questions, are no less bound than the savage, who
makes a hideous noise in order to frighten away the monster he
thinks trying to swallow the sun during an eclipse.

The strength of the church has ever lain in its power of producing fear and impelling belief in its assertion that the priesthood
alone can define the will of God, and that as His chosen servants
they but voice His will in every word they utter. Unhesitating
belief in this assertion has been required through the Christian
ages as evidence of a true son or daughter of the church, while the
cry of heresy, so frightful in its significance, so terrible in its punishment under the priesthood, has most effectively prevented
investigation and quenched the fire of rebellious thought.

The Mormon priesthood look toward the establishment of a
temporal kingdom in connection with their religion. They maintain that the civil power inherently belongs to the theocracy and
should supercede all other forms of government. Like the priesthood of other sects they claim divine guidance in the promulgation of their laws as proceeding from above while those of the
state emanate from man himself and consequently are not
binding upon the conscience, the church as a body ever claiming
to hold the keys of heaven and of hell; and the implicit belief
given to such assertion by tens and hundreds of thousands, has
ever been a most powerful method for subduing the reason. Its
anathemas, its excommunications, its denial of church rites in
marriage, in burial, its control of both temporal and spiritual
power, have ever made its weapons of the most formidable character. Fear of what may be met in a future life over which the
church assumes such knowledge and control, subjugation of the
reason, the fostering of ignorance, the denial of education and the
constant teaching that thought outside of the line formulated by

the church is deepest sin, has held the christian world in bondage during its centuries. Inasmuch as it is impossible for the candid thinker not to perceive that all forms of christianity are based upon the statement that woman having brought sin into the world rendered the sacrifice of a Saviour necessary, the reason of such persistent effort upon the part of the church for woman's entire subjugation becomes apparent. It is assumed by all theocracies that the church is a temporal kingdom, with supreme right to the control of all civil affairs. Every theocracy is therefore a political system seeking control of the civil government and however greatly suppressed in action, every theocracy proposes such control as its ulterior design. Early in 1890, an encyclical letter by the pope, declared the supremacy of the church over the state, commanding resistance to the authority of the state in case of its conflicting with the presentations of the Supreme Pontiff of the Catholic church. The Mormon theocracy and the Catholic here show their affinity. Nor are Protestants without similar pretensions as is proven by the action of the "National Reform Association" of the United States; whose aim is the union of church and state through an amendment to the Federal constitution, its ultimate purpose being that of theocratic control over the civil government of this country. These various bodies are parts of the "Christian Party in Politics," nor is this party of recent origin; as early as 1827–28 when composed almost entirely of Protestants, its designs upon the life of the republic were noted by the eloquent Scotch reformer, Frances Wright, during her travels, lectures and residence in this country. Mormonism and Catholicism do not more greatly threaten the civil and religious integrity of this republic than does the "National Reform Association," the theocracy of the Protestant church equally with that of the Catholic church constantly striving to incite congressional action in favor of obligatory religious teaching and seeking control of the common schools. Yet the history of the world proves that wherever tried, ecclesiastical schools have lowered the standard of education. Today the schools under control of the Mormon church in no respect equal those of adjacent territories. Under the plea of religious freedom the greatest dangers arise. While the Mormons affirm in reference to polygamy that their church laws concern Mormons alone, no less do other theocracies inculcate doctrines contrary to civil law; the catholic church, its spirit today[12] the same as during past ages, making civil marriage and the public school system its present objective points of opposition to the state;[13] while the general body of protestant churches more openly than the catholic churches proclaim their intention not alone to control secular education, marriage and divorce, but to unite church and state through a change in the fundamental law of the United States. A somewhat widespread fear exists in regard to the encroachment of Catholicism upon civil liberty. The most potent danger lies elsewhere, the most potent because the least perceived; the most potent because arising from a body whom the masses of native Americans, through heredity and training, look upon as supporters and defenders of both civil and religious liberty—the priesthood of the orthodox Protestant churches. Mormonism does not so fully threaten civil and religious liberty; catholicism is not making greater encroachments upon them than are the great body of the protestant clergy, under the name and the work of the "National Reform Association."

The people of the United States with careless security in the power of the principles of freedom upon which the government is based, fail to note the theocratic encroachment everywhere threatened.[14] The very nature of sacerdotalism professing as it everywhere does, to hold authority of a supernatural character, unfailingly creates a claim of supremacy over civil government. President John Taylor, of the Mormon church, a few years since openly asserted these claims, saying: "We are independent of newspapers, independent of kings, independent of governments." But it is not the Mormon priesthood alone that declares its independence of secular governments. This is the same spirit that seen through the ages of christianity has been so plainly shown by Catholicism since the temporal power in Italy has fallen into the hands of a secular monarch, and that is now so fully a part of Protestant effort. Under the overwhelming amount of biblical proof quoted in its favor by the most eminent legal and clerical minds of the christian church we must admit the doctrine of polygamy to be a component part of christianity. Although like the fagot and the stake, under the light of advancing civilization, it has somewhat fallen into disrepute with the majority of men and women, yet its renewal as an underlying principle of a new christian sect, need not be a subject of astonishment. The pulpit, the bar, and legislative halls are still under the control of man and these institutions still express the form of civilization that is due to his teachings. But as neither moral nor intellectual education is of value unless founded upon a material basis, the world now beginning to see that Wall Street, and the Bourse, with their fingers upon the business of the world, are fast becoming of greater importance in determining the future character of civilization than St. Peters, the Kremlin, or Westminster Abbey. Wendell Phillips once declared that the advance of civilization was not dependent upon either the pulpit or the press but upon commerce, and a careful study of the inventions and industries of the age, confirm this statement. Material needs, underlying all others, direct the tenor of modern civilization. But commerce of itself is not alone responsible. Within the past thirty years a new element has widely entered into the business of the world, and even the most careless observer can but in many ways note the changing customs and habits of business life, and that under this change, a new form of civilization is dawning upon the world. Woman once so carefully excluded is now everywhere seen. At the counter, behind the cashier's desk, as buyer, as business manager, and in many instances as employer, conducting business for herself. Every kind of industry is opening to her, from that of government employee at Washington with the financial interests of the nation in her grasp, to that of electrical business, woman is everywhere found. The commerce of the world is rapidly changing hands and the next quarter of a century will find woman in its full control. But few persons foresee the ultimate result of this change. With a new class at the helm, commerce will give new ideas to the world. If christianity survive the shock of coming events, it will present a different aspect within the next fifty years and its teachings in regard to woman will be totally unlike those of past ages. As woman comes into new relations with the great institutions of the world, she will cease to believe herself inferior and subordinate to man. Polygamy and all kindred degradations of her sex will become things of the past, and taking her rightful place in church and state she will open a new civilization to the world.

Notes

1. Milton's oriental views of the function of women led him not only to neglect but to prevent the education of his daughters. They were sent to no school at all, but were handed over to a schoolmistress in the house. He would not allow them to learn any language, saying with a sneer that "for a woman one tongue is enough." The miseries however that follow the selfish sacrifice of others is so sure to strike, that there needs no future world of punishment to adjust the balance. The time came when Milton would have given worlds that his daughters had learned the tongues. He was blind and could only get at his precious book—could only give expression to his precious verses through the eyes and hands of others. Whose hands and whose eyes so proper for this as his daughters? He proceeded to train them to read to him, parrot-like, in five or six languages which he (the schoolmaster) could at one time have easily taught them; but of which they now could not understand a word. He turned his daughters into reading machines. It is appalling to think of such a task. That Mary should revolt and at last after repeated contests with her taskmaster, learn to hate her father—that she should, when someone spoke in her presence of her father's approaching marriage, make the dreadful speech that it was no news to hear of his wedding, but if she could hear of his death, that was something—is unutterably painful, but not surprising.—*The Athenaeum*.

2. *The Church as It Is*.—Parker Pillsbury, pp. 32–36.

3. Report of the *Proceedings of the Missionary Conference*.—Mr. Perkins' speech.

4. The same hymns are sung, the same doctrine preached, the same necessity for salvation emphasized, and justification by faith is made the cornerstone of redemption.

5. Historians have declared that "Nowhere did the spirit of Puritanism in its evil as well as its good, more thoroughly express itself than in Massachusetts and Rhode Island." Boston, for its atrocities was known as "The Bloody Town." *The Emancipation of Massachusetts* by Brook Adams, gives a very correct account of the retarding influence of Puritan bigotry in the development of intellectual truth in the New England States.

6. *The true character of Presbyterian Pastors in Scotland in Time of Charles II.*

7. When her father's name was mentioned, Dora said, "Don't speak to me of my father, Mr. Morris, you and the whole church know that my father, prophet though you call him, broke many a woman's heart. If it is required of me to break as many hearts and ruin as many women as my father did, I should go to perdition before I would go back into the church again and—"

"Oh, sister Dora!" exclaimed the teacher in consternation at her clearness of vision.

"It is a fact and you know it," she continued, "you know that many of his wives died of broken hearts and how did he leave the rest? Look at my mother and look at all the rest of them! A religion that breaks women's hearts and ruins them is of the devil. That's what Mormonism does. Don't talk to me of my father."—Reported in the *Chicago Inter Ocean.*

8. A correspondent writing for an eastern paper from Salt Lake City, a few years since, said: "Of all the ill-conditioned, God-forsaken, hopeless-looking people I ever saw, the women here beat them all. Yesterday was supply day for the Mormons living outside the city. They bring their wives into town in dead-axle wagons, and fill the vacant room with children who look fully as bad as their mothers, if not worse. Many of them are lean and humpbacked and all look sickly and ill-clad. Two out of three women on the streets yesterday had nursing infants in their arms. One of the saints had thirteen wives and ninety-four children; another had nine wives and five nursling babies, which he exhibited with all the pride I should take in a lot of fine horses. I never realized the infernal nature of the institution nor its effect upon society as I do now."

9. *Key to Theology*, by Parley Pratt.

10. *Ibid.*

11. The following conversation took place between a mistress and an Irish servant girl: "Bridget, why are not women ever priests?" "Oh! they couldn't be; they're too wicked." "You don't believe such nonsense,

do you—you don't believe women are more wicked than men?" "Yes ma'am," replied Bridget with emphasis; "they're a dale more wicked; they can't iver be prastes, for they brought sin into the world. Eve was the very first sinner; I learned it all in the catechism."

12. In a recent Catholic Allocution, emanating from the dignitaries of that church on the Pacific Coast, it was said: "The church, like Christ, is the same yesterday, today and forever; it is the same here as in other parts of the world; its sacred laws, enacted under the guidance of the divine spirit, are as binding here as in any other place."

13. We do not, indeed, prize as highly as some of our countrymen appear to do the ability to read, write and cipher. Some men are born to be leaders, and the rest are born to be led. The best ordered and administered state is that in which the few are well educated and lead, and the many are trained to obedience.—*Catholic Review.*

14. The Mormon faith belts Idaho, Montana, Arizona, New Mexico, Nevada, Utah and Wyoming, a portion of the country that is wealthier than any other portion in its natural products. It is not simply in Utah that this power of Mormonism is found, but it is spreading in every territory. Every railroad in that section is partially built by Mormon laborers. They are spreading all over that country. They control, in three or four states there, the balance of power. They control every election that is held in Utah, and every man is dictated to in relation to his vote. They also control the ballot-box in Idaho and Wyoming, and are thus liable in time to come, should the two Mormon territories become states, to throw sixteen Senators into our Congress. They openly boast of their intention to take their plural system to your watering places here in the east, Saratoga, Newport and other resorts. I realize the struggle of the past when the manhood of our nation was put to the test, and I know there is another contest approaching. The leaders say they intend to fight this contest until Mormonism prevails.—*Mormonism and Treason to the United States Government.*

CHAPTER VIII

WOMAN
AND WORK

And unto Adam the Lord said; "Cursed be the ground for thy sake; in sorrow shalt thou eat of it all the days of thy life; thorns and thistles shall it bring forth to thee; and thou shalt eat the herbs of the field; in the sweat of thy face shalt eat thou bread, till thou return unto the ground, for dust thou art and into dust thou shalt return. Gen. 3: 17–19.

Upon man was pronounced the curse of the world's work. The Bible declares it was because of *his* sinfulness that the earth was to be cursed; for *his* punishment that he was to eat of it in sorrow all the days of his life; because of *his* wickedness that it was to bear thorns and thistles; and in consequence of *his* disobedience that he was to eat the herb of the field in the sweat of his face until he returned unto the ground from whence he came. No curse of work was pronounced upon woman; her "curse" was of an entirely different character. It was a positive command of the Lord God Almighty, that upon man alone the

413

work of the world should fall and this work he was to perform in sorrow and the sweat of his brow.

Thus far this book has been devoted to a consideration of the doctrines taught by christian men in regard to "woman's curse," and so earnestly has this doctrine been proclaimed that man seems to have entirely forgotten the "curse," also pronounced upon himself or if he has not forgotten, he has neglected to see its full import, and in his anxiety to keep woman in subordination he has placed *his* "curse" also upon her thus thwarting the express command of God. It is therefore but just to now devote a few pages to the consideration of man's "curse" and an investigation of the spirit in which he has accepted the penalty imposed upon him for his share in the transgression which cost him Paradise. At the commencement of this investigation, it will be well to remember that Eve was not banished from the Garden of Eden. Adam alone was cast out and to prohibit *his* reentrance, not hers, the angel with the flaming sword was set as guardian at its gates.

We must also recall the opposition of the church through the ages to all attempts made towards the amelioration of woman's suffering at time of her bringing forth children, upon the plea that such mitigation was a direct interference with the mandate of the Almighty and an inexcusable sin. It will be recalled that in the chapter upon witchcraft, the bitter hostility of the church to the use of anæsthetics by the women physicians of that period was shown, and its opposing sermons, its charges of heresy, its burnings at the stake as methods of enforcing that opposition. Man, ever unjust to woman, has been no less so in the field of work. He has not taken upon himself the entire work of the world, as commanded, but has ever imposed a large portion of it upon woman. Neither do all men labor; but thousands in idleness evade the "curse" of work pronounced upon all men alike. The church in its teachings and through its nonpreaching the duty of man in this respect, is guilty of that defiance of the Lord God it has ever been so ready to attribute to woman. The pulpit does not proclaim that this curse of work rests upon any man; does not preach this command to the idle, the profligate, the rich or the honored but on the contrary shows less sympathy and less respect for the laborer, than for the idle man. The influence of this neglect of its duty by the church has permeated the christian world, we everywhere find contempt for the man who amid thorns and thistles tills the ground, obeying his primal "curse" of earning his bread by the sweat of his brow; and everywhere see respect accorded to the man, who by whatever means of honest or of dishonest capacity evades his curse, taking no share in the labors of the field, nor earning his bread in the sweat of his brow.

Anaesthetics have justly been called the greatest boon ever conferred by science upon mankind. But after the persecution of the witchcraft period a knowledge of their use was lost to the world for many hundred years, but when rediscovered during the present century, their employment in mitigating the sufferings of the expectant mother, again met with the same opposition as during the middle ages upon the same ground of its interference with "the curse" pronounced by God upon woman. The question of their use at such time was violently discussed at ministerial gatherings, and when Sir James Simpson, physician to Queen Victoria, employed them at the birth of the later princes and princesses he was assailed by pulpit and press as having sacrilegiously thwarted "the curse." When the practice was introduced into the United States, prominent New England clergymen preached against their use upon the same ground, of its being an impious frustration of the curse of the Almighty upon woman. But the history of christendom does not show an instance in which the church or the pulpit ever opposed labor by woman, upon the ground of its being an interference with the "curse" pronounced upon man, but on the contrary her duty to labor has been taught by church and state alike, having met no opposition, unless, perchance she has entered upon some remunerative employment theretofore monopolized by man, with the purpose of applying its proceeds to her own individual use. Nor has objection then arisen because of the work, but solely because of its money-earning qualities. An investigation of the laws concerning woman, their origin, growth, and by whom chiefly sustained, will enable us to judge how far they are founded upon the eternal principles of justice and how far emanating from ignorance, superstition and love of power which is the basis of all despotism. Viewing her through the Christian Ages, we find woman has chiefly been regarded as an element of wealth; the labor of wife[1] and daughters, the sale of the latter in the prostitution of a loveless marriage, having been an universally extended form of domestic slavery, one which the latest court decisions recognize as still extant. It is the boast of America and Europe that woman holds a higher position in the world of work under christianity than under pagandom. Heathen treatment of women in this respect often forms the subject of returned missionary sermons from men apparently forgetful that servile labor of the severest and most degrading character is performed by christian women, is demanded from them in every christian country, Catholic, Greek, and Protestant alike, many savage and barbarous races showing superiority over christian lands in their general treatment of women.

England claiming to represent the highest result of christian civilization shows girls of the most tender years and married women with infants at the breast, working in the depths of coal mines nearly naked, where harnessed to trucks, they drag loads of coal on their hands and knees through long low galleries to the pit mouth. Among the pitwomen in England are those to whom Christianity is not even a name; one to whom the word Christ was spoken, asking "who's him; be he a hodman or a pitman?" It has been truthfully declared that England protects its hunting dogs kept for their master's pleasure, far better than it protects the women and children of its working classes. It takes about $2,500,000 annually to pay the maintenance of the 20,000 hounds owned in Great Britain, while women and children are left to slowly die at starvation wages. A few years since a commission was instituted by Parliament to inquire into the condition of women working in the coal mines and the wages paid them. The facts ascertained were of the most horrible character, no improvement being shown in the past fifty years, men and women, boys and girls, still working together in an almost naked condition.

In the Lancashire coal-fields lying to the north and west of Manchester, females are regularly employed in underground labor, and the brutal conduct of the men and the debasement of the women are well described by some of the witnesses examined by them. Betty Harris (one of numerous persons examined), aged thirty-seven, drawer in a coal pit, said: "I have a belt around my waist and a chain between my legs to the truck, and I go on my hands and feet; the road is very steep and we have to hold by a rope, and when there is no rope, by anything we can catch hold of. There are six women and about six boys or girls in the pit I work in; it is very wet, and the water comes over our clog-tops always, and I have seen it up to my thighs; my clothes are always wet." Patience Keershaw, aged seventeen, another examined, said: "I work in the clothes I now have on (trousers and ragged jacket), the bald place upon my head is made by thrusting the cones; the getters I work for are naked, except their caps; they pull off their clothes; all the men are naked." Margaret Hibbs, aged eighteen, said: "My employment after reaching the wall-face is to fill my bagie or stype with two and a half or three hundred weight of coal; I then hook it on to my chain and drag it through the seam, which is from twenty-six to twenty-eight inches high, till I get to the main road, a good distance, probably two hundred to 400 yards; the pavement I drag over is wet, and I am obliged at all times to crawl on my hands and feet with my bagie hung to the chain and ropes. It is sad, sweating, sore and fatiguing work, and frequently maims the women." Robert Bald, the government coal-viewer, states, that "In surveying the workings of an extensive colliery under ground, a married woman came forward groaning under an excessive weight of coals, trembling in every nerve, and almost unable to keep her knees from sinking under her. On coming up she said, in a plaintive and melancholy voice, 'Oh sir, this is sore, sore, sore work.' A subcommissioner said: "It is almost incredible that human beings can submit to such employment—crawling on hands and knees harnessed like horses, over soft, slushy floors, more difficult than dragging the same weight through our lowest sewers." Hundreds of pages are filled with testimony of the same revolting character. These miserable human beings are paid less than twenty cents per day. The evidence shows almost as terrible a condition of the employes of the workshops and large manufacturing establishments.

For the same kind of work men are paid three times more wages than are paid to women.

> Women in the iron trade of the Midlands are compelled, according to a labor commission witness, to work in the sheds scantily covered and in the summer have to divest themselves of nearly all their clothing while hammering nuts and bolts. They bring their children to the factories and cover them up to prevent their being burnt by red-hot sparks. Often they have to carry bundles of iron weighing half a hundred weight. For such work they earn 4s. or 5s. a week, while the men make about 14s.

As early as 1840 an inquiry into the mining affairs of Great Britain, while showing a pitiable condition of the male laborers, exhibited that of women and children in a much worse light. As the natural guardians of children, well aware of their immaturity of body and mind, no mother allows their employment in severe labor at a tender age unless herself compelled to such work and unable to save her children. But at this investigation, men, women and children were found working together in the pits all either nude or nearly so, and according to the Report, not seeing daylight for weeks at a time. Women soon to become mothers were found yoked to carts in the pits; girls carried baskets of coal on their backs up ladders; while mere children crawling like dogs, on hands and feet, hauled carts along narrow rails, the system in operation requiring these victims to remain underground for weeks at a time, breathing foul air and deprived of the light of day. The spirit of ambition is not dead among these wretched serfs, these women working out man's "curse." The most degraded woman in the English coal mine will fight for precedence. She has all the force of the man by her side whose religious equal she is not; whose political equal she is not; he possessing those elements of power, entrance to the priesthood and use of the ballot, denied to her. Through the ballot he receives higher wages for the same kind and amount of work, the church having taught his superior rights upon every point; through the ballot he influences the action of government in his own favor to the injury of his fellow work-woman. A few years since the male miners petitioned against the employment of women in the mines, when a clause to that effect was immediately introduced to the Coal Mine Bill, then before Parliament, although in the Lancashire districts where one hundred and sixty-four women were employed, all but twenty-six were widows or single women entirely dependent upon their own earnings. As severe as the work, the women were remarkable for their bright and healthful appearance as contrasted with the woman workers in the factories of Great Britain. Man, hereditarily unjust to women under the principles of the Patriarchate and the lessons of Christianity, is even more unjust in the fields of work he has compelled her to enter, than in those of education and the ballot which she is seeking for herself. Organizations, strikes, the eight-hour law demand, are largely conducted by men for men. The grim humor originating the proverb "a man's work is from sun to sun, a woman's work is never done," still clings with all its old force to women in most employments. To such small extent has man made the woman worker's cause his own, that instances are to be found even in the United States, where men and women working together and together going out upon a strike, the men have been reinstated at the increase demanded, the women forced to return at the old wages. Nor is our own country the chief sinner in this respect. It was found imperative many years since, among the women of England to organize leagues of their own sex alone, if they desired their own interest in labor to be protected; the male Trades Unions of that country excluding women from some of the best-paid branches of industry, as carpet making, cloth weaving, letter press printing.[2] In self-defense, the Woman's Protective and Provident League, and a *Woman's Union Labor Journal* were founded. The principle of exclusion has not alone been shown against woman's entrance into well-paid branches of work, but in those they have been permitted to enter they have found themselves subjected to much petty annoyance. Among the male painters of pottery a combination was formed to prevent the use by woman of the arm-rests required in this work. Tram-way trains carry London workmen at reduced rates, but a combination was entered into by male laborers to prevent women workers from using the low-priced trains. Nor in many instances are employers less the enemies of women, unions having been found necessary for the purpose of moral protection. A most deplorable evidence of the low respect in which woman is held and the slavery that work and cheap wages mean for her, is the suggestion often made by employers that she shall supplement her wages by the sale of her body. The manager of an industrial league in New York City a few years since found that no young girl escaped such temptation. Neither extreme youth nor friendliness afforded security or protection but were rather additional inducements for betrayal, most of the victims numbering but fourteen short years. The late Jennie Collins, of Boston, one of the earliest persons in the United States, to devote herself to this branch of the "woman question," said:

> It is easy for a young girl to obtain employment but let her go where she will, even in government positions at Washington, she will find her innocence assailed if not made the price at which she gets a chance to work. And that same government does not pay its women employees the same amount of wages for the same kind of work.

In the Scottish collieries women are compelled to work in mines filled with gas and flooded with water,[3] little girls commencing work in these collieries at four years of age, and at six carrying loads of one hundred and fifty pounds upon their backs. Half-clothed women work by the side of entirely nude men, dragging ponderous loads of 16,000 yards a day by means of a chain fastened to a belt, the severe labor of dragging this coal up inclined places to the mouth of the pit, testing every muscle and straining every nerve. It is a work so destructive to health that even the stoutest men shrink from it, women engaged in it seldom living to be over thirty or forty years of age.

A gentleman traveling in Ireland blushed for his sex when he saw the employments of women young and old. He described them as patient drudges, staggering over the bogs with heavy creels of turf on their backs or climbing the slopes from the sea-shore laden like beasts of burden, with heavy sand-dripping sea-weed, or undertaking long journeys on foot into the market towns bearing heavy hampers of farm produce. Man in thrusting the enforcement of his "curse" upon woman in Christian lands has made her the great unpaid laborer of the world. In European countries and in the United States, we find her everywhere receiving less pay than man for the same kind and quality of work. A recent statement regarding women workers in the foundries of Pittsburgh, Penn., where five hundred women are employed in putting heads on nails and bolts, declared they received less than one-half the sum formerly paid to men who did the same kind of work; women getting from but four to five dollars a week while the wages of men ranged from fourteen to sixteen dollars a week. But as evil as the experience of young women in the world of work, that of old women is in some respects even greater. While the young girl is almost certain to obtain work even if at small wages, it is very difficult for the woman of mature years to obtain work at all, either in households as seamstresses or in manufactories. Societies in the City of New York, for the aid of the working women find it impossible to secure employment for middle-aged women. The report of one such society stated that some of these women managed to pro-cure commitment to the Island in order to obtain food and pre-vent absolute starvation; others slowly died from want of suffi-cient food; still others, like the poor hard-working girls of Paris, sought the river as an end to their sufferings. As in the witchcraft period when the chief persecution for many years raged against old women, we still find in our own country that the woman of middle life is the least regarded in her efforts for a livelihood. The reason remains the same. Looked upon during the Christian ages from a sensual standard, the church teaching that woman was made for man still exerts its poisonous influence, still destroys woman. Not alone employers and male laborers oppress woman, but legislation is frequently invoked to prevent her entering certain occupations. The Coal Miner's Bill was one of many instances in Great Britain. Women work there also at making nails, spikes and chains. Not long since legislation prohibiting their entering this branch of work was attempted, when a deputation of women iron-workers waited upon the home secretary to protest against government interference with their right to earn a livelihood. One of these representative women had entered the work at seven years of age, being then fifty-seven. Having spent nearly half a century in this occupation she was practically incapacitated for any other form of labor.

The terrible condition of working women in Paris has attracted the attention of the French government. In but three or four trades are they even fairly well paid, and these few require a peculiar adaptation, as well as an expensive training out of reach of most women laborers. And even in these best-paid kinds of work, a discrimination in favor of man exists; at the China manufactory at Sévres where the men employed receive a retiring pension, the women do not. From fifteen to eighteen pence represents the daily earnings of the Parisian working girl, upon which sum it is impossible for her to properly support life. Many of these girls die of slow starvation, others are driven into prostitution, still others seek relief in the Seine. French women perform the most repulsive labors of the docks; they work in the mines dragging or pushing heavy trucks of coal like their English sisters, through narrow tunnels that run from the seams to the shaft; eating food of such poor quality that the lessening stature of the population daily shows the result. This decreasing size of Frenchmen especially among the peasantry, the majority not coming up to the regulation army height, has within the last fifteen or twenty years called attention of the government during conscription, yet without seeming to teach its cause as lying in the poor food and hard labor of women, the mothers of these men. The heaviest burdens of porters, the most offensive sanitary work, the severest agricultural labor in that country falls upon woman. "I pity the women, the donkeys, and the boys," wrote Mrs. Stanton when traveling in the south of France. It is the poor nourishment and excessive labor of woman which makes France today a country of rapidly decreasing birth-rate, seriously affecting its population and calling the earnest attention of statistical bureaus and physicians to this vital question; a question which affects the standing of France among the nations of the earth. According to the report of the chief of the statistical bureau, 1890, there were fewer births than deaths that year, the births amounting to 838,059, the deaths to 876,505, an excess of 38,446 deaths. Commenting upon these returns, *Der Reichsbote* of Berlin, attributed the cause to a widespread aversion to large families; acknowledging, however, that the lower classes had become weakened and dwarfed by the tasks imposed upon them. What neither the statistical bureau, the press, or the church yet comprehend is the fact that the work imposed upon its Christian women, the "curse" of man thrust upon her, is the chief cause of the lessening size and lessening population of that country. A French gentleman employing a large number of women in a flax factory was appalled at the great amount of infant mortality among the children of his employees. Believing the excessive death rate to be in consequence of the continued labor of women, he released expectant mothers for a month previous, and two months after the birth of a child, with a marked diminution of the death rate. The ordinary food of the peasantry is of poor quality and meager quantity. Those employed in the manufacture of silk largely subsist upon a species of black broth proverbial for its lack of nutritive qualities. The absence of certain elements in food both creates specific diseases and inability to combat disease. Vital stamina is closely dependent upon the number of red corpuscles in the blood, the quality of food possessing direct connection with these corpuscles. Dr. Blackwell, of the London Anthropological Society, examined the blood of different races as related to the food eaten by them, finding the number and shape of the red corpuscles to be dependent upon the kind of food eaten. Dr. Richardson, a Philadelphia microscopist, said: "Any cause which interferes with perfect nutrition may diminish the red corpuscles in number." These corpuscles are recognized as "oxygen carriers," therefore any cause which tends to diminish the number of red corpuscles also deprives the system of a portion of the oxygen required for sanitary needs. Blood not fully oxygenated is poisonous to the system. Among the causes recognized by physiologists as creating that alteration in the functions of the body which materially changes the character of the red corpuscles, are poor food, bad air and overwork. These specifically produce blood poisoning, creating new substances in the body that are injurious to the organism.

It is not alone in France that such effects are to be noted, although governmental attention has, not elsewhere been called to the condition produced, yet twenty years since, *Frazer's Magazine* in an article on "Field Farming Women in England" in reference to the poor food and overwork of women of this class, said of their children: "The boys are always very short for their age, those of fifteen being no larger than town boys of ten; girls are thin and skinny, angular and bony." Eight years ago, Dr. Rochad, who has given much time to this question, prophesied that the population of France would become stationary before the end of the century. At that time his words carried no weight; he was ridiculed as a vague theorizer, but this result has been reached in one half the time he gave and the results are even of graver character than Dr. Rochad assumed them to be. The balance has already fallen upon the opposite side and in a single year the deaths have outnumbered the births nearly 40,000. Two hundred and fifty thousand infants annually die in France because of the impoverished blood, hard work and general innutrition of French mothers. "These lives are the more precious to France which can no longer afford to lose them, since in a single year the death rate outnumbered the birth rate 40,000." Through the effort of Dr. Rochad, a society has been organized, rules for feeding infants formulated with penalties attached, and like futile methods for effecting a change suggested; while the real cause of the lessening population is left untouched. Until the condition of the mother as life-giver is held as sacred under Christianity as it was among the Greeks and Romans; until man taking his own "curse" upon himself frees woman from its penalties; until she and her young children are supplied with nourishing food and woman secures pure air to breathe and freedom from the hardships so supremely her lot under existing laws and customs, not until then will a change take place. Parker Pillsbury in *Popular Religion*, says:

> Once I journeyed among the magnificent fields, villages and vineyards in the south of France. Women tanned, browned, almost bronzed by the sun, wind and much exposure, weary and worn, many of them mothers, or soon to become such, spaded, shoveled, plowed, harrowed, often drawing harrows themselves across furrowed fields; they mowed, raked, pitched, loaded and unloaded the hay of the meadows; they harvested the crops and then hastened to haul manure and prepare the ground for other crops, rising early and toiling late, doing almost all kinds of work men do anywhere, and some kinds which neither man nor woman should ever do.

Germany, whose women were revered in the centuries before Christianity, now degrades them to the level of beasts. Women and dogs harnessed together are found drawing milk carts in the streets; women and cows yoked draw the plough in the fields; the German peasant wife works on the roads or carries mortar to the top of the highest buildings, while her husband smokes his pipe at the foot of the ladder until she descends for him to again fill the hod. To such extent is woman a laborer that she comes in competition with the railroad and all public methods of traffic. Eight-tenths of the agricultural laborers are women; they plow and sow, and reap the grain and carry immense loads of offal for fertilizing the land. As street cleaners they collect the garbage of towns, work with brooms and shovels to cleanse roadways; and harnessed alone, or with cows or dogs, perform all the most repulsive labors of the fields and streets. Nor for a knowledge of their work are we dependent upon the statements of travelers, but official documents corroborate the worst. An American consul says of a Circular Upon Labor recently issued by the German government:

An important factor in the labor of Germany is not enquired of in the circular, viz., the labor of dogs. I have heard it estimated that women and dogs harnessed together do more hauling than the railroads and all other modes of conveyance of goods united. Hundreds of small wagons can be seen every day on all the roads leading to and from Dresden, each having a dog for the "near horse" harnessed, while the "off horse" is a woman with her left hand grasping the wagon tongue to give it direction, and the right hand passed through a loop in the rope which is attached to the axle, binding the shoulder; the harnessed woman and dog trudge along together, pulling miraculous loads in all sorts of weather.

The pay of woman for this strange, degrading labor is from ten to twenty-five cents a day. Nor is that of sewing more remunerative. In March, 1892, a libel suit against an embroidery manufacturer brought to light the fact that women in his employ received but five cents a day. No burden in Germany is considered too heavy for woman until the failing strength of old age necessitates a change of occupation, when amid all varieties of weather they take the place of the newsboys of our own country, selling papers upon the streets. Munich, the capital of Bavarian Germany, is famed for its treasury of art; paintings, ancient and modern sculptures, old manuscripts of inestimable value, large libraries and splendid architecture make it the seat of the fine arts. But its women are still victims of Christian civilization. Dresden is another city whose art treasures and architectural beauty has rendered it famous among European cities as the "German Florence." Yet both of these cities employ women in the same kinds of work under the same repulsive conditions that are found in other portions of that empire.

Bavarian men wearing heavy wooden shoes drive their barefooted wives and daughters before the plough in the field, or harnessed with dogs send them as carriers of immense loads of merchandise through the cities. Says a writer:

Women become beasts of burden; still they do not grumble; they do not smile either—they simply exist. The only liberty they have is liberty to work; the only rest they have is sleep. The existence of a cow or a sheep is a perpetual heaven, while theirs is a perpetual hell.

In addition to all this out-of-door labor performed by the German women, they have that of the house and the preparation of clothing for the family. They industriously knit upon the street while doing errands; they cook, they spin and make clothing which takes them afar into the night, rearing their children amid labor so severe as forever to drive smiles from their faces, bringing the wrinkles of premature old age in their place. Switzerland, whose six hundredth anniversary was celebrated in 1888, the oldest republic, sees its women carrying luggage and blacking boots as porters at inns; propelling heavily laden barges down its romantic lakes; swinging the scythe by the side of men in the fields; bringing great baskets of hay strapped to their shoulders down the mountainside; carrying litters containing travelers up the same steep mountain top; bringing heavy baskets of fagots from the forests, and carrying in the more pleasant cutting of grapes at the vineyard harvest. From five o'clock in the morning till eight in the evening is the peasant woman's day of work. A stolid expressionless face, eyes from which no soul seems to look, a magnificent body as strong as that of the man by her side, is the result of the Swiss woman's hardships and work. It is but a few years since the laws of Switzerland compelled division of the paternal estate with sisters as well as brothers, this change provoking intense opposition from the men. On the Alps, husbands borrow and lend their wives, one neighbor not scrupling to ask the loan of another's wife to complete some farming task, which loan is readily granted with the under standing that the favor is to be returned in kind. Says one writer:

The farmers in the Upper Alps, though by no means wealthy, live like lords in their houses, while the heaviest portion of agricultural labors devolves upon the wife. It is no uncommon thing to

see a woman yoked to a plough with an ass, while her husband
guides it. An Alpine farmer counts it an act of politeness to lend
his wife to a neighbor who has too much work, and the neighbor
in return lends his wife for a few days labor whenever requested.

In Vienna, women lay the brick in building, while throughout
Austria young girls carry mortar for such work. They also work in
the fields, in the mines, pave and clean the streets, or like their
German sisters, harnessed with dogs, drag sprinklers for the street
or serve milk at the customer's door. Prussian women are also to
be found working the mines, in quarries in foundries, building
railroads, acting as sailors and boatmen, or like those of Holland,
dragging barges in place of horses on the canals, or like those of
other European countries, performing the most severe and repulsive agricultural labors. A correspondent of the *Cincinnati Commercial* traveling through Belgium, said: "No work seems to be
done except by woman and dogs. With few exceptions women do
the harvesting, working like oxen." The physiological fact that the
kind of labor and the kind of food affect the physical frame is
noticeable in Belgium the same as in France and England. Women
of all ages from fourteen to sixty, work in the coal mines, married
women sometimes carrying babies strapped to their backs into the
pit, laying the infants near them while digging coal, some mine
owners refusing to employ a miner unless he can bring one or
more members of his family into the pit with him. Employers
prefer girls and women because of their lower wages and greater
docility; for twelve hours work a woman receives but thirty cents.
Even in little Montenegro, husbands lend their wives to each other
during the harvest season, and an exceptionally strong or quick-
moving wife finds exceptional demand for her services. This little
state degrades woman to still greater extent than her sister countries, as they there form the beasts of burden in war, and are
counted among the "animals" belonging to the prince.

The Russian peasant woman under the Greek church, finds
life equally a burden, and is even to greater extent than in most
countries the slave of her husband and the priest, no form of

labor or torture being looked upon as too severe to impose upon her. The women are much more industrious than the men and the hardest work is done by them. As Russia is primarily an agricultural country it possesses immense fields of hay, oats and wheat, the work largely performed by women. The wheat sown broadcast is either harvested with sickles or the old-fashioned scythe with a broad blade. Women do the entire work of gathering up, binding and stacking the wheat, neighbors during harvest helping each other. Women of every age from the young girl to the aged grandmother, take part, assembling at daybreak. Horses are also there in number for carrying food, water, extra implements, and the men and boys of the conclave. The women, however aged, walk; the day's work lasting over eighteen hours or from daybreak until dark; in that northern land at harvest time it continues light from 3 A.M. to 9:30 P.M. Nor are mothers with young infants excused from this toil. Babies are carried into the fields where they lie all day under trees, or partially sheltered by a bough over them, covered with insects from which the mother can find no time to relieve them. Under such circumstances of neglect, it is not surprising that infant mortality is excessive. Nor do the children of a slightly larger growth receive the care requisite for their tender years, and it is estimated that eight out of every ten children in Russia die under ten years of age. But no one form of Christianity monopolizes the wrong. Everywhere, under every name and sect, man has thrown the carrying out of his "curse" on to woman. Italy, the center of Catholicism, under a careful analysis of statistics, showing that the wages of the Italian working woman do not exceed four pence a day. In Venice a traveler was recently shown some wonderfully beautiful articles of clothing; scarfs, shawls, mantles, handkerchiefs, many of them requiring six months for the production; expressing amazement at the astonishingly low price demanded for such exquisite fabrics he was told, "we pay our young girls but seven cents a day." A correspondent of the *Philadelphia Press*, writing from abroad in 1885, declared the debasement of woman to be more thorough and complete in Protestant Stockholm, than in any city of northern

Europe, as there she supplanted the beasts of burden. He spoke of her as doing all the heavy work on buildings and paid only one kroner (equivalent to a trifle over twenty-six cents) for a hard day of this toil. He found women sweeping the streets, hauling rubbish, dragging hand-carts up the hills and over the cobble-stones, unloading bricks at the quays, attending to the parks, doing the gardening and rowing the numerous ferries which abound in that city. The entire dairy business of the city is in their hands and here they have the help of neither horses nor dogs but take the entire place of the beasts, carrying the heavy cans of milk on their shoulders from door to door; he said:

> I am not altogether unfamiliar with woman's work in Europe; I have seen her around the pit mouth, at the forge, and bare foot in the brick yards of "merrie" England; filling blast furnaces and tending coke ovens in "sunny France." I have sadly watched her bearing the heat and burden of the day in the fields of the "fatherland" and in Austria-Hungary doing the work of man and beast on the farm and in the mine. I have seen women emerge from the coal pits of "busy Belgium" where little girls and young women were underground bearers of coal and drawers of carts. Aged, bent and sunburned, I have seen women with rope over shoulder toiling on the banks of canals and over dykes in "picturesque Holland." Having witnessed all this, I was yet surprised to find in a city so beautiful and seemingly so rich as Stockholm, women even more debased.

In the Connellsville coke region of Pennsylvania, United States, the Hungarian woman workers are found engaged in the severest labor under authority of the husband or father, half-nude women drawing the hot coke from the chambers. Master Workman Powderly visiting the place early one morning, said of it:

> At one of the ovens I saw a woman half naked drawing the coke from one of the chambers. She had no covering on her head and very little on her person. Her appearance was that of one whose spirit had been broken by hardship and hard work. Her attire

consisted of a chemise and a pair of cowhide boots. In a freight car close by stood another woman forking the coke as it came into the car. The woman stood in the doorway and was dressed in a rough, loose-fitting outer garment and an apron. Her person from the waist up was exposed. When she stooped over to handle the coke, she caught her hair between her teeth in order to keep it out of her way. Her babe which she brought to the works with her, lay in front of the car with scarcely any covering except the shadow of a wheel barrow which was turned up in order to protect the child from the rays of the sun.

The suffering of helpless infants and children from privation and neglect through enforced labor of the mother, is one of the most shocking things connected with this degradation of woman in labor. The ownership by the husband of the wife's services; his power under the Christian law of church and state of compelling her to work for him; the public sentiment of church and state which not alone recognizes absolute authority over the wife as inhering in the husband, but which are the creators of such belief, are the causes of illness, death, moral degradation, insanity, crime and vice of every kind. One year even, of civilized housekeeping with its routine of washing, starching, ironing, scrubbing, cooking, baking, pickling, canning, sewing, sweeping, house-cleaning, etc., etc., with all their accompanying overheating and overlifting; the care of children both night and day, whether sick or well, the constant demands upon her time and strength, thrown upon women of the Christian household, are labors more severe than fell on the old-time savage woman of America during her whole life. Until the customs of civilization reached the Indians, their wives, according to Catlin, Schoolcraft and others, were not called upon to work with half the severity of the women of today, nor had they tradition of children ever born deaf, dumb or blind. Those kinds of labor pointed to as showing the hardships of an Indian woman's life, Schoolcraft dismisses very lightly. The lodge built by her is not made of heavy posts and carpentry, but of thin poles bent over at the top, such as a child can lift. When a family changed its residence these poles were not removed; only the thin sheets of birch bark covering, were taken to the new rendezvous. The gathering of the fuel by the women, was cutting dry limbs of the forest not over eighteen inches in length, with a hatchet. The tillage of the fields shared alike by the old men, women and the boys, was very light. No oxen to drive, no plough to hold, no wheat to plant or thresh. The same corn hills were used year after year, forming small mounds that were long a puzzle to the antiquarian. The squash and the pumpkin grew luxuriantly, while the children made holidays of gathering nuts and acorns for winter use. And today Africa, "The Dark Continent" is the children's paradise, says Mrs. French Sheldon, the wonderful woman explorer, who carried peace with her everywhere and whose investigations in that part of the world exceed in value those of Livingstone or Stanley. She says:

> In all these months among the children every day, I never saw a child struck and I heard a child cry but twice while on the Dark Continent.

How different from the countries of Christian civilization where children, mere infants of three and four years, are put to the most severe labor or because of the mother's enslaved condition, die from neglect. It will be said, but these instances, especially in the United States, are exceptional. This is not so, although the work performed may be of a different character. The wife even in this country is expected to understand and perform many kinds of labor. She is cook and baker, laundress and seamstress, nurse for her children and the sick, besides a thousand and one cares which rise before her every hour. One such overworked mother acknowledged to placing the cradle where the sun would shine in the baby's eyes, thus compelling them to close, when she would push all out of the way underneath the bed. Said a German girl working "as help" in the modern kitchen of a well-to-do American family, "I plowed at home harnessed beside a cow, and the work was not as hard as in your hot kitchen." The care of children and domestic labor are not compatible with each other. One must be neglected, and she of whom, "meals on time" are demanded, can say where the neglect necessarily falls. A consistent carrying out by man of his "curse" would cause him to take upon himself the entire work of the world; not alone tilling the soil, but all household labor; the baking and brewing, the cooking and cleaning and all the multitudinous forms of work which make such wearisomely incessant demands upon woman's strength and time. From all sewing, knitting, crocheting, embroidering, she should be freed, and even beyond this, under the principles of *his* "curse," upon man should fall all the work of rearing children, as woman's "curse" so often quoted does not refer to aught but bringing them to life in sorrow and suffering. Custom, which has been defined as unwritten law, adds its force to legislative enactments and soon becomes as binding upon thought as a moral command. People soon cease to question a custom, or a law, accepting both in that conservative spirit so utterly destructive to liberty. For that reason what has long been so, is regarded as right, and even while regretting the neglect of her children so unavoidable to the ordinarily situated mothers, few women give thought to the cause bringing it about. Women are not sufficiently permeated with the meaning of personal liberty. They do not sufficiently investigate the causes of their restricted condition, and the break made within the past twenty-five to forty years against conditions, has rather been in the nature of a blind instinctive revolt, than brought about through philosophic thought except in the minds of a few, who by the protest of speech, opened the way that vast multitudes are now entering upon. Open rebellion against law is ever considered by the majority as rebellion against morality. Speaking of the moral influence of law, Sheldon Amos says:

> As soon as a law is made and lifted out of the region of controversy, it begins to exercise a moral influence which is no less intense and wide-spreading for being almost imperceptible. Though law can never attempt to forbid all that is morally wrong, yet that gets to be held as morally wrong, which the law forbids.

No less does unwritten law come to be regarded as morally right. The customs of society built up through teachings of the church, and laws of the state, have destroyed that sense of personal security among women which is the chief value of social life and of law. The very foundation of religion tends to this end even with man, but the division of rights and duties promulgated by the church as between man and woman, the changing form of laws—class legislation—has rendered the position of woman notably insecure. This usurpation is productive of immense loss to the state as France so clearly shows. Take the one article of food alone, the delicacies and the substantials alike are claimed by man. No proof of this statement other than the innumerable saloons and restaurants chiefly supported by men is required. While the dairyman, the birdfancier, the horse trainer, and even the pugilist, recognize the value of food as far as a factor of life and strength, where his own immediate money interest is concerned, neither governments, religions nor scientists have to any extent noted the influence of proper food for the mother upon the health and life of the unborn child. Victor Hugo, while upon the island of Guernsey, noted the vastly beneficial effect that even one good meal a week had upon the peasant children. Food, building muscles, nerves, the brain, what can be expected but a deterioration of humanity when mothers eat insufficient or improper food?

The effect of the kind of food eaten has recently been noted in the new industry of ostrich farming, in California, of which it is said: "Ostriches yield the best feathers if the birds are well cared for. The quality of the plumes depends upon the quality of the food. If the ostriches are well fed, their plumes are soft and big. Bad feeding makes the feathers hard and coarse." Nor are animals from whom the best products are looked for allowed to labor. Their lives are those of ease and comfort that best results may be obtained. Innutrition and the hard labor of expectant mothers are the two great factors in physical degeneration and infantile mortality. The question is not one of sentiment or of law or of religion, but of physiology. It does not alone involve the destiny of mothers but of the race. There is not a national problem, be it of war or population or finance, that is not based upon the condition of woman. Its neglect has depopulated the world in times past, it has lessened intellectual development, it has almost entirely obliterated certain kinds of morality and can no longer be regarded from the standard of either of those great institutions, church or state.

The recent official report of the Factory Inspector of the state of New York upon the condition of working women, showed a condition quite in line with the worst features of foreign lands. Overwork, bad ventilation, low wages, poor food, all combining for their physical and moral destruction. The *Churchman* under heading of "In Darkest New York" speaks of the condition of the poor in that city, both men and women; but while not forgetting the wrongs of the male laborer, we must ever remember that the condition of woman is still lower, and the results of her severe work and semistarvation, much more injurious to the world.

> We must leave the tenements without attempting to reproduce any of the shocking cases of crowded rooms in which almost incredible numbers of poor wretches are huddled together even in summer, when Mr. Riis has found the thermometer rise to 115 degrees. In some of these places there is more than struggle; there is often starvation. Every once in a while a case of downright starvation gets into the papers and makes a sensation. But this is the exception. Were the whole truth known it would come home to the community with a shock that would course it to a more serious effort than the spasmodic undoing of its pursestrings. I am satisfied that hundreds of men, women and children are every day slowly starving to death with my medical friend's complaint of "improper nourishment." Within a single week I have had this year three cases of insanity provoked directly by poverty and want. Worse than even that is the evil case of thousands of ill-fated working girls. The average wages of 150,000 of them is 60 cents per day; and that includes the incomes of the stylish "cashiers" who earn $2 a day as well as the pittance of girls who earn 30 cents a day in east-side factories. The lot of the average saleswoman who does not partly depend on her family is hard indeed.

That the average wages of the 150,000 working girls in the city of New York alone are but sixty cents a day, some receiving as little as thirty cents in the east side factories; that 30,000 young girls between the ages of twelve and fourteen employed as cash girls cannot supply themselves with food unless having parents upon whom to partially depend, are no less moral than material questions. Nor are they questions confined to that one city, or to any one portion of the United States, or of christendom, but belong to humanity itself. As all are parts of one great whole, the evil that afflicts one class touches all; all suffer because of the wrong done to even one human being. The population of the city of New York is more largely comprised of women than of men and a great proportion of this class are dependent upon their own labor for a livelihood. Although many foreign-born women emigrate to this country, over two millions having landed upon our shores within the nine years from 1881 to 1890, it is not alone upon them these conditions of severe labor fall, but native-born American women, both within and without the household, suffer from the same kind of oppression. Even upon the Pacific coast where few foreigners except Chinese are found, little girls of five and six years are put to work in the jute mills and factories by side of their drudging mothers, whose wages do not equal those of the men employed. In government clerkships at Washington, women receive but one-half the pay that men receive for the same kind and quality of work. Although the sweating system in the manufactories of clothing has called the nation's attention to its abuses, yet in the District of Columbia, under sole power of Congress, a system of similar nature exists. Nor are statistics of woman's severe work in the United States of immediately recent date. The labor Commission report of the state of Connecticut for 1876, declaring that the wives and daughters of the farmer engage in work which he can find no man to do, rising at four o'clock in the morning and working until nine in the evening. Analyzing the statistics of the Massachusetts Labor Bureau for 1891, the *Boston Globe* showed the greatly inferior payment of women laborers:

The figures simply show that in the employments in which the very lowest wages are paid, women constitute over 70 percent of the workers, while in the employments where as high as $20 a week are paid, they constitute hardly over 3 percent. In addition to all this is the humiliating fact that in some occupations, standing side by side with men, the females are paid less wages for the same work; or, what amounts to the same thing, a woman of 20 years or upwards is made to work side by side with a boy of ten at the same wages. Women are compelled, then, to fill most of the cheap places, and paid less wages for the same work at that.

In this report the shameful fact is proven through governmental statistics, that the wages paid to a girl of twenty years are no more than those paid a boy of ten, women constituting over seventy percent of the workers to whom the very lowest wages are paid. Underlying all other results are those upon woman herself. Before every question of population, is that of woman as an individual. Overwork and the undernourishment of muscle, nerve, brain, render her own proper evolution either as a physical or as a moral being impossible. To just the extent that such pressure comes upon her, does she cease to be a morally responsible being. Thousands to whom life and comforts are sweet, throw aside all scruples, entering that one avenue of escape always open to a young woman or a girl. For the statement that the majority of women entering upon immorality have been driven by actual want to this mode of life, we are again indebted to rigorous investigation and statistics for information, but the moral deterioration of the race arising from these wrongs to women can not be estimated by figures. In teaching, the only absolute equality of wages between man and woman is found in the Cherokee nation of Indians. The civilization of the Indian tribes is a question of woman's education and freedom. The world still holds a mistaken idea of force and power, those questions not so fully pertaining to the physical as to the intellectual and spiritual parts of the being. The *New York Nation* recently said, "It is absolutely essential to the preservation of the dignity and independence of women that they should be on a par with men as regards property and education, the two things that in modern times have supplanted physical force as elements of power."

Real estate possesses more power as property, than either money or jewels. The real strength of American civilization lies in the fact that almost every family owns its home. Permanent national strength lies in the division of realty. In England women are more rapidly becoming part of the governing class than in the United States, and in that country one-seventh of the landed property owners are women. These facts should be borne in mind in regard to the civilization of the native races of America. It is through the Indian women that the problem of their civilization must be answered; the title in fee simple to lands should be in the hands of the women.

The union of the state with the church in the enforcement of man's "curse" upon woman is most forcibly shown by a decision of the New York Court of Appeals rendered early in 1892 which held that the services of a wife belong to the husband and that she cannot recover wages from him even if holding his written promise to pay. This decision like that of the Agar-Ellis case in England, was upon the principle that the wife is so fully under subjection to her husband as to incapacitate her from making a contract even with that husband. In all the wife's relations to the husband she is regarded as a being without responsibility. The case upon which this decision rested is this: A woman fell down a coal-hole and sued for damages, recovering $500. The defendant asked for a new trial upon the ground that the woman was working for her husband and the court had taken into account her loss of wages. The services of the wife belonging to the husband, her claim for lost wages was a fraud. But this decision of the Court of Appeals doubtless will not interfere with the power of the husband to recover damages for loss of her time by reason of this injury which deprived him of her services. The decision of the Court recognized the right of the husband to compel the wife to perform household duties for him. When in England, 1880, the married woman's property rights bill was before parliament, a commission of inquiry was sent to New York to learn the effect of securing the control of their own property to married women. Under various amendments since the first passage of this act in 1848, the legislature of New York has further secured to married women the right of making wills, of collecting wages for work, and of entering business outside of the household, the proceeds belonging entirely to herself. But under this decision of the Court of Appeals, the ground was taken that the wife cannot collect wages from the husband, and that household work for him is compulsory upon her.[4] This decision as to compulsory housework controverts that other right recognized by legislation, of entering into business, doing work outside of the home, the proceeds to belong solely to herself. Under this decision of the Court of Appeals, a wife can be compelled to work for the husband in the house without wages, and is debarred from all outside business.

St. Augustine in his *City of God*, taunts Rome with having caused her own downfall by her treatment of her slaves. He speaks of the slaves as miserable beings put to labor only fit for the beasts of the field and even degraded below them; their condition had brought Rome to its own destruction. But Roman wives were not forced to labor. The peace made by the Sabines with the Romans after the forcible abduction of the Sabine maidens, had for one of its provisions that no labor except spinning should be required from wives. Among both the ancient Greeks and Romans, the woman about to become a mother, as heretofore shown, was held sacred; she was exempt from hard labor and no one was allowed under penalty of punishment, to vex or disturb her mind.

If degrading their slaves below the beasts of the field led to the destruction of Rome, as declared by Augustine, what may not be predicted of that Christian civilization which in the twentieth century of its existence degrades women and children to such labors as he declared unfit for the slaves of ancient Rome, suitable only for the beasts of the field; which harnesses them by side of cows, asses and dogs to do the most menial work, which robs them in wages and stints them in food in the name of "religion"?

Notes

1. See *Decision of New York Court of Appeals* 1892, pp. 463–64.

2. During the Parliament Commission inquiry, a witness, Peter Garkel, collier, said that he preferred women to boys as drawers; they were better to manage and kept time better; they would fight and shriek and everything but let anybody pass them. The *London National Reformer* states that "The first woman member (Mrs. Jane Pyne), of the London Society of Compositors was admitted by the executive on August 30 (1892). Two years ago Miss Clementine Black applied for permission to join the society but the request had to be refused on the ground that "it was not proposed that woman should be paid on the same scale as men."

3. Lecture by Felix Adler, 1892, "The Position of Woman in the Present."

4. "The New York Court of Appeals has rendered an opinion which shows that married women in that state are still in bondage. A woman fell down a coal-hole and sued for damages, recovering $500. The defendant asked for a new trial on the ground that the woman was working for her husband and the court had taken into account her loss of wages. The Court of Appeals reversed the decision and sent the case back for a new trial. It held that the services of a wife belonged to her husband, and she can not recover any wages even if she holds his written promise to pay."—*Chicago Inter Ocean*, Jan. 1892.

CHAPTER IX

THE CHURCH
OF TODAY

While under advancing civilization, a recognition of the religious rights of woman is steadily progressing among people at large, it requires but slight investigation to prove that olden church theories regarding her not only came into the reformation, but largely remain the same today. The Christianity of the ages having taught the existence of a superior and an inferior sex possessing different rights in the Christian Church, held accountable to different codes of morals, it is not strange that we do not find morality to have been more of a fundamental principle among the pastors of early Protestant churches than in the Catholic priesthood. The doctrine of "Once in grace, always in grace," carries with it a plea for vice, and the early experience of strict Calvanistic Scotland was much that of mediæval Catholic Europe. The Presbyterian Conventicles[1] early bore an extremely evil reputation. The fact that ministers of the reformed church were permitted marriage, did not change priestly teaching that woman was created solely for man, and they found apologies in the Bible for illicit conduct. These Protestant clergymen taught, as had the Catholic, that a priest was incapable of sinning; and from the Sermon on the Mount, "To the pure all things are pure" was quoted in proof of this assertion. Even when under circumstances of great personal peril and danger to life, the trust of parishioners in the morality of their shepherds was often abused, of this, Rev. David Williamson, one of the most eminent Presbyterian ministers of Edinburgh, was a conspicuous example. In defense of his immorality Mr. Williamson said, "Verily, I do not deny that with St. Paul I have a law in my members warring against the law of my mind, and bringing me into captivity unto the love of sin which is in my members." The strangest sermons, most insulting to woman and too indecorous for quotation, were constantly preached: while her inferiority and incapacity for understanding even the gospel was also as constantly declared from the pulpit. An old Presbyterian preacher, Rev. David Douglas, discovering a woman weeping in the kirk, pointed toward her, crying, "Wife, what makes you weep? I am sure thou understandeth not what I am saying; my discourse is directed to the brethren and not to the like of you." The present century, with all its enlightenment does not cease to give us glimpses of that favorite mediæval doctrine that "sin can be killed with sin as the best way of becoming innocent again," and its concomitant, that it is impossible for a person in grace to commit sin.[2] The doctrines of holiness and entire sanctification, taught by some sects today, and the theory that all experience is necessary in order to a full development of character, are of the same nature. Eastern "Wisdom Religion" declares that a person can be come neither God nor deva without passing through all experience, returning again and again to earth for this purpose.

> The departure of the soul-atom from the bosom of the
> Divinity is a radiation from the life of the Great All, who

expends his strength in order that he may grow again and live by its return. God thereby acquires new vital force, provided by all the transformation that the soul-atom has undergone. Its return is its final reward. Such is the secret of the evolution of the Great Being and of the Supreme Soul.[3]

Directions for seeking out the way:

Seek it not by any one road, to each temperament there is one road which seems the most desirable. But the way is not found by devotion alone, by religious contemplation alone, by ardent progress, by self-sacrificing labor, by studious observation of life. None can take the disciple more than one step onward. All steps are necessary to make up the ladder, one by one, as they are surmounted. The virtues of men are steps indeed, necessary—not by any means to be dispensed with. Yet, though they create a fine atmosphere and happy future, they are useless if they stand alone. The whole nature of man must be used wisely by the one who desires to enter the way. Each man is to himself absolutely the way, the truth and the life. Seek it by plunging into the mysterious and glorious depths of your own inmost being. Seek it by testing all experience, by utilizing the senses in order to understand the growth and meaning of individuality and the beauty and obscurity of those other divine fragments which are struggling side by side with you, and form the race to which you belong.[4]

The Catholic, and Calvinistic doctrines of woman's inferiority of position and intellect taught from the pulpit, are by no means relegated to past centuries, but continue to be publicly taught by the Protestant clergy of every sect, as fully as by their Catholic and Greek brethren. The first National Woman Suffrage Covention, which assembled in Washington, 1869, having invited Rev. Chaplain Gray, of the House, to open its proceedings with prayer, he referred in this petition to woman as an afterthought of the Creator, an inferior and secondary being, called into existence for the special benefit of man. The noble old Quakeress, Lucretia Mott, sitting in an attitude of devout attention, suddenly raised her head, and at close of the prayer, Bible in hand, she read aloud the account of the creation, Genesis 1.27–28, woman and man equals, both having been given dominion over nature. The thirtieth anniversary of the first public demand of woman for the recognition of her equality of right with man, held in Rochester, N.Y., July 18, 1878, passed a series of resolutions[5] asserting woman's equality and religious rights with man. Three of these proved especially obnoxious to the clergy of the country, in declaring the first duty of every individual to be self-development; the duty of every woman to be guided by her own reason rather than the authority of another; and that it was owing to the perversion of the religious element in woman that she had been so completely subjugated to priestcraft and superstition.

> *Resolved:* That as the first duty of every individual is self-development, the lessons of self-sacrifice and obedience taught to woman by the Christian church have been fatal, not only to her own vital interests, but through her, to those of the race.
>
> *Resolved:* That the great principle of the Protestant Reformation, the right of individual conscience and judgment heretofore exercised by men alone, should now be claimed by woman; that, in the interpretation of Scripture, she should be guided by her own reason, and not by the authority of the church.
>
> *Resolved:* That it is through the perversion of the religious element in woman—playing upon her hopes and fears of the future, holding this life with all its high duties in abeyance to that which is to come—that she and the children she has borne have been wrongfully subjugated by priestcraft and superstition.

These resolutions immediately called forth a sermon in opposition from the Rev. A. H. Strong, D.D., president of the Rochester Theological Seminary (Baptist), in which he said:

> She is subordinate to man in office, she is to be helper, not principal. Therefore man has precedence in the order of creation, woman is made of man, and to supply the felt need of man. The

race, therefore, is called the race of man and not the race of
woman. For this office of subordination and whether they
assert it or not, women are fitted by their very constitution, and
in the very creation of mankind in the garden of beauty unde-
filed by the slimy track of the serpent as it was, God ordained
the subordination of woman and the differences of nature that
makes her subordination inevitable. The power of rule seems to
me to have been invested in the head of the family that he may
act for them, or rather that they may act through him.

The assertion of this theologian that "the race therefore is
called the race of man and not the race of woman," is of the same
character as that of Inquisitor Sprenger in regard to the word
femina, as applied to woman, showing the intellectual calibre of
both inquisitor and theologian to be the same. But in their assertion of woman's inferiority and subordination, neither Chaplain
Gray nor President Strong proceeded quite as far as an opposing
speaker at the Philadelphia Woman Suffrage Convention of 1854,
who said, "Let woman first prove that she has a soul, both the
Bible and the Church deny it." Here we are set back to the
Macon Council of the sixth century, which debated the question
of woman's humanity.

That the church of the nineteenth century possesses the same
character as that of the fourteenth, the twelfth, the fifth, was
forcibly illustrated during the early days of the antislavery struggle,
especially in its persecution of the women who took part in that
reform. Lucretia Mott and Esther Moore were integral members
of the American Anti-slavery Society, having assisted in the convention which organized this society in 1883. Shortly afterward
the Grimke sisters of South Carolina, Sarah and Angelina, convinced of the sinfulness of slavery, left their delightful home in
Charleston, and coming North, spoke eloquently through Massachusetts against those wrongs of which they themselves had been
witnesses. The church, becoming frightened at woman's
increasing power and influence, determined to crush her work. Its
action began with the Orthodox Congregational, at that time the

largest and most influential ecclesiastical body of Massachusetts, and in 1837 the General Association of Massachusetts issued a pastoral letter calling upon all "churches under their care" to defend themselves by closing their doors against the abolitionists, who had set aside the laws of God by welcoming women to their platforms and allowing them to speak in public;[6] section third was the most significant portion of this pastoral letter.

III. We invite your attention to the dangers which at present seem to threaten the female character with widespread and permanent injury.

"The appropriate duties and influence of woman are clearly stated in the New Testament. Those duties and that influence are unobtrusive and private, but the source of mighty power. When the mild, dependent, softening influence of woman under the sternness of man's opinions is fully exercised, society feels the effects of it in a thousand forms. The power of woman is her dependence, flowing from the consciousness of that weakness which God has given her for her protection, and which keeps her in those departments of life that form the character of individuals and of the nation. There are social influences which females use in promoting piety and the great objects of Christian benevolence which we cannot too highly commend. We appreciate the unostentatious prayers and efforts of woman in advancing the cause of religion at home and abroad; in Sabbath schools; in leading religious inquirers to the pastors for instruction; and in all such associated effort as becomes the modesty of her sex; and earnestly hope that she may abound more and more in these labors of piety and love.

"But when she assumes the place and tone of man as a public reformer, our care and protection of her seem unnecessary; we put ourselves in self-defense against her; she yields the power which God has given her for her protection, and her character becomes unnatural. If the vine whose strength and beauty is to lean upon the trellis work, and half conceal its clusters, thinks to assume the independence and the overshadowing nature of the elm, it will not only cease to bear fruit, but fall in shame and dishonor into the dust. We cannot, therefore, but regret the mistaken conduct of those who encourage females to bear an obtrusive and ostentatious part in measures of reform, and countenance any of that sex who so far forget themselves as to itinerate in the character of public lecturers and teachers. We especially deplore the intimate acquaintance and promiscuous conversation of females with regard to things which ought not to be named; by which that modesty and delicacy which is the charm of domestic life, and which constitutes the true influence of woman in society is consumed, and the way opened, as we apprehend, for degeneracy and ruin.

"We say these things not to discourage proper influences against sin, but to secure such reformation as we believe is scriptural, and will be permanent."

That we may rightly judge the character of this pastoral letter, it must be remembered, that no discussion upon what is known as "the woman question" took place at those meetings, which were entirely devoted to the southern slave. This letter was written by men, emanating from a body of christian people that sustained colored slavery as an institution upon which God had as equally placed his sanction, as upon the subordination of woman. To such extent have the conscience and will been under the bondage of the priesthood, that the more timid members of the antislavery society became frightened, even some of those who believed in woman's equality, advising these speakers to yield their rights in the meetings, lest the ministers who had joined them should withdraw, taking others with them. Thus priestly intolerance and the timidity of antislavery men, had the effect of silencing the philanthropic and eloquent Grimke sisters,[7] in their efforts for the freedom of the slave. After ten months' work, their voices were heard no more. These sisters were not only persecuted in the North, under ban of the church, but in the South the State united with the Church, and by a decree of the city of Charleston they were rendered permanent exiles from home, and informed that should they return despite this, they would not be able to escape personal violence from a mob. With one noble exception, this mandate of the church and clergy had effect for a time in silencing woman's plea for the slave. For seven long years the voice of but one woman, that of Abby Kelly,[8] was heard upon the antislavery platform, and the persecutions of the church made her life one long martyrdom; her appeals for the slave, were met by mob violence, furious howls, cries, and the vilest language, being supplemented by more material efforts for silencing her voice. Were these proceedings not so thoroughly substantiated, the time so shortly past, credence could not be given as to the means used against this noble woman, to prevent her pleading for those so greatly wronged.[9] Ministers of high standing, assailed her from the pulpit, a favorite text being, "Revelations" 2–20. I "have a few things against thee, because thou suffereth that woman, Jezebel, which calleth herself a prophetess, to teach and seduce my servants to commit fornication." Not alone the Congregational body, but all Christian sects, were imbued with the same persecuting spirit, a Methodist presiding elder characterizing the Garrisonian societies, as no longer antislavery, but "no-government, no-sabbath, no-church, no-bible, no-marriage, woman's rights societies."

That woman had assumed the right to speak in public for the oppressed, was the origin of all this vituperation. Its real cause was of the same nature as that which laid 30,000 heads low, at St. Bartholamew, that woman's voice had been heard in public contrary to the teaching of the church. It was perhaps foreseen that she might, as really at a later period was done, draw a vivid illustration of the similitude between the condition of the white wife, and the black slave.[10] The unity and peace of the World's Antislavery Convention, London, 1840, was disturbed by the hostility of several clergymen, and a few bigoted laymen of the same spirit, who objected to the recognition of the women delegates sent by several American societies, among whom were Lucretia Mott and Esther Moore, members of the parent organization. After a spirited discussion their admission was decided to be a violation of the ordinances of Almighty God, and their credentials were rejected.[11]

In 1843, the Hopkinson Association of Congregational Divines, of New Hampshire, unanimously enacted a statute in opposition to women opening their lips in church, even to "sigh" or "groan" in contrition; doubtless agreeing with Minister Douglas, that they were incapable of understanding a discourse directed to the brethren, who alone were allowed to shout "Amen," "Bless the Lord," and "Glory." By a strange inconsistency women were still allowed to sing "under men as leaders." This statute of restriction, declared:

> But, as to leading men, either in instruction or devotion, and as to any interruption or disorder in religious meetings, "Let your women keep silence in the churches"; not merely let them be silent, but let them keep or preserve silence. Not that they may not preach, or pray, or exhort merely, but they may not open their lips to utter any sounds audibly. Let not your women in promiscuous religious meetings preach or pray audibly, or exhort audibly, or sigh, or groan, or say Amen, or utter the precious words, "Bless the Lord," or the enchanting sounds, "Glory! Glory!"

In 1888, forty-five years after this statute, Rev. Dr. Theodore L. Cuyler in the *New York Evangelist*, gave his opinion in regard to woman's action in reform work and her demand for a share in making the laws which govern her, in this wise:

> We can say frankly to our temperance brethren, that if they attempt to lash the wise project of prohibition of saloons, and the foolish project of female suffrage inseparably together, they will encounter fatal opposition. They will repel, tenfold more sensible voters than they will win. Their most eloquent and logical advocate, Dr. Herrick Johnson, is intensely opposed to the Lucy Stone and Elizabeth Cady Stanton doctrines of woman suffrage, as I am. Nineteen-twentieths of our Presbyterian ministers will never cast a vote which is nominally only for prohibition, and yet is really a vote for burdening womanhood with civil government. What is true of our church is true of the Episcopal, Reformed, Baptist, Congregationalist, and the most influential portion of the Methodist church.

The same year of President Strong's opposing sermon, 1878, the United Presbyterian Assembly, passed a resolution to the effect that they found no sufficient authority in Scripture to warrant the ordination of women as deacons, yet they might with profit to themselves, and great advantage to the cause of suffering humanity, and for Christ, be *allowed to act as assistants to deacons*, thus emphasizing the dominant church teaching of woman's irresponsibility and secondary position to man. The same year, however, an advance step was taken in Europe, the Synod of Born (Old Catholic), following the example of Père Hyacinth, adopted a resolution in favor of the marriage of the clergy by a vote of 76 to 22. At the same time the Old Catholics were taking this advance step, the Protestant Episcopal Diocesan Convention of South Carolina, forbade woman's voting upon church matters, although it was proven during the discussion that in some parishes there were but five male members. The Southern Baptist Convention, held in Savannah, Georgia, 1885, appointed a committee with title of, and whose business was to decide upon "Representation by Women" in church affairs. This committee reported in favor of the word "brethren" instead of "members" being incorporated in the constitution, thus confirming the right of man alone to take part in church councils. Having thus effectively closed the lips of women on discussion of church questions, the convention introduced a resolution on divorce[12] followed by a speech declaring that but one cause could exist. The convention having shut off all chance for woman's opinion upon this question of equal and even of more vital interest to her, "applaudingly and overwhelmingly adopted the resolution." At the annual election for officers of Christ Church, New Haven, Connecticut, April 1886, a discussion arose upon the right of women to become members of the society and consequently voters it in. Several ladies having signified a desire to unite with the society, Bishop Williams was consulted as to their admission; he decided the Canon was clearly against them, and on motion of the clerk their application was rejected, only one member speaking in favor.

The title of the sermons still preached upon woman, illustrate priestly thought regarding her. Among those of recent date are found, "Blighted Women"; "Sins of Women"; "Women and

Divorce"; "Women and Skepticism"; "Woman's Place and Work";
"Our Common Mother"; "The Relation of Husband and Wife";
"Marriage and Divorce"; "The Sphere of Woman"; "Husband and
Wife"; "A Mission for Women"; "The Church and the Family";
"The Duties of Wives to Husbands"; these sermons all subordi-
nating woman to man in every relation of life; all designed to
repress woman's growing tendency towards freedom, and her claim
for the same opportunities in life conceded to man. That the clerical teaching of woman's subordination to man was not alone a
doctrine of the dark ages, is proven by the most abundant testimony of today. The famous See trial of 1876, which shook not
only the Presbytery of Newark, but the whole Synod of New
Jersey, and finally the General Presbyterian Assembly of the United
States, was based upon the doctrine of the divinely appointed subordination of woman to man, and arose simply because Rev. Dr.
Isaac See admitted two ladies to his pulpit to speak upon temperance; Rev. Dr. Craven, the prosecutor, declared this act to have
been "an indecency in the sight of Jehovah." He expressed the
general clerical and church view, when he said:

> I believe the subject involves the honor of my God. I believe
> the subject involves the headship and crown of Jesus. Woman
> was made for man and became first in the transgression. My
> argument is that subordination is natural, the subordination of
> sex. Dr. See has admitted marital subordination, but this is not
> enough; there exists a created subordination; a divinely arranged
> and appointed subordination of woman as woman, to man as
> man. Woman was made for man and became first in the trans-
> gression. The proper condition of the adult female is marriage;
> the general rule for ladies is marriage. Women without children,
> it might be said, could preach, but they are under the general
> rule of subordination. It is not allowed woman to speak in the
> church. Man's place is on the platform. It is positively base for
> a woman to speak in the pulpit; it is base in the sight of Jehovah.
> The whole question is one of subordination.[13]

Thus before a vast audience largely composed of women, Dr. Craven stood and with denunciatory manner, frequently bringing his fists or his Bible emphatically down, devoted a four hours' speech to proving that the Bible taught woman's subordination to man. His arguments were the same as those of the church in the past and were based upon the same theory, viz. that woman was created inferior *to* man, *for* man, and was the first in sin. He referred to the fashions as aid in his argument, saying, "In every country, under every clime, from the peasant woman of Naples, with a handkerchief over her hair, to the women before me with bonnets, every one wears something upon her head in token of subordination." Dr. Craven made this statement in direct contradiction to historical facts which prove that the head covering is always removed in presence of a superior. To remain bareheaded is an act of deference to a higher authority. Even the Quaker custom of men's wearing the hat in meeting, originated as an act of defiance to the Anglican Church. Dr. Craven also forgot to state that flowing hair has always been regarded as an emblem of superiority and freedom; clipped hair that of a slave or prisoner. Thus Dr. Craven's appeal to fashion reacted against him in the minds of all historically informed persons, yet together with his other statements, it was fully endorsed by most of his brother clergymen present, some of whom enthusiastically shouted, "Amen!" At the close of his speech several other clergymen, gave their views. Dr. Ballentine considered the subject too simple for an argument. Dr. Few Smith, although he "admired Miss Smiley, more than almost any orator he had ever listened to, did not want her or any other woman to permanently occupy the Presbyterian pulpit." Dr. Wilson rejoiced to see so many women crowding in the lecture room; but Brother See should not take all the glory to himself. He was glad to see the women take so deep an interest in the subject under discussion; but as he looked at them he asked himself: "What will all the children do while these women are away from home?" A decision of censure against Dr. See, was agreed in by the Synod of New Jersey, and confirmed by the General Assembly of the Presbyterian Church of the United States, in session at Pittsburg.

Thus we find that the Christianity of today continues to teach the existence of a superior and an inferior sex in the church, possessing different rights and held accountable to a different code of morals. Not alone did Dr. Craven express the idea that woman's very dress was typical of her inferiority, but the Right Rev. Dr. Coxe, Bishop of the Western (Episcopal) Diocese of New York refused the sacrament in 1868, to the lady patients of the Clifton Springs sanitarium whose heads were uncovered, although the chapel was under the same roof and on the same floor with the patients' rooms. This same Right Rev. Dr. Coxe, in a speech at his installation as first president of the Ingham Seminary for young ladies, declared "the laws of God to be plainly Salic." Rev. W. W. Patten, D.D., president of Howard University, Washington, D.C., in a sermon preached at the Congregational church, upon "Woman and Skepticism," January, 1885, advanced the proposition that as soon as they (women), depart from their natural sphere, they become atheistical and immoral.[14] In March, 1891, a half-column editorial in the *Presbyterian* discussed the ethics and æsthetics of woman's dress at communions, not precisely in line with Dr. Coxe, yet of the same general character as to regulating woman's dress, in, "Should women receive the elements at communion with gloved hands?" Some authorities objected to the practice upon the ground "that nothing might come between the recipient and the mystic power contained in the bread and wine after consecration by the priest." But while, as the editor remarks, "It is after all a very small matter," it is in a historical aspect, a great one, showing such pronounced change from the church teaching of but a few centuries since, when women were forbidden to take the eucharist in their naked hands because of their impurity. Rev. Mr. Denhurst, member of the Connecticut Legislature (House), during a hearing before a committee upon that question March 10, 1886, while speaking favorably of woman suffrage still betrayed his belief in the old theological idea that women brought sin into the world, through which, her subordination to man ensued. But like Dr. See, he limited this subordination to married women, saying:

As a minister of the gospel, I deny that you can find anywhere in the Bible, woman's subordination till she sent the curse of sin upon the world, and that relates only to married women, and marriage is a matter of choice.

The spiritual and temporal superiority of man over woman is affirmed by clergymen of the present day as strongly as by those of the dark ages, and sermons in opposition to her equality of rights are as frequently preached. The entrance of woman into renumerative industries is as energetically opposed as is her demand for governmental and religious freedom. Rev. Morgan Dix, rector of Trinity church, New York, in a series of "Lenten Lectures"[15] a few years since, made woman the subject of violent attacks as an inferior and subordinate being, now attempting to pass beyond the bounds set by God for her restraint.

There is a more emphatic, a more hopeless degradation for her. It is seen when she seeks to reverse the laws of her nature and upset the economy of the universe, pushing her way out of her own sphere into a rivalry with men in their sphere and in their proper pursuits. On that must follow a degradation, greatly to be feared. When the claim for rights seems to be taking the form of a competition with man, on a field which God has reserved for man only, in a work not suited to the woman, and in professions already overstocked that must end, not in enhancing the merit of woman in his eye but in making her offensive and detestable. There is a point beyond which patience will not hold out; and of this let the woman be sure: that if she go too far the end will arise; and man having long borne her manners and finding that she is becoming a social nuisance and a general tormentor, will finally lose all respect for her and thrust her away with loathing and disgust and bid her behave herself and go back to her old inferiority.

In this series of lectures, Dr. Dix emphatically declared man's spiritual supremacy even in the household.

The father is by God's law, priest over his household; to him should they look as a witness for that God who gave him his rank and title.[16]

The sects agree in their teachings regarding woman; Rev. A. Sherman, at one time president of Bacon College, Kentucky, declaring that woman was first in transgression, that she beguiled man and was therefore put in bondage under his authority, said:

The wide-spreading contempt for this truth exhibited by the political-religious fashion and infidelity of the age, is one of the most alarming symptoms of approaching anarchy and the overthrow of our liberties. The attempt which is being made in these United States to elevate the wife to a perfect equality with the husband, or to change in any respect the relation between them, established by God himself, is rank infidelity, no matter what specious disguise it may assume.

In a sermon of his Lenten series, entitled "The Calling of a Christian Woman, and Her Training to Fulfill It," Dr. Dix said:

We, priests, who whatever our personal short comings, have a commission from above and a message to man from God, and are the mouthpiece of that church to which his handmaidens belong, may be and ought to be able to help occasionally, by merely stating what the Bible and the church declare on certain great matters, on which many lower ones depend. . . . What did Almighty God, the Creator, the wise Father of all, make woman for? What did he intend her to do? What did he not mean her to do or try to do?

He answered these questions in a lecture entitled, "A Mission for Woman," of the same series.

Looking for a mission, for a work to do, this is the attitude of many women today. . . . You hear of the education of women, of coeducation of the sexes of emancipation of woman from bonds—what bonds the Lord only knows! Here is a mission

worthy of yourselves, it is of all works that could be rendered
the fittest for a church woman, because she was at the beginning of all the trouble in the world. . . . We believe the old
story of the Bible reaffirmed by Christ and his apostles, that
Adam was not deceived by the devil, but that the woman being
deceived, was in the transgression. Now to her with whom the
wrong began, we look for the beginning of the right.
Remember that in the woman are the poles of the good and
the evil in human nature.

When she is good she is the best of all that exists; when
bad, the worst.

Another sermon of this Lenten series, expressed the views of
the reverend gentleman upon the family relation, bearing of children and divorce, in which he expressed his hatred of modern
development saying:

I feel great solicitude about the subject of this evening's lecture;
I had rather not touch it at all. You may think that its selection
is an instance of that disrespect to which I have referred. Not
so, oh, not so. I hold the old ideas. I abhor and detest the
modern development; before any woman who fears God, does
her duty, and gives us in her life and acts the picture of a true
and beautiful womanliness, I rise up and bless her and do her
reverent homage. It is thus in no spirit of assumption that I shall
say what I have to say tonight. It is rather in a tone of remonstrance, of wonder, of expostulation. Why do women err as
they do? Why lower themselves to men's level? Why should the
queens abdicate their thrones and go down to the ring and act
unseemly parts and lay their honor in the dust? Let us think this
evening of some things done by women which one would have
said that no woman with a woman's heart and a woman's sense
could, after due reflection, justify. Sins fall naturally into groups
or classes, and if I speak this evening of only one class of sins it
is because the time does not permit us to take a larger survey of
the field. We shall limit ourselves, then, to these topics.

The lack of serious views of life and the habit of turning
the thoughts exclusively to enjoyment. The degradation of the

idea of matrimony, as shown by entering into that estate for low and unworthy motives. The deliberate determination of some married women to defeat the objects for which marriage was instituted; to have no real home; to avoid first the pains and next the cares and duties of maternity. The habit, where a home exists, of neglecting it by spending most of the time away from it, running up and down in pursuit of excitement and turning their children over to the care of servants. The growing indifference to the chief of all social abominations, divorce, and the toleration of lax notions about it.

These questions of most vital import to woman, to her material condition, intellectual development and place in the church, Rev. Dr. Dix and the great body of the church, deem themselves supremely competent to adjust without woman's voice upon them. Wherever she has shown her views upon the subject of education, industries, the family, the church, to be in opposition to those of theologians, she has at once been told to remain in her old position of "inferiority" looking up to man as her divinely appointed master and spiritual head; Dr. Dix, in his lectures, but gave the views of priests of all denominations at the present day. Despite the advancing civilization of the age, and the fact that in so many avocations woman has shown her capacity for taking equal part with man, we find theology still unprogressive; a portion of the press, however, severely criticized these discourses.[17] The "Lenten Pastoral" 1886, of Rev. A. Cleveland Coxe, bishop of Western New York, to the laity of his diocese, contained a middle-age reminder to women of the impurity of motherhood, in the demand made for church cleansing subsequent to her bringing an immortal being into life:

6. Christian women, active as they often are, above all comparison with men, are yet sometimes negligent of their immediate duties as wives and mothers and fail to exert that healthful influence over the family, which God has made it the high privilege of woman to exercise in this sphere of her duty and her glory. The office for "the Churching of Women" testifies against those who neglect it, as for-

getting the dignity of motherhood and that gratitude to God
which every woman owes to the Christian religion, for enthroning
her in the household, and making the example of the "Blessed
among Women" her peculiar lesson and incentive to piety.

Many portions of this advice are an open insult to woman,
and could the divine but see it, is even from the Christian standard, an imputation upon that being he professes to revere as the
Creator of the universe.

A work was recently written by an English bishop, bearing
upon the governmental effort for repeal of the law forbidding
marriage with a deceased wife's sister or brother. This work was
written for the express purpose of proving that, while it is eminently improper and sinful for a woman to marry her deceased
husband's brother, it is eminently proper and right for a man to
marry his deceased wife's sister, and this upon the same principle
that governed the disinheritance of woman under the Salic law;
i.e., because by marriage a woman becomes merged into her husband's family. He specifically declares that the sister of the wife is
in no sense the sister of the husband, therefore it is permissable for
a man to marry his wife's sisters successively. But he affirms that to
the contrary, the widow cannot marry her deceased husband's
brother, as by the act of her marriage she became a part of her
husband's family; a second marriage to such husband's brother
thereby becoming incestuous. This is the law of England, both
religious and civil. A striking evidence of the incongruity of this
law is found in the fact that the illegitimacy of such brother is held
to destroy the relationship, as by law of both church and state, an
illegitimate child is not held as related to its father; he is the son of
nobody. A woman can marry two brothers in succession, one the
child of marriage, the other a child of the same father born outside of the marriage relation. The son of nobody, a being unfa-
thered in the eye of the law, is the brother of nobody. A striking
instance of the effect of this law occurred in England within the
past few years, when a lady successively married two brothers, the
first a natural son of the Earl of Waldegrave, the second his legiti-

mate son. The father, although not recognized as such in law, left the bulk of his property to his natural son; the title, over which he had no power of alienation, descending to the son born under authority of the church. The first husband, dying, the lady afterward married the legitimate son, thus becoming first, "Mrs." Waldegrave, and afterwards, "Lady" Waldegrave, securing both fortune and title by her marriage with the nonrecognized and lawrecognized sons of the same father, and breaking neither the law of state or church in so doing. American clergymen of the Episcopal church, have expressed views in accordance with those of the English bishop. Rev. George Zabriskie Gray, D.D., dean of the Episcopal Theological School of Cambridge, Mass., published a work in 1885 entitled *Husband and Wife*, also suggested by the constantly debated English question of State, concerning the lawfulness of marriage with a deceased wife's sister. Dr. Gray coincides with many of his reverend brethren in the declaration that with the wife, no liberty of divorce is allowable, but his reasons present somewhat the freshness of novelty. As previously stated, the nonrelationship of husband and wife was at one time the general Christian belief. While like the English bishop, Rev. Mr. Gray admits the relationship of the wife to the husband to such extent that becoming fully absorbed by him his relatives become hers; like the English bishop he further declares that in consequence of this absorption, the wife loses her former family relationship, her mother and father, her sister or brother no longer bearing relationship to her, but have become to her as strangers. He said:

> The wife becomes a member of his family, while he does not become one of her own. The equilateral idea is a physiological[18] and psychological impossibility. The unity is in the man. The woman by marriage becomes a member of the man, therefore she cannot put him away; for a member cannot put away the head; the impurity of the wife imperils the family, renders pedigree and all concerned therein, uncertain, and so she may be put away. But the husband's unchastity, while it may be as sinful, yet has no such effect. It does not render it doubtful who are rightful children of his stock, who are enti-

tled to the name that he and his wife both bear, and therefore
does not call for the severance of the marriage tie, that is, the
dissolution of the family. That is, divorce, so far as Scripture
goes seems to be a measure for the protection of the family and
of the rightful inheritance of whatever is to be transmitted to
the children, and so a remedy open only to man. There seems
to be no way of preventing the abuse of divorce, if any principle is admitted that will extend it to woman.

Under this form of reasoning, both Dr. Gray and the English
bishop, dispose with case of the state obstacle to marriage with a
deceased wife's sister. Inasmuch as by marriage the husband forms
no ties of consanguinity with the wife's family, she having
become a member of his family without his having become a
member of hers, marriage with his deceased wife's sister would be
the same as marriage with an entire stranger, saying:

> As the husband enters into no connection with the wife's family,
> her sisters are no more his sisters, than they had been before.
> Therefore he may marry one of them as freely as any one else,
> as far as any real principle involved in matrimony is concerned.

The *Christian Register*, of Boston, commenting upon Dr.
Gray's work, although itself a recognized organ of the Episcopal
church, yet in a spirit more in accord with modern thought, carefully corrected the size of type in the word "wife" upon the title-
page and outside of the book, thus: HUSBAND AND WIFE:[19]
also facetiously referring to the late Artemus Ward, who at time of
the late civil war, was ready to sacrifice all his wife's relations.[20]
These two works of the English bishop and the American dean,
are consistent with the teaching of the Christian ages in reference
to woman. Not held as belonging primarily to herself, but ever to
some man, her very relationship to the mother who brought her
into life destroyed by law, she once again through the church is
presented to the world as a being without a birthright, not even
receiving for it Esau's mess of pottage, or a father's shorn blessing,
after its loss. She is held up to view as without father, mother, or

individual existence. Rev. Knox-Little, a high church clergyman of England, traveled in the United States in the fall of 1880. During his stay in Philadelphia, he preached a "Sermon to Women," in the large church of St. Clements. As reported in the *Times* of that city, its chief features were a representation of woman's inferior intellect, her duty of unqualified obedience to her husband, however evil his life, the sinfulness of divorce and the blessedness of a large family of children. He said:

> God made himself to be born of a woman to sanctify the virtue of endurance; loving submission is an attribute of woman; men are logical, but women lacking this quality, have an intricacy of thought. There are those who think woman can be taught logic; this is a mistake, they can never by any power of education arrive at the same mental status as that enjoyed by man, but they have a quickness of apprehension, which is usually called leaping at conclusions, that is astonishing. There, then, we have distinctive traits of a woman, namely: endurance, loving submission and quickness of apprehension. Wifehood is the crowning glory of a woman. In it she is bound for all time. To her husband she owes the duty of unqualified obedience. There is no crime which a man can commit which justifies his wife in leaving him or applying for that monstrous thing, divorce. It is her duty to subject herself to him always, and no crime that he can commit can justify her lack of obedience. If he be a bad or wicked man, she may gently remonstrate with him, but refuse him, never. Let divorce be anathema; curse it, curse this accursed thing, divorce; curse it, curse it! Think of the blessedness of having children. I am the father of many and there have been those who have ventured to pity me; "keep your pity for yourself," I have replied. "They never cost me a single pang." In this matter let women exercise that endurance and loving submission, which with intricacy of thought are their only characteristics.

Such a sermon as the above preached to women under the full blaze of nineteenth-century civilization, needs few comments. In it woman's inferiority and subordination are as openly asserted as at any time during the dark ages. According to Rev.

Knox-Little, woman possesses no responsibility; she is deprived of conscience, intelligent thought, self-respect, and is simply an appendage to man, a thing. As the clergy in the Middle Ages divided rights into those of persons and things, themselves being the persons, the laity things, so the Rev. Knox-Little and his ilk of today, divide the world into persons and things, men being the persons, and women the things. Rev. Dr. T. De Witt Talmage, of Brooklyn, New York, joins his brethren in preaching of "the first, fair, frail woman; her creation, her fall and her sorrow." Speaking of the trials of housekeepers, he said:

> Again, there is the trial of severe economy. Nine hundred and ninety-nine households out of the thousand are subject to it, some under more, and some under less stress of circumstances. Especially if a man smokes very expensive cigars and takes very costly dinners at the restaurants, he will be severe in demanding domestic economies. This is what kills thousands of women; attempting to make five dollars do the work of seven. How the bills come in. The woman is the banker of the household; she is the president, and cashier, and teller, discount clerk, and there is a panic every four weeks. This thirty years' war against high prices; this perpetual study of economics, this lifelong attempt to keep the outgoes less than the income exhausts millions of housekeepers. O, my sister, this is part of divine discipline.

It should require but little thought upon woman's part to see how closely her disabilities are interwoven with present religious belief and teaching as to her inferiority and preordained subordination. If she needs aid to thought, the Cravens, the Knox-Littles, the Talmages, will help her. The spirit of the priesthood, Protestant equally with Catholic, is that of the early and middle ages. The foundation being the same, the teaching is of similar character. From the sermons referred to, we can justly declare they express the opinions of the priesthood as a body; we meet no protest against them. Not a single church has denied these degrading theories; no clergyman has preached against the doctrines mentioned, blasphemous as they are against the primal rights of the soul. These sermons stand as representatives, not only of high-church theology in regard to woman, but as expressing the belief of all churches in her creation and existence as an inferior and appendage to man. All her suffering, material or spiritual, her restrictions, her sorrows, her deprivation of the right of unrestricted conscience are depicted as parts of her divine discipline, which she must accept with endurance and loving submission. Even from the criminal, she is not to free herself, or refuse him obedience. Scarcely a Protestant sect, that has not within a few years, in some way, placed itself upon record as sustaining the doctrine of woman's subordination. The Pan-Presbyterian Council that assembled in Edinburg a few years since, refused to admit a woman even as a listener to its proceedings, although women constitute at least two-thirds of the membership of that church. A solitary woman who persisted in remaining to listen to the discussions of this body, was removed by force; "six stalwart Presbyterians" lending their ungentle aid to her ejection. The same Pan-Presbyterian body in session in Philadelphia, the summer of 1880, laughed to scorn the suggestion of a liberal member that the status of woman in that church should receive some consideration; referring to the work of the Sisters of Charity, in the Catholic church, and that of women among the Quakers. Although this question was twice introduced it was as often "met with derisive laughter," and no action was taken upon it. But had this liberal member been wise enough to have brought before this body the fact that the Presbyterian church is losing its political influence because of the great preponderance of its women members without the ballot, he would have received more consideration. As all churches seek influence in politics, we may rest assured that when the church as a whole, or any sect thereof, shall be found sustaining the political rights of woman or her religious equality in the church, it will be from the worldly wisdom of a desire to retain fleeting political power. The life or the death of the church largely depends upon its political forethought.

Differing political rights have ever been productive of diverse moral codes. What was considered right for the king and the nobility has ever been wrong for the peasant. The moral rights of the master and the slave, were ever dissimilar, while under Christianity two codes of morals have ever been extant, the lax code for man, the strict for woman. This diversity is shown by the different position that society accords to an immoral man and an immoral woman, but nowhere is the recognition of differing codes of morals for man and woman as clearly shown as in the church, as presented in discourses of clergymen. To them adultery in the husband is merely a pastime in which he can indulge without injury to his wife, who is powerless to put him away, nor has she been wronged. But to the contrary, under the same teaching, should the wife prove thus unfaithful she should immediately be cast out. Colored pastors unite with their white brethren in denying woman's moral, spiritual or personal equality with man. Rev. Alexander Crummel,[21] a colored clergyman of Washington, rector of St. Luke's (Episcopal) church, in 1881, preached a sermon upon the biblical position of woman, which was published in tract form for circulation. He referred to her as having been created inferior to man, with no right, natural or acquired, by creation or revelation, to govern herself or hold opinions of her own. This sermon—"Marriage and Divorce"— laid down the following principles:

> Marriage is a divine institution. It came from God. It is not, therefore, the creation of legislative action. It is not merely a civil contract. It is not the invention of man. The estate of matrimony is a sacred one; originated by the will of God, and governed by his law. Marriage is indissoluble. Adultery on part of the wife is ground for divorce. Thus far we have considered the case with reference to the unfaithfulness of the wife, and have shown that when a woman violates the covenant of marriage by adultery, her husband has the right to divorce her. But now the question comes, "Is not this a reciprocal right?" When husbands are unfaithful, have not wives the right to divorce them? My reply is that no warrant for such divorce can be found in the Bible. Under both covenants, the right of divorce is given exclusively to husband. The right in all cases is guar-

anteed to the man only. And so far forth we have the word of God for its specific reservation to husbands. In no case is it even hinted that a woman has the right of divorce, if even her husband be guilty of unfaithfulness. There is a broad, general obligation laid upon woman in the marriage relation. The sum of the matter respecting the woman seems to be this; the woman is bound by the ties of wedlock during the whole period of her husband's life; and even under distressful circumstances has no right to break them; i.e., by divorce.

The additional reasons presented by Rev. Mr. Crummel against woman's right of divorce, even for the infidelity of the husband, are "The hidden mystery of generation, the wondrous secret of propagated life committed to the trust of woman." In thus referring to those laws of nature whose conditions are not yet fully understood, Rev. Mr. Crummel presented the strongest reasons why the mother, and not the father, should be regarded as the true head of the family. This "hidden mystery of generation, this wondrous secret of propagated life, committed to the trust of woman," most forcibly demonstrates that she should be the one in whose power is placed the opportunity for escape from an adulterous husband, thus enabling her to keep her body a holy temple for its divine-human uses, over which as priestess, she alone should possess control. The assertion of Rev. Alexander Crummel, that an adulterous husband cannot do the same wrong to the wife that the wife does to the husband under similar circumstances, is absolutely false. By reason of certain "physiological mysteries," to which he refers, but of which he also shows absolute ignorance, the wrong done woman by reason of her potential motherhood, is infinitely greater to her than similar infidelity upon her part can possibly be to the husband. And not to her alone but to the children whom she may bring to life. His attempted justification of the husband's adultery upon the plea that "when a man begets bastard children, he does so beyond the boundary of the home," and so cannot "foist spurious children upon the household and kindred—that the family is kept together," are most sophistical and fallacious methods of reasoning, entirely inimical to truth and purity. Of an absolutely selfish and libidinous character, they have been used by profligates in the church and in the state as pleas for a license that has no regard to the rights of woman, or the duties of fatherhood, and are not only essentially immoral in themselves, but are equally destructive of personal and social purity.

The individual and not the family, is the social unit; the rights of individuals are foremost. Immorality of man, everywhere presents a more serious and destructive aspect than that of woman. Aside from the unmarried mother whom society does not recognize as longer a part of it, is the irreparable wrong done to those innocent human beings whom Rev. Mr. Crummel designates as "spurious children"; whom the Catholics call "sacrilegious" when the father is shown to be a priest, and upon whom society at large terms "illegitimate." Closely connected with injury to the innocent child, itself, thrust into being without provision for its future needs, is the detriment to society which thus finds itself compelled to assume the duties belonging to the bastard father. Such children, for whom neither home nor fatherly care awaits, are allowed by him to grow up neglected street waifs, uneducated, untrained, uncared for, filling almshouses, reformatories, and prisons of the land, perhaps to die upon the gallows. The responsibility of such fathers is not a subject of church teaching; it is simply passed carelessly by, regardless of the unspeakable wrongs connected with it. If, as the Rev. Mr. Turnstall asserts, the Bible is not for woman, if his position is true, or if that of the Jews who claim that the Ten Commandments were given to man alone, is true, it is to man alone, that adultery is forbidden. Luther asserted that the Ten Commandments applied to neither Gentiles nor Christians, but only to the Jews. It was to man alone, that Christ spoke against adultery, saying: "Whosoever looketh upon a woman to lust after her hath already committed adultery with her, in his heart." To man, Christ also said: "Owing to the hardness of their hearts, Moses permitted a man to put away his wife, but it was not so from the beginning." Man, and not woman, is commanded to leave father and mother; man is to cleave unto his wife, not woman unto her husband. It was the men of Corinth whom Paul addressed concerning lewdness, "Such fornication was never known among the heathen as that a man should take his father's wife."[22]

One of the most remarkable facts connected with church teaching is the lightness with which such positive declarations of Christ as to the relations of husband and wife are cast aside, or his teaching entirely reversed, in order that man may receive license for an immorality forbidden to woman.

It must be noted that the chief reason given by the church for assuming woman's greater guilt in commiting adultery is not based upon the greater immorality of the act, per se, but the injury to property rights, succession, etc. It must also be noted, that the great objection of the church to divorce on part of woman, lies in the fact that the wife thus escapes from a condition of bondage to one of comparative freedom. In securing a divorce she repudiates the husband's "headship," she thus subverts his authority; by this act she places herself upon an equality of moral and property rights with man, and the church not admitting such equality between man and woman, is hostile to divorce upon her part. Every new security gained by woman for the protection of her civil rights in, or out of the family, is a direct blow at the church theory of her inferiority and subordination. Her full freedom is to be looked for through her increased legal and political rights and not through the church.

During the same year of the remarkable sermon, by Rev. Alexander Crummel, 1881, Rev. S. W. Dilke read a paper before the Social Science Association at Saratoga, entitled "Lax Divorce Legislation." He showed the same disregard for the rights of the individual, when the individual was a wife, as his brother clergymen, saying : "Our lax divorce system treats the wrongs of the wife, chiefly as those of a mere individual." He was assiduous in his regard for the protection of the womanly nature, recognizing sex, "her sex" as "a profound fact in nature," but why the sex of woman should be a more "profound fact" than the sex of man, he did not show. That woman now claims a recognition of her individuality as a being possessed of personal rights, is the basis of present attack upon divorce by the church; nor is the state more ready to admit her individual representation and personal rights of self-government. In March, 1887, Rev. E. B. Hurlbert preached a sermon in the First Baptist church of San Francisco on "The Relation of Husband and Wife"; afterward published, in which he said:

> The principal objection to the Episcopal marriage service raised by the self-willed woman of the period is, that it requires her to *obey* her husband. But this objection is leveled equally against the requirement of the word of God, and, furthermore, the additional promise to honor and love him can only be kept in the spirit of obedience. This obligation is founded upon the fact that he is her husband, and if she cannot reverence him for what he is in himself, still she must reverence him for the position which he holds. And, again, she must render this submissive reverence to her husband's headship as unto the Lord, "as is fit in the Lord." She reverences him not simply as a man, but as her own husband, behind whom stands the Lord himself. It is the Lord who has made him husband, and the honor with which she regards him, though himself personally not deserving it, is in reality an honoring of the Lord. Many a Christian woman, actuated by this motive, has been most tenderly submissive, dutiful and patient, as towards the most unreasonable and despotic of husbands—inspired by the remembrance that it was a service rendered unto Christ. Let the wife, then, reverence her husband for what he is in himself, for his loving and noble qualities; but if these qualities do not belong to him, then let her reverence him for the sake of his office—simply because he is her husband—and in either event let her reverence him, because in doing so she is honoring the Lord and Savior.

It is but a short time since the pastor of the Swedenborgian church, Washington, D.C., as reported by one of his flock, expressed to that body his opinion that the church had better remain unrepresented rather than have women represent it, and this, although nine-tenths of his congregation are women. It is, however, pleasing to state that the committee for that purpose elected an equal number of women with men; the efforts of the pastor against woman, securing but seven votes. The Unitarian and Universalist churches which ordain women to preach and administer the ordinances, still make these women pastors feel that the innovation is not a universally acceptable one. In a lengthy pastoral letter issued by the Episcopal convention held in Chicago a few years since, it was asserted that the claim of the wife to an equal right with her husband, to the control of her person, her property and her earnings was "disparaging the Christian law of the household." The Methodist church still refuses to place woman upon an equality with man, either in the ministry or in lay representation, a few years since taking from them their previous license to preach, and this despite the fact that Mrs. Van Cott, a woman evangelist, did such severe work during a period of fourteen years, as to seriously injure her health, and so successful were her ministrations that she brought more converts to the church than a dozen of its most influential bishops during the same time. To such bitter lengths has opposition to woman's ordination been carried in that church, that Rev. Mr. Buckley, editor of the *Christian Union*,[23] when debating the subject, declared that he would oppose the admission of the mother of our Lord into the ministry, the debate taking on most unseemly form.[24] Miss Oliver who had long been pastor of the Willoughby Street church, in Brooklyn, appealed to the General Conference of the Methodist Episcopal Church, at its session in Cincinnati, May, 1880, for full installment and ordination, saying:

"I am sorry to trouble our dear mother church with any perplexing question, but it presses me also, and the church and myself must decide something. I am so thoroughly convinced that the Lord has laid commands upon me in this direction that it becomes with me really a question of my own soul's salvation." She then gave the reasons that induce her to believe that she is called to pastoral work, and concluded: "I have made almost every conceivable sacrifice to do what I believe to be God's will. Brought up in a conservative circle in New York City, that held it a disgrace for a woman to work, surrounded

with the comforts and advantages of ample means, and trained
in the Episcopal church, I gave up home, friends and support,
went counter to prejudices that had become second nature to
me, worked several years to constant exhaustion, and suffered
cold, hunger and loneliness; the things hardest for me to bear
were laid upon me. For two months my own mother would
not speak to me. When I entered the house she turned and
walked away, and when I sat at the table she did not recognize
me. I have passed through tortures to which the flames of martyrdom would be nothing, for they would end in a day; and
through all this time and today I could turn off to positions of
comparative ease and profit. I ask you, fathers and brethren, tell
me what would you do in my place? Tell me what would you
wish the church to do toward you, were you in my place?
Please only apply the golden rule, and vote in conference
accordingly."

In answer to this powerful and noble appeal, and in reply to
all women seeking the ministry of that church, the General Conference passed this resolution:

> *Resolved:* That women have already all the rights and privileges
> in the Methodist church, that are good for them, and that it is
> not expedient to make any change in the books of discipline
> that would open the doors for their ordination to the ministry.

The General Conference, after so summarily deciding what
was for the spiritual good of women, in thus refusing to recognize their equality of rights to the offices of that church, resolved
itself as a whole into a political convention, adjourning in a body
to Chicago before its religious business was finished, in order that
its presence might influence the National Republican Convention there assembled, to nominate General Grant for a third term
to the presidency of the United States; General Grant being in
affiliation with the Methodist church.

The Congregational church is placed upon record through
laws, governing certain of its bodies, which state that:

By the word "church" is meant the adult males duly admitted and retained by the First Evangelical church of Cambridgeport, present at any regular meeting of said church and voting by a majority.

The *New York Independent*, of February 24, 1881, commenting upon this official declaration that only "adult males" are to be considered the "church," says:

The above is Article XIV of the by-laws of the society connected with the aforesaid church. It is a matter of gratitude that the society, if it forbids females to vote in the church, yet allows them to pray and to help the society raise money.

The Rev. W. V. Turnstall, in the *Methodist Recorder*, a few years since, gave his priestly views in regard to woman, and by implication, those of the Methodist church. He declared woman to be under the curse of subjection to man, a curse not removable until the resurrection. He said that, under the Mosaic law woman had no voice in anything; that she could hold no office, yet did so in a few instances when God wished to especially humiliate the nation; that she was scheduled as a higher piece of property; that even the Bible was not addressed to her but to man alone; woman finding her salvation even under the new covenant, not directly through Jesus, but approaching him through man; his points were:

First: That woman is under a curse which subjects her to man.
Second: This curse has never been removed, nor will it be removed until the resurrection.
Third: That woman under the Mosaic law, God's civil law, had no voice in anything. That she was not allowed her oath; that she was no part of the congregation of Israel; that her geneology was not kept; that no notice was taken of her birth or death, except as these events were connected with some man of providence; that she was given no control of her children; that she could hold no office; nor did she, except in a few instances, when to reproach and humiliate the nation, God suspended his own law, and made an instrument of women for the time being. That she offered no sacrifices, no redemption

money was paid for her; that she received no religious rites; that the mother's cleansing was forty days longer, and the gift was smaller for a female child than for a male; and that in the tenth commandment—always in force—she is scheduled as a higher species of property; that her identity was completely merged in that of her husband.

Fourth: That for seeking to hold office Miriam was smitten with leprosy; and that under the new covenant, she is only permitted to pray or prophesy with her head covered, which accounts for the fashion of wearing bonnets in public to this day; that she is expressly prohibited from rule in the church or usurpation of authority over the man.

Fifth: That to vote is to rule, voting carrying with it all the collaterals of making, expounding, and executing law; that God has withheld from woman the right to rule, either in the church, the state or the family; that He did this because of her having "brought sin and death into the world, and all our woe."

Sixth: That the Bible is addressed to man and not to woman; that man comes to God through Jesus, and woman comes to Jesus through man that every privilege the wife enjoys she but receives through the husband, for God has declared that woman shall not rule man, but be subject unto him.

A more explicit statement of the opinion of the church regarding woman is seldom found. Later action of the Methodist body proves its agreement with Rev. Mr. Turnstall. The General Conference of that church convened May 1, 1888, in the Metropolitan Opera House, New York, numbering delegates from every part of the United States as well as many from foreign lands. Among these delegates were sixteen women. The question of their admission came up the first day. The senior bishop, Rev. Thomas Bowman, in his opening remarks, declared that body to stand in the presence of new conditions, in that they found names upon the roll of a class of persons whose eligibility had never been determined by the high tribunal of the church. A committee was appointed to report upon their admission. Bishop Merrill, occupying the chair upon the second day, said that "for the first time in the history of the conference, women had been sent as delegates, but the bishops did not think the women were eligible. The report of the committee was submitted, which declared that after a serious discussion they had become convinced that, while the rule was passed relating to the admission of lay delegates to the General Conference, the church contemplated admission only to men as lay delegates, and that under the constitution and laws, women were not eligible. The committee agreed that the protest against women should be sustained, and the conferences from which they were sent, be notified that their seats were vacant. A long discussion ensued. Rev. John Wiley, president of the Drew Theological Seminary of the New York Conference, spoke against woman's admission, saying:

> That if the laws of the church were properly interpreted they would prove that women are not eligible and then, besides, no one wanted them in the General Conference.

Rev. J. R. Day, the New York Conference, argued against the admission of women, saying:

> When the law was passed for the admission of lay delegates it was never intended that women should be delegates to the General Conference. It is proposed today to make one of the most stupendous pieces of legislation that has been known to Christendom. I am not opposed to woman doing the work that she is capable of doing but I do not think that she should intrude upon the General Conference. Woman has not the necessary experience; this is a tremendous question.

Rev. Jacob Rothweiler, of the Central German Conference, asserted that:

> The opponents of the report are trying to override the constitution of the church, and are making an effort to strike at the conscientiousness of 90 percent of the Christian church which has existed for the last 1,800 years. The history of Christianity shows that women were never intended to vote.

The conference was seriously divided upon this question. Although eventually lost, yet many clergymen permeated with the spirit of advancing civilization, voted in its favor, among them Rev. Dr. Hammond, of Syracuse, New York, a delegate for the episcopacy; while arrayed in bitter opposition was Rev. Mr. Buckley, editor of the *Christian Union*, also a candidate for the bishopric, and the man that when the question of the ordination of Miss Oliver came up a few years since, declared he would oppose the admission of the Mother of the Lord, to the ministry. His remark recalls that of Tetzel, the great Catholic dealer in indulgences, given in another part of this work, and illustrates to what extent of blasphemy the opponents of women's equality proceed. It was not until the seventh day of the Conference that the question of woman's admission was decided in the negative, and the great Methodist Episcopal church, put itself upon record as opposed to the recognition of more than one-half of its members. The women delegates were not even allowed seats upon the floor during the debate. Mrs. Nind, president of the Woman's Foreign Missionary Society, arose to vote, but was not counted, although the Woman's Foreign Missionary societies are making converts where men cannot reach—in the zenanas. The action of the Conference was foreshadowed by that of Baltimore a few weeks previously, when it was decided that women missionaries should not be permitted to administer communion in the zenanas as it would open the door for their ordination to the ministry and this despite the fact that women alone are admitted to the zenanas. At the Methodist minister's bimonthly meeting, Syracuse, N.Y., near time of the General Conference, Rev. Thomas Tinsey, of Clyde, read a paper entitled "Is it advisable to make women of the church eligible to all the ecclesiastical councils and the ministerial order of the church," quoting Paul in opposition to giving her a voice, saying:

> What can our modern advocates of licensing and ordaining women and electing them to annual conferences, do with the command to the Corinthians, "Let your women keep silence in

the church"; or to Timothy: "Let the women learn in silence and all subjection," Paul certainly meant something by such teaching. The position taken by the Fathers of Methodism appears to me to be the only tenable one, viz: that the prohibition applies to the legislation or official business of the church—precisely the kind of work contemplated in the effort to make them eligible to the General Conference, and to Methodist orders. Concerning these things, "Let them learn of their husbands at home."

Rev. Mr. Tinsey further gave his opinion as to the comparative uselessness of woman. He was able to conceive of no good reason for her creation, aside from that of burden bearer in the process of reproduction, saying:

> Woman is that part or side of humanity upon which the great labor, care and burden of reproduction is placed. We can conceive of no good reason for making women aside from this. Man is certainly better suited to all other work.

After discussion, the ministers present generally agreed that, because of motherhood, woman should be debarred from such official recognition.

The final ground of women's exclusion as delegates to the General Conference, is most noticeable inasmuch as appeal was ultimately made to the State. Upon the seventh day's session it was resolve to suspend the rules and continue the debate on the admission of women as lay-delegates. So anxious were men to speak that forty-one delegates at once sprung to their feet and claimed the floor. Judge Taylor, a lay delegate from the St. Louis conference, walking down the aisle with a number of law books under his arm, proceeded to argue the question on constitutional grounds, saying:

> It would do much harm to admit women at the present time. There are bishops to be elected and other important matters to be voted on, and if women are admitted and allowed to vote, and it should subsequently be decided that women should not be entitled to seats, the acts of the present General Conference would be illegal and unconstitutional.

While claiming, personally, to favor women's admission, he quoted law to sustain their rejection, and wished the question to be submitted to a vote of the church. The "vote of the church," as shown by the adoption of Rev. F. B. Neely's amendment, signifying the ministers present at annual conferences.[25] The vote upon this amendment, which excluded women from seats in the General Conference, submitting their eligibility to the decision of ministers of the annual conferences, was adopted 237 to 198. It thus requires three-fourths vote of the members present and voting at the annual conferences, this vote to be ratified by a two-thirds vote of the General Conference in order to woman's acceptance as lay delegate to such General Conference.[26] Aside from the fact of an appeal to the civil law for the exclusion of woman, thus showing the close union of church and state, one other important point must be noticed. In the declaration that the church should be consulted in regard to such an important matter, that body was defined as the ministers of the annual conference, laymen not here ranking as part of the church. The lay delegates, unnarrowed by theological studies were, as a body, favorable to woman's admission. Nor did they refrain from criticizing the clergy, declaring that the episcopacy did not interpret the law of the church, this power resting in the General Conference. But one more favoring vote would have tied the question. Gen. Samuel H. Hurst, dairy and food commissioner of Ohio, the first layman to gain the floor, defended the right of women to admission. He alluded to the opponents of the women as "old fogies." He criticized the bishop's address.

> The episcopacy does not interpret the law of the church, but the General Conference does. Woman does not come here as a strong-minded person demanding admittance, but she comes as representative of the lay conference. The word "laymen" was interpreted to mean all members of the church not represented in the ministry. That is the law, and if women are "laymen" they are entitled to admission.

The Southern Baptist Association, meeting in New Orleans in July of the same year, refused to admit women by a vote of 42 to 40. The church as of old, is still strenuous in its efforts to influence legislation. An amendment to the National Constitution is pressed by the National Reform Association, recognizing the sectarian idea of God; another placing marriage and divorce under control of the general government by uniform laws; while priestly views upon the political freedom of woman are thrust into the very faces of our lawmakers.[27] The following portions of a sermon preached at the Cathedral of the Holy Cross, Boston, February 21, 1886, by the Rev. Father J. P. Bodfish, were printed and distributed among the members of the Massachusetts Legislature that spring by the opponents of woman suffrage:[28]

> No that I would have woman step out of her sphere; the man is the natural protector, the father, the lawgiver, of his family; nor would I counsel wives to usurp the places of their husbands at the polls. I believe this to be one of the errors of modern times, to try to unsex woman, and take her from the high place she occupies and drag her into the arena of public life. What has she to do there? We might as well try to drag down the angels to take part in the menial affairs of this world as to take woman from the high place she occupies in the family, where 'tis her privilege and duty to guide, to counsel and to instruct—to lead that family in the way of righteousness. It is but offering her a degradation; Almighty God never intended it. The charm, the influence of woman, is in that purity that comes from living in a sphere apart from us. God forbid that we should ever see the day that a man, a husband or a father, is to find his will opposed and thwarted at the polls by his daughter or his wife. Then farewell to that reverence which belongs to the character of woman.
>
> She puts herself on an equal footing with man when she steps down from that place where everyone regards her with reverence, and becomes unsexed by striving to make laws which she cannot enforce, and taking upon herself duties for which she is altogether unfitted.

Decrees of various characters presenting woman as a being of different natural and spiritual rights from man, are constantly formulated by the churches. The Plenary Council of Baltimore, 1884, busied itself in the enactment of canons directly bearing upon marriage and divorce, reaffirming the sacramental character of marriage and declaring that marriages under civil rites should be resented by the whole Catholic world. This council was preceded by an encyclical from the Pope, laying out its plans by work yet leaving it within the power of the diocesan bishops to promulgate its canons according to their own wisdom. Consequently, not until three years later were those upon marriage published on the Pacific Coast, at which time the archbishop of San Francisco, the bishops of Monterey, Los Angelos and Grass Valley, addressed a pastoral letter to the Catholics of those regions, condemning civil marriage as a sin and sacrilege, illegal, and a "horrible concubinage." It was further stated that marriage unblessed by a priest, subjected the parties to excommunication. At the still later Catholic Congress, in honor of the hundredth anniversary of the Catholic Hierarchy in America, divorces were affirmed to be the plague of civilization, a discredit to the government, a degradation of the female sex, and a standing menace to the sanctity of the marriage bond. In noting these canons of the Plenary Council, and the resolutions of the Catholic Congress, it should be borne in mind that the chief secret of the long-continued power of the Catholic church has been its hold upon marriage and the subordination of woman in this relation. To these celibate priests, nothing connected with woman is sacred. Celibacy and the sacramental nature of marriage are each of them based upon the theory of woman's created inferiority and original sin. Priestly power over marriage, and the confessional, through which means it is able to wrest all family and state secrets to its own use, are powers that will not be peaceably relinquished. Their destruction will come through the growing intelligence of people, and the responsibility of political self-government. These will insure confidence in the validity of civil marriage and a belief in the personal rights of individuals. To woman, the education of political responsibility is most essential in order to free her from church bonds, and is, herefore most energetically opposed by the church. In 1890, a number of Catholic ladies of Paris formed a union for the emancipation of woman from different kinds of social thraldom.[29] Their first attack was upon the priesthood, whom they declared the mortal adversary of woman's advancement, affirming that every woman "who abets the abbes is an enemy of her sex." This open rebellion of Catholic ladies against the power of the hierarchy, is a significant sign of woman's advancing freedom.

All canons, decrees, resolutions and laws of the church, especially bearing upon the destinies of woman are promulgated without the hearing of her voice, either in confirmation or rejection. She is simply legislated for as a slave. Two of the later triennial conclaves of the Episcopal church of the United States, energetically debated the subject of divorce, not, however, arriving at sufficient unanimity of opinion for the enactment of a canon. When Mazzini, the Italian patriot, was in this country, 1852, he declared the destruction of the priesthood to be our only surety for continued freedom, saying:

> They will be found as in Italy, the foes of mankind, and if the United States expects to retain even its political liberties, it must get rid of the priesthood as Italy intends to do.[30]

Frances Wright, that clear-seeing, liberty-loving, Scotch freethought woman, noted the dangerous purpose and character of the Christian party in politics, even as early as 1829; and the present effort of this body, now organized as the "National Reform Association" with its adjunct "The American Sabbath Union," officered by priests and influential members of the Woman's Christian Temperance Union, and kindred bodies, is a perpetual menace to the civil and religious liberties of the United States. Its effort for an amendment to the Federal Constitution which shall recognize the United Sates as a Christian nation, is a determined endeavor toward the union of church and state and its success in such attempt will be the immediate destruction of both civil and religious liberty. That such a party now openly exists, its intentions no secret is evidence that the warnings of Italian patriot and the Scotch freethinker, were not without assured foundation.

As a body, the church opposes education for woman, and all the liberalizing tendencies of the last thirty-five or forty years, which have opened new and varied industries to women and secured to wives some relief from their general serf condition. Bishop Littlejohn, of the Episcopal church, at the Triennial Conclave of bishops, 1883, preached as his "triennial charge" upon "The Church and the Family," presenting the general church idea as to woman's inferiority and subordination. He made authoritative use of the words "sanctities of home," a phrase invented by the clergy as a method of holding woman in bondage; directed the church to "strictly impose her doctrines as to marriage and divorce, clash as they may with the spirit of the times and the laws of the state" (thus emulating the Catholic doctrines of the supremacy of the church). He declared that, in any respect to change the relation established by God himself between husband and wife, was rank infidelity, no matter what specious disguise such change might assume, explicitly declaring the authority of the church over marriage, as against the authority of the state; protesting against omission of the word "obey" from the marriage service, and the control of the wife over her own earnings and expenditures, saying:

If it be outside the province of the states to treat marriage as more than a contract between a man and a woman, the church must make it understood, as it is not, that it is inside her province to treat it as a thing instituted of God. Practically, we have reached a point where the wife may cease to have property interests in common with her husband, may control absolutely her own means of living, and determine for herself the scale of expenditures that will suit her tastes or her caprices. The man is no longer the head of the household, the husband. It has been made an open question whether the man or his wife will fulfill that function, and "a community of interests, with the recognized authority of the husband to rule the wife, and the recognized duty of the wife to obey that authority, is no longer deemed expedient or necessary." This rebellion against the old view of marriage is so strong that in many cases the word "obey" is omitted from the marriage service.

Even among Christianized Indians we find different laws governing man and woman. In 1886, the governor of Maine paid a visit to the governor of the Passamaquody Indians, at a time when a large council was in progress upon the St. Croix reservation. This council first assembled at the chapel, where the Revised Statutes— the whole basis of government of the Passamaquodies—are posted. These statutes having been approved by Bishop Healy, of Portland, are also looked upon as canons of the church.[31]

The statutes principally affecting women, are:

Third: No woman who is separated from her husband shall be admitted to the sacrament, or to any place in the church except the porch in summer and the back seat in winter, unless by the consent of the bishop.

Fourth: Any woman who admits men into her house by night shall be treated as a criminal and delivered to the courts.

Fifth: Any woman who is disobedient to her husband, any common scold or drunkard, shall not be permitted to enter the church, except by permission of the priest.

It will be noted that these statutes forbid the sacrament to the woman who is separated from her husband, not even permitting her an accustomed seat in church. She must remain in the porch during the summer and in a back seat during the winter, except "the bishop" otherwise permits. Also the woman not rendering obedience to her husband is denied permission to enter the church except under priestly permit. The Christian theory of woman's inferiority and subordination to man, is as fully endorsed by these statutes as in the mediæval priestly instruction to husbands.[32]

No profession as constantly appeals to the lower nature as the priestly, the emotions rather than reason, are constantly invoked;

ambition, love of power, hope of reward, fear of punishment, are the incentives presented and in no instance are such incentives more fully made use of than for purposes of sustaining the supremacy of man over woman. The teaching of the church cannot fail to impress woman with the feeling that if she expects education, or even opportunity of full entrance into business, she must not heed the admonitions of the priesthood, when, as by Dr. Dix, she is contemptuously forbidden to enter the professions on the ground that God designed these offices alone for man. When women sought university honors at Oxford, a few years since, many "incredibly foolish" letters, said *London Truth*, were written by its opponents who were chiefly clergymen. Canon Liddon's influence was against the statute; the Dean of Norwich referred to it as "an attempt to defeat divine Providence and Holy Scripture." Dr. Gouldbourne thought it would "unsex woman."[33]

"There is no sin" said Buddha, "but ignorance," yet according to Rector Dix, Rev. S. W. Turnstall, Dr. Craven and the priesthood of the present day, in common with the earlier church, woman's normal condition is that of ignorance, and education is the prerogative of man alone; and yet the dangers of ignorance have by no means been fathomed, although the latest investigations show the close relation between knowledge and life. That as intelligence is diffused, there is a corresponding increase of longevity, is proven; the most uneducated communities showing the greatest proportion of deaths. Ignorance and the death rate are parts of the same question; education and length of life are proportionately synonymous. Statistics gathered in England, Wales and Ireland a few years since showed the percentage of infantile deaths to be much greater in those portions where the mother could not read and write, than where the mother had sufficient education to read a newspaper and write her own name. In districts where there was no other appreciable difference except that of education, the mortality was the largest in the most ignorant districts.

In deprecating education for women, no organized body in the world has so clearly proven its own tyrannous ignorance as has the priesthood, and no body has shown itself so fully the enemy of mankind. Church teaching and centuries of repression acting through the laws of heredity have lessened woman's physical size, depressed her mental action, subjugated her spirit, and crushed her belief in her right to herself and the proper training of her own children. The church, in its opposition to woman's education through the ages, has literally killed off the inhabitants of the world with much greater rapidity than war, pestilence, or famine; more than one-half the children born into the world have soon died because of the tyranny and ignorance of the priesthood.[34] The potential physical energy of mankind thus destroyed,   can in a measure be estimated, but no one can fathom the infinitely greater loss of mental and moral force brought about through condemnation of knowledge to woman; only by induction can it even be surmised. Lecky points out the loss to the world because so many of its purest characters donned the garb of monk or nun. That injury was immediately perceptible, but in the denial of education and freedom to women more than ninety percent of the moral and physical energy of the world has literally been suffocated, and owing to ignorance and lack of independent thought this loss is as yet scarcely recognized. So dense the pall of ignorance still overshadowing the world that even woman herself does not yet conjecture the injury that has been done her, or of what she and her children have been deprived. Nor has the world yet roused to a full consciousness of the mischief to mankind that has been perpetrated through the falsehood and ignorant persumption of those claiming control over its dearest rights and interests. Resistance to the wrong thus done the world has been less possible because perpetrated in the name of God and religion. It has caused tens of thousands of women to doubt their equality of right with man in education, to disbelieve they possess the same authority to interpret the Bible or present its doctrines as man; neither, having been deprived of education, do they believe themselves to be man's political equal, or that they possess equal rights with him in the household. This degradation of woman's moral nature is the most direful result of the teaching of the church in regard to her. A loss of faith in one's own self, disbelief in one's own right to the fullest

cultivation of one's own powers, proceeds from a debasement of
the moral sentiments. Self-reliance, self-respect, self-confidence, are
acquired through that cultivation of the intellectual faculties which
has been denied to woman. Rev. Dr. Charles Little, of the Syracuse
University, says: "In the report of a sermon of a distinguished theologian which appeared not long ago, this striking passage
occurred: 'If I were to choose between Christianity as a life and
Christianity as a dogma, I would choose Christianity as a dogma.'
Judging from its treatment of woman and the many recent trials for
heresy, dogma rather than life is the general spirit of the churches
everywhere. It is dogma that has wrecked true religion; it is dogma
that has crushed humanity; it is dogma that has created two codes
of morals; that has inculcated the doctrines of original sin; that has
degraded womanhood; that has represented divinity as possessing
every evil attribute.

From all these incontrovertible facts in church and state, we
see that both religion and government are essentially masculine in
their present forms and development. All the evils that have
resulted from dignifying one sex and degrading the other, may be
traced to one central error, a belief in a trinity of masculine gods,
in one from which the feminine element is wholly eliminated;
and yet in the scriptural account of the simultaneous creation of
man and woman, the text plainly recognizes the feminine as well
as the masculine element in the God-head, and declares the
equality of the sexes in goodness, wisdom and power. Genesis 1,
26-27.

> And God said, Let us make man in our own image, after our
> likeness, and so God created man in his own image; in the
> image of God created He him, male and female created He
> them, and gave them dominion over the fish of the sea and
> over the fowl of the air, and over every living thing that
> moveth upon the earth.

In nothing has the ignorance and weakness of the church
been more fully shown than in its controversies in regard to the

creation. From time of the "Fathers" to the present hour, despite its assertion and its dogmas, the church has ever been engaged in discussions upon the Garden of Eden, the serpent, woman, man, and God as connected in one inseparable relation. Amid all the evils attributed to woman, her loss of Paradise, introduction of sin into the world and the consequent degradation of mankind, yet Eve, and through her, all women have found occasional defenders. A book printed in Amsterdam, 1700, in a series of eleven reasons, threw the greater culpability upon Adam, saying:

> *First*: The serpent tempted her before she thought of the tree of knowledge of good and evil, and suffered herself to be persuaded that not well understood his meaning.
>
> *Second*: That believing that God had not given such prohibition she eat the fruit.
>
> *Third*: Sinning through ignorance she committed a less heinous crime than Adam.
>
> *Fourth*: That Eve did not necessarily mean the penalty of eternal death, for God's decree only imported that man should die if he sinned against his conscience.
>
> *Fifth*: That God might have inflicted death on Eve without injustice, yet he resolved, so great is his mercy toward his works, to let her live, in (that) she had not sinned maliciously.
>
> *Sixth*: That being exempted from the punishment contained in God's decree, she might retain all the prerogatives of her sex except those that were not incidental with the infirmities to which God condemned her.
>
> *Seventh*: That she retained in particulars the prerogative of bringing forth children who had a right to eternal happiness on condition of obeying the new Adam.
>
> *Eighth*: That as mankind was to proceed from Adam and Eve, Adam was preserved alive only because his preservation was necessary for the procreation of children.
>
> *Ninth*: That it was by accident therefore, that the sentence of death was not executed on him, but that otherwise he was more (justly) punished than his wife.
>
> *Tenth*: That she was not driven out from Paradise as he was, but was only obliged to leave it to find out Adam in the earth; and that it was with full privilege of returning thither again.

> *Eleventh*: That the children of Adam and Eve were subject
> to eternal damnation, not as proceeding from Eve, but as pro-
> ceeding from Adam.

In 1580, but three hundred years since, an inquiry set on foot as to the language of Paradise, resulted in the statement that God spoke Danish; Adam, Swedish; and the serpent, French. Eve doubtless was conceded to have spoken all three languages, as she conversed with God, with Adam, and with the serpent. Hieronymus, a Father of the Church, credited Eve with possessing a much finer constitution than Adam, and in that respect as superior to him.[35] Thus, during the ages, the church through its "Fathers" and its priests has devoted itself to a discussion of the most trivial questions concerning woman, as well as to the formation of most oppressive canons against her, and although as shown, she has found an occasional defender, and even claimants for her superiority upon certain points, yet such discussions have had no effect upon the general view in which the church has presented her, as one accursed of God and man.

Notes

1. Generally these conventicles produced very many bastards, and the excuse they (the ministers) made for that, was, "where sin abounds the Grace of God superabounds; there is no condemnation in those that are in Christ." Sometimes this: "The lambs of God may sport together; to the pure all things are pure." Nay, generally they are of opinion that a man is never a true saint till he have a fall like that of David with Bathsheba, *The true character of the Presbyterian Pastors and People of Scotland*. Reign of King Charles II—and since the Revolution. P. 12.

2. Mr. Mott a member of the Salvation army in Syracuse, having led astray another member, a young girl of seventeen and being requested to do her the justice of marrying her, replies that he has a great mission in converting the world and has no time for marrying. He took an active part in the salvation meeting the other night. He says he was doing as Jesus did, and was free from sin. He carried the flag in the streets and

prayed three times. There was great disorder and indignation at Mott's impudence in praying and speaking.—*Syracuse Daily Standard.* 1883.

3. *The Book of Pitris.*

4. *Light on the Path.* 1–20.

5. Mrs. Gage, *Chairman of the Resolution Committee.*

6. Both Marie Weston Chapman, and Whittier, immortalized this letter in verse, Mrs. Chapman by a spirited poem entitled: "The Times that Try Men's Souls," and Whittier in one called "A Pastoral Letter."

This "Clerical Bull" was fulminated with special reference to those two noble South Carolina women, Sarah M. and Angelina E. Grimke, who were at that time publicly pleading for those in bonds as bound with them, while on a visit to Massachusetts. It was written by the Rev. Dr. Nehemiah Adams, of Boston, author of "A South-side View of Slavery."

7. No man who remembers 1837 and its lowering clouds, will deny that there was hardly any contribution to the antislavery movement greater or more impressive than the crusade of these Grimke sisters, from South Carolina through the New England States.—*Wendell Phillips.*

8. Who afterwards married Stephen Foster, one of the apostles of the antislavery cause.

9. Decomposed eggs, the contents of stables, and even of out-houses, were hurled at the speaker and those assembled to listen.

10. Rev. Samuel J. May, first had his attention called to the wrongs of women under Church and State, by a striking comparison of the two, from the lips of a woman.

Priestly opposition to new ideas, and to woman's taking part in reform work, still continues to be manifest, as shown by the tour of General Weaver and Mrs. Lease, through the Southern States in the fall of 1892. "The notorious Mrs. Lease," as she was termed, was met by hooting, howling, egg-throwing mobs, and in Atlanta "an eminent minister of the strongest religious denomination (Baptist) in the South" preached against the third party, September 18, five days before that on which General Weaver and Mrs. Lease were to speak in that city. This sermon, reported by the Constitution, as a "red-hot roasting" declared against the political party that would employ women as speakers, "unsex American women," as an evidence of the skepticism of the age. Nor is this the only recent instance of pulpit opposition to woman. After the formation of the Woman's National Liberal League, Washington, February 1890, clergymen in different portions of the country—Washington, Iowa, Massachusetts, etc.—hurled their anathemas against this association, as inimical to Bible morality, and especially against the women leading in this step. In addition to these sermons, a Catholic Orphanage of seven hundred children, was instructed to pray against such demoralizing ideas; and beyond this, letters passing between influential women fell under United States supervision, and were opened in transit.

11. Lucretia Mott foremost among these delegates, after this rejection decided upon holding a Woman's Rights Convention, upon her return to America, which should present the wrongs under which women suffered. This was done, 1848, at Seneca Falls, N.Y.

12. Through *Senator Joseph E. Brown.*

13. Several ladies well known for their work in the enfranchisement of their sex, attended this trial, the *New York Sun* facetiously referring to the presence of "those eminent Presbyterians, Lillie Devereux Blake, Matilda Joslyn Gage and Susan A. King."

14. Report of the Washington, D.C., *Republican.*

15. Ably reviewed each week as they appeared, by Mrs. Lillie Devereux Blake.

16. *Lenten Lectures*, pp. 56–57, 114.

17.

WOMEN AND THEIR SPHERE!

Rev. Dr. Dix, some weeks since, came to the front with a series of sermons in which, by unsupported assertion, he managed to demonstrate that women in the United States are no longer ornamental. The trouble in the mind of the reverend D. D. seems to be that women, having grown in the knowledge of the truth and of that liberty wherewith Christ maketh free, have concluded that their sphere is not to be man's slave—his plaything, a human gewgaw, to be fondled, caressed, or kicked as the masculine mind may elect. If it is important for man to "know himself," brave women have concluded that it is quite as essential for a woman to know herself, and with a heroism born of rights conferred by God Himself, women have in these latter days resolved to map out their own sphere independent of man's dictation. They have made commendable headway. They have succeeded in shaking down a number of antiquated citadels where ignorance, superstition, prejudice, despotism and cruelty found refuge, and, as they tumbled, the breath of popular indignation has blown the fragments away like chaff in the grasp of a tornado. These brave women, finding out that—"Life is real, life is earnest"—set themselves about solving its problems for themselves and for their sex. Some of them asked for the ballot. Why? Because they wanted to obliterate from the statute books such laws as restricted their liberties and circumscribed their sphere. As wives they wanted to be the equals of their husbands before the law. Why not? As mothers they wanted to be the equal of their sons before the law. Why not? A thousand reasons have been assigned why not, but they do not answer the demand. What is wanted as prudent guarantees that the ballot will be wisely wielded by those upon whom the great right has been conferred? The answer is ready—intellect, education, a fair comprehension of the obligations of citizenship, loyalty to the Government, to republican institutions and the welfare of society. It is not contended that women do not possess these qualifications, but the right is withheld from them nevertheless, and by withholding this right a hundred others are included, every one of which when justice bears sway will be granted. This done woman's sphere will regulate itself as does man's sphere. The *Boston Herald* in a recent issue takes Dr. Dix to task for narrowness of vision and weakness of grasp in discussing "the calling of a Christian woman," and then proceeds to outline its own views on the "sphere of capable women," in which it is less robust than the reverend D. D. To intimate that the Infinite Disposer of Events favors the narrow, vulgar prejudices of Rev. Dr. Dix and his organ, the *Boston Herald*, is to dwarf the Almighty to human proportions and bring discredit upon His attributes in the midst of which justice shines with resplendent glory, but the demand is that women themselves shall determine for themselves the boundaries of their sphere. It is not a question of mere sentiment, it is not a matter of fancy or caprice. It is a rugged question. It involves food, clothing, shelter. It means self-reliance. Women are not appealing to man's gallantry, nor to any quality of less importance than his sense of justice for their rights. Man is not likely to regard his mother with less affection and reverence because she is his father's equal, and if in the past, when women were more degraded than at present, the best men have found in women inspiration for their best work, good men will not find less inspiration for good work when women are emancipated from the thraldom of vicious laws, and crowned man's equal in all matters relating to "sphere," shall, by laws relating to physical and mental organism, take their chances in the world's broad field of battle, demanding and receiving for work done in any of the departments of human activities men's pay when they perform men's work.—*Indianapolis Sentinel*, May 13, 1883.

18. It is not a physiological cause which produced our present family with the father as ruler and owner of all property.—*Kemptsky*.

19. By a singular lack of oversight in making up the title page and lettering the cover, the words "Husband and Wife" have been printed as though they referred to objects of equal importance. Even the carefully trained eye of a former editor of the *Christian Register*, the Rt. Rev. F. D. Huntington, D. D. Bishop of Central New York, who furnishes a brief and cautious introduction to the volume, did not detect this error. It has been left to us to call attention to the incongruity of the title page, and to give the sentiment of the book proper typographical expression. The conventional sobriety and ecclesiasticism of the title page do not prepare one for the novelty of the contents. It is only by reading the book that we become aware of them. The sensation of the reader is somewhat the same as one would have on going into a building which from the facade appeared to be a plain, dignified Episcopal church, but which on entering he found to be a mediæval circus. Not that there is anything intentionally hilarious in the arena of this book or that it displays any athletic vigor of thought, but that it is essentially novel and revolutionary. Dr. Gray is not unconscious of the novelty of his doctrine. "It is believed," he says, "that the position of this essay is new to the discussion. It has not been urged or stated in print in England or America"; and, later on, he expresses a well-grounded belief that "some will smile" at his views as "antiquated and fanciful." All of these claims may be readily granted. First, the doctrine is new. It is new at least in its present dress—as new as Adam would seem to be, if he put on a modern costume, dyed his gray hairs, and appeared in Boston as a social lecturer.—The *Christian Register*, Boston.

20. Who has forgotten the sublime magnanimity of Artemus Ward, when he proposed on a certain occasion to sacrifice all his wife's relatives? This is exactly what Dean Gray theoretically achieves. He not only abolishes his own wife's relatives, but those of other men who have entered into the marriage relationship. He makes thorough work of it. Not only does he extinguish the wife's sister as a relative, but also her cousins and her aunts. In fact, he even abolishes the mother-in-law. The luxury of a mother-in-law is granted to the wife, who by virtue of marriage becomes related to her husband's mother, but is not granted to the husband, who has no relation whatever to the mother of his wife. As to the sisters, the cousins and the aunts, there may be a reason why Sir Joseph Porter, K.C.B., would view with dismay an equal addition to

their number through the offices of matrimony; but the majority of men not blessed with a similar superfluity would hardly wish to forego this delightful form of conjugal perquisite.—*Ibid.*

21. "One of the most learned colored men in the country is Alexander Crummel, Rector of St. Luke's Protestant Episcopal Church, Washington, D.C. When he desired to study for holy orders he applied at Kenyon College, Gambier, O., but was refused admission. He made applications elsewhere, which were equally unsuccessful. He finally went to Oxford, England, and there took a full course. He is an eloquent preacher, and his congregation embraces a large number of prominent colored citizens."

22. I Corinthians, V: 1.

23. And one of the most bitter opponents to the admission of the women lay-delegates to the Methodist General Conference.

24. As reported in Syracuse, New York *Sunday Morning Courier*, March 4, 1877.

25. Rev. F. B. Neely, of Philadelphia, said that he was in favor of submitting the question to the annual conferences. He offered the following amendment to the report of the committee:

But since there is great interest in this question, and since the church generally should be consulted in regard to such an important matter, therefore.

Resolved: That we submit to the annual conferences the proposition to amend the second restrictive rule by amending the words "and said delegates may be men or women" after the words "two lay delegates" for an annual conference so that it would read, "Nor of more than two lay delegates for an annual conference, and the said delegates may be men or women."

The amendment was seconded by Dr. Paxton.—*Telegram.*

New York, May 12.—The debate on the admission of women delegates was one of the most lengthy in the history of the church. It occupied the time of the conference during the larger part of six sessions. It is the common remark, too, that never before was a subject contested in this body with such obstinacy, not to say bitterness. The struggle to obtain recognition from the chair was a revelation to those who did not know previously how fond Methodists are of speaking in meeting. The instant the chairman's gavel fell, announcing the termination of one speech, fifty delegates or more were on their feet, and from fifty stentorian voices rang out the pitiful appeal, "Mr. Chairman!" This was the order of affairs from the beginning of the debate to the close. One delegate who was finally recognized proved to be so hoarse from his protracted efforts to get the floor that it was with difficulty he could be heard when he did get it. Correspondence, Syracuse, N.Y., *Sunday Herald*, May 13.

26. The final vote, excluding women from this conference and submitting the question of their eligibility to the annual conferences, stood: To exclude and submit, 237; against, 198—making a majority of 39 only of the total vote, while the laymen were so evenly divided that the change of one vote would have tied them. If now the annual conference shall decree by a three-fourths vote of all the ministers present and voting, that women are eligible, and if four years hence the general conference by a two-thirds vote shall ratify that decree, the fair sisters will thereafter have free course in that body. Otherwise they will be tolerated only as mere lookers-on. From the fact, that many who voted to submit the matter to the annual conference did go, not because they wish the women to come in, but merely as the best method of getting rid of a troublesome question for the time being, it looks as though their chances of gaining admittance as delegates four years hence were little better, if any, than in the present instance.—*Sunday Herald*, Syracuse, N.Y., May 13.

27.

The Priesthood

Now, too oft the priesthood wait
At the threshold of the state—
Waiting for the beck and wave
Of its power as law and God.

—From Whittier's *Curse of the Charter Breakers*.

28. From *The Woman's Journal*, Boston.

29. Headed by *Mme. Artie de Valsayre*.

30. When the temporal kingdom took possession of Italy, the rate of ignorance was 90 percent. It has now been reduced to 45 percent.

31. The *Boston Herald*, Aug. 17, 1886, heading an article upon these statutes; "Copper Colored Blue Laws."

32. A husband is entitled to punish his wife when he sees fit. At first he is to use remonstrances; if these do not avail, he is to have recourse to more severe punishment.

The confessor is at first bound not to pay much heed to women complaining of their husbands, because women are habitually inclined to lie.

33. The scene in the convocation was animated, the public at large favoring the women. The senior Proctor being slow in his figuring, one

of the "Gods in the Gallery" becoming impatient for the announcement of the numbers, shouted, "Call in one of the ladies to help you, sir."

34. In Egypt, where women received the same education as men, very few children died—a fact noted in the absence of child mummies.

35. "Eve lived 940 years, giving birth to a boy and a girl every year. Eve lived ten years longer than Adam. They must give this first woman the best constitution in the world for while her husband lived 930 years and communicated to his sons for several generations the principle of so long a life (which is no less applicable to Eve than to him), he must have been of very vigorous constitution; . . . turn the thing as you will it will always be an argument from the greater to the less to show that Eve's body was better constituted than that of her husband."

CHAPTER X
PAST, PRESENT, FUTURE

The most important struggle in the history of the church is that of woman for liberty of thought and the right to give that thought to the world. As a spiritual force the church appealed to barbaric conception when it declared woman to have been made for man, first in sin and commanded to be under obedience. Holding as its chief tenet a belief in the inherent wickedness of woman, the originator of sin, as its sequence the sacrifice of a God becoming necessary, the church has treated her as alone under a "curse" for whose enforcement it declared itself the divine instrument. Woman's degradation under it dating back to its earliest history, while the nineteenth century still shows religious despotism to have its stronghold in the theory of woman's inferiority to man. The church has ever invoked the "old covenant" as authority, while it also asserts this covenant was done away with at the advent of the new dispensation. Paul, whose character as persecutor was not changed when he veered from

Judaism to Christianity, gave to the church a lever long enough to reach down through eighteen centuries in opposition to woman's equality with man. Through this lengthy period, his teaching has united the christian world in opposition to her right of private judgment and personal freedom.

Each great division of christianity alike proclaims the supreme sinfulness of woman in working for the elevation of her sex. In this work she has been left outside of religious sympathy, outside of political protection, yet in the interest of justice she claims the right to tear down the barriers of advancing civilization and to rend asunder all beliefs that men hold most sacred. Freedom for woman underlies all the great questions of the age. She must no longer be the scapegoat of humanity upon whose devoted head the sins of all people are made to rest. Woman's increasing freedom within the last hundred years is not due to the church, but to the printing-press, to education, to free-thought and other forms of advancing civilization. The fashions of the christian world have changed but not its innermost belief. The power of the pulpit, built up by a claim of divine authority, with the priest as an immediate representative of God, has been reacting upon the priesthood itself, and now while vainly struggling for light this order finds itself bound by chains of its own creating. Today the priesthood is hampered by creeds and dogmas centuries old, yet so fully outside of practical life that the church has become the great materialistic force of the century; its ideas of a God, its teachings of a future life all falling within the realm of the physical senses; the incorporeal and spiritual are lost in the grossest forms of matter.[1] Although a body professing to inculcate pure spiritual truths, the church teaches the grossest form of materialism. It asserts principles contradictory to natural laws; it presents chaos as the normal condition of the infinite; it bids people live under faith outside of evidence, and in thus doing is guilty of immeasurable evils to mankind. A bark without compass, it steers upon a sea of night no star illumining the darkness; the control and guidance by humanity of the psychic part of being, generally spoken of as "supernatural," although the truest to nature, has become nearly lost through the materalization of spiritual truth by the church, the worst form of idolatry. Christianity was a stern reality to the men of the early and middle ages, who believing themselves to have been created nearer to God than woman also believed themselves to have lost earthly immortality through her. Permeated with this idea, it is not strange that men through many hundred years taught that woman was especially under control of the Evil One. The devil was an objective form to the clergy and people alike. Nor under such belief, is it strange that priests should warn their flocks from the pulpit against the wiles of woman, thus degrading her self-respect and teaching men to hold her in that contempt whose influence is felt today. The result of this teaching has been deplorable to humanity; men equally with women having sunk under this degradation of one-half of the race.

The most stupendous system of organized robbery known, has been that of the church towards woman, a robbery, that has not only taken her self-respect but all rights of person; the fruits of her own industry; her opportunities of education; the exercise of her own judgment, her own conscience, her own will. The unfortunate peculiarity of the history of man, according to Buckle, is that although its separate parts have been examined with considerable ability, hardly anyone has attempted to outline them into a whole and ascertain the way they are connected with each other. While this statement is virtually true as regards the general history of mankind, it is most particularly so in reference to the position of woman in its bearings upon race development. A thorough investigation of her connection with our present form of civilization, or even with that of the past, as compared with each other, or as influencing the whole, has never yet been authoratatively undertaken. This failure has not been so largely due to willful neglect as to incapacity upon the part of man to judge truly of this relation. Woman herself must judge of woman. The most remote feminine personality is not less incomprehensible to man, than the woman of today; he now as little understands the finer qualities of her soul or her high intuitive reasoning faculties as in the past. Reason is

divided into two parts, theoretical and practical; the former apper-
tains to man; the latter, composed of those intuitive faculties which
do not need a long process of ratiocination for their work, inhere
in woman. Although the course of history has given many
glimpses of her superiority, and the past few decades have shown
in every land a new awakening of woman to a recognition of her
own powers, man as man, is still as obtuse as of yore. He is yet
under the darkness of the Patriarchate, failing to recognize woman
as a component part of humanity, whose power of development
and influence upon civilization are at least the equal of his own.
He yet fails to see in her a factor of life whose influence for good
or for evil has ever been in direct ratio with her freedom. He does
not yet discern her equal right with himself to impress her own
opinions upon the world. He still interprets governments and religions as requiring from her an unquestioning obedience to laws
she has no share in making, and that place her as an inferior in
every relation of life. Ralph Waldo Emerson with keen insight
into the fallibility of lawmakers, declared that "good men must not
obey the laws too well." Woman is showing her innate wisdom in
daring to question the infallibility of man, his laws, and his interpretation of her place in creation. She is not obeying "too well,"
and yet man fails to analyze her motives in this defection. The
church and the state have long done man's thinking for him, the
ideas of the few, whose aim is power, have been impressed upon
the many; individualism is still characterized as the essence of evil;
self-thought, self-control as heretical. The state condemns both as
a crime against itself, the church as a sin against heaven. Both
church and state claiming to be of divine origin have assumed
divine right to the control of man, also asserting the divine right
of man over woman; while church and state have thought for man,
man has assumed the right to think for woman.[2]

As man under fear of eternal damnation surrendered to the
irresponsible power of church and state, so woman yielded to that
power which closed every external avenue of knowlege to her
under pretext of her sinfulness. One-tenth of the human race,
within the period covered by modern civilization, has compelled

the other nine-tenths to think their thoughts and live lives according their commands. This has been the chief effort of governments and religion. The most formidable general evil under which woman has suffered during the Christian ages, has been that of protection; a nonrecognition of her ability to care for herself, rendering watchful guardianship over her a recognized part of man's law; not alone to prevent her sinking into depths of vice but to also prevent her entire subversion of government and religion. Buckle and other writers have recognized the protective spirit as the greatest enemy to civilization, its influence causing the few to establish themselves as guardians of the many in all affairs of life. The American Revolution in proclaiming the rights of humanity struck a blow at the protective system. This system has ever based itself upon a declaration of the supreme rights of a God, and certain rights as pertaining to certain classes of men by virtue of authority from that God. The defense of such authority has ever been the chief business of church and state, and thus religions and governments have neither found time nor inclination to uphold the rights of humanity. Under the christian system, woman as the most rebellious against God in having eaten a forbidden fruit, has found herself condemned through the centuries to untold oppression in order that the rights of God might be maintained. Yet while constantly teaching that woman brought sin into the world, the church ever forgets its own corollary; that if she brought sin she also brought a God into the world, thus throwing ineffable splendor over mankind. The whole theory regarding woman, under christianity, has been based upon the conception that she had no right to live for herself alone. Her duty to others has continuously been placed before her and her training has ever been that of self-sacrifice. Taught from the pulpit and legislative halls that she was created for another, that her position must always be secondary even to her children, her right to life, has been admitted only in so far as its reacting effect upon another could be predicated. That she was first created for herself, as an independent being to whom all the opportunities of the world should be open because of herself, has not entered the thought of the church; has not yet become one of the conceptions of law; is not yet the foundation of the family.

But woman is learning for herself that not self-sacrifice, but self-development, is her first duty in life; and this, not primarily for the sake of others but that she may become fully herself; a perfectly rounded being from every point of view; her duty to others being a secondary consideration arising from those relations in life where she finds herself placed at birth, or those which later she voluntarily assumes. But these duties are not different in point of obligation, no more imperative upon her, than are similar duties upon man. The political doctrine of the sovereignty of the individual, although but partially recognized even in the United States, has been most efficacious in destroying that protective spirit which has so greatly interfered with the progress of humanity. This spirit yet retains its greatest influence in the family, where it places a boundary between husband and wife. Of all circumstances biasing the judgment and restricting the sympathies, none have shown themselves more powerful than physical differences, whether of race, color or sex. When those differences are not alone believed to be a mark of inferiority, but to have been especially created for the pleasure and peculiar service of another, the elements of irresponsible tyranny upon one side, and irremediable slavery upon the other, are already organized. If in addition, that inferior is regarded as under an especial curse for extraordinary sin, as the church has ever inculcated in reference to women; and when as in the case of woman and man an entire separation of interests, hopes, feelings and passions is impossible, we have reached the extreme of injustice and misery under the protective system. Consequently no other form of "protection" has possessed so many elements of absolute injustice as that of man over woman. Swedenborg taught, and experience declares, that morality cannot exist except under conditions of freedom. Hence we find much that has been called morality is the effect of dependence and lessened self-respect, and has really been immorality and degradation. While in every age, the virtues of self-sacrifice have been pointed to as evidence of the highest morality, we find those women in whom it has been most apparent, have been those doing least justice where justice first belongs—to themselves. Justice as the foundation of the highest law, is a primal requirement of the individual to the self. It is none the less a serious impeachment of the religious-moral idea, that the doctrine of protection and the duty of woman's self-sacrifice, were taught under the theory of divine authority. No faith was more profound, none could be more logical if resting on a true foundation, than the church theory regarding woman. Life assumed a sterner reality to men who believed themselves in point of purity and priority nearer their Creator than woman. Thereafter, she was to be protected from herself, the church and man cheerfully assuming this duty. Under the protective spirit it is not so very long since men sold themselves and their families to some other man in power, either lay or religious, under promise of protection, binding themselves to obey the mandates of such lord evermore. The church protected and directed the thought of the world. To think for one's self, is not even now the tendency of mankind; the few who dare, do so at great peril. It will require another hundred years of personal and political freedom for men to appreciate what liberty really is—for them to possess confidence in their own judgment upon religious questions—for the man of humble station to fully believe in himself and in his own opinions when opposed to the authority of church or state.

Women of the present century whose struggle for equal opportunity of education with men; for a chance to enter the liberal professions; for a fair share of the world of work; for equal pay in that work; for all demands of equality which make the present a noted age in the world's history, have met their greatest opposition from this protective spirit. No less than during the darkest period of its history does the church still maintain the theory that education[3] and public life are not fitting for woman—indelicate for herself and injurious to the community. During the Christian ages, the church has not alone shown cruelty and contempt for woman, but has exhibited an impious and insolent disregard of her most common rights of humanity. It has robbed her of responsibility, putting man in place of God. It has forbidden her the offices of the church and at times an entrance within its doors. It has denied her independent thought, declaring her a secondary creation for man's use to whom alone it has made her responsible. It has anathematized her sex, teaching her to feel shame for the very fact of her being. It has not been content with proclaiming a curse upon her creative attributes, but has thrust the sorrows and expiations of man's "curse" upon her, and in doing these things the church has wrought her own ruin. A religious revolution of the most radical kind, has even now assumed such proportions as to nearly destroy the basic creeds of various sects, and undermine the whole fabric of christendom. It everywhere exists, although neither the world nor the church seem to realize the magnitude of its proportions. As a legitimate result of two opposing forces, a crisis in the life of the church is at hand; nay, even upon it. While we see it making organized effort for extension of power and entire control of the state, we also find great increase of radical thought, and development of individual conscience and individual judgment. With thought no longer bound by fear of everlasting punishment, mankind will cease to believe unproved assertions, simply because made by a class of men under assumed authority from God. Reason will be used, mankind will seek for truth come whence it may, lead where it will, and with our own Lucretia Mott, will accept "truth for authority and not authority for truth."

In knocking at the door of political rights, woman is severing the last link between church and state; the church must lose that power it has wielded with changing force since the days of Constantine, ever to the injury of freedom and the world. The immeasurable injustice to woman, and her sufferings under christianity, her intellectual, moral and spiritual servitude, will never be understood until life with its sorrows shall be opened to our vision in a sphere more refined than the present one. The superstitions of the church, the miseries of woman, her woes, tortures, burnings, rackings and all the brutalities she has endured in the church, the state, the family, under the sanction of christianity, would be incredible had we not the most undeniable evidence of their existence, not alone in the past but as shown by the teachings, laws and customs of the present time.[4] "She has suffered under a theology which extended its rule not only to her civil and political relations, but to her most insignificant domestic and personal concerns, regulating the commerce of husband and wife, of parent and child, of master and servant, even prescribing her diet and dress, her education and her industries." Edmund Noble speaks in like manner of the ancient Russians under the tyrannical provisions of the Greek church, saying, "Clearly, such a system of theocratic supervision and direction as this, is compatible only with the lowest possible spiritual condition of the subject, or the lowest possible conception of God." Possessing no proof of its premises, the church has ever fostered unintelligent belief. To doubt her "unverified" assertion has ever been declared an unpardonable sin. The supreme effort of the church, being maintenance of power, it is but recently that woman has been allowed to read history for herself, or having read it, dared to draw her own conclusions from its premises. Ignorance and falsehood created a sentiment in accord with themselves, crushing all her aspirations. In the family, man still decides the rights and duties of the wife, as of old. As legislator and judge, he still makes and executes class laws. In the church, he yet arrogates to himself the interpretation of the Bible; still claims to be an exponent of the Divine will, that grandest lesson of the reformation, the right of private interpretation of the scriptures, not yet having been conceded to woman. The premises upon which the church is based being radically false, it is a necessary corollary that its conclusions must be equally false, and this, most especially in everything relating to woman. Trained from infancy by the church to a belief in woman's inferiority, and incapacity for self-government; men of the highest station have not hesitated to organize societies in opposition to her just demands. As early as 1875, an antiwoman's franchise association was formed in London, under name of "Association for Protecting the Franchise from the Encroachment of Women"; Hon. Mr. Bouverie, a leading opponent of Woman Suffrage in the House of Commons, being its chairman. Among the promoters of the movement were Sir

Henry James, formerly attorney general (for the Crown), Hon.
Mr. Childers, late First Lord of the Admiralty, Mr. Claflin and Mr.
Leathers, correspondent of the *New York Tribune*.

Since this period, a number of women distinguished as "the
wives of" have petitioned legislative bodies for protection against
freedom for themselves, and all others of their sex, in asking that
legislatures shall not recognize woman's self-governing right. The
deepest depth of degradation is reached when the slave not only
declares against his own freedom, but strives to tighten the bonds
of fellow slaves; and the most cruel wrong resulting from such
slavery, is the destruction of self-respect in the enslaved, as shown
by the course of these women petitioners. The protective theory
reached its lowest depth for woman by an attack upon her already
vested rights of the ballot, in the former territory, now State of
Washington, on the Pacific coast, in case of Nevada M. Bloomer
[a woman] against John Wood and others, to have the women of
that territory deprived of their already existing right of suffrage.[5]
In line with the general opposition to the enfranchisement of
woman, men of even the most liberal tendencies declare that her
political freedom will be used to sustain the church, apparently forgetting that man alone has placed the church in power and that
man alone holds it in power. And proof of man's complicity is
even greater than this. Despite what is said of the larger church
membership of women, the most noted modern evangelist,
Moody, recently declared that he "found men ten-fold, aye, an
hundred-fold" more receptive of his preaching than women.
While speaking in Farwell Hall, Chicago, 1886, he said, "For fifteen years I have preached to women in the afternoon and very
often as near as I could, have preached the same sermon to men at
night, and in ninety-nine cases out of a hundred have had five
times more result in preaching to men than to women." This
pseudo-argument, as to woman's susceptibility to church teaching,
brought up by the enemies of her freedom, possesses no more real
value than the pseudo-political argument sometimes presented in
opposition to woman's admission into active politics; that is, her
emotional temperament. To one who has been present at four

great presidential nominating conventions and several large state conventions, knowledge upon this point is practical. When one has seen a cordon of police enforced by the mayor upon the platform, protecting the officers of such convention, while its members, standing upon seats, stamped, shouted, gesticulated, threatened with revolvers, acting more like uncaged wild beasts than like men[6] when one has witnessed the wildest enthusiasm at the mention of a name, the waving of flags, of hats, of handkerchiefs, the shaking of umbrellas, chairs, canes, with violent stamping, amid a hubbub of indistinguishable voices, all shouting; screaming so loud that people for blocks away are roused from slumber[7] in affright of a fire, or the approach of an ungovernable mob, such objections to woman's freedom as her "emotions" fall to their lowest value.

In Church and in State, man has exhibited the wildest passions, the most ungovernable frenzy—has shown himself less controlled by reason than possible for woman under the most adverse circumstances. Judaism, and its offspring, Christianity, show the results of the Patriarchate in some of its most degenerate forms; industrial servitude, educational restrictions, legal thraldom, political slavery, false religious teachings, are but a portion of the evils existing under its most enlightened forms, and equally with the more pronounced polygamy and infanticide they show a total perversion of moral ideas. Woman dearly pays for the rights she has secured. Labor opposes, in less pay for the same work; literature, at first welcoming her only through the cook book, next compelled her to conceal her sex under a male pseudonym, in order that her writings might be received with the same respect as those of man; art has given her similar experiences, and while today admitting her to the same advantage of study with man, yet compels her to pay twice the price for the same instructions.

The careful student of history will discover that christianity has been of very little value in advancing civilization, but has done a great deal toward retarding it.[8] "Civilization, a recognition of the rights of others at every point of contact," has been carried forward by means of rebellion against church teaching and church authority. The experience of science is familiar to all, even schoolchildren quoting Gallileo and Dr. Faust. What are called reformations in religion, the work of Huss, of Luther, of the Waldenses, the Huguenots, are equally familiar instances to the youngest student, of rebellion against the church. These and a myriad of others known to the historian, have all been brought about by refusal to accept the authority of the church as final. The Peasant War, in France, the struggles of Wat Tyler and of Hampden in England, the French and the American revolutions looking toward equality of rights; and a thousand minor forms of political progress have all been opposed by the church as rebellions against its teachings, yet all have been marked steps in civilization. The church and civilization are antipodal; one means authority, the other freedom; one means conservatism, the other progress; one means the rights of God as interpreted by the priesthood, the other the rights of humanity as interpreted by humanity. Civilization advances by free-thought, free speech, free men. The uprising of the women of all peoples in assertion of their common humanity with man, is exemplification of that fact recognized in the Declaration of Independence, that while patient endurance of wrongs to which persons are accustomed, always long borne rather than by change perhaps to meet evils they know not of, shows its absolutely certain ultimate effect, no matter how long delayed, in rebellion. A time comes in the history of souls, as of nations, when forbearance ceases to be a virtue, and self-respecting life is only to be retained through defiance of and rebellion against, existing customs. The soul must assert its own supremacy or die. It is not one woman, or the women of one nation that have thus suddenly shown desire to rule themselves—to act for themselves alone. A strange identity of thought prevades all parts of the world—India, China, Japan, Russia and all of Europe, North and South America, the vast continents of the southern seas and the isles thereof, and even barbaric Africa, all evince proof of the wide psychic undercurrent which seething through women's souls, is overthrowing the civilizations built upon the force principles of the patriarchate, and will soon reinstate the reign of truth and justice. During those long ages of priestly intolerance, of domestic and governmental tyranny, in which woman seemed to accept the authority of the priest as that of God, there still existed a consciousness hardly perceptible to herself, that she was an independent being to whom by virtue of her humanity all opportunities in life belonged. From century to century mothers transmitted this scarcely developed perception to daughters, until suddenly within the past fifty years, these dominant ideas woke to thought, and the women of all nations begun to proclaim their same right to self-control as that claimed by man.

It is impossible to write of the church without noticing its connection with the great systems of the world, during its course of life. The history of christendom is the history of the myriad institutions which have arisen through its teachings, or that have been sustained by its approval. The world has not grown wise under it, except with a wisdom that is leading the purest humanitarian thought in a direction contrary to its footsteps. Slavery and prostitution, persecutions for heresy, the inquisition with its six hundred modes of torture, the destruction of learning, the oppression of science, the systematized betrayal of confiding innocence, the recognized and unrecognized polygamy of man, the denial to woman of a right to herself, her thought, her wages, her children, to a share in the government which rules her, to an equal part in religious institutions, all these and a myriad more, are parts of what is known as christian civilization. Nor has the church ever been the leader in great reforms. During the anti-slavery conflict, the American Church was known as "the bulwark of American slavery." Its course continues the same in every great contest with wrong. A memorial history of the American Episcopal church, an extensive work in two volumes of seven hundred pages each, published within the past few years, devotes but seven pages to "the Attitude of the Church during the Civil War," and the general refusal of the church to take part in the great struggle for national life, is referred to with complacent satisfaction. Penitentiaries and prisons, asylums and reformatories, all institutions of a repressive character which the church prides herself as having built up, are no less evil than the convents, monasteries and religious orders belonging to it. They have all risen through perversion of nature.

Crimes and criminals are built up and born because of the great wrong first done to mothers; they are the offspring of church and state. Science now declares crime to be a disease, but it has not yet discovered the primal cause of this disease. It is an inheritance from centuries of legalized crime against woman, of which the church in its teachings is prime factor.

Woman will gain nothing by a compromising attitude toward the church, by attempt to excuse its great wrong toward her sex, or by palliation of its motives. On the contrary, a stern reference to facts, keeping the face of the world turned toward its past teachings, its present attitude, is her duty. Wrongs of omission equal in magnitude those of commission.

Advance for woman is too well established, woman has had too much experience, has borne too much ridicule, misrepresentation and abuse to now hesitate in an attack upon the stronghold of her oppression—the church. She possesses too full knowledge of its subtle touch upon civil law to dare leave it alone; it has become one of woman's first duties, one of her greatest responsibilities, to call public attention to its false doctrines and false teachings in regard to the origin, condition and subjection of woman. She has engaged in too many battles, weathered too many storms to longer hesitate in exposure of its stupendous crimes toward one-half of humanity. Let those who fear, hide themselves, if they will, until the storm is past. Let those who dare, defiantly rejoice that they are called upon to bear still more, in order that woman may be free. A brighter day is to come for the world, a day when the intuitions of woman's soul shall be accepted as part of humanity's spiritual wealth; when force shall step backward, and love, in reality, rule the teachings of religion; and may woman be strong in the ability and courage necessary to bring about this millennial time. The world is full of signs of the near approach of this period; as never before is there an arousing sense of something deeper, holier in religion than the christian church has given. The world has seemingly awaited the advent of heroic souls who once again should dare all things for the truth. The woman who possesses love for her sex, for the world, for truth, justice and right, will not hesitate to place herself upon record as opposed to falsehood, no matter under what guise of age or holiness it appears. A generation has passed since the great struggle began, but not until within ten years has woman dared attack upon the veriest stronghold of her oppression, the Church. The state, agent and slave of the church, has so long united with it in suppression of woman's intelligence, has so long preached of power to man alone, that it has created an inherited tendency, an inborn line of thought toward repression. Bent in this line before his birth, man still unwittingly thinks of woman as not quite his equal, and it requires a new creation of mind to change his thought. A second generation has arisen, in whom some slight inherited tendencies toward recognition of a woman's right to herself are seen. In the next generation this line of inherited thought will have become stronger, both Church and State more fully recognizing woman's inherent right to share in all the opportunities of life; but at what cost to all who have taken part in the great struggle.

Has woman no wrongs to avenge upon the church? As I look backward through history I see the church everywhere stepping upon advancing civilization, hurling woman from the plane of "natural rights" where the fact of her humanity had placed her, and through itself, and its control over the state, in the doctrine of "revealed rights" everywhere teaching an inferiority of sex; a created subordination of woman to man; making her very existence a sin; holding her accountable to a diverse code of morals from man; declaring her possessed of fewer rights in church and in state; her very entrance into heaven made dependent upon some man to come as mediator between her and the Saviour it has preached, thus crushing her personal, intellectual and spiritual freedom. Looking forward, I see evidence of a conflict more severe than any yet fought by reformation or science; a conflict that will shake the foundations of religious belief, tear into fragments and scatter to the winds the old dogmas upon which all forms of christianity are based. It will not be the conflict of man with man upon rites and systems; it will not be the conflict of science upon church theories regarding creation and eternity; it will not be the light of biology illuminating the hypothesis of the resurrection of the body; but it will be the rebellion of one half of the church against those theological dogmas upon which the very existence of the church is based. In no other country has the conflict between natural and revealed rights been as pronounced as in the United States; and in this country where the conflict first began, we shall see its full and final development. During the ages, no rebellion has been of like importance with that of Woman against the tyranny of Church and State; none have had its far-reaching effects. We note its beginning; its progress will overthrow every existing form of these institutions; its end will be a regenerated world.

Notes

1. *As the resurrection of a material body to dwell in a spiritual heaven.*

2. When a quarter of the human race assume to tell me what I must do, I may be too much disheartened by the circumstance to see clearly the absurdity of this command. This is the condition of women, for whom I have the same compassion that I would have for a prisoner so long cramped in a narrow cage that he could not use his limbs. While many women are thinking their own thoughts there are others without so potent a brain, who have as yet, failed to see the absurdity of allowing others to think for them. For this condition of mental and moral blunders the church is responsible.—*Ralph Waldo Emerson.*

3. When reading was first taught women in America, said Dr. Clemence S. Lozier, it was opposed on the ground that she would forge her father's or husband's name should she learn to read and write. Geography met with like opposition on the ground of its tendency to make her dissatisfied with home and desirous of travel, while the records of history shows that the first public examination of women in Geometry, 1829, raised a cry of disapproval over the whole country.

4. There are hard and ugly facts in this Christendom of ours, and its history includes the serfdom and nihilism of Russia, the drudgery of German women; the wrongs of the Irish peasant girl; the 20,000 little English girls sold each year to gratify the lusts of the aristocracy; all the horrors

of the inquisition; all the burnings of the witches; the slavery and polygamy of America and the thousand iniquities all around us; all these belong to the history of Christendom.—The *Woman's Tribune*, Clara Colby, editor,

5. This case decided adversely to woman's right of suffrage by the territorial Supreme Court, was appealed to the Supreme Court of the United States, through the efforts of Mr. A. S. Austin, a young and energetic attorney of Olympia, the state capital; the points raised by Mr. Austin were, *First;* that the Bloomer case is a collusive one between the original plaintiff and defendants, and is a fraud upon all friends of equal suffrage in the state. *Second;* that the decision of the Supreme Court of Washington Territory was erroneous in two respects, to-wit; that the statute of the territory conferring suffrage was constitutional, and that women are citizens.

6. At a *Democratic State Convention*, Syracuse, N.Y.

7. This was the case at the Republican nominating convention, Chicago, 1880.

8. The liberty and civilization of the present are nothing else than the fragments of rights which the scaffold and stake have wrung from the strong hands of the usurpers.—*Wendell Phillips.*

Index